The Archaeology of Household Activities

As a medium for the investigation of past household behaviour, houses alone produce a prescriptive view. Documentary sources for domestic behaviour tend to provide specific perspectives and anecdotal evidence on relationships between household members. *The Archaeology of Household Activities* expands the parameters of this investigation, providing a fuller understanding of changing domestic behaviour through a critical analysis of the complete record of household material culture – the house, its content and their spatial relationships.

This edited collection brings together case-studies of the household material culture from later prehistoric periods, including pre-Roman Britain, Classic Mayan, Greek, Roman, colonial Australia and the Americas. Engaging with recent research in different branches of the archaeological discipline, the book explores the archaeology of households to develop a greater understanding of household structure. The essays take an artefact-based approach to both material and textual evidence for household activities, irrespective of geographical region, and explore household behaviour through the distribution of material culture. Theoretical issues concerning concepts of household constitution are also addressed and provide a less structured approach to issues of spatial, gender and status organization.

The Archaeology of Household Activities provides a comprehensive and accessible study for undergraduates and postgraduates into the material record of past households, and is an essential source for a wider understanding of our own domestic development.

Penelope M. Allison holds a Research Fellowship in Archaeology at the University of Sydney, Australia. Her main research is concerned with Roman art and material culture in a domestic context and household archaeology of colonial and post-colonial Australia.

The Archaeology of Household Activities

Edited by Penelope M. Allison

London and New York

First published 1999 by Routledge
11 New Fetter Lane, London EC4P 4EE

Simultaneously published in the USA and Canada
by Routledge
29 West 35th Street, New York, NY 10001

Routledge is an imprint of the Taylor & Francis Group

Selection and editorial matter © 1999 Penelope M. Allison

Individual chapters © 1999 individual contributors

Typeset in Garamond by Keystroke, Jacaranda Lodge, Wolverhampton
Printed and bound in Great Britain by TJ International Ltd, Padstow, Cornwall

British Library Cataloguing in Publication Data
A catalogue record for this book is available from the British Library

Library of Congress Cataloging in Publication Data
A catalog record for this book has been requested

ISBN 0–415–18052–X (HB)
ISBN 0–415–20597–2 (PB)

Contents

Figures

Tables

Contributors

Rani T. Alexander, Assistant Professor, Department of Sociology and Anthropology, New Mexico State University, Las Cruces, NM 88003-8001, USA.
E-mail: raalexan@nmsu.edu

Penelope M. Allison, U2000 Post-doctoral Research Fellow, Department of Archaeology, University of Sydney, NSW 2006, Australia.
E-mail: Pim.Allison@archaeology.usyd.edu.au

Bradley A. Ault, Assistant Professor, Department of Classics, 712 Clemens Hall, State University of New York at Buffalo, N.Y. 14260, USA.
E-mail: clarbrad@acsu.buffalo.edu

Marilyn Y. Goldberg, Chair, Department of Ancient Studies, University of Maryland Baltimore County, 1000 Hilltop Circle, Baltimore, MD 21250, USA.
E-mail: goldberg@umbc.edu

Vincent M. LaMotta, Ph.D. candidate, Department of Anthropology, University of Arizona, Tucson, Arizona 85721, USA.
E-mail: vml@u.arizona.edu

Susan Lawrence, Lecturer, Department of Archaeology, LaTrobe University, Bundoora, Melbourne, Australia 3083.
E-mail: S.Lawrence@latrobe.edu.au

Eleanor Leach, Professor, Department of Classical Studies, Indiana University, Bloomington, Indiana 47405, USA.
E-mail: Leach@indiana.edu

Brian R. McKee, Ph.D. candidate, Department of Anthropology, University of Arizona, Tucson, Arizona 85721, USA.
E-mail: bmckee@u.arizona.edu

Karen Meadows, Ph.D. candidate, Department of Archaeology and Prehistory, University of Sheffield, Northgate House, West Street, Sheffield S1 4ET, UK.

Lisa C. Nevett, Lecturer, Department of Classical Studies, Faculty of Arts, The Open University, Milton Keynes, MK7 6AA, UK.
E-mail: L.C.Nevett@open.ac.uk

Michael B. Schiffer, Professor, Department of Anthropology, University of Arizona, Tucson, Arizona 85721, USA.
E-mail: schiffer@u.arizona.edu

Suzanne M. Spencer-Wood, Associate, Peabody Museum of Archaeology and Ethnology, Harvard University, USA.
E-mail: smwood@core.fas.harvard.edu

Preface

This book had its beginnings at the Annual Meeting of the Archaeological Institute of America in San Francisco in December 1990, where I met Nicholas Cahill for the first time and where we discussed the lack of good contextualized material culture studies in Classical archaeology, particularly of artefact assemblages in domestic contexts. At the AIA meeting in New Orleans in 1992 Nicholas and I started to draw up a list of potential contributors to produce a colloquium on the subject and, with Stephen Dyson's urgings, included archaeologists with research interests in parts of the world not normally represented at the AIA meetings. At the Theoretical Archaeology Conference in Durham in 1993 Lisa Nevett and I met each other (finally!) and at the Australian Women in Archaeology Conference in Sydney in February 1995 I met Suzanne Spencer-Wood, Marilyn Goldberg and Susan Lawrence. As a result of these encounters, a colloquium called 'Household Archaeology' took place at the AIA meeting in San Diego in December 1995. Suzanne Spencer-Wood encouraged me to prepare it for publication. Versions of all the papers in the original colloquium have been included in the book, along with three others.

Therefore I must first express my gratitude to all the organizers of the above conferences for facilitating these international contacts and especially to the Archaeological Institute of America Conference Fund for making it possible for Lisa Nevett and myself to take part in the colloquium in San Diego. I am also especially grateful to Stephen Dyson for all his encouragement, to all the original participants of the colloquium and to the contributors to this book. A visiting fellowship in the Department of Archaeology at the University of Sheffield and a U2000 Post-doctoral Research Fellowship in the Department of Archaeology at the University of Sydney have provided me with the time and intellectual input to prepare this book for publication. I would like to thank the staff and students of both departments for their support. I am grateful to Lisa Nevett and Eleanor Leach for assistance in the editing of the papers. Finally, I wish to thank Vicky Peters, Steven Jarman and Nadia Jacobson of Routledge for their patience and support in preparing this work for publication.

Chapter One

Introduction

Penelope M. Allison

Science is built up of facts, as a house is built of stones; but an accumulation of facts is no more a science than a house is a heap of stones.

(Henri Poincaré, *Science and Hypothesis* 1905)

The dwellings and dwelling spaces we inhabit house the attitudes and traditions through which we both conform to and confront the world beyond (Bourdieu's *habitus*). That world has the potential to bring innovation into dwelling spaces but the dwelling spaces also provide the security through which we learn to negotiate acceptable relationships with these new ideas, and to formulate and test our own. The forms and patterns of dwellings (the architecture) can act as a medium through which the outside world (the wider community) can exercise control over the activities within. At the same time the physical structures provide the means to separate these activities from the direct influence of that wider society – 'a sanctuary from the perils outside' (Ardener 1993: 11). For these reasons, architecture can never totally dictate the behaviour within its spaces. Its façades, and its internal divisions, serve as shields of social conformity behind which the traditions and the patterns of human interrelationships are formulated and enacted. Dwellings serve both 'to reveal and display' and 'to hide and protect' (Carsten and Hugh-Jones 1995: 2).

The place of houses and households in the study of the past, and especially in archaeological approaches to the past, is significant. Households constitute the bulk of the population in ancient societies (Smith 1992a: 30). Concern for households in the past has traditionally been for their role as measurable socio-economic units of the wider community (e.g. Kramer 1980; Kolb 1985: esp 581; Blanton 1994). Such concerns have frequently been based in assumptions that a 'mean family size' can be calculated through average house size at a site (cf. Kolb 1985: 582) and, therefore, that the number of households, and hence total population, of an archaeological site can be measured. However:

> We can describe the associations between material culture and social phenomena from which we estimate population but we have no model that can explain that relationship . . . The use of average figures for particular levels of socio-economic organisation may prevent our recognising gradual change when we reconstruct communities which we have identified as moving from one level to another.
>
> (Fletcher, comments in Kolb 1985: 592)

Wilk and Rathje (1982) stressed the importance of households as essential building blocks in the reconstruction of past societies. An understanding of the nature of change in household organization would bridge the existing 'mid-level theory gap' in archaeology (ibid.: 617). Households were seen as an essential level of inquiry in order to move 'from grand theories of cultural change and evolution to the practical archaeology of potsherds and stone tools'. At the level of the household 'social groups articulate directly with economic and ecological processes' (ibid.: 618). Blanton has subsequently argued that households were probably the major arena in which social productive strategies are played out (1994: esp. 20).

However, beliefs that the actual compositions of households are known, and are relatively standardized and unchanging phenomena, have permeated such studies. Thus, studies of the internal dynamics and intrarelationships of a household have been viewed as trivial and insignificant pastimes in the investigation of the patterns of human behaviour. The mechanisms and ideologies which construct the household as a unit of reproduction to contribute to society's production (see e.g. Gregory 1984: esp. 14) have been considered of little consequence. Beliefs in unproblematic compositions of households stem from perspectives that the head of the household controls the activities and behaviours of his [*sic*] socio-economic unit. The contributions of the other members to its formation and to its interaction with the community are mitigated through that household head, and therefore largely irrelevant (see Hendon 1996: 46–8).

The deconstruction of such perspectives can only lead to an awareness that household dynamics are important factors in the social, political and economic roles of the household in the wider community, not as a unit but as a system of membership (see e.g. vom Bruck 1997). '[T]o understand the power of domestic space as a social construct, one must look beyond ritual action and grand cosmological belief systems and into the practical actions of daily life' (Pader 1993: 114). To validate a conception of households as productive entities there needs to be a well-founded comprehension of what such entities might be composed of – the potential diversities of their internal organization (physical and ideological) both within a society and cross-culturally.

This book, therefore, concentrates on an essential level of inquiry – the constitution and organization of households themselves. Only when the spatial, status, gender and age relationships in the organization and structure of households are more fully explored can the complexity and diversity of the roles of households, as social and productive units in the wider community, be better understood.

ETHNOGRAPHY

Without some structured perspective on the nature of households in the past they become an elusive concept. Archaeologists do not dig up households. They dig up dwellings and domestic artefacts but not social units (Wilk and Rathje 1982: 618). A household is an ethnographic phenomenon, not an archaeological one. Yet Wilk and Rathje's definition (1982: 621) of a household as a centre for production, distribution, transmission and reproduction, draws on the ethnographic category (see Smith 1992a: 29) to construct approaches to the archaeological remains of past households. Wilk and Rathje (1982: 613) have argued that the embedding of household archaeology in a comparative ethnographic matrix is vital to any approach which will allow archaeologists to draw inferences about past household behaviour. And Blanton (1994) has attempted to develop methods for analysing the archaeological remains of households which are wholly dependent on ethnographic material.

However, the use of ethnographic and ethnohistorical analogy to explain archaeological phenomena can have the effect of normalizing past domestic behaviour and accentuating, or even constructing and superimposing, patterns of household behaviour from different temporal, cultural or spatial situations (see e.g. Fletcher, comments in Kolb 1985: 592. For the broader issue: Fletcher 1995: part I). As Ciolek-Torello argued (1984: 129), studies which have relied heavily on architectural parallels between historic and prehistoric puebloan rooms have ignored the potentially 'significant alteration of domestic activity space and organization' since prehistoric times. Likewise, an archaeologist's use of his/her own domestic behaviour as baseline ethnographic data stems from the philosophy that assumes the internal dynamics of a household are self-evident.

This is not to say that ethnography should be peripheral to the study of households in archaeology; rather, it is fundamental to it. However, the procedure should not be simply to use ethnographic data to describe household behaviour in the past but to use it also to highlight the potential for diversity and change in domestic worlds (see Wylie 1985: esp. 97–107). Ethnography should be employed as a *signifier* of complexity rather than a *prescriber* of household behaviour. Blanton's work has stressed the importance of cross-cultural studies and comparative methodologies to deepen our understanding of archaeological assemblages (Nevett 1994). However, it has not actually dealt with the problem of using archaeological remains for the insights which they are capable of providing into households and household activities in the past which are not represented in the ethnographic record. He assumes that archaeology is only capable of following an agenda set by anthropology.

TEXT

Ethnography and ethnohistory are essential tools for *exploring the possibilities* for household composition and activities from the prehistoric past, but many studies of household archaeology have been concerned with the households of historical periods (e.g. Beaudry 1984; Gibb and King 1991; Wallace-Hadrill 1994). The availability of written documentation for the archaeology of the Classical, medieval, post-medieval and colonial worlds, and for much of the Near East, provides the researchers of these areas with an often very full body of data for the investigation of household behaviours and relationships (see Beaudry 1984). But the relationships between the textual and the archaeological material can be as complex and as difficult to grasp as the relationships between archaeology and ethnography, or the interrelationships of the members of households in the past. While, in many situations in post-medieval or colonial archaeology, at least some of the members of a specific archaeologically identified household may also be identified through documentary evidence (e.g. Karskens 1997: 156), attempts to relate archaeological remains to extant textual evidence must be sensitive to the 'selective and unrepresentative nature of . . . texts' (Hijmans 1996: 81). For example, textual material often emphasizes and reinforces the roles of society's élites, while archaeology can frequently provide evidence of household behaviour across a much broader social spectrum. This is not to say that the writers of texts are isolated from social structures (see Moreland 1992: 116). Rather, attempts to read the archaeological record through direct associations with documentary sources, without regard for the specific social and ethnic contexts of that archaeological record, for the specific agenda of the texts, or for the precise relationships between these sets of data, lead to a normalization of past domestic behaviour which denies it historicity, or its regional or status specificity. Such readings not only serve to perpetuate perspectives of the inconsequence of household dynamics in the writing of history, they also compromise the ability of archaeological data to provide information which cannot be directly associated with textual information.

ARCHITECTURE

Not only are perspectives of household uniformity in the past derived from inappropriate associations of the archaeological record with often extraneous ethnographic or textual material, but studies which have concerned themselves with the archaeology of households have often been dominated by investigations of architectural remains to describe household behaviour. This is particularly evident in the predominance of studies which emphasize domestic architecture (e.g. Kent 1990; Blanton 1994). Investigations of the physical structures of dwellings from the past are frequently assumed to be investigations of domestic behaviour in the past (e.g. Laurence 1994; cf. Small 1996 and Tsakirgis 1996). Not only are houses physical units and not households (i.e. not social units). The investigation of structural remains may lead to an understanding of cultural patterning of space but does not, necessarily, lead to an understanding of the perceptions of those who built the buildings, still less to an understanding of the behaviour of those who inhabited them.

Rapoport has argued (1990: 15–20) that designers and users of the built environment are a far from homogeneous group and that 'designers tend to react to environments in perceptual terms' whereas 'the users, react to environments in associational terms'. While some buildings are built by some of the subsequent occupants, users of buildings frequently inhabit spaces designed by the builders of an earlier period or by other, more dominant, social or cultural groups who may have imposed the structures on them. A belief that most will build the house in which they will dwell (Rippengal 1993: 93) essentially stems from a belief that the head of the household is the only important member of it. While cases may exist where all household members are involved in the construction of their dwelling, many household members live in dwellings which were constructed by close relatives or associates during their lifetime but into whose construction or into decisions about its form they had little or no input (see Blanton 1994: 8). Many others live in houses built by unrelated individuals or distant ancestors. It would, therefore, be truer to say that the vast majority of individuals will not build the house in which they will dwell. Even when members of the household have contributed to the building of their own dwelling, these members can often be more concerned outwardly to imitate other socially dominant groups, in the con- struction of their dwelling, than to conform to the expected lifestyle of the household members. In such situations 'buildings [can act] as repressive mechanisms and authoritarian representations' (Miller 1987: 164). However, while such dwellings can serve to constrain those lifestyles they can never completely reformulate them (see Pader 1993). To view architecture as a prescriber and dictator of household behaviour is to bias analysis towards the perspectives of the builder or the head of the household as the signifier of domestic behaviour and, once more, to undermine the significance of the activities of the other inhabitants in the structuring of dwellings as social spaces. Fletcher argues (1995) that there is no 'proper' relationship between architecture, meaning and the social behaviour of either its producers or its consumers (cf. Rapoport 1996: 416).

Another important point, when investigating households archaeologically, is that the term 'architecture' is frequently used to refer to floor plans alone, because these are generally all that remains of dwellings from the past. For this reason, investigations of the social arrangements of domestic space tend to see dwellings as a two-dimensional concepts. The application of Hillier and Hanson's approach to social space (1984) to archaeological remains which are still three- dimensional (e.g. Grahame 1997) serves only to perpetuate a limited approach to the archaeology of households. Great emphasis has been placed on the layout of architectural remains at the expense of their three-dimensional proportions, windows, perspectives and decoration (e.g. Blanton 1994: esp. 24–37). For Roman archaeology, where such architectural remains are extant, Andrew Wallace-Hadrill's study of Pompeian households (1994: esp. 3–61) can be seen as an important departure from this, interweaving more descriptive and art-historical approaches to extant architectural remains with historical material.

The archaeology of households is also not limited to the archaeology of individual structures. It has been adequately demonstrated (e.g. Fletcher 1977; Kent 1984) that household groups can inhabit more than one structure or, alternatively, that more than one household can inhabit one structure. This leads to considerable difficulty in the conception of a household in archaeological terms, particularly if structural remains are the only archaeological evidence employed in the analysis. Thus, it is important to break free from the idea of a household, in archaeological terms, as an architecturally dominated entity. But this is also important for the many cases in archaeology where the structural remains of dwellings are either not extant in the archaeological record or they never existed. That is, a household, as a social entity, is not bounded by the identification of its 'house'.

Comments

It has been claimed that the investigation of households is an inappropriate inquiry for archaeology and that, because of its association with concepts of kinship, and a need for ethnography, ethnohistory and history to interpret spatial patterning, household archaeology is a misnomer (see Alexander, this volume). Some would argue that material remains cannot tell us anything about household behaviour. The problem here is not that archaeological remains cannot provide information on domestic behaviour in the past but rather that archaeological data is not always capable of answering the kinds of questions which anthropologists and social-historians might ask of their own data (see Wilson 1993: esp. 21).[1]

Household archaeology which can use material remains to contribute to our knowledge of household behaviour in the past must set up questions which archaeological data is capable of answering and which will provide insights into human behaviour in past societies, rather than illustrations of textual or ethnographic information. Such insights may then be compared to such ethnographic, ethnohistorical or textual data for similarities and differences. The differences are not necessarily errors on the part of the investigator; rather they may help us to understand that the diversity of human behaviour in the past is often blurred or even obliterated by use of analogy, even at the level of household activities.

ARTEFACT ASSEMBLAGES

If we argue that the uses of text, ethnography and architecture to interpret household behaviour in the past can contribute to prescriptive views and normalizing processes, what do we have left? As Wilk and Rathje have pointed out (1982: 618), households not only live in but also use material culture. While it is true to say that archaeologists do not dig up households it is also true to say that they do not just dig up houses. Whenever they dig settlement sites they invariably dig up household material culture. The architectural remains are only part of that material culture. As ethnography and history can serve to flesh out these remains, so it can serve to warn us of the role of this architecture in concealing household behaviour. Ciolek-Torello objected (1984: 152) 'to the specific ethnographic model which has been used as a substitute for quantitative examination of a broad range of archaeological context data without adequate consideration regarding the appropriateness of such data'. He turned to 'identifying recurrent patterns of spatial distribution of archaeological remains' (ibid.: 130) and argued that 'artefactual remains of activities are a far better indication of room function than are room size and other architectural features' (ibid.: 134). Ellen Pader (1993: esp. 130) has eloquently demonstrated how the architecture and projected ideologies of Mexicans who have lived in the United States reflect their experiences, but the actuality of domestic practice, by themselves and by other members in their households, follows more long-standing local traditions. These phenomena were not articulated through the architecture or even through direct ethnographic study. Insights into such phenomena were provided not only by chance discussions with relatives but also by the patterns of house contents.

It is these house contents, the 'nonfixed-feature' elements (Rapoport 1990: 96–101), of which there may often be considerable wealth in archaeological remains, which are not part of the architecture but which are evidently part of the household and which must surely constitute a major contribution to insights into household behaviour and relationships between social action and the material. While it is very difficult to use this material to identify the nature and quantity of the members of a household and their interrelationships, the patterns which this material produces, however ephemeral and whether or not delimited by architectural remains, must surely give us a greater comprehension of the range and distribution of the activities, and possibly behaviour and ideologies, within these households.

While studies of house floor assemblages for assessing spatial distribution of household activities have their beginnings in the south-west of the United States in the 1970s (see LaMotta and Schiffer, this volume), studies in branches of Old World archaeology have only recently included more holistic approaches to the archaeological record and specifically to the distribution of household artefacts within dwelling spaces (e.g. Roaf 1989; Cahill 1991; Nevett 1992; Daviau 1993; Allison 1992b; Ault 1994).

Thus, it is in this area, on this level and with this type of approach, that the material culture of past households can contribute particularly to our knowledge of past household behaviour. That is, the investigation of household activities, their spatial distribution and their changing temporal patterns are appropriate levels of inquiry for the nature of the archaeological record. To this end, this book concentrates on examining the material cultural remains of houses – the structures and their contents – which form the archaeological record. It places emphasis on the spatial patterning of structures and other artefacts to throw light on household organization of production and consumption. It investigates relationships between archaeology, text and ethnography. It includes case-studies which demonstrate various methodological and theoretical perspectives for the study of household activities in the past, within these parameters.

TYPES OF SITES

These case-studies are chosen from a wide geographical range but it is intended that they concentrate on regions, chronological periods, dwelling types and site types with suitable material remains for investigating relationships between the patterning of material culture and distribution of household activities and relationships between archaeological, ethnographic and historical data.

Four of the chapters in this book involve sites in the European region – three in the Mediterranean region (Goldberg, Ault and Nevett, Allison) and one in Britain (Meadows). Four chapters are concerned principally with the United States and Central America (Spencer-Wood, LaMotta and Schiffer, McKee, Alexander) and one with Australia (Lawrence). The types of sites range from Goldberg's study of urban housing in Classical Athens and Spencer-Wood's of public cooperatives in colonial Boston, to Meadow's, McKee's and Alexander's largely rural settings, to Lawrence's temporary mining settlement. Thus, the similarities and differences between the types of sites and the approaches to them are not necessarily regionally specific.

Important issues in the approach to archaeological remains for studying household activities are the depositional circumstances and the processes of abandonment. Many of the case-studies here concern sites which have experienced relatively rapid and often complete abandonment. The chapters by Allison, on Pompeii, and by McKee, on the sixth–seventh century AD Cerén site in El Salvador, deal with sites abandoned during volcanic eruption. Although the actual process of this abandonment, and its effect on the remaining material culture, is not necessarily as rapid and as complete as that proposed by the 'Pompeii Premise' (Schiffer 1985; cf. Allison 1992a), both sites produce a complex dataset of a type which is seldom preserved in archaeological contexts.

Alexander's study of house lots in Yaxcaba in the Yucatan, Mexico and possibly Ault and Nevett's study of Hellenistic Halieis in the southern Argolid in the Greek Peloponnese, involve sites with a documented abandonment date – that in Yaxcaba after a century of rapid political and economic change. The tenuousness of existence and the rapid social change at Lawrence's Morrabol diggings has likewise contributed to fairly swift abandonment. However, while rapid abandonment, sometimes textually recorded, is a feature of many of the case-studies in this book, it is also evident, from studies like those of Goldberg, Spencer-Wood and Meadows, that it is not a prerequisite for studies in the archaeology of households. From LaMotta and Schiffer's chapter it is also apparent that the actual process of abandonment is not always as easily read as has been assumed.

In addition, the excavation processes and the questions which the excavators and subsequent investigators wish to address are as pertinent to the nature of the information on household behaviour which is extractable from such sites, as is the actual abandonment process and the extant material record. A number of the studies in this book involve the investigation of sites which were not excavated by the current investigators but by previous archaeologists, with quite different theoretical and methodological frameworks. This is frequently the situation in Classical archaeology which has tended to produce large volumes of excavated material, often without including good contextual information, in the hope that it will one day be useful to someone (Allison 1997)! These investigators have, therefore, to extrapolate information on household activity from excavation reports whose data collection techniques fall very short of today's standards. Ault and Nevett's chapter highlights this problem for the study of household archaeology in Classical and Hellenistic Greece. However, rather than dismiss this material as unusable, Goldberg, Ault and Nevett and Allison demonstrate approaches to such excavation recordings which can provide information on household behaviour.

READING MATERIAL CULTURE

One of the aims of this book is to demonstrate that the study of household material culture provides information on domestic behaviour which may elucidate, be contradictory to, or alternatively not be evident in, related textual and ethnographic material. As Miller has discussed (1987), there exists a long-standing and widespread belief that the study of objects is an inferior academic pursuit to the study of language, because material culture is seen to be incapable of contributing to information gleaned from literary material. Furthermore, Miller has argued that it is the 'pervasive influence of linguistic methodology upon such studies of objects' which has contributed to 'crude and clumsy' approaches to 'objects of everyday interaction' (ibid.: 95–8), and thus served to substantiate this belief. As Miller has stated (ibid.: 110), archaeology affirms the significant potential of material culture to provide information on past human behaviour which might not be available through linguistic or literary sources. Fletcher (1992: 37–8) has pointed out that the work of Hodder and others since the 1980s has introduced to archaeology 'the role of material entities as potentially active components of human behaviour'. Furthermore he has argued that the 'enduring material component of human behaviour . . . exerts selective pressure on social action, even though it is originally derived from that action' (see also Fletcher 1995).

While views of the superiority of the study of languages over the study of material culture are not generally held by archaeologists, many do hold a view of the superiority of the study of architectural remains over less evident past material culture in providing information about past human behaviour. This is particularly evident in much of the archaeology of historical periods with substantial structural remains, where the investigation of the material culture for household behaviour has often ignored the information which the smaller objects related to these structures can provide. The concentration on architectural remains, as the archaeological evidence of households from the past, is not only a compromise of the archaeological evidence but it denies the individuality of the members of the household who inhabited these spaces. It is not merely through architectural remains of past dwellings that we can use material culture to learn about past domestic behaviour – the complete archaeological assemblage can provide much richer information (Miller 1987; Shanks and Tilley 1987).

The authors in this book stress the importance of a more holistic approach to the material remains of households and the nature of the evidence which that approach can provide. Goldberg highlights the adaptability of domestic space and furniture to argue that investigation of architectural remains alone is a misleading approach to household behaviour. McKee incorporates structural and non-structural evidence to assess the distribution of household activites and Lawrence, likewise, demonstrates how the identification of activities in temporary structures is as dependent on their contents as on their architecture, if not more so. Alexander and Meadows emphasize how the distribution of material culture, at sites which are largely devoid of architectural remains, can be used to map activity areas and behaviours at the household level. And Spencer-Wood explores the active role which domestic inventions of the late nineteenth century had on structuring domestic activities.

PRODUCTION AND CONSUMPTION

As discussed above, studies of household archaeology in the past have been largely concerned with elucidating evidence of the household as a unit of production, both economic and social. But dwellings are generally the principle location for the consumption of material culture. Hendon (1996: 50) has argued that activities like food and cloth production are important household activities (see also Gardner and Wiedemann 1991: 72) but that these have not figured much in discussions of household organization or function. There has been a tendency to separate house-hold activities which are concerned with production and distribution outside the household from those which are concerned with production or consumption within the household. Such separation of specialization, surplus production and household consumption applies artificial, uniform and generalized parameters to household behaviour (Hendon 1996: 55) which cannot be verified historically or cross-culturally.

This book discusses the information that the study of household material culture can provide on the production and consumption activities of a household without unwarranted assumptions about such separations of household-focused tasks. To this end many of the chapters concentrate on the consumption of material culture, but this is by no means straightforward. Some of the principle reasons for difficulties in studies of material culture consumption stem from assump-tions, both in capitalist and Marxist systems, of a hierarchy of production over consumption rather than a reciprocity, with consumption as a logical outcome of production rather than as an active agent in the process of that production (see Miller 1987: 46–8). Ault and Nevett discuss how the types of questions usually asked by Classical archaeologists render a study of household consumption difficult. And this is exemplified in Allison's chapter which demonstrates that investigations of household activities, and particularly of consumption, first require an unravelling of past scholarship which has frequently depended on unsubstantiated analogies between text, archaeology and contemporary domestic behaviour and has overemphasized material culture production. Spencer-Wood stresses the role of colonial women in household production, and in the invention of domestic machines for the production and consumption of food outside the private household. Lawrence uses both textual evidence and the distribution of material cultural remains to demonstrate the complex relationships between household production and consumption activities, both social and economic. She also uses bone assemblages to dispel myths about limited diet on goldfields. Meadows is likewise concerned with culinary habits, focusing on social, cultural, political and economic motivations for types of food consumption and its relationship to settlement structures and 'romanization'. Alexander considers household consumption through quantitative comparisons of non-local material culture and its relationship to a community's political and economic status.

CLASSIFICATION

Investigations of material culture consumption also highlight the issue of category (Wittgenstein 1963), particularly the process of classifying archaeological remains, and thereby demonstrate the effects which this issue is having on our ability to use archaeological data to ask more sociological questions. As Miller has demonstrated, objects are classified through language which is not always adequate or appropriate. Despite overriding concerns in archaeology for production processes, objects from the past are usually labelled on the basis of their forms, thereby providing them with assumed functions (Miller 1985: 51–74). But, as Miller has again argued (1987: 116), this procedure does not account for the fact 'that form and function are not inherently related' and that there is a 'distance between form and function in non-industrial as well as industrial societies'. This is particularly important in household archaeology where assumed relationships between form and function produce a normalizing effect on domestic behaviour and a sense of familiarity which is not necessarily warranted.

Because of such difficulties, on a more practical level, investigations of household consumption are often thwarted by the lack of usable models. Therefore, attempts in the chapters of this book to deal with issues of household consumption may seem limited and relatively insignificant. However, these attempts involve a critical approach to this issue which attempts to break free from past prejudices in this area of research. Allison's chapter seeks to show how classification systems in Roman archaeology mislead us into believing that Roman household behaviour is a well-known and familiar phenomenon. The exceptional state of preservation at the Cerén site, and more recent approaches to its excavation than to that of Pompeii, has permitted McKee to demonstrate that the reuse of material culture within the dwelling structure shows ongoing and changing consumption of material culture which is not so apparent in more usual archaeological sites. His examples also demonstrate that the labelling of pottery sherds can be unrelated to their final functions. Such examples warn that traditional studies of the production and distribution of material culture can benefit by paying more attention to the consumption of material culture.

GENDER AND VISIBILITY

The importance of a study of past household activities is evident through the need to deconstruct perceptions that households are largely unchanging and known socio-economic entities, with a known set of power structures. Such perceptions have been created by the application of analogy with contemporary western societies to the study of past domestic behaviour, such as views that the house is the locus for consumption (Miller 1994: 8) and the woman's domain (see also Rapoport 1990: 187) but under the authority of the male head of the household. Rather ironically, they have even led to David's assumptions (1971: 128) of 'the *male* [my emphasis] tendency towards archaeological invisibility' in households because of a belief that the material culture of households would inform mainly about female activities. However, Bourdieu's celebrated study of the Kabyle house in Algeria (1970) has done much to inspire subsequent scholars to investigate the arrangements of household material culture for more sensitive and informed insights into gender and spatial distributions of domestic activities. Nevertheless, it has also led many scholars to concentrate on binary gender oppositions in the domestic worlds of other cultures (e.g. Blanton 1994: esp. 12). Kent's study of contemporary Navajo, Euroamericans and Spanish-Americans tested for sex specific and mono-functional spaces in domestic contexts and generally found that such divisions are ideologies of modern European societies (1984: esp. 1, 187). More recently, vom Bruck (1997) has shown that the Kabyle model cannot even be applied to other parts of the Arab world, where domestic spatial relationships are much more complex and fluid.

Cultural and gender biases in investigations of past household behaviour can be exposed, and potentially even removed, through engendered approaches to archaeology, particularly those which address the issues concerning divisions of labour and the visibility of gender. Wilk has stated (1991: 6) that 'a vital part of that very cultural context [i.e. household decisions] is gender-based divisions of labour within the household', but this should not be assumed to be uniform across time, space and status. To quote Tringham (1991: 101), 'strong implicit assumptions about generic gender relations form the foundation of many formulations of household archaeology studies'. It is largely through the use of analogies with western societies, through preconceived ideas about activities and through concerns for the perspectives of a male head of the household, rather than through anything readable in the archaeological data, that assumptions have been made about gender roles, gender distribution of activities and spaces, and an invisibility of certain members of the household. As Tringham (1991: 93) has emphasized, gender is not visible in the architectural remains, nor in archaeological remains. In the archaeological record of dwelling spaces, without some outside analogical inferences, males are no more or less visible than females, élites no more or less visible than subordinates. Notions of the invisibility of only certain members of the household in the archaeological record are determined by assumptions that other members are more visible. Moore and Scott (1997) include diverse approaches to concepts of invisibility in the archaeological record but, as Hodder warns (1997a: 75–8), we must continue to be critical of our own prejudices in our attempts to highlight biases and to redress the balance. Hendon has pointed out (1996: 49) that the 'most productive archaeological studies of the household have focused on gender as a symbolic system that structures social and economic relations within the household and the larger community'.

Chapters in this book rely on engendered approaches to textual analogy to identify gender relationships. Goldberg stresses the importance of individual agency in the breakdown of presumptions of the passivity of non-dominant groups in households of Classical Athens. She argues for the lack of archaeological evidence for engendered space and that binary oppositions in the Greek world might be more evident in status, or between households and the world beyond, than they are between male and female spaces (cf. Wallace-Hadrill 1994: 8). Through evidence from similarly engendered readings of Classical literature and from social movements of the late nineteenth century, particularly domestic reform, Spencer-Wood vehemently opposes assumptions about continued gender separation of activities in western society.

Allison demonstrates that the misuse of textual analogy and assumptions about task division in interpretations of Pompeian household material culture are often the cause of any invisibility of the activities of 'subordinate' members of the household. Lawrence sees households as the logical place to increase the visibility of women and uses material culture consumption to distinguish all-male households from those with a female presence. She demonstrates that production and consumption activities are not divided along strictly gender lines, even in a nineteenth-century, largely European, society.

PRIVACY

Another concept which has pervaded household studies in the past, and particularly in the western world, is that of a binary opposition between public and private lives. The recent series by Philippe Ariès and Georges Duby, *A History of Private Life*, is a case in point. This series draws on masculinist perspectives which classify private life as that pertaining to women, children and slaves, and the household as being made up of elements which 'serve' the master. It perpetuates the domination of written documentation, as opposed to material culture, in the study of European domestic behaviour, thus producing largely male and bourgeois perspectives of domestic life in the past. As Hendon has stressed (1996: 47) 'cross-cultural studies of gender have [now] undermined the domestic/public opposition as universal or even particularly meaningful' and serve to demonstrate that such approaches to studies of the functions of archaeological space (cf. Wallace-Hadrill 1994: 8–16) once again have an unwarranted normalizing effect on our understanding of past household behaviour.

In this book, Goldberg likewise argues that assumptions about public/private space are part of the cultural baggage of the modern scholar. Through her evidence of the subsistence farming activities of women and children, Lawrence demonstrates that the association of women with private and men with public space are aspects for upper and middle class Europeans which have become reified in historical documentation. Spencer-Wood discusses the public roles of women in Classical Greece and also demonstrates that the instigation of public cooperative housekeeping in the nineteenth century challenges the traditional definition of household as private and extends women's 'private' roles to the 'public' community.

SYMBOLISM

As well as neglecting the role of household consumption, studies of household archaeology have tended to ignore the roles of ritual and symbolism in household behaviour and in the deposition of household material culture. This is in notable contrast to Carsten and Hugh-Jones's claim for 'a tendency in anthropology . . . to focus on the ritual aspects of social life' rather than the 'everyday activities, carried on without ritual' (Carsten and Hugh-Jones 1995: 45). I believe that one of the main problems is the assumption that 'everyday', or routine, and 'ritual' are separate phenomena. For example, the 'everyday' activity of morning coffee is a 'ritual'. The important issues are that 'routine' activities often have their own symbolic qualities and ritual activities can be part of everyday routine. Such symbolism is inherent in the archaeological record of households.

In this context, Meadows discusses the daily ritual of eating, as well as ritual eating on celebratory occasions, and the symbolism involved in the adoption of 'Roman' material culture by native populations. Spencer-Wood highlights the acquisition of cult status of many aspects of women's routine domestic roles, and the manner in which this could be symbolically expressed through material culture. Similarly, Lawrence discusses the roles of women in the maintenance of the household's cultural identity and as guardians of morality and respectability. She also stresses the symbolic nature of household material culture in structuring and reinforcing social status, and particularly in articulating aspirations of Victorian gentility. Goldberg has less material evidence but uses textual information to draw our attention to aspects of household religion and the place of Athenian women in public worship, which might enable them to acquire levels of authority and thus constitute an added dimension to spatial and gender relations within the household.

LaMotta and Schiffer stress the importance of ritual in the depositional processes of material culture within a dwelling. They introduce the significance of ritual abandonment in the life cycle of domestic structures and point out that, while the 'least effort model of abandonment behaviour' is often used to relate types of assemblages to types of abandonment, 'ritual abandonment processes' can often play a large part in enriching floor assemblages and can complicate more processual readings of abandonment processes.

TEMPORALITY

One of the most important factors in the relationship between household material culture and household behaviour concerns temporality, both in terms of the daily life cycle and the life cycle of the household itself. Smith (1992a) has argued for the impossibility of isolating the remains of a single household in the past, except at sites with catastrophic abandonment as at Pompeii and the Cerén site. I would argue that even at such sites one cannot isolate a single, quantified, household. Likewise, in cultures where dwellings might be specifically built for one generation, the original individuals may remain, but other occupants grow, multiply and move away (Laslett 1972: 371; Goody 1969). Rather, the developmental life cycles of dwellings, both cross-culturally and in most abandonment contexts, practically guarantee that all archaeological sites involve Smith's household series. Thus, house floor assemblages are always a palimpsest of activities which may cover several generations. Archaeological contexts are not systemic contexts, even at Pompeii (see Allison 1992a). The material culture remains of households might therefore be best employed to investigate patterns of household behaviour which are likely to persist over generations. Alexander discusses the issue of potential variation in household organization over time, its links to means of production and residential mobility, and the resulting problems of using ethnohistory to explore this issue.

But an investigation of household behaviour through material culture must also bear in mind the changing use of space throughout the day. Bourdieu has demonstrated potential for the daily changing relationships between people, household objects and space (see also vom Bruck 1997). Given the difficulties in isolating the activities of single households from the past it is only too evident that separating out daily routines through archaeological remains, without textual and ethnographic analogy, is practically impossible. Rather, the potential for the use of and access to particularly household spaces to change throughout the day serves to warn scholars from making oversimplistic associational relationships within assemblages or from ascribing static functions to such spaces. Such issues are important to Goldberg's study of Athenian houses.

METHODS OF ANALYSIS

The chapters in this book demonstrate a number of methodological approaches for the analysis of household activities through archaeological remains. Only through combinations of methods and critical appraisals of the appropriateness of such methods, in each case, can archaeological remains be employed to throw light on past household behaviour.

Ethnographic and textual analogy

As mentioned above, ethnographic and textual analogy are important analytical tools in archaeology and particularly in household archaeology. However, as Smith (1992b: 52) has complained for studies in Postclassic central Mexico, 'many "archaeological" interpretations . . . are so permeated by historical constructs that their archaeological reliability or accuracy is difficult to judge'. A type of analogy which is in constant use, particularly when concerned with domestic life, is analogy with contemporary western cultures. Wilk and Rathje have argued (1982: 619) that we can use our knowledge of a society's economy and subsistence to infer the kinds of household units which were present and that we can use material evidence to test these inferences. While any type of analogy has the potential to bias interpretations of archaeological remains, if used critically analogy provides essential data for the modes of inquiry for most of the case-studies in this volume. The issue is not whether analogy is appropriate *per se* but whether the particular analogical inferences made are appropriate to the particular archaeological data (Wylie 1985).

Alexander argues for a reconsideration of ethnoarchaeological and ethnohistorical approaches to household archaeology in Mesoamerica. She uses ethnographic studies from agricultural communities in the Maya lowlands to investigate the spatial arrangements of house lots in precolonial and colonial communities in Yaxcaba Parish, but warns of the danger of the undue synchronicity and descriptive approach to past behaviour that such analogy imposes on the archaeological record, rather than explaining the variation between the two sets of data. LaMotta and Schiffer draw on an array of ethnographic studies in the south-west of the United States and other parts of the world to investigate the diversity of depositional processes in houses and to highlight the potential for 'unanticipated' processes in the life cycles and abandonments of dwellings.

Goldberg highlights textual tyranny in Greek archaeology but also demonstrates that a re-reading of the same texts, from a feminist perspective and with a critical re-investigation of their relationship to the archaeological remains, can substantially alter our interpretations of domestic behaviour in Classical Athens. In a similar vein, Lawrence combines documentary and archaeological evidence to challenge perceptions of goldfields in colonial Australia as being male dominated. Spencer-Wood stresses the need for critical analysis of both archaeological and documentary data to comprehend relationships between ideologies and actual practice, but she also emphasizes the usefulness of documentary evidence to locate sites of domestic reform. Allison discusses the processes whereby potentially inappropriate analogical inference has been used to order and normalize the Roman domestic world and, in so doing, to imbue past societies with our own concerns and ideologies and to create a belief in an enduring western tradition of domestic behaviour.

Pictorial analogy

Another important body of analogical material, which can often have a good chronological and social proximity to the archaeological data, is pictorial representation. This can include depictions of dwellings and household objects and activities in artistic or commemorative representations – sculpture, paintings, etchings, drawings or even early photography. However, like textual evidence, pictorial evidence can be imbued with its own agenda and can reproduce ideal rather than actual behaviour.

Goldberg employs Greek vase-painting, depicting men and women in association with moveable furniture and engaged in household activities, as a major source of evidence for the engendering of those activities. Lawrence is able to make use of artists' depictions of gold-mining settlements to explain and interpret the fragmentary remains of temporary dwellings. Spencer-Wood relies on architectural and design drawings to comprehend the workings of public kitchens and their apparatus. Allison discusses relationships between objects depicted in Pompeian wall-paintings and interpretations of found objects.

Thus, available contemporary pictorial material can be extremely useful in providing relevant information on household behaviour but it can also serve to distort our view of the material past if not treated with caution and appropriately contextualized. Like textual and ethnographic material, it embodies the world-view of the creator which cannot necessarily be seen as representative of the world-views or practice of those being depicted, or of those in analogous situations.

Artefact assemblages

Subsequent to Sherratt's claims (1992: 135, 140) of the 'continuing capacity of archaeologists and historians to ignore each other's existence' and that 'Archaeology will have come of age when historians arrange symposia etc. on what historians can learn from archaeologists', some historians, particularly social historians, are starting to realize the importance of the archaeological record. However, there is a belief among many such scholars, who have come to this realization in the interdisciplinary post-modern world (e.g. Laurence 1997: esp. 10), that post-processual archaeology requires a rejection of processual method in order to answer more sociological questions. While the objectivity of processual method does need to be questioned (Hodder 1997b), such beliefs often demonstrate a lack of understanding of the strengths and limitations of the archaeological record and of the need to comprehend site formation processes to exploit this record appropriately before questions can be asked, and answered, about relationships between household behaviour and the archaeological record. Schiffer's detailed approach to site formation processes and 'Cultural Transforms' is fundamental to the interpretation of archaeological sites and to their use in household archaeology, even in this post-modern world. Attempts to reject such approaches constitute an ignorance of the very nature of the archaeological record. To quote Fletcher (1992: 40) 'opponents of processualism [have] had to revert to individual-based humanism'.

For this reason, at the very least, LaMotta and Schiffer's synthesis of their own work and of the ethnographic studies of others stresses the accretion and depletion processes which contribute to floor assemblages and which occur during habitation, abandonment and post-abandonment. They present a clear outline of the effect which various activities and processes during the domestic life cycle have on different types of objects and how these processes, which include the role of human thought (see Shanks 1997: 397), can change to almost the complete opposite during the abandonment phase. Thus they offer a pragmatic approach to provide a guideline to dealing with the processes through which house contents reach their archaeological context, isolating the main pitfalls faced in using artefactual assemblages to study habitual household activities. The importance of this approach to archaeological process in the study of house-hold activities is amply demonstrated by its employment in many of the chapters here.

Ault and Nevett argue that the concentration on structural remains in the study of Greek houses has led to their treatment as 'empty shells'. They use a step by step approach to Schiffer's methodogy to examine the artefactual assemblages and to extract information, however elusive and fragile, about the spatial distribution of household activities at Halieis. McKee's work is also explictly derived from Schiffer's, in that he employs the Cerén as a 'laboratory' to examine specific pre-abandonment formation processes which are often obscured at other archaeological sites. His assemblages are important in that they include much organic material which is either not preserved at other sites or not recorded at sites with less careful excavation and recording procedures (see Allison 1995: 152–4). His analysis includes the identification of patterns of reuse and discard in household contexts which warn of the difficulties of tying assumed artefact functions with spatial functions. Alexander employs this method in surface survey to investigate spatial patterns of household activities.

The chapters of Spencer-Wood, Allison, Lawrence and Meadows are less explicit in the application of such an approach but, nonetheless, rigorous processual method is evident in their data processing.[2] Meadows employs environmental data to establish the presence of habitation and to indicate dietary habits. Spencer-Wood stresses that material culture which expresses nineteenth-century domestic reforms may be found above or below ground. She also highlights the significance to the archaeological deposit of levels of rubbish removal in differing urban areas and notes the types of artefacts which might be found and which might be symptomatic of domestic reform practices.

Artefact distribution, as a level of inquiry, is given considerable emphasis in this volume, in many cases because of its role in contributing to less prescriptive approaches to the distribution of household activities. As evidenced in the chapters in this book, the use of computerized databases and statistical analyses have greatly facilitated such approaches to household material culture. To carry out a study of household activities there is a need for a 'rich' description of all domestic remains, such as is lacking in Blanton (1994) and many similar studies.

CONCLUSIONS

Considerable chronological and geographical gaps between the study areas of this book are obvious, but the aim is not to produce a comprehensive study of all households in the past. Rather it is to assess the nature of the information which can be elicited through combinations of theoretical and methodical frameworks in differing archaeological contexts. The main emphasis is on the exploration of possibilities for contextualizing assemblages at settlement sites with varying depositional conditions, towards a better understanding of household space and house-hold activity. It is also to take a critical perspective on the extent to which archaeological assemblages provide important information on household activities and the extent to which analogy is useful for interpreting this data or, conversely, presents biased or distorted perspectives of the meanings of household material culture. At the same time it must be acknowledged that we can never get more than biased views of the past.

Thus, this book discusses some of the problems which archaeology, as a discipline which deals with material culture from both historical and prehistorical periods, faces in attempting to identify households and household activity through the archaeological record before the role of the household as a socio-economic entity can be discussed.

It is immediately apparent that the case-studies in this book concern some of the principal areas which have traditions of not just western, but, more specifically North American scholarship which has been the most prominent in its concern for the archaeology of households (e.g. Kent 1984; Wilk and Ashmore 1988; Wilk and Rathje 1982). One of the main aims of this book, which stems from the objectives of the original colloquium, is to integrate Classical archaeology with other archaeologies which have traditionally employed more anthropological approaches to the archaeological record (see Dyson 1989). But this integration is not a one-way process. The re-investigation of the rich dataset of the Classical world, which is often the envy of archaeologists working in fields less well endowed with material and textual remains, can serve to expose many of our preconceived ideas about relative uniformity in western domestic traditions and exemplify the variability of household composition, activities and relationships in the past. Likewise, as Spencer-Wood demonstrates, a more critical perspective of gender ideologies in the Classical world and their role in constructing nineteenth-century ideologies is important for exposing the biases which contemporary scholars bring to their investigations of households.

It is not seen as the role of this book to replace established frameworks of domestic behaviour with a new set of criteria. It was felt that there exists a need for a study which concentrates on the role of archaeology in leading to a better comprehension of the complexity of spatial relationships in the domestic sphere in the past and of the constant renegotiations of those relationships. There is a need to break free from the normalizing effects which much ethnographic, textual and contemporary analogy can have on this area of inquiry. Thus, this book aims to highlight the lack of evidence for many all-encompassing models of household behaviour and to show how an attempt to comprehend the agencies which formulate a household can lead to a better compre-hension of the roles of households in the wider community. At the same time it demonstrates that largely processual approaches to household archaeology are necessary to produce well-grounded datasets to which more sociological theoretical frameworks, concerned with consumption, privacy, gender, symbolism, household series and an historiographic approach to the nature of a household, can be applied. As might be expected the chapters in this book are not necessarily all in agreement on these issues, with me or with the other contributors, but I hope this book will go some way, at least, to achieving some of these objectives.

ACKNOWLEDGEMENTS

I would like to thank Roland Fletcher and Jean Ellard for reading versions of this introduction and for their useful comments.

NOTES

1 A case in point is Laurence and Wallace-Hadrill (1997), where many of the contributors have explored archaeological remains to find expressions of social phenomena which are known from textual information (e.g. slaves). Such approaches assume that a site like Pompeii provides an ethnographic record which has a direct and easily readable relationship to textual phenomena (cf. Allison 1992b: esp. 100). Any lack of such expression is attributed to the inadequacies of archaeology rather than, more appropriately, to the problems arising from 'mixed epistemologies' and the confusion of 'macroprocesses' and 'micro-processes' (Wilson 1993: 22).
2 This method was very much part of my original study of Pompeian house contents (Allison 1992a, 1992b, 1995).

BIBLIOGRAPHY

Allison, P. M. (1992a) 'Artefact Assemblages: Not the "Pompeii Premise"', in E. Herring *et al.* (eds) *Papers of the Fourth Conference in Italian Archaeology* 3, no. 1, London: Accordia Research Centre: 49–56.
—— (1992b) 'The Distribution of Pompeian House Contents and its Significance', Ph.D. thesis, University of Sydney, Ann Arbor: University Microfilms no. 9400463 (1994).
—— (1995) 'House Contents in Pompeii: Data Collection and Interpretative Procedures for a Reappraisal of Roman Domestic Life and Site Formation Processes', *Journal of European Archaeology* 3, 1: 145–76.
—— (1997) 'Why Do Excavation Reports Have Finds Catalogues?', in C. Cumberpatch and P. Blinkhorn (eds) *Not So Much a Pot More a Way of Life: Recent Approaches to Artefact Studies*, Oxford: Oxbow Books: 77–84.
Ardener, S. (1993) *Women and Space* (2nd revised edition), Oxford: Berg.
Ariès, P. and Duby, G. (1985–7) *Histoire de la vie privée*, vols 1–5, Paris: Seuil.
Ault, B. (1994) 'Classical Houses and Households: An Architectural and Artifactual Case Study from Halieis, Greece', Ph.D. thesis, Indiana University, Ann Arbor: University Microfilms no. AA195-18532.
Beaudry, M. (1984) 'Archaeology and the Historical Household', *Man in the Northeast* 28: 27–38.
Blanton, R. E. (1994) *Houses and Households: A Comparative Study. Interdisciplinary Contributions to Archaeology*, London and New York: Plenum Press.
Bourdieu, P. (1970) 'La maison Kabyle ou le monde renversé', in J. Pouillon and P. Maranda (eds) *Échanges et Communications: Mélanges offerte à Claude Lévi-Strauss* II, Paris and La Hague: Mouton: 739–58.
—— (1977) *Outline of a Theory of Practice* (trans. R. Nice), Cambridge: Cambridge University Press.
Carsten, J. and Hugh-Jones, H. (eds) (1995) *About the House: Lévi-Strauss and Beyond*, Cambridge: Cambridge University Press.
Cahill, N. D. (1991) 'Olynthus: Social and Spatial Planning in a Greek City', Ph.D. thesis, University of California, Berkeley, Ann Arbor: University Microfilms no. 9228589.
Ciolek-Torello, R. (1984) 'An Alternative Model of Room Function from Grasshopper Pueblo, Arizona', in H. Hietala (ed.) *Intrasite Spatial Analysis in Archaeology*, Cambridge: Cambridge University Press: 127–53.
Daviau, M. (1993) *Houses and their Furnishings in Bronze Age Palestine: Domestic Activity Areas and Artefact Distribution in the Middle and Late Bronze Ages* (*Journal for the Study of the Old Testament*, Supplement no. 143), Sheffield: Sheffield Academic Press.
David, N. (1971) 'The Fulani Compound and the Archaeologist', *World Archaeology* 3,1: 111–31.

Dyson, S. L. (1989) 'The Role of Ideology and Institutions in Shaping Classical Archaeology in the Nineteenth and Twentieth Centuries', in A. L. Christensson (ed.) *Tracing Archaeology's Past: The Historiography of Archaeology*, Carbondale and Edwardsville: Southern Illinois University Press: 127–35.

Fletcher, R. (1977) 'Settlement Studies (Micro and Semi-micro)', in D. L. Clarke (ed.) *Spatial Archaeology*, London: Academic Press: 47–162.

—— (1992) 'Time Perspectivism, *Annales* and the Potential for Archaeology', in A. B. Knapp (ed.) *Archaeology, Annales and Ethnohistory*, Cambridge: Cambridge University Press: 35–49.

—— (1995) *The Limits of Settlement Growth*, Cambridge: Cambridge University Press.

Gardner, J. and Wiedemann, T. (1991) *The Roman Household: A Sourcebook*, London: Routledge.

Gibb, J. G. and King, J. A. (1991) 'Gender, Activity Areas and Homelots in the 17th Century Chesapeake Region', *Historical Archaeology* 25: 109–31.

Goody, J. (ed.) (1969) *The Developmental Cycle in Domestic Groups*, Cambridge: Cambridge University Press.

Grahame, M. (1997) 'Public and Private in the Roman House: The *Casa del Fauno*', in R. Laurence and A. Wallace-Hadrill (eds) *Domestic Space in the Roman World: Pompeii and Beyond* (*Journal of Roman Archaeology* Supplement 22): 137–64.

Gregory, C. A. (1984) 'The Economy and Kinship: A Critical Examination of Some of The Ideas of Marx and Lévi-Strauss', in M. Spriggs (ed.) *Marxist Perspectives in Archaeology*, Cambridge: Cambridge University Press: 11–21.

Hendon, J. A. (1996) 'Archaeological Approaches to the Organization of Domestic Labor: Household Practice and Domestic Relations', *Annual Review of Anthropology* 25: 45–61.

Hijmans, S. E. (1996) 'Contextualizing Sol Invictus: an Essay in the Role of Post-processual Archaeology in the Study of the Roman Sun-God', in C. M. Gulliver, W. Ernst and F. Scriba (eds) *Archaeology, Ideology and Method: Inter-academy Seminar on Current Archaeological Research 1993*, Rome: Canadian Academic Centre in Italy: 77–96.

Hillier, B. and Hanson, J. (1984) *The Social Logic of Space*, Cambridge: Cambridge University Press.

Hodder, I. (1997a) 'Commentary: the Gender Screen', in J. Moore and E. Scott (eds) *Invisible People and Processes: Writing Gender and Childhood into European Archaeology*, London and New York: Leicester University Press: 75–8.

—— (1997b) 'Towards a Reflexive Excavation Methodology', *Antiquity* 71, 273: 691–700.

Karskens, G. (1997) *The Rocks: Life in Early Sydney*, Carlton, Victoria: Melbourne University Press.

Kent, S. (1984) *Analyzing Activity Areas: An Ethnoarchaeological Study of the Use of Space*, Alberquerque: University of New Mexico.

—— (ed.) (1990) *Domestic Architecture and the Use of Space: An Interdisciplinary Cross-cultural Study*, Cambridge: Cambridge University Press.

Kolb, C. (1985) 'Demographic Estimates in Archaeology: Contributions from Ethnography on Meso-american Peasants', *Current Anthropology* 26: 581–99.

Kramer, C. (1980) 'Estimating Prehistoric Populations: an Ethnoarchaeological Approach', in M.-T. Barrelet (ed.) *L'Archéologie de l'Iraq: Perspectives et Limites de l'Interprétation Anthropologique des Documents* (Colloques internationaux du C.N.R.S. 580), Paris: 315–34.

Laslett, P. (1972) *Household and Family in Past Time*, Cambridge, Cambridge University Press.

Laurence, R. (1994) *Roman Pompeii: Space and Society*, London: Routledge.

—— (1997) 'Space and Text', in R. Laurence and A. Wallace-Hadrill (eds) *Domestic Space in the Roman World: Pompeii and Beyond* (*Journal of Roman Archaeology Supplement* 22), Portsmouth: 7–14.

Laurence, R. and Wallace-Hadrill, A. (eds) (1997) *Domestic Space in the Roman World: Pompeii and Beyond* (*Journal of Roman Archaeology* Supplement 22), Portsmouth.

Miller, D. (1985) *Artefacts as Category*, Cambridge: Cambridge University Press.

—— (1987) *Material Culture and Mass Consumption*, Oxford: Blackwell.

—— (1994) *Modernity: An Ethnographic Approach*, Oxford: Berg.

Moore, J. and Scott, E. (eds) (1997) *Invisible People and Processes: Writing Gender and Childhood into European Archaeology*, London and New York: Leicester University Press.

Moreland, J. (1992) 'Restoring the Dialectic: Settlement Patterns and Documents in Medieval Central Italy', in A. B. Knapp (ed.) *Archaeology, Annales and Ethnohistory*, Cambridge: Cambridge University Press: 112–29.

Nevett, L. (1992) 'Variation in the Form and Use of Domestic Space in the Greek World in the Classical and Hellenistic Periods', Unpublished Ph.D. thesis, University of Cambridge.

—— (1994), 'Review of R. E. Blanton, *Houses and Households: A Comparative Study*', *Antiquity* 68, 260: 666–7.

Pader, E. J. (1993) 'Spatiality and Social Change: Domestic Space in Mexico and the United States, *American Ethnologist* 20, 1: 114–37.

Rapoport, A. (1990) *The Meaning of the Built Environment: A Nonverbal Communication Approach*, Tucson: University of Arizona.

—— (1996) 'Review of M. Parker Pearson and C. Richards, *Architecture and Order: Approaches to Social Space*', *American Journal of Archaeology* 100: 416–17.

Rippengal, R. (1993) '"Villas as a Key to Social Structure"? Some Comments on Recent Approaches to the Romano-British Villa and Some Suggestions Towards an Alternative', in E. Scott (ed.) *Theoretical Roman Archaeology: First Conference Proceedings* (Worldwide Archaeology Series 4), Avebury: 79–101.

Roaf, M. (1989) 'Ubaid Social Organization and Social Activities as seen from Tell Madhhur', in E. F. Henrickson and I. Thuesen (eds) *Upon this Foundation – The Ubaid Reconsidered*, Copenhagen: Museum Tusculanum Press: 91–146.

Schiffer, M. B. (1985) 'Is there a Pompeii Premise?', *Journal of Anthropological Research* 41: 18–41.

Shanks, M. (1997) 'Archaeological Theory: What's on the Agenda?', *American Journal of Archaeology* 101: 395–99.

Shanks, M. and Tilley, C. (1987) *Re-constructing Archaeology*, Cambridge: Cambridge University Press.

Sherrat, A. (1992) 'What can Archaeologists Learn from Annalistes? in A. B. Knapp (ed.) *Archaeology, Annales and Ethnohistory*, Cambridge: Cambridge University Press: 135–42.

Small, D. B. (1996) Review of R. Laurence, *Roman Pompeii: Space and Society* (1994), *American Journal of Archaeology* 100, 2: 430.

Smith, M. (1992a) 'Braudel's Temporal Rhythms and Chronology Theory in Archaeology', in A. B. Knapp (ed.) *Archaeology, Annales and Ethnohistory*, Cambridge: Cambridge University Press: 23–34.

—— (1992b) 'Rhythms of Change in Postclassic Central Mexico', in A. B. Knapp (ed.) *Archaeology, Annales and Ethnohistory*, Cambridge: Cambridge University Press: 51–74.

Tringham, R. (1991) 'Households with Faces: the Challenge of Gender in Prehistoric Architectural Remains', in J. M. Gero and M. W. Conkey (eds) *Engendering Archaeology: Women in Prehistory*, Oxford: Blackwell: 93–131.

Tsakirgis, B. (1996) 'Houses and Households', *American Journal of Archaeology* 100, 4: 777–81.

Vom Bruck, G. (1997) 'A House Turned Inside Out', *Journal of Material Culture* 2, 2: 139–72.

Wallace-Hadrill, A. (1994) *Houses and Society in Pompeii and Herculaneum*, Princeton: Princeton University Press.

Wilk, R. R. (1991) 'The Household in Anthropology: Panacea or Problem?', *Reviews in Anthropology* 20,: 1–12.

Wilk, R. R. and Ashmore, W. (eds) (1988) *Household and Community in the Mesoamerican Past*, Albuquerque: University of New Mexico Press.

Wilk, R. R. and Rathje, W. L. (eds) (1982) 'Archaeology of the Household: Building a Prehistory of Domestic Life', *American Behavioral Scientist* 25, 6: 611–725.

Wilson, S. M. (1993) 'Structure and History: Combining Archaeology and Ethnohistory in the Contact Period Caribbean', in D. J. Rogers and S. M. Wilson (eds) *Ethnohistory and Archaeology*, New York: Plenum Press: 19–29.

Wittgenstein, L. (1963) *Philosophical Investigations* (trans. G. E. M. Anscombe), Oxford: Blackwell.

Wylie, A. (1985) 'The Reaction against Analogy', *Advances in Archaeological Method and Theory* 8, New York: Academic Press: 63–111.

Chapter Two

Formation processes of house floor assemblages

Vincent M. LaMotta and Michael B. Schiffer

INTRODUCTION

With the advent of processual archaeology in the mid-1960s, the analysis of house floor assemblages came to play a central role in archaeological reconstructions of social, economic, and demographic characteristics of prehistoric populations, particularly in the US Southwest (e.g. Hill 1968, 1970; Jorgensen 1975; Longacre 1970). The early studies tended to assume that variability in house floor assemblages – i.e. differences and similarities in the kinds and quantities of artefacts – could be attributed to differences in the activities carried out in those structures. Since the mid-1970s, however, there has been a concerted effort to identify additional sources of variability contributing to house floor assemblages, principally the formation processes of the archaeological record – both cultural and noncultural (for a survey of formation processes, see Schiffer 1996; for additional principles and case-studies, see e.g. Cameron and Tomka 1993; Goldberg *et al.* 1993; Kristiansen 1985; Nash and Petraglia 1987; Needham and Spence 1997; Rosen 1986; Staski and Sutro 1991; Stein 1992; Waters 1992). As a result, many recent studies have offered reconstructions that are based on the attempt to identify, and control for, the effects of at least some relevant formation processes of house floor assemblages (e.g. Cameron 1990, 1991; Cameron and Tomka 1993; Ciolek-Torrello 1978, 1985; Deal 1985; Gorecki 1985; Joyce and Johannessen 1993; Kent 1984, 1987; Lightfoot 1993; Montgomery 1993; Reid and Whittlesey 1982; Rothschild *et al.* 1993; Savelle 1984; Scarborough 1989; Schiffer 1976, 1985, 1989; Seymour and Schiffer 1987; Stevenson 1985; Sullivan 1989; Szuter 1991). As part of this new focus on formation processes, especially abandonment modes, house floor assemblages have also come to be used to gauge the causes of, and constraints upon, structure and site abandonment (Baker 1975; Bonnichsen 1973; Cameron 1990, 1991; Joyce and Johannessen 1993; Kent 1993; Lange and Rydbeg 1972; Longacre and Ayres 1968; Robbins 1973; Schiffer 1972, 1976, 1985; Stevenson 1982).

In this chapter we synthesize the myriad formation processes pinpointed thus far within a general model of the life history[1] of a domestic structure. This model outlines the timing of different types of cultural and noncultural formation processes in relation to a domestic structure's life history stages, including use (habitation), abandonment, and post-abandonment stages. Drawing upon ethnoarchaeological and ethnographic examples of formation processes, especially from the US Southwest, we assess the types of behavioural inferences that may be obtained from the analysis of house floor assemblages. In light of recent research in the US Southwest, we emphasize the roles that ritual abandonment processes can play in creating house floor assemblages (see Cameron 1990, 1991; LaMotta 1996a, 1996b; Lightfoot 1993; Montgomery 1992, 1993; Schlanger and Wilshusen 1993; Seymour and Schiffer 1987; Varien and Lightfoot 1989; Walker 1995a, 1995b; Wilshusen 1986, 1988) and suggest that such processes may have greater consequences for the interpretation of house assemblages worldwide than many archaeologists presently realize.

LIFE HISTORY OF A DOMESTIC STRUCTURE

The processes that create house floor assemblages can be divided into two broad families: accretion processes result in the deposition of objects within a domestic structure, and depletion processes either (a) remove objects from archaeological deposits within a house or (b) prevent objects once used within the domestic structure from being deposited at their locations of use. Both accretion and depletion processes contribute to the formation of floor assemblages.

At different times in a structure's life history, different types of cultural and noncultural formation process can occur. We recognize three stages (cf. Deal 1985; Stevenson 1985): (1) habitation; (2) abandonment; and (3) post-abandonment (see Table 2.1). During these stages, we submit, there is patterning in the occurrence of various accretion and depletion processes.

The recognition that the formation of house floor assemblages involves both accretion and depletion processes, and that these are patterned in relation to the stages of a structure's life history, permits us to highlight two central themes in the study of formation processes (see Rathje and Schiffer 1982: ch. 5; Schiffer 1976, 1985, 1989, 1996): (1) there is no necessary one-to-one relationship between objects found in a structure and prehistoric activities that took place in the space bounded by that structure; all objects used in a house are not likely to be deposited where they were used, nor were all objects deposited in a structure necessarily used there; and (2) the archaeological record preserved in house assemblages may be a palimpsest of deposits related to different phases of that structure's life history; house assemblages cannot simply be interpreted *a priori* as tool-kits or 'household inventories' related to activities of the habitation stage.

Table 2.1 Formation processes of house floor assemblages

Stage	Accretion processes	Depletion processes
Habitation	Primary and loss refuse deposition Provisional refuse deposition	Secondary refuse deposition
Abandonment	*De facto* refuse deposition Ritual refuse deposition	Curation Ritual depletion
Post-abandonment	Re-use refuse deposition Secondary refuse deposition Structural collapse Disturbance	Scavenging Disturbance Decay

We develop these two themes by discussing accretion and depletion processes specific to the three stages of a house's life history (see Table 2.1). In the following, we make use of selected ethnographic, ethnoarchaeological, and archaeological examples of formation processes, mainly exploiting work done in the US Southwest where both authors have worked.

HABITATION STAGE, DEPOSITIONAL PROCESSES

Activities comprising habitation stage processes are primarily related to the maintenance of the commensal unit (such as a family), including food processing, preparation, and consumption, sleeping, manufacture and maintenance of tools and other artefacts, activity-area maintenance, enculturation, and household ritual (Rathje and Schiffer 1982: 46). The material residues of these activities can make their way into the archaeological record through three major depositional processes (for another rendering of these processes, see Needham and Spence 1997).

1 *Primary deposition* is the accretion process by which objects enter the archaeological record at their location(s) of use, either through discard as 'primary' refuse (Schiffer 1972, 1977, 1996) or through accidental deposition as 'loss' refuse (Fehon and Scholtz 1978; Schiffer 1996: 76–9). For archaeologists interested in reconstructing social, economic, or demographic characteristics of households, an assemblage comprised mostly of objects both used in a house and deposited in that same house potentially provides the strongest line of evidence.

Regrettably, as Murray's (1980) cross-cultural ethnographic research has demonstrated, primary deposition (through primary refuse) is the ultimate fate of few material residues of household activities. In a sample of seventy-nine societies, Murray found that most activity areas are cleaned up periodically and the refuse deposited elsewhere. A detailed example of activity-area maintenance is furnished by the ethnoarchaeological work of Hayden and Cannon (1983) among the contemporary Maya. They report that in frequently maintained activity areas, such as house floors, refuse that is either (1) bulky and an obstruction to the performance of activities, or (2) potentially hazardous to humans, is rapidly collected and deposited away from the activity area as secondary refuse. Any remaining primary refuse most likely includes objects that had a low potential for hindering ongoing activities, especially objects small enough to escape cleaning technology (McKellar 1983; Schiffer 1996: 66–7; Tani 1995). The penetrability of the floor matrix also plays a large role in determining which objects directly enter the archaeological record (e.g. an unconsolidated sand floor captures more artefacts than a less penetrable matrix like hard-packed clay – see Schiffer 1996: 126–8). As a rule, microartefact studies (for examples see Hull 1987; Metcalfe and Heath 1990; Rosen 1986) on the floor matrix are required for isolating reliable samples of primary refuse from assemblages in well maintained houses.

2 *Secondary deposition* is a depletion process that involves the removal of refuse from an activity area, and its deposition in a spatially removed location such as a midden, toft, landfill, abandoned structure, or cemetery (Schiffer 1972, 1977, 1996; see also Rathje and Murphy 1992). As ethnoarchaeologists have demonstrated, many objects used and expended by a household ultimately wind up as secondary refuse. For example, Clark's (1991) work among the Lacandon Maya illustrates the techniques used by flintknappers to prevent the residues of biface production from being deposited on house floors. This debris is collected, stored, and ultimately discarded in a midden located a safe distance from footpaths and other activity areas, thus leaving little trace of the knapping activities in the archaeological record of house structures themselves. Such practices underscore our position that house floor assemblages cannot be presumed to be fossilized representations of past activities, an assumption that Schiffer (1985) has referred to as the 'Pompeii Premise' (cf. Ascher 1968 and Binford 1981).

3 The third major depositional process that occurs during the habitation phase is *provisional discard*. In this process, broken or worn-out objects are not discarded *per se*, but are stored or cached with the expectation that they will serve a useful purpose later (Deal 1985; Hayden and Cannon 1983; Schiffer 1996: 99). An additional contributor to provisional refuse is functionally obsolete items – broken or still usable – that are nonetheless retained instead of discarded. Gould (1987: 149) terms this the 'nostalgia effect', suggesting that people can keep items that took part

in earlier activities in their own lives; for example, the Finnish 'farmers' he studied hang on to old farm equipment even though they no longer practice farming. Sometimes old items acquire new functions as a part of displays, as in collections; such cases exemplify secondary use (a kind of reuse) rather than provisional discard (Schiffer 1996: ch. 3).

One needs to look no further than one's own garage or attic to find convenient examples of provisional discard. These examples also demonstrate the generality of an observation made by Hayden and Cannon (1983), that provisionally discarded objects are frequently cached in out of the way places – not in the middle of activity areas. For this reason, provisionally discarded items left in domestic structures are likely to comprise only a small fraction of floor assemblages, usually forming clusters along walls or under features such as beds or tables. This spatial patterning provides archaeologists with one tool for distinguishing provisionally discarded objects from abandonment refuse (see below), secondary refuse, and other deposits of broken objects.

ABANDONMENT PHASE, DEPOSITIONAL PROCESSES

From our discussions of primary, secondary, and provisional deposition, it should be clear that relatively little cultural deposition occurs within house structures during their habitation phase, certainly not enough to account for the large assemblages of objects sometimes recovered from archaeological house floors. During the abandonment phase, however, changes occur both in household activities and in patterns of deposition as the domestic unit prepares to move itself and some of its belongings to a new location (see Schiffer 1985 for a discussion of the specific changes in primary and secondary deposition expected immediately prior to abandonment).

De facto refuse deposition and curate behaviour are two sides of the same coin; the former an accretion process, the latter a depletion process. Deposition of *de facto* refuse involves the abandonment of still usable objects within a structure (Schiffer 1996: 89–97), while curate behaviour (adapted from Binford 1973) is defined as the transfer of objects from the old to the new activity location (for studies of curate behaviour, see Hayden 1976; Schiffer 1985, 1996: 90–6; Tomka 1993; for critiques of the curation concept, see Nash 1996; Shott 1996). Obviously, the selective abandonment of certain objects on a house floor will skew reconstructions of prehistoric household activities (Schiffer 1985). While there may be no way of knowing for certain which specific objects were curated upon abandonment (Cordell *et al.* 1987), it may be possible to predict which kinds of objects will be differentially abandoned or curated. Objects likely to be curated upon site or structure abandonment are quite portable, have high replacement costs, and are still fairly usable; such items are considered to have a high curate priority (*sensu* Schiffer 1985). Objects likely to be left behind as *de facto* refuse are difficult to transport, easy to replace, and/or have little residual utility. A floor assemblage composed entirely of bulky, broken, and fairly ubiquitous objects is therefore one likely to have been heavily depleted by curation processes, and would not provide a representative household inventory (Stevenson 1982).

The concept of curate priority is based on a least-effort model of abandonment behaviour (see Zipf 1949). It is assumed that, when abandoning a settlement or structure, the inhabitants will transport as much of their household assemblage as is economical, given the conditioning factors of (1) replaceability, (2) transport costs, and (3) conditions of abandonment (Schiffer 1985; Stevenson 1982). In studies of abandonment, archaeologists sometimes hold the first two factors constant in order to infer the conditions under which a settlement or structure was abandoned – its 'abandonment mode' (e.g. see Baker 1975; Bonnichsen 1973; Cameron 1991; Joyce and Johannessen 1993; Kent 1993; Lange and Rydberg 1972; Longacre and Ayres 1968; Robbins 1973; Schiffer 1972, 1976, 1985; Stevenson 1982). A structure whose floor assemblage includes many portable, valuable, and/or usable objects, for example, is typically inferred to have undergone a rapid, unplanned abandonment. In contrast, an assemblage that appears to be highly depleted by curation – i.e. one with only large and/or broken objects – is usually ascribed to a slow, planned abandonment. Although a least-effort model can explain much variability in archaeological floor assemblages, another family of processes, 'ritual formation processes', results in deposition that departs markedly from least-effort expectations (cf. Szuter 1991: 219). In particular, ritual formation processes often result in enriched floor assemblages that can be easily confused with abundant *de facto* refuse. Clearly, failure to acknowledge and identify these processes can severely bias inferences based on house assemblages, leading, for example, to erroneous conclusions about abandonment mode.

In the New World, there is a rich and underexploited body of ethnographic literature on ritual formation processes. In the Greater Southwest, and indeed in much of North America, many indigenous peoples living in mud-and-brush pit structures are reported to have burned their houses upon abandonment, usually as a result of the death of one or more of the occupants. Ethnographers commonly report that some portion of the deceased's material possessions, among other objects, were destroyed within a house when it was burned. These accounts, coupled with a growing experimental literature on the difficulties of accidentally burning mud-covered structures (Glennie 1983; Glennie and Lipe 1984; see also Bankoff and Winter 1979; Friede and Steel 1980), strongly suggest that deposits contained within many of the burned pit structures excavated throughout the US Southwest may have been heavily affected by abandonment rituals (Cameron 1990, 1991; Seymour and Schiffer 1987; Walker 1995a, 1995b).

Ethnographic accounts from the US Southwest among the Navajo, Cocopa, and Quechan record the abandonment of an entire household assemblage on the floors of structures burned upon an occupant's death (Kelly 1952: 29; Kent 1984: 140). These accounts have been used occasionally by Southwesternists to justify the assumption that floor assemblages from burned pit structures represent complete household inventories. As other ethnographic observations testify, however, household inventories are often systematically depleted before being burned in house structures, and foreign objects are occasionally deposited on house floors as part of the abandonment ritual, a phenomenon Lightfoot (1993: 174) has termed 'abandonment assemblage enrichment'.

For example, some groups in north-east California burn only the deceased's most personal possessions, while other groups burn only broken or no longer usable objects (Wheeler-Voegelin 1942: 137–8, 231). The Navajo frequently avoided the mass destruction of household objects by moving a dying person to an empty, makeshift structure, which was then burned (Ward 1980: 31–3). Other groups practised differential disposal of the deceased's possessions: while some objects were destroyed or abandoned on house floors, others were interred with the individual (Pima – Ezell 1961: 90; Papago – Fontana 1964: 54; Havasupai – Spier 1928: 292; Tarahumara – Bennett and Zingg 1976: 236), dumped in specialized refuse areas (Yuma – Spier 1933: 303), or redistributed (Apache – Buskirk 1986: 108; Havasupai – Spier 1928: 234; Tarasco – Lumholtz 1902: 242–3), sometimes for reuse as relics of the deceased (Lumholtz 1902: 242–3).

Seymour and Schiffer (1987: 571) have proposed that similar ritual formation processes may partly explain the severely depleted condition of pit house assemblages from the Hohokam site of Snaketown in southern Arizona. Noting that a single cemetery cache of ceramics at Snaketown contained more whole vessels than did all the house floors from the Sacaton phase combined (see also Haury 1976: 183), they suggest that the selective disposal of some component of the household assemblage in ritual caches played a substantial role in the formation of house floor assemblages.

Other ritual abandonment processes introduce 'foreign' objects to floor assemblages. Wilshusen (1986), for example, has noted the differential burning and abandonment of Anasazi pit structures that contain human remains, while Lightfoot (1993) has suggested that some portion of floor assemblages of pit structures containing human interments may have been introduced as mortuary offerings. In regard to puebloan sites, LaMotta (1996b) has suggested that floor assemblages in domestic rooms containing subfloor infant burials may include objects that were deposited upon abandonment as 'offerings' for an individual buried beneath the floor. In many cases, such floor assemblages include artefact types that were otherwise deposited primarily in non-domestic contexts, such as adult human burials, canine and avian burials, and in ceremonial structures. Although there is no parallel from Southwestern ethnography for such a mode of ritual deposition, the Andaman Islanders have been reported to emplace, upon abandonment of a settlement, offerings on the floors of structures containing subfloor infant burials (Radcliffe-Brown 1933: 109).

Behaviours unrelated to mortuary ritual may also add objects to house floor assemblages. Walker (1995a, 1995b), for example, has argued that Anasazi pit structure assemblages may contain 'ceremonial trash', or worn-out objects from ceremonial activities. Like Wilshusen (1988), Walker has proposed that structures used for household or community rituals experience depositional processes distinct from those of non-ritual structures, both during and after abandonment, including the preferential discard of ceremonial trash from other activity areas on their floors and in their fill.

Site abandonment rituals may also heavily impact the contents of house floors. Montgomery (1992, 1993), for example, has discussed the ritual cremation and burial of the Mogollon pueblo of Chodistaas in east-central Arizona. As many as thirty whole vessels, among other objects, were left on room floors at Chodistaas before the site was burned and the rooms filled with trash from the surrounding middens. Chodistaas is an excellent example of a ritual abandonment that could easily have been mistaken for a rapid, unplanned, and perhaps even catastrophic site abandonment in which large quantities of still usable objects were left on room floors.

Two major themes stand out in our brief discussion of ritual formation processes: (1) ritual abandonment processes can mimic other forms of cultural deposition, especially provisional and *de facto* refuse deposition, leading archaeologists to misinterpret them as whole or partial household inventories (Cameron 1991; Deal 1985); and (2) least-effort models of abandonment cannot be applied directly to floor assemblages without controlling for the effects of ritual accretion and depletion processes. Much more comparative research needs to be conducted on specific processes of ritual deposition before we will be able fully to recognize the end-products of these behaviours in the archaeological record (see Walker 1995a for a discussion of method and theory in the analysis of ritual deposits).

POST-ABANDONMENT PROCESSES

Finally, we briefly call attention to the fact that the life history of a structure does not end with its abandonment; many processes of accretion and depletion can alter house assemblages in the post-abandonment stage. For example, the reuse of a structure, either for habitation or other purposes, may introduce a new set of primary, secondary, and provisional depositional processes, possibly obscuring all traces of earlier occupations (Rothschild *et al.* 1993; Schiffer 1985, 1996: 28, 40–4).

As is well known, abandoned structures are often used as rubbish dumps, leading to accumulations of refuse varying in depth, quantity, and artefact content. In some cases, these deposits are readily identified as secondary or even 'tertiary' refuse (see Scarborough 1989: 415) on the basis of various traces on the artefacts and on the characteristics of the deposits. For example, traces such as small and heavily abraded sherds permitted Scarborough (1989) to identify house deposits as tertiary refuse – secondary refuse that had been previously deposited in an extramural area, subjected to trampling, and then redeposited in an abandoned structure. Sometimes stratigraphic evidence furnishes definitive evidence of secondary refuse in a structure deposit. In any event, it may be difficult to distinguish artefacts deposited on floors in habitation and abandonment stages from secondary or tertiary refuse thrown in after abandonment. As Walker has suggested (1995a, 1995b; see also Walker *et al.* 1996; Lightfoot 1993; Lightfoot and Varien 1988; Walker and LaMotta 1995; Wilshusen 1988), however, the types of objects deposited secondarily in an abandoned structure may not be totally random with respect to the functions of that structure in its habitation stage; the possible interrelationship of depositional modes in the habitation, abandonment, and post-abandonment phases of a structure is another area that requires far more archaeological and ethnoarchaeological research.

Structural collapse can also introduce objects onto room floors, primarily through the deposition of objects (e.g. chinking sherds, artefacts in adobe) used as construction materials (Schiffer 1985, 1996).

Finally, a slew of cultural and non-cultural processes can remove objects from room floors after abandonment. Scavenging (Gorecki 1985), collecting, and a wide range of cultural and non-cultural disturbance processes, including faunal- and floral-turbation, organic decay, pot hunting, and archaeological excavation, deplete archaeological deposits and further transform house floor assemblages; regularities that govern these processes have been summarized by Schiffer (1996: 207–12) and others (e.g. Wood and Johnson 1978; Erlandson 1984).

CONCLUSION

It should be clear from our brief outline of the life history of a domestic structure that all house assemblage formation processes are not created equal, neither in their relative contributions to floor assemblages, nor in the behavioural inferences that they permit. We have emphasized that primary deposition of objects at their locations of use is a fairly rare phenomenon in heavily maintained activity areas, such as house floors. Objects left on house floors are therefore more likely to be the product of abandonment processes or of post-abandonment deposition. In our discussion of abandonment, we have placed particular emphasis on processes of ritual deposition. We believe that these types of formation processes have been overlooked by archaeologists for too long; clearly it is time that method and theory be developed for isolating ritual deposits in the archaeological record (see Walker *et al.* 1996; Walker 1995a, 1995b). The occurrence of ritual abandonment processes is certainly not a phenomenon unique to the American Southwest (e.g. see Merrifield 1987; Hill 1995), and thus archaeologists working in many regions must develop the implications of these behaviours for reconstructing abandonment mode and household activities.

The impact of ritual formation processes, not only on structure floor assemblages but also on fill assemblages, leads us, finally, to question the strict analytical dichotomy that is often drawn between floor and fill contexts (Walker *et al.* 1996; Schiffer 1976: 133–8; Walker and LaMotta 1995). Given that under certain circumstances both floor and fill may be created by the same, or related, depositional processes, and, furthermore, that these deposits are often stratigraphically indistinguishable, is it justifiable arbitrarily to privilege floor-contact assemblages in the analysis of structure deposits? We suggest that understanding the complete depositional history of a structure, from habitation through abandonment and post-abandonment stages, is the best way to successfully partition all sources of variability in the highly complex archaeological records of domestic structures (e.g. see Kobayashi 1974; Schlanger and Wilshusen 1993; Walker 1995b; Wilshusen 1986, 1988).

NOTE

1 *Sensu* Binford (1968: 21–2) and Schiffer (1996: 13–15).

BIBLIOGRAPHY

Ascher, R. (1968) 'Time's Arrow and the Archaeology of a Contemporary Community', in K. C. Chang (ed.) *Settlement Archaeology*, Palo Alto: National Press Books: 43–52.

Baker, C. M. (1975) 'Site Abandonment and the Archaeological Record: An Empirical Case for Anticipated Return', *Arkansas Academy of Science Proceedings* 23: 10–11.

Bankoff, H. A. and Winter, F. A. (1979) 'A House-Burning in Siberia', *Archaeology* 32, 5: 8–14.

Bee, R. L.(1983) 'Quechan', in A. Ortiz (ed.) *Southwest*, Handbook of North American Indians, vol. 10 (W. C. Sturtevant, general editor), Washington, DC: Smithsonian Institution: 86–98.

Bennett, W. C. and Zingg, R. M. (1976) *The Tarahumara: An Indian Tribe of Northern Mexico*, Chicago: University of Chicago Press.

Binford, L. R. (1968) 'Archaeological Perspectives', in S. R. Binford and L. R. Binford (eds) *New Perspectives in Archaeology* Chicago: Aldine: 5–32.

—— (1973) 'Interassemblage Variability – The Mousterian and the "Functional" Argument', in C. Renfrew (ed.) *The Explanation of Culture Change: Models in Prehistory*, London: G. Duckworth: 227–53.

—— (1981) 'Behavioral Archaeology and the "Pompeii Premise"', *Journal of Anthropological Research* 37: 195–208.

Bonnichsen, R. (1973) 'Millie's Camp: An Experiment in Archaeology', *World Archaeology* 4: 277–91.

Buskirk, W. (1986) *The Western Apache*, Norman: University of Oklahoma Press.

Cameron, C. M. (1990) 'Pit Structure Abandonment in the Four Corners Region of the American Southwest: Late Basketmaker III and Pueblo I Periods', *Journal of Field Archaeology* 17: 27–37.

—— (1991) 'Structure Abandonment in Villages', in M. B. Schiffer (ed.) *Archaeological Method and Theory*, vol. 3, Tucson: University of Arizona Press: 155–94.

Cameron, C. M. and Tomka, S. A. (eds) (1993) *Abandonment of Settlements and Regions: Ethnoarchaeological and Archaeological Approaches*, Cambridge: Cambridge University Press.

Ciolek-Torrello, R. (1978) 'A Statistical Analysis of Activity Organization: Grasshopper Pueblo, Arizona', Unpublished Ph.D. dissertation, University of Arizona, Tucson, Ann Arbor: University Microfilms.

—— (1985) 'A Typology of Room Function at Grasshopper Pueblo, Arizona', *Journal of Field Archaeology* 12: 41–63.

Clark, J. E. (1991) 'Flintknapping and Debitage Disposal among the Lacandon Maya of Chiapas, Mexico', in E. Staski and L. D. Sutro (eds) *The Ethnoarchaeology of Refuse Disposal*, Anthropological Research Papers no. 42, Arizona State University: 63–79.

Cordell, L. S., Upham, S. and Brock, S. L. (1987) 'Obscuring Cultural Patterns in the Archaeological Record: A Discussion from Southwestern Archaeology', *American Antiquity* 52: 565–77.

Deal, M. (1985) 'Household Pottery Disposal in the Maya Highlands: An Ethnoarchaeological Interpretation', *Journal of Anthropological Archaeology* 4: 243–91.

Erlandson, Jon M. (1984) 'A Case Study in Faunalturbation: Delineating the Effects of the Burrowing Pocket Gopher on the Distribution of Archaeological Materials', *American Antiquity* 49: 785–90.

Ezell, P. H. (1961) 'The Hispanic Acculturation of the Gila River Pimas', *American Anthropological Association* 5, 2: Menasha, Wis.

Fehon, J. R. and Scholtz, S. C. (1978) 'A Conceptual Framework for the Study of Artifact Loss', *American Antiquity* 43: 271–3.

Fontana, B. L. (1964) 'The Papago Indians', Manuscript on file, Arizona State Museum, University of Arizona, Tucson.

Friede, H. M. and Steel, R. H. (1980) 'Experimental Burning of Traditional Nguni Huts', *African Studies* 39: 171–81.

Glennie, G. D. (1983) 'Replication of an A.D. 800 Anasazi Pithouse in Southwestern Colorado', Unpublished MA thesis, Washington State University, Pullman.

Glennie, G. D. and Lipe, W. D. (1984) 'Replication of an Early Anasazi Pithouse', Paper presented at the 49th Annual Meeting of the Society for American Archaeology, Portland, Oreg.

Goldberg, P., Nash, D. T. and Petraglia, M. D. (eds) (1993) *Formation Processes in Archaeological Context*, Monographs in World Archaeology no. 17, Madison, Wis.: Prehistory Press.

Gorecki, P. (1985) 'Ethnoarchaeology: The Need for a Post-Mortem Enquiry', *World Archaeology* 17, 2: 175–90.

Gould, R. A. (1987) 'The Ethnoarchaeology of Abandonment in a Northern Finnish Farming Community', *Nordia* 21: 133–52.

Haury, E. W. (1976) *The Hohokam: Desert Farmers and Craftsmen. Excavations at Snaketown 1964–1965*, Tucson: The University of Arizona Press.

Hayden, B. (1976) 'Curation: Old and New', in J. S. Raymond, B. Loveseth, C. Arnold and G. Reardon (eds) *Primitive Art and Technology*, Calgary: Archaeological Association, University of Calgary: 47–9.

Hayden, B. and Cannon, A. (1983) 'Where the Garbage Goes: Refuse Disposal in the Maya Highlands', *Journal of Anthropological Archaeology* 2: 117–63.

Hill, J. D. (1995) *Ritual and Rubbish in the Iron Age of Wessex: A Study on the Formation of a Specific Archaeological Record*, British Archaeological Reports, British Series no. 242, Oxford.

Hill, J. N. (1968) 'Broken K Pueblo: Patterns of Form and Function', in S. R. Binford and L. R. Binford (eds) *New Perspectives in Archaeology*, Chicago: Aldine:103–42.

—— (1970) *Broken K Pueblo: Prehistoric Social Organization in the American Southwest*, University of Arizona, Anthropological Papers no. 18, Tucson.

Hull, K. L. (1987) 'Identification of Cultural Site Formation Processes Through Microdebitage Analysis', *American Antiquity* 52: 772–83.

Jorgensen, J. (1975) 'A Room Use Analysis of Table Rock Pueblo, Arizona', *Journal of Anthropological Research* 3: 149–61.

Joyce, A. A. and Johannessen, S. (1993) 'Abandonment and the Production of Archaeological Variability at Domestic Sites', in C. M. Cameron and S. A. Tomka (eds) *Abandonment of Settlements and Regions: Ethnoarchaeological and Archaeological Approaches*, Cambridge: Cambridge University Press: 138–56.

Kelly, W. H. (1952) 'Cocopa Ethnography', Manuscript on file, Arizona State Museum, University of Arizona, Tucson.

Kent, S. (1984) *Analyzing Activity Areas*, Albuquerque: University of New Mexico Press.

—— (1987) 'Understanding the Use of Space: An Ethnoarchaeological Approach', in S. Kent (ed.) *Method and Theory for Activity Area Research: An Ethnoarchaeological Approach*, New York: Columbia University Press: 2–60.

—— (1993) 'Models of Abandonment and Material Culture Frequencies', in C. M. Cameron and S. A. Tomka (eds) *Abandonment of Settlements and Regions: Ethnoarchaeological and Archaeological Approaches*, Cambridge: Cambridge University Press: 54–73.

Kobayashi, T. (1974) 'Behavioral Patterns Reflected in Pottery Remains – The Jomon Period', *Arctic Anthropology* XI (Supplement): 163–70.

Kristiansen, K. (ed.) (1985) *Archaeological Formation Processes: The Representativity of Archaeological Remains from Danish Prehistory*, Copenhagen: Nationalmuseets Forlag.

LaMotta, V. M. (1996a) 'The Use of Human Remains in Abandonment Ritual at Homol'ovi', Unpublished MA Report, Department of Anthropology, University of Arizona.

—— (1996b) 'A Life-History Framework for Explaining Variability in the Deposition of Human Remains', Paper presented at the 61st Annual Meeting of the Society for American Archaeology, New Orleans, La., 12 April.

Lange, F. W. and Rydberg, C. R. (1972) 'Abandonment and Post-Abandonment Behavior at a Rural Central American House-Site', *American Antiquity* 37: 419–32.

Lightfoot, R. R. (1993) 'Abandonment Processes in Prehistoric Pueblos', in C. M. Cameron and S. A. Tomka (eds) *Abandonment of Settlements and Regions: Ethnoarchaeological and Archaeological Approaches*, Cambridge: Cambridge University Press: 165–77.

Lightfoot, R. R. and Varien, M. D. (1988) *Report of 1987 Archaeological Investigations at the Duckfoot Site (5MT3868), Montezuma County, Colorado*, Cortez, Colo.: Crow Canyon Archaeological Center.

Longacre, W. A. (1970) *Archaeology as Anthropology: A Case Study*, University of Arizona, Anthropological Papers no. 17, Tucson.

Longacre, W. A. and Ayres, J. E. (1968) 'Archaeological Lessons from an Apache Wikiup', in S. R. Binford and L. R. Binford (eds) *New Perspectives in Archaeology*, Chicago: Aldine: 151–9.

Lumholtz, C. (1902) *Unknown Mexico, A Record of Five Years' Exploration among the Tribes of the Western Sierra Madre; in the Tierra Caliente of Tepic and Jalisco; and among the Tarascos of Michoacan*, vol. II, New York: AMS Press (reprinted 1973).

McKellar, J. A. (1983) 'Correlates and the Explanation of Distributions', *Atlatl, Occasional Papers* 4, Anthropology Club, University of Arizona.

Merrifield, R. (1987) *The Archaeology of Ritual and Magic*, New York: New Amsterdam Books.

Metcalfe, D. and Heath, K. M. (1990) 'Microrefuse and Site Structure: The Hearths and Floors of the Heartbreak Hotel', *American Antiquity* 55: 781–96.

Montgomery, B. K. (1992) 'Understanding the Formation of the Archaeological Record: Ceramic Variability at Chodistaas Pueblo, Arizona', Unpublished Ph.D. dissertation, University of Arizona, Tucson, Ann Arbor: University Microfilms.

—— (1993) 'Ceramic Analysis as a Tool for Discovering Processes of Pueblo Abandonment', in C. M. Cameron and S. A. Tomka (eds) *Abandonment of Settlements and Regions: Ethnoarchaeological and Archaeological Approaches*, Cambridge: Cambridge University Press: 157–64.

Murray, P. (1980) 'Discard Location: The Ethnographic Data', *American Antiquity* 45: 490–502.

Nash, D. T. and Petraglia, M. D. (eds) (1987) *Natural Formation Processes and the Archaeological Record*, British Archaeological Reports, International Series, no. 352.

Nash, S. E. (1996) 'Is Curation a Useful Heuristic?', in G. H. Odell (ed.) *Stone Tools: Theoretical Insights into Human Prehistory*, New York: Plenum Press: 81–99.

Needham, S. and Spence, T. (1997) 'Refuse and the Formation of Middens', *Antiquity* 71: 77–90.

Radcliffe-Brown, A. R. (1933) *The Andaman Islanders*, Cambridge: Cambridge University Press.

Rathje, W. L. and Murphy, C. (1992) *Rubbish! The Archaeology of Garbage*, New York: HarperCollins.

Rathje, W. L. and Schiffer, M. B. (1982) *Archaeology*, New York: Harcourt Brace Jovanovich.

Reid, J. J. and Whittlesey, S. M. (1982) 'Households at Grasshopper Pueblo', *American Behavioral Scientist* 25: 687–703.

Robbins, L. H. (1973) 'Turkana Material Culture Viewed from an Archaeological Perspective', *World Archaeology* 5: 209–14.

Rosen, A. M. (1986) *Cites of Clay*, Chicago: University of Chicago Press.

Rothschild, N. A., Mills, B. J., Ferguson, T. J. and Dublin, S. (1993) 'Abandonment at Zuni Farming Villages', in C. M. Cameron and S. A. Tomka (eds) *Abandonment of Settlements and Regions: Ethnoarchaeological and Archaeological Approaches*, Cambridge: Cambridge University Press: 123–37.

Savelle, J. M. (1984) 'Cultural and Natural Formation Processes of a Historic Inuit Snow Dwelling Site, Somerset Island, Arctic Canada', *American Antiquity* 49: 508–24.

Scarborough, V. (1989) 'Site Structure of a Village of Late Pithouse–Early Pueblo Period in New Mexico', *Journal of Field Archaeology* 16: 405–25.

Schiffer, M. B. (1972) 'Archaeological Context and Systemic Context', *American Antiquity* 37: 156–65 (reprinted in Schiffer 1995: 25–34).

—— (1976) *Behavioral Archeology*, New York: Academic Press.

—— (1977) 'Toward a Unified Science of the Cultural Past', in S. South (ed.) *Research Strategies in Historical Archeology*, New York: Academic Press: 13–50.

—— (1985) 'Is There a "Pompeii Premise" in Archaeology?', *Journal of Anthropological Research* 41: 18–41 (reprinted in Schiffer 1995: 201–18).

—— (1989) 'Formation Processes of Broken K Pueblo: Some Hypotheses', in R. D. Leonard and G. T. Jones (eds) *Quantifying Diversity in Archaeology*, Cambridge: Cambridge University Press: 37–58.

—— (1995) *Behavioral Archaeology: First Principles*, Salt Lake City: University of Utah Press.

—— (1996) *Formation Processes of the Archaeological Record*, Salt Lake City: University of Utah Press (originally published in 1987 by University of New Mexico Press, Albuquerque).

Schlanger, S. H. and Wilshusen, R. H. (1993) 'Local Abandonments and Regional Conditions in the North American Southwest', in C. M. Cameron and S. A. Tomka (eds) *Abandonment of Settlements and Regions: Ethnoarchaeological and Archaeological Approaches*, Cambridge: Cambridge University Press: 85–98.

Seymour, D. J. and Schiffer, M. B. (1987) 'A Preliminary Analysis of Pithouse Assemblages from Snaketown, Arizona', in S. Kent (ed.) *Method and Theory for Activity Area Research: An Ethnoarchaeological Approach*, New York: Columbia University Press: 549–603.

Shott, M. J. (1996) 'An Exegesis of the Curation Concept', *Journal of Anthropological Research* 52: 259–81.

Spier, L. (1928) 'Havasupai Ethnography', *Anthropological Papers of the American Museum of Natural History* 29: 232–99.

—— (1933) *Yuman Tribes of the Gila River*, Chicago: University of Chicago Press.

Staski, E. and Sutro, L. D. (eds) (1991) *The Ethnoarchaeology of Refuse Disposal*, Arizona State University, Anthropological Research Papers no. 42.

Stein, J. (ed.) (1992) *Deciphering a Shell Midden*, Orlando: Academic Press.

Stevenson, M. G. (1982) 'Toward an Understanding of Site Abandonment Behavior: Evidence from Historic Mining Camps in the Southwest Yukon', *Journal of Anthropological Archaeology* 1: 237–65.

Stevenson, M. G. (1985) 'The Formation Processes of Artifact Assemblages at Workshop/Habitation Sites: Models from Peace Point in Northern Alberta', *American Antiquity* 50: 63–81.

Sullivan, A. P. III (1989) 'The Technology of Ceramic Reuse: Formation Processes and Archaeological Evidence', *World Archaeology* 21: 101–14.

Szuter, C. R. (1991) *Hunting by Prehistoric Horticulturalists in the American Southwest*, New York: Garland.

Tani, M. (1995) 'Beyond the Identification of Formation Processes: Behavioral Inference Based on Traces Left by Cultural Formation Processes', *Journal of Archaeological Method and Theory* 2, 3: 231–52.

Tomka, S. A. (1993) 'Site Abandonment Behavior among Transhumant Agro-Pastoralists: The Effects of Delayed Curation on Assemblage Composition', in C. M. Cameron and S. A. Tomka (eds) *Abandonment of Settlements and Regions: Ethnoarchaeological and Archaeological Approaches*, Cambridge: Cambridge University Press: 11–24.

Varien, M. D. and Lightfoot, R. R. (1989) 'Ritual and Non-Ritual Activities in Mesa Verde Region Pit Structures', in W. D. Lipe and M. Hegmon (eds) *The Architecture of Social Integration in Prehistoric Pueblos*, Occasional Paper no. 1, Crow Canyon Archaeological Center, Cortez, Colo.: 73–88.

Walker, W. H. (1995a) 'Ritual Prehistory: A Pueblo Case Study', Unpublished Ph.D. dissertation, University of Arizona, Tucson, Ann Arbor: University Microfilms.

—— (1995b) 'Ceremonial Trash?', in J. M. Skibo, W. H. Walker, and A. E. Nielsen (eds) *Expanding Archaeology*, Salt Lake City: University of Utah Press: 67–79.

Walker, W. H., and LaMotta, V. M. (1995) 'Life-Histories as Units of Analysis', Paper presented at the 60th annual meeting of the Society for American Archaeology, Minneapolis, Minn., 5 May.

Walker, W. H., Adams, E. C. and LaMotta, V. M. (1996) 'Finding and Interpreting Ritual Behavior in the Archaeological Record', Paper presented at the 1996 Southwest Symposium, Arizona State University, Tempe, Ariz., 9 February, for the Symposium 'The Spread of Religious Systems'.

Ward, A. E. (1980) *Navajo Graves: An Archaeological Reflection of Ethnographic Reality*, Center for Anthropological Studies Ethnohistorical Report Series no. 2, Albuquerque, N.Mex.

Waters, M. (1992) *Principles of Geoarchaeology*, Tucson: University of Arizona Press.

Wheeler-Voegelin, E. (1942) *Culture Element Distributions: XX, Northeast California*, Berkeley: University of California Press.

Wilshusen, R. H. (1986) 'The Relationship between Abandonment Mode and Ritual Use in Pueblo I Anasazi Protokivas', *Journal of Field Archaeology* 13: 245–54.

—— (1988) 'The Abandonment of Structures', in E. Blinman, C. J. Phagan and R. H. Wilshusen (eds) *Dolores Archaeological Program Supporting Studies: Additive and Reductive Technologies*, Denver: Bureau of Reclamation, Engineering and Research Center: 673–702.

Wood, R. W. and Johnson, D. L. (1978) 'A Survey of Disturbance Processes in Archaeological Site Formation', in M. B. Schiffer (ed.) *Advances in Archaeological Method and Theory* vol. 1, New York: Academic Press: 315–81.

Zipf, G. K. (1949) *Human Behavior and the Principle of Least Effort*, Cambridge, Mass.: Addison-Wesley.

Chapter Three

Household archaeology and cultural formation processes: Examples from the Cerén site, El Salvador

Brian R. McKee

INTRODUCTION

Household archaeology has grown in recent decades to become a focus of many studies in the Old and New Worlds. Household studies can provide information regarding production, distribution, transmission, and reproduction (Wilk and Rathje 1982) among cooperative co-residential groups in past societies through the analysis of material remains. The archaeological record is not a direct reflection of past activities, however. Numerous cultural and non-cultural processes intervene between past behaviours of interest and their recovery through archaeological inference (Schiffer 1972, 1976, 1987). In order to reconstruct and explain past behaviours we must understand those processes and how they act to help form the archaeological record.

The Cerén site provides an excellent laboratory to examine formation processes of the archaeological record. The site was catastrophically buried by the eruption of a nearby volcano in AD 590 ± 90. This eruption preserved structures, artefacts, fields, and even plants in the locations they occupied prior to the eruption. The deep burial has limited the effects of many cultural and non-cultural formation processes. Paradoxically, this allows us to study other formation processes in a fashion not possible in most other archaeological sites. This study examines the role of a class of cultural formation processes, discard and reuse processes, in forming the archaeological record at Cerén. I begin with a brief summary of archaeological investigations at Cerén. This is followed by an examination of discard and reuse processes and their presence at Cerén. Finally, I summarize the role that cultural and non-cultural formation processes have had in creating the archaeological record at Cerén, and the implications of Cerén for the study of other sites.

THE CERÉN SITE

The Cerén site was accidentally discovered in 1976 during the construction of grain storage silos (Sheets 1979). According to local residents, a bulldozer operator exposed and destroyed parts of two structures buried beneath approximately five metres of volcanic ash. Informants noted that one or more additional structures were completely destroyed. Because of the exceptional preservation, the bulldozer operator and local residents believed the remains were recent, as did a representative of the National Museum who visited the site in 1976 (Sheets 1989).

Formal investigations at Cerén began in 1978. At that time, a team from the University of Colorado, directed by Dr Payson Sheets, was surveying the Zapotitán Valley, where the site is located. A goal of this survey was to explore the effects of the second to third century AD eruption of Ilopango volcano on the inhabitants of the region. Residents of the area informed project members that a house had been found buried under a more recent eruption. The Colorado team cleaned the bulldozer cut to better expose the structure, and encountered Classic Period sherds on the floor. A sample of burned roofing thatch was collected and submitted for radiocarbon dating. The resulting date was AD 590 ± 90 (Zier 1983). The 1978 excavations exposed portions of two structures and surrounding areas and a prehistoric cornfield (ibid.). The research team returned in 1979 and 1980 to conduct geophysical research to locate more buried structures (Loker 1983). Ground-penetrating radar and soil resistivity located several anomalies that were subsequently tested with a soil drill (ibid.; McKee 1989a). The stratigraphy indicated buried structures at the locations of these anomalies. Excavations in the 1980s and 1990s have found additional structures where there were no anomalies (Sheets and McKee 1989, 1990), and the effectiveness of the remote sensing techniques is being re-evaluated (Spetzler and McKee 1990; Doolittle and Miller 1992). A more recent study using high resolution ground-penetrating radar has shown more promise (Conyers 1995), but the results of this study have not yet been systematically evaluated through excavation.

The Salvadoran Civil War erupted in 1980, and investigations were halted until 1989, when Sheets returned with a multidisciplinary team, and investigations have continued since then (Sheets and McKee 1989, 1990; Sheets and Kievit 1992; Sheets and Simmons 1993; Sheets and Brown 1996). The peace accords of 1992 have provided increased security since that time. To date, eleven structures have been at least partially excavated (Figure 3.1), and the locations of at least five others are known.

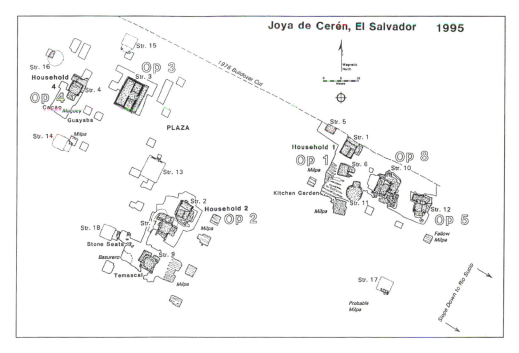

Figure 3.1 The Cerén site, El Salvador, with locations of excavations and structures. Figure by Payson Sheets.

VOLCANISM AT CERÉN

The Zapotitán Valley has been frequently affected by volcanism during the last 2,000 years. Ilopango volcano erupted violently in the second or third century AD. The vent, located near San Salvador, approximately 40 km from the site, rapidly ejected 20–50 cubic km of material (Hart and Steen-McIntyre 1983). The heavy ash cover affected western El Salvador and surrounding portions of Guatemala and Honduras (Sheets 1979). The depth of Ilopango ash, which has been called the *tierra blanca joven* (*tbj*), at Cerén varies from 20 cm to more than 1 m (McKee 1989a). The Zapotitán Valley was abandoned for at least several decades following this eruption (Sheets 1979).

The inhabitants of Cerén were among the first to recolonize the valley (Black 1983). Some time later they were impacted by another eruption: Loma Caldera volcano, located approximately 0.8 km north of Cerén, erupted in AD 590 ± 90. This eruption was smaller than the Ilopango eruption, but was locally devastating. The Cerén site was buried by 3–7 m of ash (McKee 1989a) while still occupied. The eruption was phreatomagmatic in character, caused by the interaction of hot magma and water. The phases of the eruption resulted in three types of deposits. One type was deposited by base surges. Base surges are caused by steam explosions propelling accidental material from around the vent out laterally as diffuse clouds of hot, wet mud at temperatures of about 100°C and velocities of 100–300 km/hr (Cas and Wright 1988). Base surges deposited fine-grained sediments over and around structures, artefacts, and organic materials. The base-surge deposits alternated with airfall deposits of basaltic pumice and ballistic fragments, and deposits from one pyroclastic flow (Miller 1989). The airfall and pyroclastic surge deposits were emplaced at temperatures of greater than 575°C (Hoblitt 1983). Ballistic blocks up to one metre in diameter are present at Cerén. The hot airfall deposits ignited roofs and other organic materials as well as burying structures and surrounding areas. Ballistic fragments crashed through structure roofs and walls, and impacted many artefacts.

The site was probably abandoned by its inhabitants, as we have not encountered human remains, but they took little with them when they left (McKee 1990a). This is evidenced by the presence of small but valuable items inside various structures. According to C. Dan Miller (pers. comm. 1990), people inside structures could have survived the initial base surge, and there may have been a few hours to leave the site between the end of that phase and the beginning of the succeeding hot airfall eruption.

The volcanic stratigraphy provides many unique opportunities. By excavating in stratigraphic levels, we can determine which artefacts were in contact with the floor at the time of the eruption, and which were stored above the floor and fell during the eruption. We can accurately infer the sequence of events during the eruption, and see when artefacts and architectural elements fell. The deposits have also preserved organic

Figure 3.2 Cerén: plaster cast of enigmatic feature consisting of corn plants lashed together with agave fibre twine.
Photograph by Brian McKee.

materials in at least four ways: direct preservation, carbonization, mineral replacement, and preservation of the forms of organic materials as moulds. In the latter case, the fine grained base surge deposits packed around the materials which then decomposed, leaving a void. When these voids are encountered during excavation, we fill them with dental plaster. The ash is then excavated, leaving a cast as a direct replica of the form of the original item (Figures 3.2, 3.3).

The volcanoes of the area have not been quiescent since the eruption of Loma Caldera. At least seven additional eruptions have occurred within 10 km of the site since the Ilopango eruption (Miller 1992). It is very likely that other eruptions have occurred that are not yet recognized.

THE OCCUPATION OF CERÉN

The Cerén site is located immediately north of the Río Sucio, in the northern portion of the Zapotitán Valley. It was apparently a village or small town, although its total extent is not yet

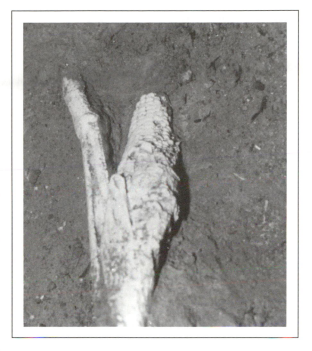

Figure 3.3 Cerén: plaster cast of corn cob. Photograph by Brian McKee.

known. Eleven structures and surrounding areas have been partially or completely excavated (Figure 3.1). Each household used several functionally specialized structures that include domiciles, storage structures or *bodegas*, kitchens, and small ramada-like structures. Seven structures have been tentatively assigned to three households on the basis of proximity and access (Sheets 1992), while the other four are considered to either be communal structures or their affiliation is not known.

Household 1

Four structures have been excavated from Household 1 (Structures 1, 5, 6, and 11). Structure 1 (Zier 1983; Beaudry and Tucker 1989) was identified as the domicile. The northern portion of the structure was destroyed by a bulldozer in 1976, and its dimensions are not known. However, based on comparisons with other structures, the missing portion appears to be minimal; the remaining portion measures 4.45 × 3.7 m (Beaudry and Tucker 1989). The structure was built on a clay platform, the walls are of *bajareque* (wattle and daub), and the roof is of grass thatch. There are two rooms with a large bench in the interior room. Many artefacts, including ceramic vessels, were found in Structure 1.

Structure 5 was a small, unwalled, roofed platform north-west of Structure 1; it measured 2.75 × 1.9 m when excavated, but the northern portion was destroyed during silo construction. Few artefacts were associated with this structure (Zier 1983).

Structure 6 is interpreted as the *bodega* or storehouse of Household 1. It was built on a clay platform, and had some walls made of organic materials and some of *bajareque* (Beaudry and Tucker 1989; Mobley-Tanaka 1990). The structure contained numerous artefacts, including chipped stone, grinding stones, and ceramic vessels, many with contents in place (Beaudry and Tucker 1989).

Structure 11 is round in plan with a small rectangular porch, and was largely built with organic materials (Mobley-Tanaka 1990). There is no prepared clay platform, and the floor consists of slightly mounded up *tbj* ash. The walls were built of vertical poles and were covered with thatch, as was the roof, and a three-stone hearth was present. This structure is interpreted as a kitchen (ibid.; Sheets 1992). The artefact assemblage included chipped and ground stone, modified bone, and polychrome painted gourds, as well as a relatively large ceramic assemblage. We have excavated considerable areas outside the structures in Operation 1. Most of the area was covered by a cornfield (Zier 1983; Tucker 1990), and a garden plot used for the cultivation of several species (Tucker 1990; Reyna de Aguilar 1991). Features such as the *surcos* or growing ridges and small drainage ditches are present in these gardens (Tucker 1990). Other areas around the structures include possible footpaths and highly trampled areas used for various activities.

Household 2

Two structures are believed to have been used by Household 2 (Structures 2 and 7). Structure 2, was identified as the domicile (McKee 1989b), and is similar to Structure 1, with *bajareque* walls built on top of a clay platform and is covered with a thatch roof. It has two rooms, with a clay bench in the interior room. Structure 2 measures 3.42 × 4.33 m (ibid.). Artefacts recovered included ceramics, a painted gourd, a bivalve shell, chipped and ground stone, and bone tools. An informal hearth consisting of two rocks and some charcoal was present under the western eaves, but saw little use.

Structure 7 is immediately south of Structure 2 (McKee 1990b). It is a single room *bajareque* structure with a thatch roof and measures approximately 3 metres square. An irregular porch on the north side of the platform extends 1.5 m to the north. This structure was identified as a *bodega*, and contained large numbers of ceramics, foodstuffs, chipped and ground stone artefacts, jadeite beads, shell beads, bone tools, a bone figurine, and two types of pigment, specular haematite and cinnabar. Several distinct deposits of wood ash from elevated contexts may have been used for food processing (ibid.).

Household 3

Household 3 refers to a known but largely unexcavated structure, Structure 16. This appears to be a kitchen structure similar in construction to Structure 11 (Gerstle 1992b), but until further excavations are carried out we can only speculate regarding its nature and relationship to other structures.

Household 4

Only one structure has been excavated from Household 4. This is Structure 4, which contained many artefacts and stored foodstuffs, and has been identified as a *bodega* (Gerstle 1990). This structure has two rooms with *bajareque* walls above a clay platform and a thatch roof, with no bench in the interior room. Artefacts include numerous ceramic vessels, painted gourds, a corn crib made of small poles lashed together above a mat of leaves (ibid.), red pigment, wood ash balls similar to those found in Structure 2, chipped and ground stone artefacts, bone artefacts, and the contents of the vessels and corn crib.

Other structures and features

Four additional structures that have not yet been assigned to households have been excavated. They may have been used by several households or by the entire community. Structure 3 measures approximately 8.2 × 5.3 m, and was built with solid clay walls over a massive clay platform and a thatch roof (Gerstle1989). There are two rooms, with two large benches in the exterior room. The few artefacts recovered from this structure included two ceramic vessels, one bone tool, one biconically perforated 'doughnut' stone, and another piece of modified stone. The structure has been tentatively assigned an unspecified public function (ibid.; Sheets 1992).

Structure 9 is about 5 m south of Structure 7, but its relationship with Household 2 is not known (McKee 1990c). This structure has solid clay walls above a clay platform, and is covered with a *bajareque* dome. The dome was covered by a thin roof of grass thatch (ibid.). The platform extends past the walls on the north and west sides to form a bench. There is a rounded firebox inside the structure constructed of river cobbles and clay, and the inside floor is covered with exfoliated andesite slabs and a layer of ash from Ilopango eruption. No artefacts have been found associated with Structure 9, but very little of the interior has been excavated (ibid.). The structure has been interpreted as a sweat bath (McKee 1990b).

Structure 12 (Sheets and Sheets 1990) is of *bajareque* on a solid clay platform. It is a complex structure with at least four rooms characterized by restricted and difficult access, in the form of low doorways and multiple turns to enter interior rooms. Portions of one wall are painted bright red (Sheets and Sheets 1990). The artefact assemblage is unusual, and artefacts do not appear to be functionally related. They include ceramics, chipped and ground stone, figurines and shell fragments. Many were found in niches created by the complex architecture. Sheets (1992) hypothesizes that the structure may have had a ritual function, possibly as the location where a shaman practised.

A likely ritual function has also been inferred for Stucture 10 (Gerstle 1992a, 1993), which is *c*. 8 m west of Structure 12. It is a two room *bajareque* structure built on a clay platform with a thatch roof. The platform measures 3.7 m on one side, and clay columns are present at the corners (Gerstle 1992a). The artefacts included ceramics, a painted gourd, obsidian blade fragments, and a probable headdress, consisting of the painted upper portion of a deer skull with the antlers still attached (ibid.).

Several additional areas excavated outside of structures should be mentioned. A cornfield (*milpa*) was found east of Structure 9 (McKee 1990c). Excavations west of Structure 9 revealed several upright *lajas* (exfoliated andesite) slabs with horizontal slabs at their bases (ibid.). The use of these features is not known. A midden located in a large depression was found south of these features and immediately to the west of Structure 9 (ibid.; McKee 1992). Testing of the midden encountered ceramic, obsidian, and bone artefacts, as well as complex sediments consisting of wood ash, clay, and volcanic ash. An agave (maguey) garden was encountered just south of Structure 4 (Gerstle 1990). Excavations to allow the placement of support posts for protective roofing encountered small additional areas of cultivation and possible plaza areas (Gerstle 1992b).

The Cerén site is characterized by a diverse set of structures and activity areas. Some of the structures can be grouped together to form household clusters, but the relationships between other structures are not known. Each household utilized multiple, specialized structures and had gardens or cornfields close to their structures.

DISCARD PROCESSES

Many archaeologists have viewed the archaeological record as a 'fossil' of past cultural and behavioural systems (Binford 1964). The archaeological record is a material record of past societies, but it does not come to us unaltered. Many cultural and non-cultural formation processes intervene between past behaviours of interest and what we recover as the archaeological record (Schiffer 1987). One of the principal cultural formation processes of the archaeological record is discard. Normally, most of what is seen in the archaeological record is the garbage left behind by site inhabitants.

In order to understand the processes involved in the formation of the archaeological record, it is necessary to distinguish between systemic and archaeological context. Items in systemic context are undergoing use and manipulation by people, and items in archaeological context have, at some point, been in systemic context, but are now isolated from cultural processes, and are only modified by natural processes (Schiffer 1972). Discard processes are the primary way in which items pass from systemic to archaeological context.

Discard is the endpoint of the use cycle of an artefact. Deal (1983) has devised a useful model to examine the use cycles of ceramics based on ethnoarchaeologial work in highland Chiapas. In his model, pottery has a primary function for which it was manufactured. Pottery may also have secondary uses that are generally not related to the primary use, and separate cycles of use and reuse can occur. A vessel is used for its primary function until it becomes unsuitable for that function, through wear, breakage, or fulfilling its original purpose. A vessel that becomes unusable can either be repaired, discarded permanently, or provisionally discarded. Items in provisional discard can be repaired and returned to their original function, or reused in either modified or unmodified form. Vessels at any point in the use or reuse cycle can also be permanently discarded. Provisional discard occurs in a variety of locations. Deal (1983) notes that provisionally discarded vessels are usually placed in locations where they do not interfere with ongoing activities, but are still easily retrievable. The same model can be applied to non-ceramic items.

Permanently discarded items have been found in three contexts at Cerén. The first is a low density scatter that is present throughout the site. Discarded items are present in cornfields (Zier 1983; McKee 1990c), gardens (Gerstle 1990; Tucker 1990), possible plazas, and in other areas between structures. These items vary in size and in density, but have not yet been systematically analysed. Limited excavations below the pre-Loma Caldera eruption ground surface indicate that Classic Period sherds extend from the occupation surface down to the contact with the pre-Ilopango eruption ground surface (Gerstle 1992b). The porous, sandy *tbj* soil allows for downward movement of sherds due to trampling or other processes.

A second area where discarded sherds have been encountered is in the clay platforms of the structures. Examination of the edge of Structure 1 cut by the bulldozer revealed sherds in the clay matrix. It is not known if these inclusions were intentional or inadvertent.

The final area of discard was in the midden near Structure 9 (McKee 1990c). The midden is in a large depression, the edge of which is only 1.5 m west of Structure 9. This depression slopes steeply down to the south-west. The depression may be natural, possibly the edge of a drainage, or it may be artificial. Large quantities of clay were required for the construction of nearby Structures 2, 7 and 9, and this depression may indicate a borrow pit used to mine the clay. Two test pits were excavated in the midden (McKee 1992, 1993), which were characterized by complex stratigraphy, including deposits of clay, *tbj*, and wood ash, as well as discarded ceramics, lithics, bone, and other organic materials (McKee 1992, 1993). The wood ash may result from dumping from the nearby sweat bath, Structure 9.

The nearby Río Sucio is another area where discard may have occurred. We have not excavated near the river, but indications are that the river flowed in the same location where it does today during the site occupation. Discard of household wastes into rivers is common in El Salvador today, and according to William A. Longacre (pers. comm. 1993), the same practice is common in the Philippines. If the Río Sucio was heavily utilized for refuse disposal during the Classic Period, then this may bias our sample of discarded artefacts. Test pits excavated near the river could help to clarify how much dumping of this sort occurred.

There are a number of problems in obtaining a representative sample of the discarded assemblage at Cerén. A sampling design stratified by functional areas (gardens, plazas, footpaths, etc.) and excavated to the pre-Loma Caldera ground surface could help control the first type of discard. An accurate definition of a representative sample may have to await clearer definitions of the site boundaries. A representative sample of the midden should be readily obtained, once its horizontal and vertical extents are clarified. Unfortunately, until we clear the nearly 7 m of deposits down to the pre-eruption ground surface we will not be certain of its horizontal extent. The number of sherds included in structural clay will be difficult to quantify, but my impression is that a relatively small number of sherds are included in this category when compared to the other two. Finally, the excavation of some test pits near the Río Sucio should help to resolve the question of whether a significant number of ceramics were discarded in this area.

REUSE PROCESSES

Schiffer (1987) describes several reuse processes that can keep items in systemic context that might otherwise be transferred to archaeological context or that can bring items out of archaeological context into systemic context. These processes include lateral cycling, which involves a change in the user of an item without modification or change in use and is usually invisible in the archaeological record.

Recycling involves the modification and use of an artefact for a purpose other than that for which it was originally intended. There is evidence of several recycling processes at Cerén. One of the most interesting examples involves the use of handles from large storage jars as architectural elements (Figure 3.4). The handles of broken pots were lashed to the upright poles of *bajareque* structures and then the body of the sherd was plastered over with mud (McKee 1989b, 1990b; Gerstle 1990). In the solid clay structures, the handles were apparently just embedded into the wet clay (Gerstle 1989). The most common locations for these handles are at the corners of doorways, where they were used to attach doors made of canes that were lashed together (McKee 1989b; Gerstle 1990). A ceramic handle was also found embedded in a hole in the clay platform of Structure 7. This handle apparently served as a tie-down, possibly being used to secure roofing or other architectural elements in the event of wind (McKee 1996). Broken sherds were also ground into discs in some cases (Beaudry and Tucker 1989; McKee 1990b). Some discs were perforated and used for spindle whorls (Beaudry and Tucker 1989), and another sherd disc was used as a lid for a vessel (McKee 1990b). A vessel found in Structure 1 had been repaired by the insertion

Figure 3.4 Cerén: fallen eastern wall of Structure 2. Note ceramic handle embedded in wall in foreground. Another handle (above the first one) has been dislodged by the impact of a volcanic bomb.
Photograph by Brian McKee.

of a small, ground, rounded plug into a hole (Beaudry 1989). Numerous other examples of recycling have been mentioned in the ethnoarchaeological literature (Deal 1983).

Secondary use involves the use of an object for a purpose other than that for which it was originally designed, without modification (Schiffer 1987). Large sherds were found in the roofing of several structures (Beaudry and Tucker 1989; McKee 1990b; Gerstle 1990). These sherds may have been used as plates to store perishable organic materials in the rafters. They may have also been in provisional discard locations prior to reuse (Beaudry-Corbett 1990). Deal (1983) notes that the Tzeltal Maya placed broken vessels on roofs in provisional discard, or along ridgelines to repair leaky roofs.

An important distinction that must be made in the study of discard processes is that between primary and secondary refuse. Primary refuse consists of artefacts or waste products discarded at locations of use or manufacture, and artefacts discarded elsewhere are secondary refuse (Schiffer 1987). Most discarded items found at Cerén, as well as at most other sites occupied by sedentary populations, are secondary refuse (McKee 1990a). People in these sites tend to perform regular maintenance to keep work areas free of debris.

Another variable relevant to the study of discard processes is the nature of abandonment. Abandonment is the process by which a place is transformed from systemic to archaeological context (Schiffer 1987; Cameron 1991). Many processes can be involved in abandonment, including the scavenging of usable artefacts and structural elements (Lange and Rydberg 1972). Most valuable and portable artefacts are quickly removed at the time of abandonment, and less valuable or bulkier items may be removed later. *De facto* refuse consists of the still usable materials that are left behind when a site is abandoned (Schiffer 1972). Cerén is a classic example of what Schiffer (1987) has labelled catastrophic abandonment. When the inhabitants left the site, they took with them few if any artefacts, even leaving behind valuable and portable items such as necklaces of jadeite beads (McKee 1990b). The majority of the items recovered at Cerén, other than those in clearly discarded context, are *de facto* refuse. The rapid abandonment of Cerén has minimized the effects of the cultural formation processes usually associated with abandonment.

THE DISCARD EQUATION

Several researchers have independently developed equations to study the effects of discard on the formation of archaeological assemblages. Baumhoff and Heizer (1959) were the first to note the relationships between the number of ceramic vessels used by a group, the duration of site occupation, and rates of discard. Foster (1960), in a pioneering ethnographic study, studied rates of breakage and the number of vessels used by households to improve our understanding of these variables. At least three researchers have proposed equations to relate the frequencies of artefacts in archaeological assemblages to systemic assemblages, the use-lives of these artefacts and the duration of site occupation (David 1972: 142; Schiffer 1976: 60; Schiffer 1987; de Barros 1982: 310).

Schiffer's equation (1976) has been more widely applied than the others (Deal 1983; Mills 1989; Lightfoot 1992), and is presented as follows:

$$TD = \frac{S \times t}{L}$$

where TD = the total discarded assemblage, S = the number of artefacts typically in use in the systemic inventory, L = the use-life of the artefact, and t = time. When one knows any three of the variables, it is a simple matter to solve for the fourth.

Schiffer (1987: 54) discusses several assumptions that must be made to apply the model. The first is that there is no reuse. This is clearly not true at Cerén. Many broken vessels experienced secondary uses and recycling before their final discard. It should be possible to quantify this variable and integrate it into the discard equation, but the ethnographic data are not present at this time to systematize this variable. No one, to my knowledge, has attempted to study the use-life of reused artefacts. Deal (1983) states that 21 per cent of the household inventories were being reused at the time of his survey. The equation is further complicated by the fact that different portions of the same vessel may undergo different cycles of reuse. Handles for large storage jars at Cerén, for example, would likely be preferentially reused. Vessel rims might also be reused to protect seedlings (ibid.), a factor that has major implications for traditional ceramic studies. Fortunately, at Cerén, we are able to recognize most of the ceramics that were undergoing reuse. Although reused sherds cannot generally be recognized in their permanent discard contexts, total weights and frequencies should reflect the final discard process. An important factor in the analysis of reused ceramic artefacts is that they are rarely used for their primary purpose after breakage. The majority are probably used for functions that would not otherwise be served by unbroken vessels (Barbara J. Mills, pers. comm. 1993). Therefore, most reused portions of vessels should be considered to be discarded, at least relative to their original uses and use-lives.

A second assumption noted by Schiffer (1987) is that the use-life and systemic number should remain relatively constant through time. Deal (1983) has shown that the developmental cycle of the household group can affect both of these variables in the short term, but an extended period of occupation may minimize these effects.

Schiffer's (1987) third assumption is that artefacts should not be exchanged in or out of the area of study or used outside of this area. I believe that this assumption is unnecessary, as long as the size of the systemic assemblage remains relatively constant. The source of the vessels is not important, and the most important factor is that vessels used by the group of interest are discarded within the study area. Exchange could create problems if household members are preferentially trading out old vessels, but if the size of the systemic assemblage remains relatively constant and few old vessels are traded out or in, then exchange should have minimal effects. Schiffer's final assumption is that the artefact type is functionally homogeneous. This factor must be controlled during data collection.

DISCUSSION, SUMMARY AND CONCLUSIONS

The purpose of this chapter was to outline some basic principles useful for the study of the formation of the archaeological record of households. The Cerén site provides useful examples of many cultural formation processes. These processes occurred at most archaeological sites, but they are usually difficult to observe because of succeeding cultural and non-cultural formation processes. The sudden burial of Cerén by volcanic ash and its rapid abandonment allows the clear distinction of many reused items. In the future, I would like to examine in more detail the various categories of refuse at Cerén, and to apply the discard equation. Provided that the underlying assumptions of the discard equation work at Cerén, it should be possible to arrive at the duration of the occupation. Unfortunately, we are still far from having sufficient data to quantify adequately all relevant variables on a site-wide basis.

Studies of discard processes are important for understanding the archaeological record. At most sites, the majority of the archaeological record represents items that were discarded after breaking or serving their original functions. Floor contact *de facto* refuse approximating the systemic assemblage is rare, and archaeologists must usually infer the behaviourally significant systemic assemblage on the basis of these broken and discarded artefacts. The Cerén site in El Salvador provides an ideal laboratory to develop and test methods of making these inferences. The catastrophic burial of the site by a volcanic eruption preserved the systemic assemblage largely intact, and the discovery of a midden used by site inhabitants allows us to compare the systemic ceramic assemblage with the discarded assemblage. Considerable field and analytical work remains before we can make reliable inferences, but they should be possible. Ultimately, through the use of the discard equation (Schiffer 1987), we may be able to determine the duration of the site occupation. This information will aid us in making behavioural inferences regarding the occupation of the site. At the least, by the comparison of systemic assemblages at various areas with the locations of discard, we should be able to understand preferential patterns of discard by different groups. This could allow the application of other models relevant to the study of discard processes, such as the waste stream model (ibid.). By applying these models to a nearly ideal situation at Cerén, we may clarify the use of quantitative models in more common archaeological situations.

ACKNOWLEDGEMENTS

Many people have contributed directly or indirectly to this chapter. Mike Schiffer, Pim Allison, Janet Griffitts, Vince LaMotta and Marcy Rockman read and commented on an earlier version, resulting in a clearer presentation. Thanks to Pim Allison for organizing the AIA session and to all of the symposium participants for helpful criticism. The fieldwork that provided the data used for this chapter relied on too many people to be mentioned. First, I would like to thank the people and government of El Salvador for the opportunity to work at Cerén, and our Salvadoran field crew for many seasons of enjoyable work and companionship. Finally, I would like to thank all the Cerén Project members and especially Dr Payson Sheets.

BIBLIOGRAPHY

Baumhoff, M. A. and Heizer, R. F. (1959) 'Some Unexplored Possibilities in Ceramic Analysis', *American Antiquity* 15: 308–16.

Beaudry, M. (1989) 'Ceramics', in P. D. Sheets and B. R. McKee (eds) *1989 Archaeological Investigations at the Cerén Site, El Salvador*, Boulder: Dept. of Anthropology, University of Colorado: 81–90.

Beaudry, M. and Tucker, D. (1989) 'Household 1 Area Excavations', in P. D. Sheets and B. R. McKee (eds) *1989 Archaeological Investigations at the Cerén Site, El Salvador*, Boulder: Dept. of Anthropology, University of Colorado: 29–40.

Beaudry-Corbett, M. (1990) 'Joya de Cerén Ceramics: Classification and Preliminary Analysis of Household Inventories', in P. D. Sheets and B. R. McKee (eds) *1990 Investigations at the Cerén Site, El Salvador: A Preliminary Report*, Boulder: Dept. of Anthropology, University of Colorado: 154–75.

Binford, L. R. (1964) 'A Consideration of Archaeological Research Design', *American Antiquity* 29: 425–41.

Black, K. (1983) 'The Zapotitán Valley Archeological Survey', in P. D. Sheets (ed.) *Archaeology and Volcanism in Central America: The Zapotitán Valley of El Salvador*, Austin: University of Texas Press: 62–97.

Cameron, C. M. (1991) 'Structure Abandonment in Villages', in M. B. Schiffer (ed.) *Archaeological Method and Theory* 3, Tucson: University of Arizona Press: 155–94.

Cas, R. A. F. and Wright, J. V. (1988) *Volcanic Successions, Modern and Ancient*, London: Unwin Hyman.

Conyers, L. (1995) 'The Use of Ground-Penetrating Radar to Map the Buried Topography and Structures, Cerén Site, El Salvador', Ph.D. dissertation, Department of Anthropology, University of Colorado, Boulder, Ann Arbor: University Microfilms.

David, N. (1972) 'On the Life Span of Pottery, Type Frequencies, and Archaeological Inference', *American Antiquity* 37, 1: 141–2.

Deal, M. (1983) 'Pottery Ethnoarchaeology Among the Tzeltal Maya', Unpublished Ph.D. dissertation, Simon Fraser University.

de Barros, P. L. F. (1982) 'The Effects of Variable Site Occupation Span on the Results of Frequency Seriation', *American Antiquity* 47, 2: 291–315.

Doolittle, J. and Miller, F. (1992) '1992 Geophysical Investigations at the Cerén Site, El Salvador', in P. D. Sheets and K. A. Kievit (eds) *Investigations at the Cerén Site, El Salvador: A Preliminary Report*, Boulder: Dept. of Anthropology, University of Colorado: 10–19.

Foster, G. M. (1960) 'Life Expectancy of Utilitarian Pottery in Tzinzuntzan, Michoacan, Mexico', *American Antiquity* 25, 4: 606–9.

Gerstle, A. I. (1989) 'Excavations at Structure 3', in P. D. Sheets and B. R. McKee (eds) *1989 Archaeological Investigations at the Cerén Site, El Salvador*, Boulder: Dept. of Anthropology, University of Colorado: 59–80.

—— (1990) '1990 Operation 4 Preliminary Report', in P. D. Sheets and B. R. McKee (eds) *1990 Investigations at the Cerén Site, El Salvador: A Preliminary Report*, Boulder: Dept. of Anthropology, University of Colorado: 154–75.

—— (1992a) '1992 Excavations at Structure 10, Joya de Cerén', in P. D. Sheets and K. A. Kievit (eds) *1992 Investigations at the Cerén Site, El Salvador: A Preliminary Report*, Boulder: Dept. of Anthropology, University of Colorado: 30–54.

—— (1992b) 'Summary of Text Excavations in Joya de Cerén, 1990–1992: Operations 3, 4, 6, and 7', in P. D. Sheets and K. A. Kievit (eds) *1992 Investigations at the Cerén Site, El Salvador: A Preliminary Report*, Boulder: Dept. of Anthropology, University of Colorado: 61–71.

—— (1993) '1993 Excavations at Structure 10, Joya de Cerén', in P. D. Sheets and S. Simmons (eds) *Preliminary Report of the Cerén Research Project, 1993 Season*, Boulder: Dept. of Anthropology, University of Colorado: 46–90.

Hart, W. J. E. and Steen-McIntyre, V. (1983) '*Tierra Blanca Joven* Tephra from the A.D. 260 eruption of Ilopango Caldera', in P. D. Sheets (ed.) *Archaeology and Volcanism in Central America: The Zapotitán Valley of El Salvador*, Austin: University of Texas Press: 14–34.

Hayden, B. and Cannon, A. (1982) 'Where the Garbage Goes: Refuse Disposal in the Maya Highlands', *Journal of Anthropological Archaeology* 2: 117–63.

Hoblitt, R. P. (1983) 'Volcanic Events at the Cerén Site', in P. D. Sheets (ed.) *Archaeology and Volcanism in Central America: The Zapotitán Valley of El Salvador*, Austin: University of Texas Press: 14–34.

Lange, F. W. and Rydberg, C. R. (1972) 'Abandonment and Post-Abandonment Behavior at a Rural Central American House Site', *American Antiquity* 37: 419–32.

Lightfoot, R. R. (1992) 'Archaeology of the House and Household: A Case Study of Assemblage Formation and Household Organization in the American Southwest', Ph.D. dissertation, Washington State University.

Loker, W. M. (1983) 'Recent Geophysical Explorations at Cerén', in P. D. Sheets (ed.) *Archaeology and Volcanism in Central America: The Zapotitán Valley of El Salvador*, Austin: University of Texas Press: 254–74.

McKee, B. R. (1989a) 'Core Drilling Program', in P. D. Sheets and B. R. McKee (eds) *1989 Archaeological Investigations at the Cerén Site, El Salvador*, Boulder: Dept. of Anthropology, University of Colorado: 22–6.

—— (1989b) 'Excavations at Structure Complex 2', in P. D. Sheets and B. R. McKee (eds) *1989 Archaeological Investigations at the Cerén Site, El Salvador*, Boulder: Dept. of Anthropology, University of Colorado: 41–58.

—— (1990a) 'The Pompeii Premise Revisited: Formation Processes and Activity Areas at the Cerén Site, El Salvador', MA thesis, University of Colorado, Boulder.

—— (1990b) 'Excavations at Structure 7', in P. D. Sheets and B. R. McKee (eds) *1990 Investigations at the Cerén Site, El Salvador: A Preliminary Report*, Boulder: Dept. of Anthropology, University of Colorado: 68–89.

—— (1990c) 'Excavations at Structure 9', in P. D. Sheets and B. R. McKee (eds) *1990 Investigations at the Cerén Site, El Salvador: A Preliminary Report*, Boulder: Dept. of Anthropology, University of Colorado: 90–107.

—— (1992) '1992 Excavations in Operation 2', in P. D. Sheets and K. A. Kievit (eds) *1992 Investigations at the Cerén Site, El Salvador: A Preliminary Report*, Boulder: Dept. of Anthropology, University of Colorado: 20–9.

—— (1993) 'Archaeological Investigations in Operation 2', in P. D. Sheets and S. Simmons (eds) *Preliminary Report of the Cerén Research Project, 1993 Season*, Boulder: Dept. of Anthropology, University of Colorado: 125–37.

—— (1996) 'Archaeological Excavations in Operation 2', in P. D. Sheets and L. Brown (eds) *Preliminary Report of the Cerén Research Project 1996 Field Season*, Boulder: Dept. of Anthropology, University of Colorado: 5–9.

Miller, C. D. (1989) 'Stratigraphy of Volcanic Deposits at El Cerén', in P. D. Sheets and B. R. McKee (eds) *1989 Archaeological Investigations at the Cerén Site, El Salvador*, Boulder: Dept. of Anthropology, University of Colorado: 8–19.

—— (1992) 'Summary of 1992 Geological Investigations at Joya de Cerén', in P. D. Sheets and K. A. Kievit (eds) *1992 Investigations at the Cerén Site, El Salvador: A Preliminary Report*, Boulder: Dept. of Anthropology, University of Colorado: 10–19.

Mills, B. J. (1989) 'Integrating Functional Analyses of Vessels and Sherds', *World Archaeology* 21, 1: 133–47.

Mobley-Tanaka, J. L. (1990) '1990 Excavations in Operation 1, Cerén, El Salvador', in P. D. Sheets and B. R. McKee (eds) *1990 Investigations at the Cerén Site, El Salvador: A Preliminary Report*, Boulder: Dept. of Anthropology, University of Colorado: 36–47.

Reyna de Aguilar, M. L. (1991) 'Una Verdadera Joya . . . Joya de Cerén; Flora Autoctona Salvadoreña', *Pankia* 10, 2: 3–9 (Jardin Botanico, San Salvador, El Salvador).

Schiffer, M. B. (1972) 'Archaeological Context and Systemic Context', *American Antiquity* 37, 2: 156–65.

—— (1976) *Behavioral Archaeology*, New York: Academic Press.

—— (1987) *Formation Processes of the Archaeological Record*, Albuquerque: University of New Mexico Press.

Sheets, F. and Sheets, P. D. (1990) 'Excavations of Structure 12, Cerén', in P. D. Sheets and B. R. McKee (eds) *1990 Investigations at the Cerén Site, El Salvador: A Preliminary Report*, Boulder: Dept. of Anthropology, University of Colorado: 138–47.

Sheets, P. D. (1979) 'Environmental and Cultural Effects of the Ilopango Eruption in Central America', in P. D. Sheets and D. Grayson (eds) *Volcanic Activity and Human Ecology*, New York: Academic Press: 525–64.

—— (1989) 'Introduction', in P. D. Sheets and B. R. McKee (eds) *1989 Archaeological Investigations at the Cerén Site, El Salvador*, Boulder: Dept. of Anthropology, University of Colorado: 1–5.

—— (1992) *The Cerén Site: A Prehistoric Village Buried by Volcanic Ash in Central America*, Fort Worth: Harcourt Brace Jovanovich.

Sheets, P. D. and Brown, L. (eds) (1996) *Preliminary Report of the Cerén Research Project 1996 Field Season*, Boulder: Dept. of Anthropology, University of Colorado.

Sheets, P. D. and Kievit, K. A. (eds) (1992) *1992 Investigations at the Cerén Site, El Salvador: A Preliminary Report*, Boulder: Dept. of Anthropology, University of Colorado.

Sheets, P. D. and McKee, B. R. (eds) (1989) *1989 Archaeological Investigations at the Cerén Site, El Salvador*, Boulder: Dept. of Anthropology, University of Colorado.

—— (1990) *1990 Investigations at the Cerén Site, El Salvador: A Preliminary Report*, Boulder: Dept. of Anthropology, University of Colorado.

Sheets, P. D. and Simmons, S. E. (eds) (1993) *Preliminary Report of the Cerén Research Project, 1993 Season*, Boulder: Dept. of Anthropology, University of Colorado.

Spetzler, H. and McKee, B. R. (1990) 'Resistivity Survey of Lot 189B, Cerén, El Salvador', in P. D. Sheets and B. R. McKee (eds.) *1990 Investigations at the Cerén Site, El Salvador: A Preliminary Report*, Boulder: Dept. of Anthropology, University of Colorado: 27–33.

Tucker, D. B. (1990) 'Investigations in Operation 1, Feb.–March, 1991', in P. D. Sheets and B. R. McKee (eds) *1990 Investigations at the Cerén Site, El Salvador: A Preliminary Report*, Boulder: Dept. of Anthropology, University of Colorado: 48–67.

Wilk, R. and Rathje, W. (1982) 'Household Archaeology', *American Behavioral Scientist* 25: 617–39.

Zier, C. J. (1983) 'The Cerén Site: A Classic Period Maya Residence and Agricultural Field in the Zapotitán Valley', in P. D. Sheets (ed.) *Archaeology and Volcanism in Central America: The Zapotitán Valley of El Salvador*, Austin: University of Texas Press: 1–13.

Chapter Four

Digging houses: Archaeologies of Classical and Hellenistic Greek domestic assemblages[1]

Bradley A. Ault and Lisa C. Nevett

ABSTRACT

Archaeologists in general and Classical archaeologists in particular are frequently criticized for their failure to take into account implications of the full complement of artefactual assemblages when interpreting the results of excavation. Nowhere are such omissions more glaring than in the domestic context. Several examples of ambivalent attitudes toward and selective treatment of domestic assemblages are cited. These are contrasted with a number of excavations of Greek houses which have striven not only for more comprehensive recovery of domestic assemblages but also for their fuller presentation and integration into subsequent interpretation.

   While advocating the latter approach, the authors acknowledge a number of potential stumbling blocks which must be taken into consideration when associating and interpreting the numerically great and typologically diverse components of the domestic artefactual assemblage. Among these are the importance of distinguishing between primary *de facto* assemblages of synchronic significance (with an attendant caveat that these may reflect abandonment rather than habitation scenarios), primary refuse which has accumulated gradually as a result of primary activities (making for a diachronic assemblage), and secondary refuse introduced from another location. Finally, the notion of an archaeological household as the subject of an anthropologically analogous ethnographic study is dispelled in favour of recognizing the more fluid and dynamic notion of a household series or cycle circumscribed by the built environment of the house.

Traditionally, Classical archaeologists have tended to display relatively little interest in exploring the domestic context in comparison with the attention which has been paid to public monuments and funerary sites. When they have been studied, both domestic architecture and the artefacts found in domestic contexts tend to be viewed as isolated objects to be categorized and typologized, while questions about the nature of life in the ancient world have usually been left to those working with textual, rather than with archaeological material.[2]

   Recently, however, the influence of the New Archaeology has led Classical archaeologists to realize that their data will allow them to ask a broader range of questions. Using the material record they are able to look at aspects of the ancient world, such as social and economic relations, which are only partially covered by the documentary sources, compare and contrast different geographical regions and assess long-term change.[3] Nevertheless, our lack of knowledge about the domestic environment and about many of the activities which took place there has begun to stand out as a factor which is preventing us from using archaeology to address some of these major questions. For example, we do not yet have detailed models to explain the processes by which the artefacts found in the archaeological record were deposited there. We return to this problem below, but for now, several quotes from the recent literature, their ceramocentric emphasis notwithstanding, will suffice to underscore that this problem is one which deserves recognition and rectification:

> little is known about rates of ceramic consumption and discard in either town or country contexts . . .
>
> (Alcock *et al.* 1994: 169–70)

> Pottery has probably been the subject of more study and discourse by archaeologists than any comparable class of artifacts. In spite of such attention, archaeologists have shown too little interest in how pottery is treated and used in the domestic household. Most research directed at this question, in fact, has been ethnographic rather than archaeological.
>
> (Hally 1983: 163)

> To date, archaeologists have made little use of such information [i.e. the relation between vessel form and function, composition of vessel assemblages, the use-life of pottery vessels, the recycling of broken vessels, and patterns of pottery discard] in their investigations of archaeologically derived pottery collections.
>
> (Hally 1983: 163)

In short, we remain woefully uninformed about many of the patterns of social and economic relationships within and between households, and we lack the models which would help us to interpret artefactual assemblages.

A number of the excavations which have revealed areas of Classical or Hellenistic housing have highlighted various reasons why such material has not received the attention which we feel it deserves. Perhaps the most impressive house remains, in terms both of their number and standard of preservation, are those on Delos (for relevant bibliography, see Bruneau and Ducat 1983). Some of the structures at the site are among the first Greek houses to have been excavated. From the early publications it seems that, for the excavators, the main interest lay in the architecture, while the finds were generally simply cleared away and received little attention in the publications. Thus, although these houses offer a vivid impression of the nature of the city during the late Hellenistic and early Roman periods, they are in fact empty shells, and the early excavators seem to have taken little interest in how they might have further informed us about daily life. The material published from the more recent work on the Insula of the House of the Comedians gives some idea of the information about daily life which has been lost (Bruneau and Vatin *et al.* 1970). Also, recent interpretative studies of domestic decorative programmes from the island offer an indication of some of the kinds of questions which can be raised, not only about the appearance of these houses but also about the patterns of social relationships taking place within them, and which might be better addressed if more detailed evidence were available from a larger proportion of the excavated houses.[4]

A range of related problems occur also with other more recently excavated domestic assemblages. At Athens, for example, a large number of houses have come to light during excavation in and around the city centre. The excavators of the Agora report finding several dozen houses, although architectural details and plans of only a handful have been published.[5] Despite the fact that large numbers of finds have been recovered from the Agora area and that many of the published items, in particular the pottery, are likely to have been in everyday use in domestic contexts, the publications include little information about either the architectural contexts in which they were recovered or what other objects were found with them.[6] Thus, where they are published, both artefacts and architecture are studied as isolated entities, and the main topic of interest lies, for the architecture, in clarifying its form and phasing, and for the finds, in looking at style and creating a typological framework for dating. Again, there seems to have been little attention to the value of looking at complete assemblages with an eye to answering social questions.[7]

A rather different approach has been adopted by the excavators of the area near the Silenus Gate on Thasos (Grandjean 1988). In publishing the results of the excavations of houses located here, the excavators take a step towards linking the architectural spaces and the objects which were found within them by including partial inventories of the different spaces during successive phases of occupation (ibid.: passim) Nevertheless, the excavators are discouraged by the fact that the houses seem to have been emptied prior to their abandonment, by the fragmentary state of most of the pottery, and by the 'modest quality and repetitive character' (ibid.: 251) of the finds in general. Such an attitude to the material suggests that the main interest of the objects found in the houses was still perceived as being intrinsic to those objects themselves rather than lying in the picture created by the assemblage as a whole. As a result, only a limited number of the finds are published and their principal use is inevitably as tools for dating the different phases of the building rather than contributing to the reconstruction of patterns of domestic activity.

If the circumstances which attended the abandonment of the houses on Thasos left only a disappointingly small and fragmentary artefactual assemblage, the same cannot be said for the House with the Mosaics at Eretria, which was destroyed by fire *c.* 270 BC, preserving an array of non-combustible household equipment. Such circumstances should offer an ideal opportunity to study in detail the distribution of movable objects within the domestic context, and to draw conclusions about the nature and organization of such activities conducted there (Ducrey *et al.* 1993: 12). Nevertheless, good preservation brings with it different, but associated, problems. In this case, although large numbers of everyday 'minor' items were preserved, it became difficult to justify the expense of publishing everything that was found, and decisions were therefore made about the value of presenting information against the cost of publication. Again, the selection of material for inclusion in the recent final publication of the house appears to have been made on the basis of the intrinsic interest of individual pieces and their value for dating the architecture, and any merit which might have lain in the full publication of whole assemblages has lost out to financial considerations.[8]

Even where fuller artefactual assemblages have been published, the excavators do not always seem to have been aware of the questions which can potentially be addressed using such information, so that it is not always clear what their aims were by including it. The publications of both the Dema Wall and Vari Cave farmhouses in Attica (Jones *et al.* 1962, 1973), which included extensive inventories of the pottery and other small finds from the sites, do not include details of where the majority of the objects were found, so that although they offer a valuable picture of domestic assemblages as a whole, the opportunity to reconstruct patterns of activity within the houses is lost, and although the excavators seem to have been interested in the contents of the houses, that interest does not extend to the way in which individual spaces were used.

A common feature of these various studies is that the artefactual material is expected to answer few questions beyond confirming the general layout of individual houses and the date of each phase of occupation. One project which has attempted to move beyond this, in that it involved some recognition of the potential of the finds to assist in recognizing and interpreting patterns of activity within households, is the excavation of Olynthus, which, although it took place more than fifty years ago, produced a monumental final report of fourteen volumes publishing many individual finds along with a concordance of their find-spots (Robinson *et al.* 1929–52).[9] Although a fifteenth volume, which was to include a synthesis and interpretation of the artefactual material as whole, was ultimately rejected as being unnecessary, subsequent analysis of the material has demonstrated the value of the recovery and publication of such detailed information.[10]

Nevertheless, the approach taken at Olynthus raises its own problems: although the intention from the outset was to keep a thorough record of all the finds recovered from the different areas, in reality the sheer volume of material generated meant that it was impossible for the envisioned standard to keep pace with excavation itself. This was in part due to the scale of the operation, with a hundred-odd workers being employed, as well as to the opening up and working of such a large area over a mere four field campaigns. Especially in the final season, the excavators themselves acknowledge that complete recording of artefact provenance was impossible (Robinson *et al.* 1929–52 [1941]: v–vi). Subsequent renewed excavation of limited areas at the site also revealed that there was likely to have been rather more material present than the average of three finds per room which are recorded in the original publications (Drougou and Vokotopoulou 1989).

Elsewhere, more recent concentrated excavation of fewer numbers of houses has allowed much fuller recording and publication of associated finds. At Halos, for instance, several houses have so far been revealed, and the architecture and contents of one house have already been published (Reinders 1988). Similar work at Thorikos has also been directed at recovering detailed artefactual assemblages from a small number of houses (e.g. Mussche *et al.* 1990). The slower pace of excavation, coupled with its equally gradual publication, reveals the painstaking nature of this work. At the same time, the limited number of excavated houses at such sites makes it more difficult to generalize about the nature of household organization there. Nevertheless, such detailed study is surely necessary if we are to build up models which will allow us to interpret less detailed information which has been collected elsewhere. By looking closely at all of the ceramic and other finds from excavated houses it should be possible to explore patterns of use, storage and discard, which will inform our interpretation of artefacts found in other contexts, in particular those recovered during field survey. In order to make full use of detailed data on artefactual assemblages, however, we also need effective behavioural models which will help us to interpret this kind of information. It is to this problem that we would now like to turn.

In order to examine some aspects of the variability present in well documented domestic assemblages, we will here consider several deposits recovered at the small Archaic to early Hellenistic *polis* of Halieis in the southern Argolid. Excavated in the 1960s and 1970s by Indiana University and the University of Pennsylvania, portions of the city's acropolis, lower town and fortification system have been explored, as has an extramural sanctuary of Apollo.[11] Halieis appears to have been abandoned early in the third century BC. While the historical circumstances of this event are obscure, but should probably be connected with the activities of Antigonos Gonatas in the area (Jameson *et al.* 1994: 88–9), the net result for archaeology is an ancient Greek town emptied of its population (along with much of its portable wealth) and left to decay unimpeded and undisturbed. Although not recovered on the scale of Olynthus, Halieis offers a picture of urban and domestic life complementary to that site. One of the many noteworthy aspects of the houses excavated at Halieis is the fact that virtually every scrap of associated artefactual material was collected by stratigraphic unit, identified, and recorded. Study of this data has revealed significant information about the nature of the domestic economy, its scale and its spatial configuration.[12]

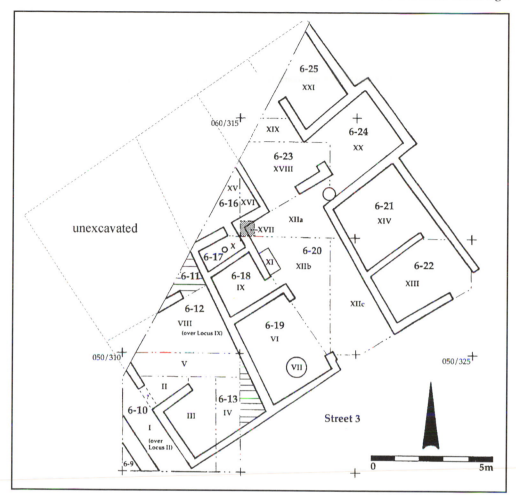

Figure 4.1 House E, Halieis: Rooms and loci. Locus XVII shaded.

Not that the wealth of data provided by careful excavation and recording at Halieis is without a whole host of problems as well as potential interpretative scenarios. For example, from the fourth-century habitation levels of House E (Figure 4.1) more than 4,100 ceramic objects and 3,300 roof tile fragments were recovered (in addition to less numerous categories such as lamps, stone and metal artefacts, shells, terracotta figurines, coins, etc.). Among the ceramic finds only thirty-six survived as whole vessels, but using a standard measure for determining the minimum number of vessels (MNV) represented on the basis of rim and base counts,[13] a total of 580 vessels can be accounted for. This illustrates once again the richness of datasets, already alluded to above, that can and should be recovered from the archaeological context.

Moving from quantification to interpretation, at the most basic level three sorts of depositional processes can be distinguished which account for how and why material enters the archaeological record. M. B. Schiffer has termed these 'Cultural Transforms'.[14] The first of these processes is of a type easily recognized by archaeologists, and which perhaps most causes their collective pulses to quicken, since it often results in the recovery of complete artefacts. Termed '*de facto* deposits', these represent the abandonment or deposition of artefacts in essentially the place where they were last used in the living context. They therefore stand in a one to one relationship to events in the past. Returning to House E, a *de facto* deposit there has been used to strengthen the identification of the only partially excavated Room 6–16. While its identification as a kitchen was already deemed highly likely on architectural grounds (that is, it was paved with a plaster floor and a small bathroom, Room 6–17, opened off its south side),[15] the deposit from Locus XVII (Figure 4.1) adds considerable weight to this identification. Eleven whole vessels and large portions of several others were recovered from this deposit. A tabular listing of the whole vessels, by ware, function and shape appears in Table 4.1, along with their Halieis Pottery (HP) catalogue numbers.[16]

Table 4.1 Halieis, House E, Locus XVII: whole vessels recovered

Fine ware	Coarse ware
Food	*Food*
Serving and consumption:	Preparation and serving
1 salt-cellar (HP2154)	1 bowl (HP2170)
	1 strainer (HP2155)
Drink	Cooking:
Consumption:	1 griddle (HP 2159)
2 bolsals (HP2151, HP2156)	1 lopas (HP 2161)
1 stemless cup (HP2164)	
Serving and pouring:	
2 jugs (HP2157, HP2158)	
Other	
1 squat lekythos (HP2153)	

Although the deposit lay in the north-west corner of the courtyard (Room 6–20), it actually began atop the stone socle of Room 6–16's south-east corner and spread into the court, indicating that the material probably either hung from pegs or rested on shelves in this corner of the kitchen, the mudbrick wall of which had collapsed backwards out into the yard.

At the same time, primary *de facto* deposits may also be indicative of abandonment rather than strictly habitation scenarios. From the neighbouring House D a massive amount of artefactual material was found spread across Room 6–36 and the south-eastern half of Room 6–35 (Figure 4.2: Loci XIV and XVI). This included a minimum number of vessels (MNV) from among the *c.* 1,700 ceramic items recovered here of 276 (not including loomweights, lamps, miniature vessels,[17] and roof-tiles), nearly 46 per cent of all those from the entire house. Of the 276 vessels represented from these two rooms, some thirty-four were whole and another eight survived with full profiles intact. A tabular listing of the whole vessels, by ware, function and shape is shown in Table 4.2, and includes respective Halieis Pottery (HP) catalogue numbers.

Adding to these the several loomweights (six), lamps (seven MNV), miniature vessels (seven MNV), the base of a terracotta figurine, nine coins, and more than thirty other objects of bronze, iron and lead, there is the strong indication that some quite specific set of circumstances accompanied the abandonment of the house. What we are probably confronted with, in this instance, is a palimpsest of habitation, caching, dumping and clean-up or maintenance of debris associated with abandonment itself.

The second and third depositional processes we want briefly to discuss and illustrate in the context of the Greek household, already alluded to in the previous example from House D, specifically involve one category of material with which many archaeologists are obsessed, whether, particularly in the case of 'Classical' archaeologists, they want to admit it or not – namely refuse. Refuse may be classified according to whether it is primary or secondary. 'Artifacts

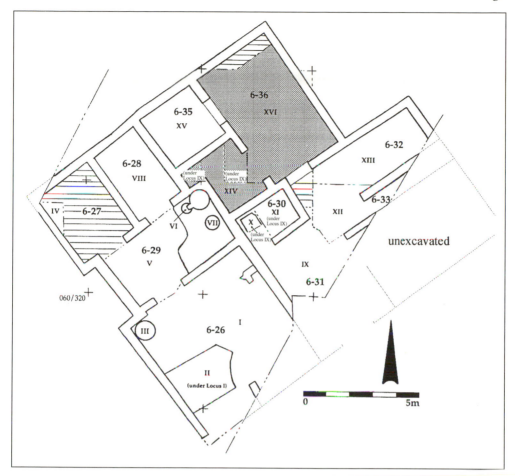

Figure 4.2 House D, Halieis: Rooms and loci. Loci XIV and XVI shaded.

discarded at their locations of use are termed primary refuse; those discarded elsewhere are known as secondary refuse' (Schiffer 1996: 58).[18]

A clear cut case of secondary refuse at Halieis is to be found in House C (Figure 4.3). Here, in a small room (Room 6–56) opening off a transverse corridor, another huge concentration of artefactual material was encountered. Out of 5,935 ceramic items recovered from the latest habitation levels of the house (not including lamps, miniatures, loomweights, and roof tiles), nearly 25 per cent came from this room. Moreover, from this deposit, which continued for a depth of over 0.40 m, only two whole vessels were recovered (in fine ware: a stemless cup [HP2190] and an askos [HP2186]). While the origin of all this material remains in question (does it represent debris from House C or was it contributed to by neighbouring houses?), as do its precise chronological implications (does it predate, is it contemporary with, or post-date abandonment?), its status as a dump is relatively unambiguous.

De facto deposits and secondary refuse represent two ends of the depositional spectrum. The third and in many ways, we would argue, the most informative depositional process which needs to be accounted for in the domestic context, is primary refuse. Nearly 4,200 ceramic objects were strewn across and embedded in the latest living surfaces of the twelve architecturally bounded spaces which comprise House 7 (Figure 4.4). Again, this figure does not include *c*. 1,800 roof tiles

Table 4.2 Halieis, House D, Loci XIV and XVI: whole vessels recovered

Fine ware

FOOD
Serving and consumption:
    7 bowls (HP2500, HP2502, HP2552, HP2553, HP2555, HP2556, HP2557)
    4 salt-cellars (HP2496, HP2548, HP2551, HP2566)

DRINK
Consumption:
    3 bolsals (HP2573, HP2583, HP2599)
    7 skyphoi (HP2554, HP2637, HP2638, HP2639, HP2640, HP2690, HP2886)
    2 stemless cups (HP2557, HP2558)
Serving and pouring:
    1 trefoil oinochoe (HP2481)

OTHER
    1 askos (HP2565)
    1 pyxis lid (HP2576)
    1 squat lekythos (HP2587)

Plain ware
FOOD
Preparation and serving:
    2 mortars (HP2560 [or shallow bowl], HP2561)

Coarse ware
FOOD
Cooking:
    1 lid (HP2522)
    3 lopades (HP2591, HP2647, HP2650)

FOOD AND DRINK
Containing and storage:
    1 askos (HP2666)
    1 pithos lid (HC[lay]827)

and the other less numerous categories of ceramic artefacts noted in the two previous examples. Among the pottery forms represented, only eight constituted complete vessels. This fact suggests that the artefacts peppering the house floors are residue from the breakage of vessels and the subsequent loss of certain fragments from collection during clean-up. With the additional proviso that breakage and loss occurred in proximity to areas of use, this material may be usefully classified as primary refuse.[19]

Using the measure of sherd counts noted above, the 4,200 ceramic objects from the latest use phase of House 7 can be taken to represent a minimum number of 497 vessels (Table 4.3). Coupled with architectural analysis, the spatial patterning represented by the find-spots for this material gives clear indications as to distinct areas for storage, food preparation, and consumption of food and drink within the house. In brief, the overwhelming evidence for storage vessels in the vicinity of the courtyard (Room 7–7) can be seen in Table 4.3: Locus IV, where there are thirty-two MNV in plain ware associated with the storage and containment of food and drink.[20] This

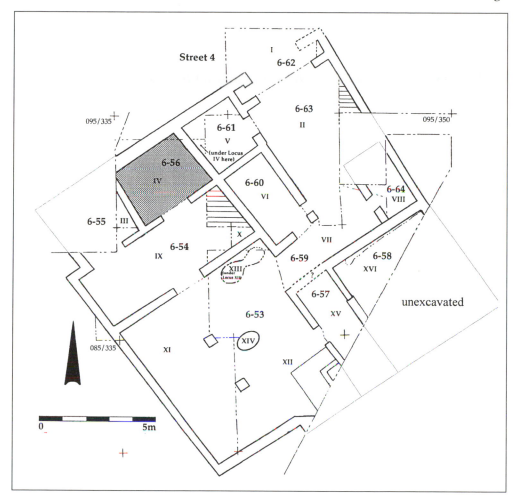

Figure 4.3 House C, Halieis: Rooms and loci. Locus IV shaded.

can be taken as evidence for the use of these vessels (mostly amphorae), if not their emplacement there. It actually seems that the interiors of Rooms 7–14 and 7–15 would have been best suited to the function of long-term storage. The identification of Rooms 7–16 and 7–17 as a site of kitchen activity is confirmed by the presence of a hearth at the end of the spur wall dividing the two, as well as the twenty-four MNV for coarse ware cooking vessels and nine MNV for plainware food preparation and serving vessels recovered from Loci V–VI and Loci XXIV–XXVIII. Finally, from Loci XVII–XIX, which correspond largely to Room 7–12, there is a concentration of fine ware material associated with the consumption of food and drink (primarily forms of drinking cups). Lying just off the open porch Room 7–13, Room 7–12 likely served as one of the primary living spaces of House 7 beyond the courtyard and kitchen already discussed.

Does the time and effort taken to recover, record and interpret such quantities of artefactual material make a difference in our appreciation or understanding of how household space was used? We believe it does, and have attempted to show as much with the examples drawn from Halieis. What this material does not do, nor should we expect it to, is provide us with some synchronic view of a household's inventory, consumption or discard patterns on anything

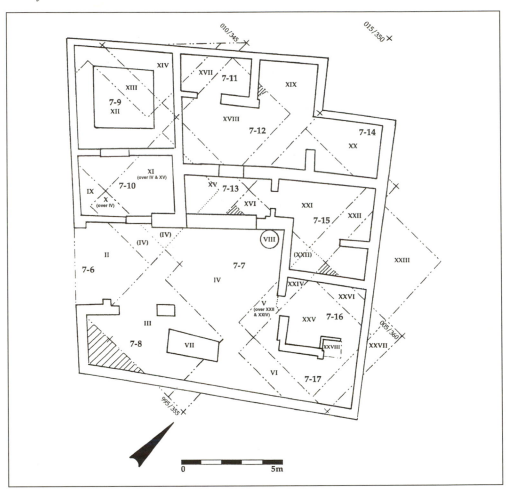

Figure 4.4 House 7, Halieis: Rooms and loci.

approximating an ethnographic 'moment in time'. Instead, we are confronted by a select and diachronic sample of debris reflecting patterns of use and behaviour over an extended period, perhaps a century of the household's (or households') operation in the case of Halieis. The household 'cycle' or 'series' represented by this material must be recognized as taking into account the wax and wane of families and their fortunes, and as such represents an absolutely necessary step in bridging what is sometimes seen as the impasse between artefacts and society, between archaeology and history. Finally, as a perceived impediment, it has ultimately been taken by many to justify the disregard for classes of artefacts all too often remembered only as 'small things forgotten'.[21]

Table 4.3 Halieis, House 7: minimum numbers of vessels represented from latest living surfaces

Locus	II	III	IV	V–VII XXIV–XXVIII	IX–XIV	XV–XVI	XVII–XIX	XX	XXI–XXIII	Total
Room(s)	6	7/8	7	16/17	9/10	13	11/12	14	15	7
Fine ware										
FOOD										
Serve/consume	1	7	15	7	1	4	5	—	7	47
DRINK										
Consume	1	30	20	20	4	15	22	3	16	131
Serve/pour	—	3	11	4	1	1	2	—	7	29
Serve/contain	—	4	7	2	—	—	2	—	4	19
OTHER	1	3	7	1	—	1	3	—	5	21
Plain ware										
FOOD										
Prepare/serve	—	10	14	9	2	—	4	—	4	43
DRINK										
Serve/pour	1	6	9	10	1	—	—	1	4	32
FOOD AND DRINK										
Store/contain	—	2	32	1	3	1	3	—	2	44
OTHER	—	2	8	—	—	—	—	—	—	10
Coarse ware										
FOOD										
Prepare/serve	—	3	4	—	—	1	—	1	—	9
Cook	—	15	34	24	—	4	7	2	11	97
DRINK										
Serve/pour	—	2	2	—	1	—	1	1	—	7
FOOD AND DRINK										
Contain/store	—	—	3	—	—	—	1	—	1	5
OTHER	1	—	—	—	—	—	—	—	—	1
Roman	—	—	—	1	—	—	—	—	—	1
Modern	—	—	—	—	1	—	—	—	—	1
MNV per locus	5	87	166	79	14	27	50	8	61	497

NOTES

1 The authors would like to thank Penelope Allison for her invitation to participate in the conference proceedings and series of papers which culminate in this volume. Bradley Ault acknowledges the support of the Arts and Letters Travel Fund administered by the Dean's Office at the University at Buffalo for helping to defray travel expenses for attending the conference itself. Lisa Nevett extends special thanks to the British Academy for its support while this paper was being written, and the Archaeological Institute of America and the Department of Archaeology, University of Durham, for helping make possible her presence at the conference.

2 It is this tendency towards compartmentalized scholarship which Morris (1994) has, most recently, traced the history of and railed against in Classical archaeology.

3 Exemplary exhortations to this end are those of Humphreys (1967) and Snodgrass (1985). The initial chapters of Snodgrass (1987) provide an extended treatment of the situation, while Spencer (1995) has recently offered a series of studies illustrating these theories put to practice.

4 While Kreeb (1988) is concerned solely with Delos, Harward (1982) considers finds of sculpture from houses at Olynthos, Priene, etc., in addition to Delos. More recently, Rauh (1993) incorporates a good deal of evidence from the Delian houses and households into his social history of the island.

5 For example, in the most recent survey of work conducted in the Athenian Agora, only two pages of text are devoted specifically to domestic architecture (Camp 1986: 148–50). A comprehensive bibliography (prior to 1970) of the remains of ancient houses in Athens can be found in Travlos (1971: 392–3). The thoroughgoing publication of the domestic architecture from the Agora and its environs which was to be undertaken by the late J. W. Graham, is now being overseen by B. Tsakirgis (Tsakirgis 1997).

6 Similarly, a great many wells have been excavated in the area of the Agora. As of the mid-1970s, sixty-eight wells of the Classical period were known, thirty-four of which had been dated to the fifth century, twenty-eight to the fourth century, and six indeterminate as to their date (Camp 1977: 142–3). Given the attention paid to their study and the fact that many of them were associated with domestic structures, it is surprising that we lack any published studies of well assemblages which could in turn shed light on domestic inventories.

7 To give a sense of the sheer quantity of material recovered from the Agora excavations, in Sparkes and Talcott's fundamental study of the black gloss, plain and coarse ware pottery (1970), some 2,040 pieces were published. They note that, as of 1963, there were three times as many inventoried pieces in the Agora storerooms and many thousands of uninventoried examples (ibid.: 2). Elsewhere, the figures for painted pottery from the Agora are put at over 1,500 examples of black- and red-figured wares (Hannestad 1988: 224).

8 Ducrey *et al.* (1993: 97). There it is stated that it remains the intent of the excavators to present the full complement of artefactual material in a separate volume which will also treat the entire Area E/5, where the House with the Mosaics is located. It should also be noted that, appearing concurrently with the final report on the House with the Mosaics, was a volume treating the red-figure and white-ground pottery from Eretria (Gex 1993). For a discussion of the domestic context of some of this material (ibid.: 41–2).

A number of other, similarly well-preserved fourth-century houses have also been excavated at Eretria since the House with the Mosaics, these having been treated in a series of preliminary reports. See, most recently, Reber (1993).

9 For the 'Master Concordance of Proveniences' at Olynthus, see Robinson *et al.* (1929–52 [1952]: 465–509).

10 For reference to the projected and abandoned fifteenth volume, see Robinson *et al.* (1929–52 [1952]: v). For recent efforts to reconstruct and study select domestic assemblages from Olynthus, see Cahill (1991), Nevett (1992: esp. 63–85; forthcoming).

11 See Jameson (1969), for an early overview of the site; Boyd and Rudolph (1978), for a general introduction to the lower town; McAllister (1973), for the fortifications; and Jameson (1974) for the sanctuary of Apollo. For a general survey of the history and remains of Halieis, see Ault (1994: 23–59).

12 See Ault (1994: esp. 60–78) for discussions of excavation strategy at the site and the methodology employed in the analysis of artefactual materials.

13 Cf. the discussions of methods for quantifying sherd material in Orton (1989: 94–5) and Rice (1987: 290–3).

14 It is Schiffer's work with archaeological formation processes that has provided the discipline with a common vocabulary for identifying and discussing these events. See, most recently, Schiffer (1996).

15 This paired arrangement of kitchen and bath was first identified as a standard one in the houses at Olynthus; cf. Robinson and Graham (Robinson *et al.* 1929–52 [1938]: 185–204), Mylonas (Robinson

et al. 1929–52 [1946]: 369–97), and Graham (1954). While bathrooms at Olynthus occasionally contained the *in situ* remains of a tub, this example at Halieis yielded a cylindrical terracotta stand which once supported a basin (*loutarion*) for washing.

16 Discussions of the shapes and names of Greek household pottery from this period may be found in Sparkes and Talcott (1970).

17 Miniatures had a wide variety of functions, probably ranging from toys to votives in cult practice (ibid: 185–6).

18 Due to limitations of study involving the Halieis material (discussed below in note 19), we are side-stepping here the issue of residuality which affects, in very different ways, both primary and secondary refuse. 'Small artifacts not removed by maintenance processes in activity areas are termed *residual* primary refuse' (Schiffer 1996: 62). Secondary residual refuse is that which is intrusive on a deposit from an earlier time period. Thus, secondary residuality is relative depending on how one wishes to chronologically bracket the material in question. Peña's article (forthcoming), in a set of conference papers devoted to the topic, provides a good discussion and recent case-study of the perimeters of residuality.

19 That is, it is not refuse which was brought in from outside the house. Nor is it assumed to have moved a great distance within the house from its last point of use, breakage, and loss. Finer distinction of the material as to its status as primary or secondary refuse is not possible since analysis has only been possible at second-hand through the medium of the excavation notebooks (which record, in addition to numbers of sherds present within given stratigraphic units, identifications by fabric, shape and anatomical variables represented). Subsequent to recovery and recording, much of the ceramic material (particularly in the case of body sherds which form both a numerical and volumetric majority) was discarded.

20 Table 4.3 purposely excludes material from Locus I, which lies outside the house, and Loci VII and VIII, which occupy negative features, the *kopron* (a refuse pit) and well respectively.

21 With apologies to Deetz (1977). An overview of positions regarding the household as representative of a 'series' is provided by Smith (1992). Using a variety of evidence, Gallant (1991: 11–33) has actually formulated hypothetical life cycles for Classical Greek households.

BIBLIOGRAPHY

Alcock, S. E., Cherry, J. F. and Davis, J. L. (1994) 'Intensive Survey, Agricultural Practice and the Classical Landscape of Greece', in I. Morris (ed.) *Classical Greece: Ancient Histories and Modern Archaeologies*, Cambridge: Cambridge University Press: 137–70.

Ault, B. A. (1994) 'Classical Houses and Households: An Architectural and Artifactual Case Study from Halieis, Greece', Ph.D. dissertation, Indiana University, Ann Arbor: University Microfilms no. AAI95-18532.

Boyd, T. D. and Rudolph, W. W. (1978) 'Excavations at Porto Cheli and Vicinity, Preliminary Report IV: the Lower Town of Halieis, 1970–1977', *Hesperia* 47: 333–55.

Bruneau, P. and Ducat, J. (1983) *Guide de Délos*, Paris: École française d'Athènes (*Sites et monuments – I*).

Bruneau, P., Vatin, C. *et al.* (1970) *Exploration Archéologique de Délos, XXVII: L'îlot de la Maison des comédiens*, Paris: École française d'Athènes.

Cahill, N. D. (1991) 'Olynthus: Social and Spatial Planning in a Greek City', Ph.D. dissertation, University of California, Berkeley, Ann Arbor: University Microfilms no. 9228589.

Camp, J. McK., II (1977) 'The Water Supply of Ancient Athens from 3000 to 86 BC', Ph.D. dissertation, Princeton University, Ann Arbor: University Microfilms no. 77–14,245.

—— (1986) *The Athenian Agora. Excavations in the Heart of Classical Athens*, London: Thames and Hudson.

Deetz, J. (1977) *In Small Things Forgotten. The Archaeology of Early American Life*, New York: Doubleday.

Drougou, S. and Vokotopoulou, I. (1989) 'Ολυνθος– η οικία BVII1', *Το Αρχαιολογικό Εργο στη Μακεδονία και Θράκη* 3: 339–50.

Ducrey, P., Metzger, I. R. and Reber, K. (1993) *Eretria – Fouilles et recherches, VIII: Le Quartier de la Maison aux mosaïques*, Lausanne: École suisse d'archéologie en Grèce.

Gallant, T. W. (1991) *Risk and Survival in Ancient Greece. Reconstructing the Rural Domestic Economy*, Stanford: Stanford University Press.

Gex, K. (1993) *Eretria – Ausgrabungen und Forschungen IX: Rotfigurige und weissgründige Keramik*, Lausanne: École suisse d'archéologie en Grèce.

Graham, J. W. (1954) 'Olynthiaka, 5–6', *Hesperia* 23: 320–46.

Grandjean, Y. (1988) *Études thasiennes, XII: Recherches sur l'habitat thasien à l'époque grecque*, Paris: École française d'Athènes.

Hally, D. J. (1983) 'The Interpretive Potential of Pottery from Domestic Contexts', *Midcontinental Journal of Archaeology* 8: 163–96.

Hannestad, L. (1988) 'The Athenian Potter and the Home Market', in J. Christiansen and T. Melander (eds) *Proceedings of the 3rd Symposium on Ancient Greek and Related Pottery, Copenhagen August 31–September 4, 1987*, Copenhagen: National Museum, Ny Carlsberg Glyptotek, Thorvaldsens Museum: 222–30.

Harward, V. J. (1982) 'Greek Domestic Sculpture and the Origins of Private Art Patronage', Ph.D. dissertation, Harvard University, Ann Arbor: University Microfilms no. 8222641.

Humphreys, S. C. (1967) 'Archaeology and the Social and Economic History of Classical Greece', *La parola del passato* 22: 374–400.

Jameson, M. H. (1969) 'Excavations at Porto Cheli and Vicinity, Preliminary Report, I: Halieis, 1962–1968', *Hesperia* 38: 311–42.

—— (1974) 'The Excavation of a Drowned Greek Temple', *Scientific American* 231: 111–19.

Jameson, M. H., Runnels, C. N., and Van Andel, Tj. H. (1994) *A Greek Countryside: The Southern Argolid from Prehistory to the Present Day*, Stanford: Stanford University Press.

Jones, J. E., Graham, A. J. and Sackett, L. H. (1973) 'An Attic Country House Below the Cave of Pan at Vari', *The Annual of the British School at Athens* 68: 355–452.

Jones, J. E., Sackett, L. H. and Graham, A. J. (1962) 'The Dema House in Attica', *The Annual of the British School at Athens* 57: 75–114.

Kreeb, M. (1988) *Untersuchungen zur figürlichen Ausstattung delischer Privathäuser*, Chicago: Ares Publishers.

McAllister, M. H. (1973) 'The Fortifications of Ancient Halieis', Ph.D. dissertation, Bryn Mawr College, Ann Arbor: University Microfilms no. 76–13,775.

Morris, I. (1994) 'Archaeologies of Greece', in I. Morris (ed.) *Classical Greece: Ancient Histories and Modern Archaeologies*, Cambridge: Cambridge University Press: 8–47.

Mussche, H. F. *et al.* (1990) *Thorikos, IX: 1977/1982. Rapport préliminaire sur les 13ᵉ, 14ᵉ, 15ᵉ, et 16ᵉ campagnes de fouilles*, Gent: Comité des Fouilles belges en Grèce.

Nevett, L. C. (1992) 'Variation in the Form and Use of Domestic Space in the Greek World in the Classical and Hellenistic Periods', Unpublished D.Phil. thesis, University of Cambridge.

—— (forthcoming) *House and Society in the Ancient Greek World. An Archaeological Study*, Cambridge: Cambridge University Press.

Orton, C. (1989) 'An Introduction to the Quantification of Assemblages of Pottery', *Journal of Roman Pottery Studies* 2: 94–7.

Peña, J. T. (forthcoming) 'Aspects of Residuality in the Palatine East Pottery Assemblage', in *I residui nello scavo archeologico*, Rome: École française de Rome.

Rauh, N. (1993) *The Sacred Bonds of Commerce: Religion, Economy and Trade Society at Hellenistic and Roman Delos*. Amsterdam: Gieben.

Reber, K. (1993) 'Die Grabungen in Haus IV von Eretria', *Antike Kunst* 36: 126–31.

Reinders, H. R. (1988) *New Halos. A Hellenistic Town in Thessalia, Greece*, Utrecht: Hes.

Rice, P. M. (1987) *Pottery Analysis. A Sourcebook*, Chicago: University of Chicago Press.

Robinson, D. M. *et al.* (1929–52) *Excavations at Olynthus, Parts I–XIV*, Baltimore: The Johns Hopkins Press.

Schiffer, M. B. (1996) *Formation Processes of the Archaeological Record*, Salt Lake City: University of Utah Press (originally published in 1987 by University of New Mexico Press, Albuquerque).

Smith, M. E. (1992) 'Braudel's Temporal Rhythms and Chronology Theory in Archaeology', in A. B. Knapp (ed.) *Archaeology, Annales, and Ethnohistory*, Cambridge: Cambridge University Press: 23–34.

Snodgrass, A. M. (1985) 'The New Archaeology and the Classical Archaeologist', *American Journal of Archaeology* 89: 31–7.

—— (1987) *An Archaeology of Greece. The Present State and Future Scope of a Discipline*, Berkeley: University of California Press.

Sparkes, B. A. and Talcott, L. (1970) *Black and Plain Pottery of the Sixth, Fifth, and Fourth Centuries B.C.: The Athenian Agora XII*, Princeton: American School of Classical Studies at Athens.

Spencer, N. (ed.) (1995) *Time, Tradition and Society in Greek Archaeology: Bridging the 'Great Divide'*, London: Routledge.

Travlos, J. (1971) *Pictorial Dictionary of Ancient Athens*, New York and Washington: Praeger Publishers.

Tsakirgis, B. (1997) 'Houses and Housing Districts Shed New Light on Life in Ancient Athens', *Newsletter. American School of Classical Studies at Athens* 39: 1, 13.

Chapter Five

Labels for ladles: Interpreting the material culture of Roman households

Penelope M. Allison

INTRODUCTION

On a general level, Roman domestic behaviour is perceived to be a relatively well understood phenomenon. It is widely believed that problems which face investigations of household behaviour in other archaeologies are easily solved for the Roman world (e.g. Ascher 1961: 324 n.21; McKay 1977: 6; Schiffer 1987: 237). To some extent this is true. Textual references abound and the extraordinary site formation processes at Pompeii and Herculaneum provide an archaeological record of domestic material which inspired generations of scholars to concern themselves with Roman social life. In fact, in times when other branches of archaeology had been restricted – by the nature of their data, the state of their methodology and the impetus of their theories – from concerning themselves with such mundane and specific levels of inquiry as household behaviour, the nature and extent of the material remains of the Roman world were leading scholars to confront questions concerning the domestic lives of individuals in the past.

However, I would like to demonstrate that this wealth of data and this long history of research has resulted in current perspectives of Roman domestic life which are still entrenched in antiquarian approaches to material culture, and which, to a large extent, have tended to ignore changing approaches to the archaeological record (see Hijmans 1996). While other disciplines (e.g. social history and anthropology) and other branches of archaeology have been re-evaluating the principles behind their own perceptions on past domestic life, these antiquarian approaches to Roman domestic life have continued to be embellished unquestioningly.

I would also like to demonstrate that such traditional perspectives of Roman domestic life do not fully exploit the available archaeological data, but that they are based on levels of analogy-based inference which, in branches of archaeology which are less well-endowed with data, would have been the subject of much critical soul-searching (e.g. Wylie 1985; Davidson 1988). At the same time, I would like to emphasize that these perspectives continue to present a static view of domestic life in the Roman world – a view based on nineteenth- and early twentieth-century perspectives that a named and identified culture, i.e. a Roman culture, is a unified phenomenon with a specific historical relevance, which can even be used to set up parameters for the investigation of domestic behaviours of other cultures (e.g. the foundation of anthropological kinship studies in Roman law: see Saller 1997). On the contrary, the term 'Roman culture' must surely stand for what was a very multicultural society spanning many continents and many centuries.

In this chapter, I want to discuss the roles of nineteenth-century scholarship, textual analogy and contemporary analogy in current identifications of Roman household objects, and the importance of such identifications in interpretations of Roman household space and Roman household activity. I want to show, particularly, that the material culture of South Italian towns of the first century AD, like Pompeii, has been taken to represent a concept of Roman domestic life which displays little sensivity to regional, social or chronological differentiation. I would also like to demonstrate that little consideration has been given to the role of the archaeological context of this material culture in providing a fuller picture of household behaviour in this specific region, before these archaeological remains can be employed for any credible presentations of more generalized perspectives of Roman domestic life.

POMPEIAN HOUSEHOLD ASSEMBLAGES

I am specifically concerned with the investigation of household assemblages in Pompeian houses towards a better understanding of Pompeian domestic life. I have carried out a study of the artefact assemblages in a sample of thirty Pompeian houses (Allison 1992b),[1] and, more recently, I have been carrying out a detailed study of the artefacts in the assemblages from one urban block in Pompeii, the *Insula del Menandro*. This block of residential and, possibly, non-residential units was excavated in the 1930s (Maiuri 1933; Elia 1934) and is now being reinvestigated by the British Pompeii Research Committe (Ling 1997). The purpose of my study of these finds is to produce a detailed catalogue and an analysis of the room and house assemblages from the units in this *insula*, towards a better comprehension of the use of space and of the state of occupancy in these buildings at the time of the eruption of Mt Vesuvius in AD 79.

The presentation of material culture from excavations of Roman settlement sites usually consists of the allocation of the loose finds to specialists to write typological catalogues of each artefact category, with the objective of facilitating studies concerned with the production and trade patterns of each category (e.g. Stead and Rigby 1986; Sackett *et al.* 1992; Harris 1993). The aim of my current project is to present the finds as they were excavated, in the location of their end-use. Rather than a typological catalogue, it will include a provenance-oriented catalogue which is concerned with the specific context and with the consumption of each artefact. Thus, the objective of employing this format is to systematize these artefacts according to house floor assemblages and to use these for investigations of the spatial distribution of activities around the houses.

To date, studies concerned with spatial function in Roman houses have been dominated by investigations which concentrate on the relationship of architectural remains and their decoration to textual references to Roman houses (e.g. Thébert 1987; Clarke 1991: 1–30; Wallace-Hadrill 1994: 3–41). The actual house contents, which constituted the house floor assemblages, have long been removed for typological catalogues. At the same time, at sites like Pompeii and Herculaneum, it has been assumed by non-Romanists (e.g. Schiffer 1985: 18) that these house floor assemblages constitute 'artefacts of a systemic inventory' which give valuable insights into human activity (cf. Allison 1992a). However, these artefacts have actually received little attention in studies of Roman household activity. As Dunbabin has noted (1995) in her review of Wallace-Hadrill (1994) 'a history of Pompeii and Herculaneum which makes full use of the archaeological material' has yet to be written.

In order to employ artefacts and artefact assemblages in an assessment of the spatial distribution of household activities, a reliable system for ascertaining the functions of the artefacts in these assemblages is required. Through my assessment of prior research into Roman artefacts and their functions, for such usable resources, I have become sceptical of the process by which Roman, and

Classical, artefacts have been 'labelled' and thereby given a function. In addition, I have also been frustrated by the attitudes of more recent scholars who, in their studies of Roman artefacts, may justifiably claim to have abandoned such labelling, but who have chosen to limit their investigations on questions concerning artefact production and have not considered artefact consumption as an important part of their inquiry (Allison 1997b).

APPROACHES TO ROMAN MATERIAL CULTURE

The concentration on the use of Roman artefacts for production-oriented studies was part of a mid-twentieth-century shift in Roman archaeological research from antiquarianism towards an increased concern for the impact of presumed Roman technological achievements and innovations on the Roman political and economic world. However, as seems to be the main problem for Roman archaeology and its wealth of data, while archaeologists in other branches of the discipline have since moved on to concern themselves more with social contexts, the Romanists seem to feel too weighed down with these quantities of data to absorb and apply fully and successfully new lines of inquiry to it.

On the other hand, Roman archaeologists have always been concerned with social history. Since the first excavations in the Campanian region revealed objects of daily life, scholars have been isolating individual artefacts, usually of intrinsic or aesthetic value, for antiquarian study. However, during this 'ransacking' of the ancient remains of Pompeii and Herculaneum in particular, the excavators could not help but be aware that these sites were not merely repositories of ancient works but that they represented the materialization of ancient daily life (e.g. Marquardt 1886). A relationship between Roman material culture and the contribution it can make to understanding social systems of the past has long been part of Roman archaeology. It is just that much past scholarship and many of its methodologies are still being used to investigate this relationship, without critical reappraisal.

The following discussion has arisen from problems and frustrations which I, personally, am facing in trying to use the Pompeian catalogues, and the mountains of past scholarship in Roman archaeology, to produce a meaningful study of the distribution of Pompeian household material culture. If I appear to be criticizing terms and scholarship, considered outmoded by some Romanists, it is because more recent scholarship hasn't dealt more usefully with this material and these questions. If the last twenty years of research of Roman material culture has not produced more meaningful ways of viewing domestic life in the Roman world, then it is time to reassess the purpose and objectives of much of this research in the light of such extensive remains for social life from this period.

NINETEENTH-CENTURY PERSPECTIVES AND TEXTUAL ANALOGY

In 1875 Messieurs Charles V. Daremburg and Edmond Saglio published the first of six large volumes of *Dictionnaire des Antiquités grecques et romaines*.[2] In the introduction Saglio observed that the state of the 'lettres grecques et latines' was such that no one had any clear and exact notion of ancient society. Daremburg and Saglio's aim, in compiling this dictionary, was to try to rectify this situation. Their method was: (1) to search the written texts for references to the specific objects of the Greek and Roman material world; (2) to cite these references; (3) to interpret the function of these objects on the basis of this textual information; and finally, (4) to illustrate their dictionary with extant material remains which had been discovered in archaeological contexts.

Thus, their objective was to give Latin names to found objects and thereby provide relevant illustrations to ancient literary texts. However, at the same time they were providing found objects with an identity which determined their function or functions. The following are some examples of such labelled objects and the effect which unsubstantiated labels are having on our interpretation of the archaeological record.

Arca or armaria

Daremburg and Saglio (1881: 362–4) quoted the ancient authors Varro and Servius to describe an *arca* as a chest, of indeterminate form and size, for storing clothes, silver and the necessities of life. They illustrated their dictionary entry with two iron and bronze chests which had been found during the excavations of the forecourts of Pompeian houses (ibid.: figs 459–60) and other depictions of similar containers on Greek vases. While they warned that there is no direct proof of a relationship between the textual term and the Pompeian finds, subsequent scholars (e.g. Dwyer 1982: 114; Armitt 1993: 240) have used this dictionary entry to conclude that the standard furnishings of these so-called *atria* in Pompeian houses consisted of such a strong box which held the household treasure.[3] In turn, this association of text and material culture has supported such scholars' perceptions of these forecourts as spacious and elegant display foyers befitting urban élites in Pompeii (e.g. McKay 1977: 35; Dwyer 1982: 115). In my particular sample of thirty Pompeian '*atrium*' houses, which include many of the largest and seemingly most élite houses, in the forecourt of only one house, the *Casa dei Vettii* (Figure 5.1), could such strong boxes be identified. One of the two strong boxes in this forecourt is in fact that which was used by Daremberg and Saglio to illustrate this entry.

Close investigation of the remains of furnishings in these forecourts in Pompeii actually indicates that more frequent forms of storage furniture were upright wooden cupboards (Allison 1992b: 44–6, 1993: 4–6), such as those found in the forecourt of the *Casa dei Quadretti teatrali* (Maiuri 1929: 404 fig. 29; Baldassarre 1990: 374 fig. 24) and that for which a plaster cast still stands in the forecourt of the *Casa dei Ceii* (Michel 1990: figs 92, 97, 98). The recorded discovery of a variety of domestic utensils, and particularly pottery, bronze vessels and glassware in such cupboards in the *Casa del Sacello Iliaco* (Della Corte 1913: 30–3), in the *Casa della Venere in Bikini* (Armitt 1993: 240) and in the *Casa del Fabbro* (Elia 1934: 292–7), indicates that these cupboards were often used for general domestic storage. They, therefore, present a picture of this forecourt as an area of more utilitarian domestic activity than is the traditional, rather bourgeois, perspective (Allison 1993: 4–7, 1992b: 44–6; Wallace-Hadrill 1994: 116–17). Such cupboards have been called *armaria* by Elia (1934: 292). This Latin label, which Daremburg and Saglio (1881: 432–3) described as a type

Figure 5.1 Chest in forecourt of the *Casa dei Vettii*, Pompeii. Photograph by Penelope M. Allison.

of *armoire*, used for storing clothes, vases, provisions, jewellery and numerous objects, would seem appropriate.

Despite this more usual form of storage containers in Pompeian forecourts, and this seemingly more acceptable label for them, the presence of such cupboards has received little attention in discussions of domestic activity in the forecourts of Pompeian houses, which have been considered as formal display areas that the excavators could equate with the entrance halls of the residences of nineteenth-century European élites (e.g. Ames 1982: 212–13). In fact, when such cupboards have been identified in this location in Pompeian houses they have often been considered 'dislocated', due to repair activity after earthquake damage (e.g. Spinazzola 1953: 283; Maiuri 1929: 405). Besides the fact that they do not equate with nineteenth-century analogies for the use of this area of the house, there are a number of further possible reasons for the assumption that they do not belong in this space. The first is that no ancient texts have located *armaria* in *atria*. The second, possibly as a consequence of the first, is that, unlike the circumstances for metal chests as in the *Casa dei Vettii*, any trace of them was often removed from its context at the time of excavation. Being largely of organic material, and usually in a very fragmentary state, they were not intrinsically valuable or aesthetic to early excavators (see Allison 1992b: 24) . Therefore, scholars who use extant *in situ* remains in Pompeii for their interpretations of Roman domestic life (e.g. Dwyer 1982: 114–15; Clarke 1991: 7–10), have not included these cupboards, or the significance of their presence, in their studies. But perhaps a third, more crucial, reason for such treatment of the archaeological record is that these cupboards might be associated with the activities of subordinate rather than dominant groups in the Pompeian household (see Beaudry *et al.* 1991: 155–6).

However, a consistent pattern for the location of such cupboards in Pompeian forecourts (Allison 1992b: 43, 1993: 6 table 2) warns of the need for more critical analyses of the relationships between textual references to household activities and the material culture remains at specific Roman period sites. In this case such an analysis could lead to a better understanding of the relationship between these excavated forecourts and their related activities; the activities which are described in texts for the '*atria*' in Roman houses; the activities in comparable spaces in houses in other parts of the Roman world; and the activities of household members not well represented in these written records.

Cartibulum

Varro (L.L. V, 125) described a *cartibulum* as an oblong stone table with a single support. He stated that, when he was a young boy, such tables had often stood in houses near the opening in the roof (the *compluvium*) with bronze vessels set on and around them. Daremburg and Saglio (1881: 929) paraphrased Varro's description in their dictionary entry to imply that the *cartibulum* stood near the pool in the *atrium*. Again, they used examples of tables found in this location in the forecourts of Pompeian houses to illustrate this entry. However, as they have noted, the tables found in Pompeii usually have two feet (e.g. in the *Casa del Principe di Napoli*: Strocka 1984: figs 61, 63; Wallace-Hadrill 1994: figs 3.15–3.16), sometimes even three, and they are often not oblong but circular (e.g. in the *Casa dei Ceii*: Michel 1990: figs 91–2).

Tables which more aptly fit Varro's description of a *cartibula* are more frequently found in the garden areas of Pompeian houses (e.g. in the *Casa del Principe di Napoli*;[4] *Casa del Sacerdos Amandus*: Wallace-Hadrill 1994: pl. 3a) than next to this pool or even in the so-called *atria* (Allison 1992b: 58). Nevertheless, the excavators of Pompeii have used such textual analogy to move excavated tables and thus adjust the archaeological evidence so that it will comply with this labelling of the domestic objects. For example, three marble table legs, in the form of feline legs, were found in the garden area of house I 6, 8–9 (Maiuri 1929: 394 fig. 22), a house which appears to have been used for more commercial, as opposed to residential, activities (Allison 1992b: 246–52). The exavators used their knowledge of Varro's description to reconstruct and to relocate these table legs so that they now stand at the head of the pool in the forecourt of the neighbouring, seemingly grander, house, the *Casa dei Quadretti teatrali* (Allison 1992a: fig. 1).

Such direct and overly simplistic treatment of a relationship between cultural history, archaeological remains, written documents and household behaviour is of the kind which has been justifiably criticized by Beaudry *et al.* (1991: 160) as being of 'limited utility'. In the first place Varro's childhood was probably a century before the eruption of Mt Vesuvius buried Pompeii and its domestic life in AD 79. An investigation of the function of household artefacts could more usefully concentrate on *assessing* the relationship between domestic behaviour in Varro's childhood and that unearthed at Pompeii for any concordance, not *constructing* a concordance. The presence of marble tables in Pompeian forecourts might draw our attention to differences between the Roman centre and its provincial towns, even in Italy (see Mau 1899: 248). Whether or not the tables in Pompeian forecourts can be labelled *cartibula*, could their presence in this location conceivably indicate a Pompeian élite who were preserving, or mimicking, behaviours of the Roman élite from a bygone republican era to establish their credentials as Roman élites? Can such an interpretation be validated through critical appraisal of textual information or is it largely an analogy with British colonial behaviour? This example demonstrates that the methodologies used by Daremburg and Saglio, and accepted by subsequent scholars, assume that the texts offer a pattern of normative behaviour, rather than observations drawn from diversity, which present static and generalized perspectives of Roman life and culture.

Daremberg and Saglio also provided 'labels' for pottery, glass and metal vessels from the Classical world. These labels often continue to be used by investigators of Roman material culture today, in a belief, seemingly, that an ancient label will better explain the specific, unique function of an excavated vessel than will its context or any possible remains of contents.

Fritillus

The word '*fritillus*' was used by Roman authors such as Juvenal, Martial and Seneca (Daremburg and Saglio 1892: 1341 n.1). On the basis of these references, Daremburg and Saglio explained that this term is generally applied to a dice thrower. Since the late nineteenth century, Roman scholars, and particularly the cataloguers of Pompeian material, have used the label '*fritillus*' for two similar types of small pottery vessels, thereby designating them as gaming instruments (Annecchino 1977a: 198–9). One of these vessel types is approximately 7–15 cm high with an oval body, wide flaring mouth and small flattened knob base such that it stands more securely on its mouth than on the base (ibid.: figs 1, 3). The other vessel is similar in size and shape, but with a more cylindrical body, smaller mouth and low foot on which it stands securely (ibid.: figs 2, 4; here Figure 5.2). Annecchino argued that only the first type was a *fritillus* and that the second was a drinking vessel. Her argument is based largely on the discovery of die and *astragali* in two Pompeian houses, in which examples of the first type of vessel were also found although not in direct association, and on the depiction of similar vessels in painting and relief sculpture, sometimes in gaming scenes. However, even if such evidence could be used to argue that this vessel type could have been used in gaming activities, it is of a very simple form and not very different from the second type which Annecchino dismisses from having such a function because they are less well designed for dice-throwing.

Annecchino seems to have argued from the premise that each Pompeian artefact type had its own, very individual, function. This assumption must stem from a perspective that this past society could be considered analogous to our own which has a plethora of mass-produced goods, many of which are assigned precise individual tasks. However, we have no specific reason to assume that many of the objects in a Pompeian household repertoire, where each artefact is individually made, might not each have had a variety of functions. It is therefore not valid to use the presence of a so-called *fritillus* as evidence of gaming activities. In fact, to my knowledge, no such vessels have been found in *direct* association with artefacts which can be identified definitively as gaming objects, such as gaming boards and die. Daremberg and Saglio illustrated a very different object as a '*fritillus*'. A more rigorous assessment for any repeated associations of these vessel types might assist in ascertaining whether in fact they were habitually associated with other identifiably gaming implements or whether each vessel type occurs in a variety of assemblages. The presence alone of such a vessel cannot be indicative of any specific activity. In fact, the discovery of so-called *fritilli* containing traces of paint, in the forecourt of the *Casa del Quadretti teatrali*, suggests

Figure 5.2 So-called *fritillus* from house VI 6,22 (Pompeii inv. no. 409).
Photograph by Joyce Agee.

that these vessels, at least, had not been used as dice-throwers immediately prior to the demise of Pompeii. We should work from the premise of diversity of use rather than expecting to find a clear pattern for many such artefacts.

Lagoena

Daremburg and Saglio (1904: 907) suggested that the term '*lagoena*' was applied to a pottery vessel used in Greece and Italy which contained wine for filling drinking vessels. They argued that this vessel was analogous to our carafe or bottle. They illustrated their dictionary entry (ibid.: 904 figs 4326, 4327) with two vessels, each of which has an inscription identifying it as a *lagoena*. However, each vessel which they illustrated is notably of quite a different form.

An inscribed wall-painting from so-called *caupona* VI 14, 36 (i.e. shop or tavern) in Pompeii shows a woman pouring wine from a small jug into a drinking vessel (Fiorelli 1876–7: 108; for inscription, see Sogliano 1879: no. 657). Annecchino has, therefore, cited this painting as evidence that a jug found in Pompeii was called a *lagoena* and therefore proved to be a wine jug (Annecchino 1977b: 112, 119 no. 41, fig. 5). The jug illustrated by Annecchino is of a type which is frequently found in Pompeian houses. This type is made of a coarse yellowish clay; it has a ring base, spheroid body, short conical neck, and strap handle, and varies in height from approximately 7–33 cm. Two such jugs, one 29.6 cm high and the other 14 cm high (Figure 5.3), were found in court 41 in the *Casa del Menandro* (Allison 1997a: fig. 13.3).

In the excavation notebooks (the *Giornali degli Scavi*) and inventories, jugs of this type found in Pompeii have also been variously labelled '*urceus*', '*oleare*', '*olpe*' or '*oinochoe*'. To date, any

Figure 5.3 Jug from south-east corner of court 41, *Casa del Menandro* (Pompeii inv. no. 4981).
Photograph by Joyce Agee.

discussion on the functions of pottery and bronze jugs found in Pompeii, and elsewhere in the Roman world, has frequently centred around which Latin term to use for which particular known jug type (e.g. Annecchino 1977b: 111–13). Annecchino, Hilgers (1969: 61) and White (1967: 162–3) all suggested that the label '*lagoena*' should be applied to swollen-bellied, handled jugs with longer narrower necks than vessels which they labelled '*urcei*'. But the two inscribed vessels, as illustrated by Daremburg and Saglio (1904: 907 figs 4326–7), indicate that this label applied to at least two quite different jug types, suggesting that a direct relationship between Latin or Greek label and shape is particularly spurious.

A special need for Roman archaeologists to establish a relationship between textual nomenclature and excavated artefacts seems to have arisen because of the requirement for archaeologists to categorize many artefacts by shape, and hence the need to give names to these shape categories. For the same reason a need has also been seen to assume a correlation between ancient and modern categories, as discussed below. Such classification systems, which had preoccupied eighteenth- and nineteenth-century scientists (Knight 1981: esp. 16), have been of paramount importance in the establishment of artefact typologies in archaeology (Adams and Adams 1991; Trigger 1993: 156–8). The principle objectives of such typologies, and their resulting sequences, have involved investigations of the chronological and spatial distribution of the production of such artefacts (Allison 1997b). If a specific Latin term could be feasibly applied to a particular jug shape then it has been assumed that all concerned would be able to 'picture' the type of jug so labelled and locate it in its appropriate typology. This classification system and its related labelling may be very helpful to catalogue writers and to pottery specialists concerned with the manufacture and trade of such items, or to museum designers. These specialists are not really concerned with the consumption of these artefacts. However, this labelling can make assumptions about fixed and often specific functions for particular artefacts on the bases of textual analogy rather than any available archaeological information, such as residue analysis, the artefact's context, its associations or indeed inscriptional evidence. Such assumptions have led to discussions on archaeological evidence for wine-drinking, often based on the identification of particular vessels as wine jugs (e.g. Cunliffe 1988: 141).[5] The failure of this system to produce reliable and usable identifications for excavated pottery and the often misleading assumptions which it makes about specific functions of particular jug types is evident from the lack of agreement among Roman pottery cataloguers about how such jugs should be labelled (cf. Annecchino 1977b: 112–13 fig. 5 ['*urceus*' and '*lagoena*' and '*nasiterna*'] with Conticello *et al.* 1990: 212 figs 138–140 ['*olpe*' and '*fiasca*']).

The jugs from court 41 in the Casa del Menandro were found in the corner, together with a bronze cooking pot (with traces of ash and smoke-blackening), part of a stone handmill, some pottery and glass dishes (possibly tableware) and a few glass-paste beads. This assemblage is not particularly diagnostic but suggests that these jugs could as easily have held liquids related to food preparation (e.g. oil, vinegar, etc.) as those related to serving activities, such as pouring wine. The presence of other cooking implements (e.g. a tripod) in other parts of this court may sway the evidence towards these jugs having been used for food-preparation activities. The inscription on the small jug (Figure 5.3), 'LIQUAM' (Della Corte 1933: 302 no. 229), indicates that this vessel had been intended to be, and possibly was once, used to contain fish sauce. Literary references indicate that *Liquamen* was used for medical purpose and that it was similar to *garum* (Curtius 1991: 7–8 n.8). Roman recipes indicate that it was used in food-preparation (Salsa Prina Ricotti 1993: 14–15), while some references to *garum* indicate that this was also a drink (Pliny N.H. 31.95). The inscription on this jug suggests that the sauce was either purchased or stored in it. However, it does not give us any indication of whether or not this sauce was also served from this vessel. Nevertheless, it does warn us of the potential multifunctional aspects for this jug type, and indeed of its contents.

Comments

Daremberg and Saglio's dictionary exemplifies a late nineteenth-century formalization of practices which had dominated the investigation of the material remains of the ancient Greek and Roman world since the Renaissance. Classical literature was of paramount importance to Renaissance intellectuals for providing, in their quest for a highly ordered world, 'a glorious past for the emerging Italian city states' (Trigger 1993: 35). Thus, it was to Classical literature that Renaissance scholars turned to seek explanations for the material remains of the Roman past, and through which they interpreted these remains for their own glorification. Out of this grew the antiquarian practice of isolating individual monuments of the Classical past and providing them with a label from the textual remains, to facilitate concentrated and detailed study. Ancient texts were seen as the key to a comprehension of the social reality behind found artefacts. The formalization process witnessed in Daremburg and Saglio's dictionary epitomises a nineteenth-century view that collections of material culture provided the illustrations either to textual data of the past or to ethnographic data from non-European cultures of the present (see e.g. Laurencich-Minelli 1996).

The use of Latin terminology was the standard naming method employed in the eighteenth-, nineteenth- and early twentieth-century classification systems in the natural sciences (Knight 1981: 24–8). But in the study of Roman material culture this method is not purely a convention because it uses the language of those being classified as the classifier. It, therefore, purports to provide precise information on terms for material culture, and consequently on their functions, as used by these people in the past. For the studies of the Classical world, Daremberg and Saglio gave validity to this classification method, such that it became the prime method of archaeological investigation of Greek and Roman material culture. Their work continues to be a fundamental study employed by scholars who needed to catalogue, and therefore label, such artefacts. However, rather than being considered a foundation for continued investigation of the material culture of the Classical world, this dictionary should be critically appraised in the light of contemporary perspectives on the use of text-based analogy in archaeology (e.g. Beaudry *et al.* 1991: esp. 174).

CONTEMPORARY ANALOGY

Roman period sites like Pompeii also provide us with an immense volume of material culture, to which it has not been considered possible to apply such Latin labels. In such cases, contemporary analogy has frequently been used to give labels to found artefacts. It is a common and widely accepted practice, in the cataloguing of archaeological remains, to choose the names of contemporary objects for excavated artefacts when the basic shapes and general functions are apparently synonymous (e.g. the names 'jug' or 'table'). However, some of the labels which excavators and subsequent cataloguers have given to artefacts excavated in Pompeii do not give such generalized shape identifications. Rather they can be seen to provide these artefact types with very specific functions.

Forma di pasticceria

For example, the Pompeian cataloguers have applied the label '*forma di pasticceria*' (pastry or confectionery mould) to two different types of bronze vessels and have consequently intimated that such labelled vessels had a known culinary function. This label suggests analogies with moulds used by European pastry-makers in the recent past (e.g. Tannahill 1968: fig. 52), or the types of moulds used to mould delicacies to produce an attractive display at a Victorian dinner table (e.g. jelly: Brett 1968: 100). Its use, therefore, serves to link Pompeian eating habits with those of the modern European world.

Figure 5.4 Forma di pasticceria with basin (Pompeii inv. no. 4932), from room 38 in the *Casa del Menandro* (Pompeii inv. no. 4933). Photograph by Penelope M. Allison.

One of the so-labelled vessel forms is oval in shape, often *c.* 7 cm high and *c.* 20 cm in total length, with straight flaring sides and plain rim (Figure 5.4). Suzanne Tassinari (1993: I, 233) has recently suggested that this bronze vessel form was more probably used for toilet activities. However, as she warns, they might have had other uses. This particular form has been found on a number of occasions in Pompeian houses in assemblages which also include a large basin (e.g. in room 38 of the *Casa del Menandro*, Figure 5.4; in the forecourt of the *Casa della Venere in Bikini*; in the forecourt and in room 'k' in the *Casa di Principe di Napoli*; in room 'f' in the *Casa dei Ceii*; in room 'u' in the *Casa di Trebius Valens*; and in room 'o' in house VI 15, 5). The basins in the *Casa del Menandro*, the *Casa dei Ceii* and the *Casa di Trebius Valens* are of a particular large sub-hemispherical type with two small vertical handles attached to the body, the terminals of which are often the form of fish-tails. Tassinari has suggested, independently (1993: I, 231), that this type of basin was also used for ablutions.

The other vessel form, which has been labelled '*forma di pasticceria*' is in the form of a shell, often *c.* 5 cm high and *c.* 10–15 cm in diameter (Figure 5.5), sometimes with a low base and a suspension or loop handle (e.g. Borriello *et al.* 1986: 178 nos. 38–9; Conticello *et al.* 1990: 188 no. 86). In 1900, through a careful analysis of the forms of these so-called shell-shaped *forma di pasticceria*, Erich Pernice (1900: 185–7) demonstrated the inappropriateness of this label for this particular vessel type.[6] However, in spite of his exposure of the fallacy of using this label, publications as recent as 1990 continue to apply it to this bronze vessel type (e.g. Conticello *et al.* 1990: 188 no. 86; Borriello *et al.* 1986: 178 nos. 38–9). The shell shape of this vessel suggests that a function associated with water might be appropriate for this type as well. Its scoop-like form is suitable for pouring water over oneself, in a manner not dissimilar to that of bathing women in the wall-painting in the bath complex of the Casa del Menandro (Maiuri 1933: 154 fig. 73).[7] The small suspension handle on some of these vessels makes it portable when empty. This would seem an improbable attachment for a pastry mould, but more useful on a vessel used in ablutions.

Casseruola

Another bronze vessel which is frequently found in Pompeian houses has a deep bowl (often *c.* 15 cm in diameter) and a long handle (often *c.* 13 cm in length; Figure 5.6) and is labelled either a '*casseruola*', a casserole, or '*tegame*', a frying pan (e.g. Tassinari 1975: 25–36; Borriello *et al.* 1986: 176 nos. 22–5). Both terms imply that it served as a cooking vessel. Tassinari has noted (1993 I: 232) that, of the 190 such vessels now stored in the Pompeii Collection and the hundreds stored in the Naples Museum, none show any traces of blackening from smoke, which might verify such a function. White (1975: 192–3 fig. 53) believed that this vessel type was called a '*trulla*' and was a ladle or a dipper. One of the uses of a *trulla* was that it was employed at the table, particularly to take wine out of a larger recipient (see also den Boersterd 1956: xxi). That this vessel type also occurs in silver with gold inlay (e.g. de la Bédoyère 1989: 78 fig. 46), implies that it was designed for serving or table use rather than for a cooking function. Despite this, the form continues to bear the label '*casseruola*' in Italian, or 'casserole' or 'skillet' in English (e.g. Cameron 1986: 64, 69, 73).

Abbeveratoio

A small spouted pottery vessel, *c.* 5 cm in height, is frequently found in domestic contexts in Pompeii (Figure 5.7) and has been labelled an '*abbeveratoio*' or '*abbeveratoio d'uccello*' in the inventories and excavation notebooks. This suggests that this vessel has a specific known function, that of a birds' drinking vessel. At first, this seemed a totally fanciful term

Figure 5.5 Forma di pasticceria (Pompeii inv. no. 2375–5498). Photograph by Joyce Agee.

Figure 5.6 Casseruole from north-west corner of court 41, *Casa del Menandro* (Pompeii inv. nos 4947–49 with shells inv. nos 4951). Photograph by Penelope M. Allison.

Figure 5.7 *Abbeveratoio* from house VIII 2,5 (Pompeii inv. no. 6298B).
Photograph by Joyce Agee.

to me. However, the custodians of the Pompeian storerooms assure me that, when they were young, small pots of this type were tied to stakes in the garden and used to feed birds. So far my investigations in the local pet shop to find the modern counterpart have only produced small plastic vessels with no similarities to this type, but I am informed that there is a bird shop in Scafarti, the next village to modern Pompeii, which still stocks the kind in which I am interested. I have yet to explore there. However, even if these modern vessels prove to be analogous in form, if such vessels had been also used in this way in Roman times one might expect them to have been found in Pompeian gardens and open spaces. Vessels of this type, though, are frequently found in internal spaces, often in closed rooms (e.g. room 43 in the *Casa del Menandro*; room 14 in the *Casa della Caccia Antica* [Allison and Sear, n.d.]; room 2 in the *Casa del Fabbro*; room 12 in house I 10, 8) and in association with other domestic utensils. This suggests that any possible modern analogy might be misleading or that such vessels might have had a variety of functions in Roman times.

Comments

Thus, many labels for Roman household artefacts, whether derived from Roman textual analogy or modern analogy, provide such objects with an often very specific function. As a consequence this labelling suggests Pompeian household behaviour, and by extrapolation Roman household behaviour, with which we can feel a familiarity and a certain comfort. While it might be argued that this is a necessary approach for an archaeology, and especially a famous site, which has high public appeal, I find it an extremely dangerous attitude to public archaeology which purports to give contemporary domestic worlds historical precedent which has not, and probably cannot, be validated.

PRODUCTION-ORIENTED TYPOLOGIES

Current specialist cataloguers of Roman material remains might argue that many of the above labels are redundant. However, rather than explore other possible approaches to dealing with the functional and consumption aspects of these artefacts, the prevailing attitude (with a few recent and generalized exceptions – e.g. Evans 1993; Willis 1996; Hawthorne 1997), seems to be to ignore them.

Terra sigillata and red-ware

A case in point is the study of *terra sigillata* pottery, fine red-ware consisting principally of open dishes or bowls and generally considered to be tableware. There are numerous publications of this pottery type, the most recent being that of the *Conspectus Formarum Terrae Sigillatae Italico Modo*

Confectae published in 1990 (Ettlinger *et al.* 1990). These studies concentrate on appropriate typologies for the forms, and on the makers' stamps found at the base of these vessels of this widely distributed pottery. Analyses of the shapes has been dominated by redefinitions of those isolated by Dragendorf in 1895!

Because *terra sigillata* pottery is found at sites throughout the Roman world, it is of paramount importance, not only for dating contexts at Roman period sites but also for studies of the manufacturing and trading patterns of Roman fine-ware pottery (e.g. Willis 1997). However, vessels of this type also have the potential to provide interesting functional information. From sites like Pompeii, large quantities of complete vessels are available for study (e.g. Carandini 1977; Pucci 1977). Studies of use attrition on these vessels, the range of shapes and the potential reasons for this range could provide insights into Roman eating habits and their variability across the Empire.

A number of such vessels found in Pompeii, and now in the Pompeii storerooms, contained food such as olives, plums, cereals and figs (Conticello *et al.* 1990: 188 nos. 81–4). Unfortunately, for many of these, no precise provenance was recorded and therefore their associations are untraceable. If *terra sigillata* is indeed tableware, and not used in food preparation, then these finds could alert us to certain aspects of Pompeian eating habits. These vessels generally have a height between approximately 4.5–5 cm and a diameter between 11–18 cm. Each contains one type of food only. One might perhaps assume that such bowls were placed on a table for diners to sample, unless one Pompeian could eat a whole bowl of plums! However, Pompeian dining rooms had space for only a very small table (see Dunbabin 1996: esp. 68), not for such buffet-style eating. These vessels could easily be held in the hand. This might imply communal eating habits, where the bowl is passed around amongst the diners (see Petronius 66; Evans 1993: 104). Communal dishes appeared to have been the norm for modern European dining until the mid-eighteenth century (Deetz 1977: 51–2; Miller 1987: 141), and Hawthorne's assumption that it did not exist in a pre-Christian context (1997: 33–6) seems unfounded. An investigation of use attrition on these particular bowls might also confirm whether such dishes were ever used with utensils or, in fact, food was always removed from them with the fingers.

My artefact studies do not, as yet, have suitable assemblages and provenance information on *terra sigillata* pottery from Pompeii.[8] However, an assemblage of so-called Pompeian red-ware dishes was found in the *Casa del Menandro* – which seems useful for providing some insights into Pompeian eating behaviour and some reasons for the prevalence of open dishes in Roman ceramic assemblages. This pottery, like *terra sigillata* ware, consists mainly of platters, bowls and lids and is widely distributed throughout the Roman world (Peacock 1977: 147). Some sixteen vessels of this fabric (Pompeii inv. nos. 4268A–R, see Figure 5.8) were found in a recess under the stairway in room 2, a small service room off the forecourt of this house.[9] Two of these vessels (Pompeii inv. nos. 4268B and R) appear to be lids (Peacock 1977: 156–8 and fig. 3 nos. 2 and 11). The remaining plates or dishes fall into four main size categories:

- size I: one large dish (A) with a rim diameter of 39.8 cm;
- size II: two dishes (C and D) with rim diameters of 32.3–36 cm;
- size III: five dishes (M–Q) with rim diameters of 22.6–23.1 cm;
- size IV: six dishes of smallest size (E–L) with rim diameters *c.* 15.3–15.7 cm

Similar size divisions were noted by the excavator, Maiuri (1933: 454). Traces of use, in the form of soot on the outside base, are found on one of the size II dishes and three of size III. But no such traces are found on any of the six smallest dishes, size IV. It is tempting to suggest that the medium-sized dishes were used for heating food over a brazier or heating apparatus.[10] In a number

Figure 5.8 Pompeian red-ware dishes from room 2, *Casa del Menandro* (Pompeii inv. nos 4268A, C, E and O). Photograph by Penelope M. Allison.

of Pompeian houses (e.g. *Casa dell'Efebo, Casa del Menandro, Casa del Fabbro, Casa degli Amanti, Casa di Julius Polybius* and possibly house VIII 5,9) such braziers have been found in, or just outside, rooms which are thought to be dining-rooms and, thus, were likely to have been used for food-preparation (Salsa Prina Ricotti 1978: 240–1). Perhaps the smaller size IV dishes show no signs of soot because they would have been used at the table, possibly with food served into them from the larger dishes. These size IV dishes are similar in size to the *terra sigillata* dish which was discovered containing figs (Conticello *et al.* 1990: 188 no. 84).

ASSEMBLAGE STUDIES

Interpretations of Pompeian household activities have in the past made some use of evidence from artefact assemblages and their provenances. However, such interpretations have often been based on rather subjective and uncritical assessments of the archaeological remains and have led to unvalidated assumptions about spatial division of activities, specialization in Roman households and the nature of the urban landscape.

Loomweights

For example, fifty-seven loomweights found in the forecourt of house I 10,8 caused Elia, in the 1930s, to call this house a *textrinum*, a weaver's shop (Elia 1934: 317). Small quantities of loomweights are frequently included in the assemblages found in the forecourts of Pompeian houses (e.g. *Casa dei Quadretti teatrali, Casa del Sacerdos Amandus, Casa dei Ceii, Casa del Sacello Iliaco* and house VIII 2,29–30). Thus, it is highly probable that weaving was a standard activity in this well-lit part of the house. It was the large number of loomweights in this particular house which led to Elia's assumption that this was the house of a specialist tradesperson.

But Jongman has noted (1988: 163) the amount of loomweights found in house I 10,8 is equivalent to that which could have been required for one, or possibly two, warp-weighted looms (e.g. Wild 1970: table M and pl.10a–b). Comparable numbers of loomweights were also found in other houses in Pompeii – fifty-four under the stairs in the *Casa del Principe di Napoli* and sixty in a room off the forecourt of house VI 16,26. This quantity in the forecourt of house I 10,8 would, therefore, be commensurate with the existence of such looms in this area for domestic use. It does not necessitate the identification of this house as the establishment of a specialist tradesperson. One might, therefore, expect that the label 'house of the weaver' would be irrelevant in today's scholarship. However, in spite of Jongman's criticism of Moeller's more recent reiteration (1976: 93–4) of the identification of this house as an *officina textoriae* (a weaving workshop), La Torre (1988: 82 n.68) has included it as such in his study concerning the distribution of commercial and workshop sites in Pompeii. Like many recent studies of Roman society (see Foss 1996: 351 esp. n.1), La Torre's synthetic approach has based its identification of household activity on Eschebach's 1970s (1970: 120) reiteration of a 1930s interpretation, with little critical appraisal of the validity of such an interpretation. Rather than indicate a specialist function for this house, these loomweights point to the role of the forecourt of Pompeian houses as a centre for the domestic activities of a pre-industrial household which was both a producer and a consumer. As Wallace-Hadrill (1994: 117) has reminded us, literary references do, in fact, indicate that women carried out tasks like spinning and weaving in such central areas of the house. However, Asconius had considered the use of looms in the *atrium* as ceremonial by 52 BC (Clark 1907: 43).

UNLABELLABLE OBJECTS

There are large numbers of artefacts excavated from domestic contexts in Pompeii, with good provenance information and now held in the Pompeian storerooms, which do not have any such seemingly convenient labelling qualities as some of the examples given above. It is apparent that, because such artefacts cannot be labelled, they tend to be totally ignored both by cataloguers and investigators of Roman household activities.

Wooden *tondo*

A flat circular piece of wood was found in room B in the *Casa del Menandro* in the same underground storage area that the famous silver treasure was found (Maiuri 1933: esp. 245–53).

This piece of wood is now in fragments (Figure 5.9). It had an original diameter of *c.* 18 cm and is plastered on one side. On the same side as the plaster it also has a bronze boss and a small bronze handle. A number of curved fragments of wood, possibly related, were found in the same location. In the same room, in addition to the silver artefacts, were found other large quantities of wooden fragments and bronze fittings, indicating that at least one wooden chest, and possible several, had been stored in this room. The remains of numerous metal, glass and pottery vessels were also found here and may have been stored in the chests. Maiuri's publication of this house (ibid.) concentrated the best part of two volumes on the silver objects found here. This wooden disc did not warrant a mention, presumably because it could not be 'labelled'.

Thus, artefacts from Pompeii, for which no ancient textual or modern analogy can easily be drawn, but which perhaps characterize what was potentially uniquely Pompeian, or Roman, have been ignored in the interpretation of the site, seemingly because it is difficult to discuss them without 'labelling' them. The bronze boss and handle, with which this piece is furnished, are similar to those on a number of small chests and

Figure 5.9 Wooden disc from room B, *Casa del Menandro* (Pompeii inv. no. 4728).
Photograph by Penelope M. Allison.

caskets found in Pompeii. This artefact was found in a space which seems to have been used to store an array of domestic material. Could it have been one end of a small barrel-shaped container? If so, does its plastered surface indicate that it was a luxury object, possibly containing valuable contents, or is it an indication that it was roughly sealed, possibly for insulation. The decorative boss and fine handle would appear to point to it having been a luxury item. Only by publicizing such 'unlabellable' objects can we start to learn more about them, their role in the Pompeian household and the real differences between Pompeian household artefacts and activities, household activities in other parts of the Roman world, and our own conceptions of household material culture and household behaviours.

CONCLUSIONS

Functional terms are frequently given to artefacts purely because they provide convenient labels (Miller 1985: 51–5). Such labels, or categories, often assume a direct relationship between form and function. This chapter has presented examples of the processes by which artefacts from the Roman world have been 'labelled' through analogy, and thereby provided with a function. It has demonstrated that it is this, often unjustified, 'label' and not the artefact which has frequently been used to provide the basis for supposed material cultural approaches to Roman domestic life.

The material remains from Pompeii do provide extremely valuable data for the investigation of the nature of domestic activities at that site. This data can best be used for this purpose if these remains are studied within their precise contexts and artefact assemblages. However, this material has been vastly compromised by the decontextualization of individual artefacts either for inclusion in typological studies, which are usually concerned with questions external to these houses and even to Pompeii, or to illustrate textual analyses to provide a generalized picture of Roman domestic behaviour.

It is not the intention of this chapter to launch an attack on all past scholarship or to argue that the use of analogy-based inference is wrong. The work of Daremburg and Saglio is extremely important and should not be dismissed lightly. It should, however, be viewed for what it is – a careful and thorough turn-of-the-twentieth-century attitude to Roman material culture. As Wylie argued: 'There are criteria and associated methodologies for strengthening and evaluating analogical inferences, if not for "proving" them, that clearly provide a basis for weeding out and decisively rejecting those cases of false analogy' (Wylie 1985: 107). She proposed: 'exploring more fully the potential for raising the credibility of those necessarily ampliative and usually analogical inferences on which archaeology must rely if it is to bring *unfamiliar* and otherwise inaccessible aspects of the past into view' (ibid.).

There is a real need for a rigorous approach to Roman material culture remains so that analogy does not go full circle and this material culture, which has been 'labelled' through textual analogy, becomes the evidence which Roman historians then use to substantiate their interpretations of ancient written sources. An obvious case of this is when rooms in Pompeian houses are 'labelled' from textual analogy and then the so-labelled rooms are used to illustrate social and architectural history (e.g. McKay 1977: esp. 36–44; Clarke 1991: esp. 2–6; Shelton 1988: 59–62. Cf. Allison 1993, 1994, 1997a; Leach 1997; Nevett 1997). Likewise the labelling of Roman household artefacts from contemporary analogous material has the danger of justifying closer links between Roman domestic life and contemporary domestic life than can be validated by the state of our current knowledge.

This chapter aims to demonstrate that, as I investigate domestic artefacts for an assemblage study of household activity in a group of Pompeian houses, I am constantly frustrated by the inbuilt assumptions about an ordered world which pervade our perceptions of Roman household behaviour. Many of these give specificity of meaning to individual objects within the domestic realm which is unsubstantiated by the material and the textual evidence. I am likewise frustrated by the vast amount of Roman material culture which has been 'processed' in the last twenty years with little evident reflection on the limitations of this 'processing' for investigations of Roman social life. It is perhaps the very overburden of data which has caused many Roman material culture analysts to accept the methodologies and assumptions of past scholarship and process the new data accordingly.

I believe that my approach presents an attempt, at least, towards a disentanglement of some of these assumptions and a re-analysis of archaeological data for new interpretative procedures which account for ambiguity and fluidity of category and a Roman world which is likewise ambiguous and changing. This process is proving to be extremely slow, arduous and frequently negative but I hope it will produce new and more acceptable, if less specific, perspectives of Pompeian household activity which first take full account of the archaeological evidence at that site. Only when context is fully accounted for should archaeological evidence be assessed for its relationship to Roman textual information and for its potential to contribute to fresh and less subjective understandings of domestic life in the Roman world more generally.

ACKNOWLEDGEMENTS

I am very grateful to Professor B. Conticello and Professor P. G. Guzzo and the staff of the Soprintendenza archeologica di Pompei for the permission and facility to carry out this research in Pompeii. I am particularly indebted to Dr Antonio D'Ambrosio, Dott.ssa Greta Stephanie and the custodians of the *deposito* – Franco Striano, Luigi Matrone and Ciro Sicigniano – for their assistance and support. I would also like to thank Roger Ling and the British Pompeii Research Committee for the opportunity and access to funding to carry out research of the finds from the *Insula del Menandro* in Pompeii. This paper has had many 'airings': seminar for School of Archaeology, Classics and Ancient History, University of Sydney; colloquium at American Institute of Archaeology Annual Meeting, San Diego, December 1995; seminar for the Department of Archaeology and Prehistory, University of Sheffield; seminar for the Faculty of Classics, Cambridge University; seminar for Research Centre for Roman Provincial Archaeology, University of Durham; and postgraduate seminar for Department of Archaeology, University of Glasgow. I am grateful to those who listened to me and for their useful comments. I would also like to thank especially Estelle Lazer, Tom Hillard, Chris Cumberpatch, John Barrett and Eleanor Leach for reading drafts of the paper and for their suggestions. I am also indebted to Paul Rainbird for his assistance in labelling this chapter. Any errors remain my own.

NOTES

1 The information on artefacts and their locations and assemblages in Pompeian houses, discussed in this chapter, has resulted from this research.
2 The fifth and final volume of Daremburg and Saglio appeared in 1919, after Saglio's death.
3 For discussions on the labelling of domestic space in Roman houses see Allison (1993, 1994); Leach (1997).
4 It is perhaps noteworthy that Strocka did not actually illustrate this second, seemingly dislocated, table, in his publication of the *Casa del Principe di Napoli* (Strocka 1984). A table supporting bronze vessels and fitting Varro's description was found in subsidiary court 41 in the *Casa del Menandro* (Maiuri 1933: 432 fig.163), not in the main entrance court to this house.
5 Cunliffe has twice used the presence of a dish and jug as evidence for wine-drinking (1988: 141, 185). It is conceivable that these were the sets which have been identified by Nuber (1972) as those used for washing hands during the meal.

6 Pernice gives no reasons for his alternative suggestion that such vessels were used for holding fruit at the table.

7 In the *Casa del Menandro* painting the water is being poured from a jug by an assistant or companion.

8 A collection of ninety *terra sigillata* vessels, at least some of which were neatly stacked in a wooden chest, was found in room 'f', the so-called '*tablinum*', in house VIII 5,9 in Pompeii (see Morel 1979: 251).

9 The *Giornale degli Scavi* A,VI,6 566 records thirteen dishes found on 7 August 1928. Maiuri initially reports thirteen (1933: 55) and then sixteen (ibid.: 454) dishes, and provenances them to the wrong room (room 10). The quantity listed in the inventory was originally thirteen, but this numeral was subsequently crossed out and replaced with the numeral 16 with a different pen. This suggests that three of the vessels may have been discovered later, but it is also possible that they were found in another location. Maiuri seems of the opinion that they were all from the same location. Sixteen vessels are now stored in the Pompeii Collection at this inventory number. Either the extra three were found at a later date and not recorded in the *Giornale degli Scavi*, or these dishes were not in fact from this room. It is now impossible to ascertain which three of the stored and inventoried vessels these might have been.

10 Evans (1993: 105–7) observes soot on dishes from northern England in the third and fourth centuries AD. However, he attributes this to the continuation of local iron age cooking traditions. Unfortunately, he gives no indication of the possible sizes of these dishes.

BIBLIOGRAPHY

Adams, W. Y. and Adams, E. W. (1991) *Archaeological Typology and Practical Reality*, Cambridge: Cambridge University Press.

Allison, P. M. (1992a) 'Artefact Assemblages: not the Pompeii Premise', in E. Herring, R. Whitehouse and J. Wilkins (eds) *Papers of the Fourth Conference of Italian Archaeology, London 1990* 3, 1, London: Accordia Research Centre: 49–56.

—— (1992b) 'The Distribution of Pompeian House Contents and its Significance', Ph.D. thesis, University of Sydney, Ann Arbor: University Microfilms no. 9400463 (1994).

—— (1993) 'How Do We Identify the Use of Space in Roman Housing?', in E. M. Moormann (ed.) *Functional and Spatial Analysis of Wall Painting, Proceedings of the Fifth International Congress on Ancient Wall Painting*, BABESCH Suppl. 3, Leiden: 1–8.

—— (1994) 'Room Use in Pompeian houses', in J.-P. Descoeudres (ed.) *Pompeii Revisited: The Life and Death of a Roman Town*, Sydney: Meditarch: 82–9.

—— (1997a) 'Artefact Distribution and Spatial Function in Pompeian Houses', in B. Rawson and P. Weaver (eds) *The Roman Family in Italy: Status, Sentiment, Space*, Oxford: Clarendon Press: 321–54.

—— (1997b) 'Why Do Excavation Reports Have Finds Catalogues?', in C. Cumberpatch and P. Blinkhorn (eds) *Not So Much a Pot More a Way of Life: Recent Approaches to Artefact Studies*, Oxford: Oxbow Books.

Allison, P. M. and Sear, F. (n.d.) *The Casa della Caccia Antica*, Häuser in Pompeji Series, Munich: Hirmer.

Ames, K. L. (1982) 'Meaning in Artefacts: Hall Furnishings in Victorian America', in T. J. Schlereth (ed.) *Material Culture Studies in America*, Nashville, Tenn.: American Association for State and Local History: 206–21.

Annecchino, M. (1977a) 'Fritillus, un piccolo vaso di terracotta', *Cronache Pompeiane* 3: 198–213.

—— (1977b) 'Suppellettile fittile da cucina di Pompei', in A. Carandini *et al.*, *L'Instrumentum domesticum di Ercolano e Pompei*, Rome: L'Erma di Bretschneider: 105–20.

Armitt, M. (1993), 'La Casa della Venere in Bikini (I 11, 6–7)', in L. F. dell'Orto (ed.) *Ercolano 1738–1988: 250 anni di ricerca archeologica*, Soprintendenza archeologica di Pompei, monografie 6, Rome: L'Erma di Bretschneider: 235–41.

Ascher, R. (1961) 'Analogy in Archaeological Interpretation', *Southwestern Journal of Anthropology* 17: 317–25.

Baldassarre, I. (ed.) *Pompei: Pitture e Mosaici*, I (1990), II (1990), III (1991), IV (1993), Rome: Istituto della Enciclopedia Italiana.

Beaudry, M. *et al.* (1991) 'Artifacts and Active Voices: Material Culture as Social Discourse', in R. H. McGuire and R. Painter (eds) *The Archaeology of Inequality*, Oxford: Blackwell: 150–91.

Borriello, M. R. *et al.* (1986) *Le Collezioni del Museo Nazionale di Napoli: i mosaici, le pitture, gli oggetti di uso quotidiano ecc.*, Naples: De Luca.

Brett, G. (1968) *Dinner is Served: A History of Dining in England 1400–1900*, London: Rupert Hart-Davis.

Cameron, F. (1986) 'Dictionary of Roman Pottery Terms', *Journal of Roman Pottery Studies* 1: 58–78.

Carandini, A. (1977) 'La terra sigillata african', in A. Carandini *et al.*, *L'Instrumentum domesticum di Ercolano e Pompei*, Rome: L'Erma di Bretschneider: 23–4.

Clark, A. C. (1907) *Q. Asconii Pediani* (trans.), London: Clarendon Press.

Clarke, J. R. (1991) *The Houses of Roman Italy: 100 BC–AD 250*, Berkeley: University of California Press.

Conticello, B. *et al.* (1990) *Rediscovering Pompeii*, Rome: L'Erma di Bretschneider.

Cunliffe, B. (1988) *Greeks, Romans and Barbarians*, London: Batsford.

Curtius, R. L. (1991) *Garum and Salsamenta: Production and Commerce in Materia Medica*, Leiden: Brill.

Daremburg, C. V. and Saglio, E. *Dictionnaire des Antiquités grecques et romaines*, I (1881), II (1892), III (1904), Paris: Librairie Hachette (3rd edn).

Davidson, I. (1988) 'The Naming of Parts: Ethnography and the Interpretation of Prehistory', in B. Meehan and R. Jones (eds) *Archaeology with Ethnography: An Australian Perspective*, Canberra: Dept. of Prehistory, Research School of Pacific Studies, Australian National University: 17–32.

Deetz, J. (1977) *In Small Things Forgotten: The Archaeology of Early American Life*, New York: Doubleday.

De la Bédoyère, G. (1989) *The Finds of Roman Britain*, London: Batsford.

Della Corte, M. (1913) 'Pompei – continuazione dello scavo della via dell'Abbondanza', *Notizie degli Scavi di Antichità*: 28–35.

—— (1933) 'Pompei – iscrizioni dell'isola X della Regione I', *Notizie degli Scavi di Antichità*: 227–318.

Den Boersterd, M. H. P (1956) *The Bronze Vessels in the Rijksmuseum xxi* (Dep. van Onderwigs, Kunsten en Wetenschappen 31), Nijmegen.

Dragendorf, H. (1895) 'Terra sigillata. Ein Beitrag zur Geschichte der griechischen und römischen Keramik', *Bonner Jahrbuch* 96: 18–155.

Dunbabin, K. M. D. (1995) 'Houses and Households in Pompeii: Review of Wallace-Hadrill 1994', *Journal of Roman Archaeology* 8: 387–90.

—— (1996) 'Convivial Spaces: Dining and Entertainment in the Roman Villa', *Journal of Roman Archaeology* 9: 66–80.

Dwyer, E. J. (1982) *Pompeian Domestic Sculpture: A Study of Five Pompeian Houses and their Contents*, Rome: Georgio Bretschneider.

Dyson, S. L. (1989) 'The Role of Ideology and Institutions in Shaping Classical Archaeology in the Nineteenth and Twentieth Centuries', in A. L. Christensson (ed.) *Tracing Archaeology's Past: the Historiography of Archaeology*, Carbondale and Edwardsville: Southern Illinois University Press: 127–35.

—— (1993) 'From New to New Age Archaeology; Archaeological Theory and Classical Archaeology – a 1990s Perspective', *American Journal of Archaeology* 97, 2: 195–206.

Elia, O. (1934) 'Pompei – Relazione sullo scavo dell'Insula X della Regio I', *Notizie degli Scavi di Antichità*: 264–344.

Eschebach, H. (1970) *Die Städtebauliche Entwicklung des Antiken Pompeji*, Mitteilungen des Deutschen Archäologischen Instituts, Römisch Abteilung. Ergänzungsheft 17.

Ettlinger, E. *et al.* (1990) *Conspectus Formarum Terrae Sigillatae Italico Modo Confectae*, Bonn: Rudolf Habelt.

Evans, J. (1993) 'Pottery Function and Finewares in the Roman North', *Journal of Pottery Studies* 6: 95–118.

Fiorelli, G. (1876–7) 'Notizie degli Scavi di Antichità, novembre – decembre', *Atti della R. Accademia del Lincei* I: 87–123.

Foss, P. (1996) 'Pompeii: a social city – review of R. Laurence, Roman Pompeii', *Journal of Roman Archaeology* 9: 351–2.

Harris, W. V. (ed.) (1993) *The Inscribed Economy: Production and Distribution in the Roman Empire in the Light of Instrumentum Domesticum*, Ann Arbor: Journal of Roman Archaeology Supplement 6.

Hawthorne, J. W. J. (1997) 'The Role of African Red Slip Ware Vessel Volume in Mediterranean Demography', in K. Meadows, C. Lemke and J. Heron (eds) *TRAC 96. Proceedings of the Sixth Annual Theoretical Roman Archaeology Conference, Sheffield 1996*, Oxford: Oxbow Books: 29–37.

Hijmans, S. (1996) 'Contexualising Sol Invictus – An Essay on the Role of Post-processual Archaeology in the Study of the Roman Sun-God', in K. Gilliver, W. Ernst and F. Scriba (eds) *Archaeology, Ideology, Method: Inter-academy Seminar on Current Archaeological Research, 1993*, Rome: Canadian Academic Centre in Italy: 77–96.

Hilgers, W. (1969) *Lateinische Gefässnamen. Bezeichungen, Funktion und Form den römischer Gefässe nach den antiken Schriftquellen*, Beihefte der Bonner Jahrbücher 31, Düsseldorf.

Jongman, W. (1988) *The Economy and Society of Pompeii*, Amsterdam: Gieben.

Knight, D. (1981) *Ordering the World: A History of Classifying Man*, London: Burnett Books.

La Torre, G. F. (1988) 'Gli impianti commerciali ed artigianali nel tessuto urbano di Pompei', in *Pompei. L'informatica al servizio di una città antica*, Rome: L'Erma di Bretschneider: 73–102.

Laurencich-Minelli, L. (1996) 'Notes on the History of Americanistic Ethnoarchaeology', *Bollettino del XIII Congresso dell'Unione Internazionale delle Scienze Preistoriche e Protostoriche* 3, Italy: Forlì: 65–76.

Leach, E. (1997) 'Oecus on Ibycus: Investigating the Vocabulary of the Roman House', in R. Jones and S. E. Bon (eds) *Sequence and Space in Pompeii*, Oxford: Oxbow Monograph 77: 50–72.

Ling, R. (1997) *The Insula del Menandro in Pompeii I: The Structures*, Oxford: Clarendon Press.

McKay, A. G. (1977) *Houses, Villas and Palaces in the Roman World*, Southampton: Thames and Hudson.

Maiuri, A. (1929) 'Pompei – Relazione sui lavori di scavo dall'aprile 1926 al dicembre 1927', *Notizie degli Scavi di Antichità*: 354–438.

—— (1933) *La Casa del Menandro e il suo Tesoro di Argenteria*, Rome: La Libreria dello Stato.

Marquardt, J. (1886) *Das Privatleben der Römer*, Handbuch der römischen Altertümer, dritte Auflage, Bd 7 (A. Mau ed.), Leipzig.

Mau, A. (1899) *Pompeii: Its Life and Art*, trans. by F. W. Kelsey, London: Macmillan and Co.

Michel, D. (1990) *Casa dei Cei*, Häuser in Pompeji 3, Munich: Hirmer.

Miller, D. (1985) *Artefacts as Categories: A Study of Ceramic Variability in Central India*, Cambridge: Cambridge University Press.

—— (1987) *Material Culture and Mass Consumption*, Oxford: Blackwell.

Moeller, W. O. (1976) *The Wool Trade in Ancient Pompeii*, Leiden: Brill.

Morel, J.-P. (1979) 'La ceramica e il vetro', in F. Zevi (ed.) *Pompei 79*, Naples: Gaitano Macchiaroli: 241–64.

Nevett, L. (1997) 'Perceptions of Domestic Space in Roman Italy', in B. Rawson and P. Weaver (eds) *The Roman Family in Italy: Status, Sentiment, Space*, Oxford: Clarendon Press: 299–319.

Nuber, H. U. (1972) 'Kanne und Griffshale. Ihr Gebrauch in taglichen Leben und die Beigabe in Grabern der römischen Kaiserzeit', *Bericht der römisch-germanischen Kommission* 53, Frankfurt am Mainz: 1–232.

Peacock, D. P. S. (1977) 'Pompeian Red Ware', in D. P. S. Peacock (ed.) *Pottery and Early Commerce*, London: Academic Press: 147–62.

Pernice, E. (1900) 'Bronzen aus Boscoreale', *Archäologischer Anzeiger* 15: 177–98.

Petronius (1922 edn) *Satyricon*, trans. and notes by J. M. Mitchell, London: Routledge.

Pliny, *N.H. Naturalis historia*, trans. by D. E. Eichholz (1962), Cambridge, Mass.: Harvard University Press.

Pucci, G. (1977) 'Le terra sigillate italiche, galliche e orientali', in A. Carandini *et al.*, *L'Instrumentum domesticum di Ercolano e Pompei*, Rome: L'Erma di Bretschneider: 9–21.

Sackett, L. H. *et al.* (1992) *Knossos from Greek City to Roman Colony: Excavations at the Unexplored Mansion II*, London: Thames and Hudson.

Salsa Prina Ricotti, E. (1978) 'Cucine e quartieri servili in epoca Romana', *Rendiconti Atti della Pontificia accademia Romana di archeologia* 51–2: 237–94.

—— (1993) *Ricette della Cucina Romana a Pompei*, Rome: L'Erma di Bretschneider.

Saller, R. (1997) 'Roman Kinship: Structure and Sentiment', in B. Rawson and P. Weaver (eds) The *Roman Family in Italy: Status, Sentiment, Space*, Oxford: Clarendon Press: 7–34.

Schiffer, M. B. (1985) 'Is there a Pompeii Premise?', *Journal of Anthropological Research* 41: 18–41.

—— (1987) *Formation Processes in the Archaeological Record*, Alberquerque: University of New Mexico Press.

Shelton, J.- A. (1988) *As the Romans Did: A Sourcebook in Roman Social History*, Oxford: Oxford University Press.

Sogliano, A. (1879) 'Le pitture murali campane, scoperte negli anni 1867–79', in *Pompei e la regione sotterrata dal Vesuvio nell'anno 79*, Naples.

Spinazzola, V. (1953) *Pompei alle luce degli Scavi Nuovi di Via dell'Abbondanza (anni 1910–1923)* I–III, Rome: La Libreria dello Stato.

Stead, I. M. and Rigby, V. (1986) *Baldock, the Excavation of a Roman and pre-Roman Settlement, 1968–72*, Britannia monograph series 7, London: Society for the Promotion of Roman Studies.

Strocka, V. M. (1984) *La Casa del Principe di Napoli*, Häuser in Pompeji 1, Tübingen: Wasmuth.

Tannahill. R. (1968) *The Fine Art of Food*, London: Folio Society.

Tassinari, S. (1975) *La vaisselle de bronze romaine et provinciale au musée des antiquité nationales, 29th supplément à Gallia*, Paris: CNRS.

—— (1993) *Il vasellame bronzeo di Pompei*, Soprintendenza archeologica di Pompei cataloghi 5, Rome: L'Erma di Bretschneider.

Thébert, P. (1987) 'Private Life and Domestic Architecture in Roman Africa', in P. Veyne (ed.) *A History of Private Life I, from Pagan Rome to Byzantium*, trans. by A. Goldhammer, Cambridge, Mass.: Harvard University Press: 313–409.

Trigger, B. (1993) *A History of Archaeological Thought*, Cambridge: Cambridge University Press (reprint of 1989 edition).

Varro, *De Lingua Latina*, trans. by R. G. Kent (1958), Cambridge, Mass.: Harvard University Press/Loeb.

Wallace-Hadrill, A. (1994) *Houses and Society in Pompeii and Herculaneum*, Princeton: Princeton University Press.

White, K. D. (1967) *Agricultural Implements of the Roman World*, Cambridge: Cambridge University Press.

—— (1975) *Farm Equipment of the Roman World*, Cambridge: Cambridge University Press).

Wild, J. P. (1970) *Textile Manufacture in the Northern Roman Provinces*, Cambridge: Cambridge University Press.

Willis, S. (1996) 'The Romanization of Pottery Assemblages in the East and North-East of England during the First Century AD: A Comparative Study', *Britannia* 27: 179–221.

—— (1997) 'Samian: beyond dating', in K. Meadows, C. Lemke and J. Heron (eds) *TRAC 96. Proceedings of the Sixth Annual Theoretical Roman Archaeology Conference, Sheffield 1996*, Oxford: Oxbow Books: 38–54.

Wylie, A. (1985) 'The Reaction against Analogy', *Advances in Archaeological Method and Theory* 8, New York: Academic Press: 63–111.

Chapter Six

Mesoamerican house lots and archaeological site structure: Problems of inference in Yaxcaba, Yucatan, Mexico, 1750–1847

Rani T. Alexander

ABSTRACT

Ethnoarchaeological research in Mesoamerican households is crucial to linking material signatures in the house lot or *solar* to the activities and function of the household. This chapter first reviews ethnoarchaeological models of the spatial structure of house lots in Mesoamerica. A fundamental problem in household archaeology is that ethnographic and ethnoarchaeological models are relatively synchronic, whereas the archaeological record reflects diachronic processes and organization. Second, the house lot models are applied to an archaeological case study of settlements in the parroquia de Yaxcaba, Yucatan, Mexico, which were occupied from 1750–1847. The period spans a time of rapid political–economic change resulting from implementation of the Bourbon reforms and Mexican Independence from Spain. I evaluate the archaeological signatures of the specific components of the Mesoamerican house lot model through quantitative analysis of surface collection units. Site structural analysis of the survey data indicates significant differences in production strategies among agriculturalists living in *pueblos*, *ranchos*, and *haciendas* in the early nineteenth century. Comparison of the archaeological and historical records suggests that house lot size and the numbers of ancillary features are sensitive to variation in tax structure, population density, and land stress within the parish. In attempting to isolate the archaeological remains of dwellings, patios, and gardens in different communities, one can estimate the effects of the duration of occupation on house lot site structure. Neither households nor archaeological house lots are synchronic. Further advances in household archaeology depend on the implementation of appropriate diachronic units of analysis.

Over the last two decades, the household has become a favourite unit of analysis among Mesoamerican archaeologists. Household studies have demonstrated substantial advances in ethnography, ethnohistory, ethnoarchaeology, and archaeology. One reason for this resurgence is traceable to the ethnographic research conducted in the early 1980s which proposed a new definition for the household – the activity group (Netting *et al.* 1984; Wilk and Rathje 1982b). Households can be categorized on the basis of their function, including production, consumption, pooling of resources, co-residence, reproduction, transmission, and shared ownership (Ashmore and Wilk 1988; Hammel 1984; Wilk and Netting 1984). Examining activity sets and 'householding' shifts the unit of analysis toward a more dynamic behavioural perspective, capable of addressing culture change.

The concept of 'householding as a verb' (Netting 1993) accomplishes two things for archaeologists. First, it removes household morphology from the realm of kinship and residence and links it to ecology and political economy. Households are important because they represent the unit of production necessary to support greater levels of integration, the level at which social groups articulate directly with economic and ecological processes, and the level at which adaptation can be studied (Wilk 1991; Wilk and Rathje 1982b). Second, by providing a workable definition with material implications, it makes it possible for archaeologists to study households. Archaeological analyses of settlement, domestic midden contents, site structure, and activity areas can link material evidence of discrete behaviours to interpretations of household activities and their organization. Two customary approaches are employed for generating inferences in household archaeology. The first derives information from the analysis of domestic artefact assemblages, whereas the second acquires information from site structural analysis of dwellings, extramural areas, and their associated artefacts, middens, and features (Santley and Hirth 1993b: 5). In Mesoamerica, archaeological interest in households has culminated in several volumes that collectively indicate that household form and function are sensitive to variation in people's access to basic resources (Hayden and Cannon 1984; Manzanilla 1986; Santley and Hirth 1993a; Wilk and Ashmore 1988).

Nevertheless, a disjunction has emerged between actualistic investigations of household material systems, based in ethnoarchaeology and cross-cultural ethnography, and their application to the prehistoric archaeological record in Mesoamerica. Archaeologists who define the household as an activity group recognize the need for methods that link inferences of household behavioural organization to archaeological signatures. These methods must account for natural formation processes, post-depositional and reuse processes, processes of abandonment, patterns of refuse disposal, and residential maintenance as well as specific activities and production organization. Middle range ethnoarchaeological research in Mesoamerican households is consequently voluminous (Binford 1981: 21–30; e.g. Arnold 1991; Deal 1983, 1985; Dore 1996; Hayden and Cannon 1983, 1984; Killion 1990; Lee and Hayden 1988; Smyth 1990; Sutro and Downing 1988; Widmer and Sheehy 1990). Ethnoarchaeological studies are complemented by cross-cultural and ethnographic research which provides the fundamental link to general anthropological theory by examining variation of household form and dwelling form with reference to ecology and political economy (e.g. Blanton 1994; Cook 1982, 1984; Cook and Binford 1990; Netting 1993; Wilk 1991; Wilk and Netting 1984).

Applications of ethnoarchaeological and ethnographic models to purely archaeological situations in Mesoamerica, however, have been restricted for the most part to contexts where the relevance of ethnoarchaeological findings can be argued on the basis of the direct historical approach. For example, ethnoarchaeological research in the Tuxtlas mountains of Veracruz has been applied principally to Matacapan (Arnold and Santley 1993; Killion 1992a; Pool and Santley 1992; Santley 1992, 1994; Santley *et al.* 1989; Santley and Kneebone 1993). The Coxoh project in Chiapas implements ethnoarchaeological findings from Hayden and Cannon's and Deal's work in Chiapas and Highland Guatemala (e.g. Hayden 1988; Lee and Bryant 1988; Deal 1988). The Sayil project in Yucatan uses ethnoarchaeological research in households and communities in the Puuc region to interpret settlement and intracommunity patterning (Killion *et al.* 1989; Tourtellot *et al.* 1989; Smyth and Dore 1992). Ethnoarchaeological research in Mesoamerica that treats spatial relationships among dwellings, patios, gardens, and refuse areas is seldom applied to archaeological sites outside of the region in which the study was conducted.

Recently, the question was raised whether actualistic studies, especially ethnoarchaeology, could make significant contributions to general anthropological theory (O'Connell 1995). When ethnoarchaeological findings are applied to the archaeological record as conventional analogies, the results are of limited utility, because they are descriptive of past behaviour rather than explanatory of variation in behaviour (ibid.: 216–17). Models that treat the site structure of extramural space, in particular, are thought to be too specific to their given ethnographic situations, although they are sometimes useful when the archaeological record is sufficiently fine grained and representative of equivalent temporal and spatial scales. While actualistic studies of the household are not a panacea for archaeological inference, I submit, to the contrary, that they are a necessary first step for developing general theory. They indicate how the form and function of archaeological households are related to such fundamental issues as differential access to basic resources, craft specialization, and agricultural intensification (Arnold 1991; Hirth 1993; Stone 1996). Nevertheless, archaeologists have encountered difficulties in applying ethnoarchaeological findings to aid interpretation in purely archaeological situations. The problem of ethnoarchaeology's limited contributions to anthropological theory perhaps lies in the perceived breadth of its archaeological application. We have not developed the arguments of relevance to apply these findings as widely as they might be. Paradoxically, ethnoarchaeology is presently an underutilized resource in Mesoamerican household archaeology.

I would argue that the present disjunction between ethnoarchaeological research and Mesoamerican household archaeology is unnecessary, and household studies would benefit from a reconsideration of ethnoarchaeological models and their use. Below I will review the principal problems in using the household as a unit of analysis and in applying ethnoarchaeological models to the archaeological record. Second, I will consider the application of the house lot model to a case-study in historical archaeology from the parroquia de Yaxcaba, Yucatan, Mexico. Using data from the settlement survey and surface collections, I will demonstrate which aspects of the house lot model are recognizable in this archaeological situation. Third, with reference to documentary evidence, I will evaluate the sensitivity of house lot site structure to variation in access to basic resources, specifically access to land. Finally, I will examine the implications of the ethnoarchaeological house lot model for diachronic analysis of household series and its potential for developing anthropological theory.

HOUSEHOLDS AND HOUSEHOLD SERIES

Household archaeology has been criticized on two fronts, and the first critique concerns the difficulty of identifying archaeological households. Archaeologists have struggled with the age old problem of finding archaeological correlates for social units. In linking settlement patterns to social organization, units of social integration were equated with spatial clusters of dwellings and structures predicated on the principle of abundance and the nearest neighbour principle (e.g. Ashmore and Wilk 1988; Haviland 1966; Michels 1979; Tourtellot 1983). Settlement pattern studies often designated plaza groups, dwelling clusters, or basal platforms with multiple superstructures as spatial correlates of the household (e.g. Ashmore 1981; Haviland 1966, 1981, 1988; Tourtellot 1983, 1988; Willey and Leventhal 1979). The household was usually identified by isolating the smallest, redundantly occurring, modular unit of settlement (e.g. Clarke 1972). This approach continues to be refined in light of ethnographic and ethnoarchaeological studies. More recently for example, Santley and Hirth (1993b: 6–8) have proposed three spatial correlates of co-residential units in Mesoamerica: the house lot, the house compound, and the dwelling unit. The three forms illustrate how population density affects variability in the size and use of residential and extramural space.

The relationships between spatial units of settlement, social co-residential groups, and the composition of the household, however, are not self-evident, and attempts to understand these relationships constitute a focus of ethnographic and ethnoarchaeological research (Wilk and Rathje 1982a). Collectively, these works demonstrate that household archaeology is a misnomer. Archaeologists do not actually study households; they study spatial patterns of settlement that include dwellings, compounds, and house lots. Ethnographic research that shows the difficulty of comparing household form to function also indicates the complexity of equating dwelling form, a spatial unit, to household morphology, a social unit (Blanton 1994; Hammel 1984; Wilk and Rathje 1982b).

This criticism has been addressed largely by redefining the household as an activity group whose members share in production, consumption, transmission, distribution, reproduction, and co-residence (Wilk 1991; Wilk and Netting 1984). The concept of 'householding' bridges the theoretical impasse for archaeologists and provides a workable point of departure for site structural analysis. Site structure is the study of the spatial relationships and patterns among artefacts, ecofacts, features, and structures on archaeological sites with the aim of developing inferences about the behavioural processes responsible for those patterns (Binford 1987; Clarke 1977; O'Connell 1995). When the household or co-residential group can be securely linked to a specific place where co-residential activities are performed, such as a house lot or compound, archaeological patterns should faithfully reflect variation in household and community organization.

Household organization is the arrangement of different behaviours and economic tactics that comprise the overall adaptive strategy of the co-residential unit (Chayanov 1986; Sahlins 1972; Wilk 1991). As a household undergoes change, specific behaviours or activities may be dropped or added to the household repertoire, or the proportions of different activities may change relative to others. These changes affect the spatial configurations of artefacts, features, dwellings, and extramural areas. Ethnoarchaeological investigations of these processes among peasant agriculturalists indicate that production, access to land and labour, and strategies for overcoming subsistence shortfalls can be monitored through the site structure of residential units (Arnold 1990, 1991; Binford 1978; Deal 1985; Hayden and Cannon 1983, 1984; Killion 1987, 1990; Santley and Hirth 1993b; Smyth 1990).

The second criticism of household archaeology is more difficult to resolve than the first. The archaeological remains of households reflect diachronic processes and organization, not synchronic behaviour. Households have a patterned longevity recognized as the family or domestic cycle (Fortes 1958; Goody 1958). Households undergo a regular sequence of changes as members are added or lost, until the original household is dissolved and replaced by one or more similar units (Fortes 1958: 2–5). Ethnoarchaeological research demonstrates that the developmental cycle affects dwelling form and sequences of construction (see Oswald 1987; Stone 1996). Archaeological residential units, however, represent durational time that includes domestic cycles as well as periods of even longer temporal scales (Tourtellot 1983, 1988; Smith 1992a). We have not yet reconciled the temporal scales of residential units with variation in the domestic cycle. As a result, Smith (1992a) and Hirth (1993) have proposed that the appropriate archaeological unit of analysis is not the household but the household series. A household series is 'the sequence of households that successively inhabit a given structure or house over a span of more than one generation' (Smith 1992a: 30). In effect, most archaeological residential units represent household series, even within single component sites.

The concept of household series raises new questions. Can archaeologists distinguish different stages in the domestic cycle and partition the household series? Does variation among household series reflect different trajectories of change in household organization? The problems of working with household series have provoked renewed interest in archaeological chronology (Smith

1992b). Archaeological phases in Mesoamerica do not provide sufficient temporal resolution to address the aforementioned questions. Consequently, many investigations have attempted to refine existing chronologies through seriation aided by multivariate statistics combined with radiocarbon and obsidian hydration dating (e.g. Cowgill 1996; Evans and Freter 1996; Hare and Smith 1996; Nichols and Charlton 1996).

Hirth (1993) explores the implications of using households and household series as units of analysis in prehistoric situations. He suggests that archaeologists are unlikely to find abundant evidence of changes in household strategies in prehistoric Mesoamerica for several reasons. First, the infrastructure of production, transportation, and communication that impels rapid rates of change in the modern world did not characterize prehistoric societies. Because prehistoric households had a relatively narrow range of economic opportunities available to them, and because access to the means of production (technology, land, labour) was structured principally by social relations, prehistoric household series are likely to reflect stability. Prehistoric non-élite agrarian households will not demonstrate vast differences in their organization, as do modern agrarian households that must adjust to fluctuating conditions of political economic integration (ibid.: 23–8). Second, in prehistoric societies household variation increases appreciably only when households are able to diversify their activities beyond the traditional agrarian sector, typically through craft specialization and social stratification. For households engaged in agriculture, the structure of the land tenure system and access to land and labour necessary for cultivation are the principal determinants of relatively minor household variation (ibid.: 28). Household series may reflect variation in access to basic resources only at the larger scale. Third, it is unknown how aggregate data from successive co-residential groups relates to successive household adaptations. Under some conditions, household series may mask intrahousehold change, whereas in other situations it may not.

Although Hirth's arguments cast doubt on the utility of ethnoarchaeological models to prehistoric situations, especially agriculturalists, he indirectly poses an open question. Can we use modern ethnographic and ethnoarchaeological cases to recognize variation in household organization within and among household series, even though these actualistic investigations have been conducted from a synchronic perspective? To what degree are access to basic resources, land, and labour detectable in archaeological agrarian households that are expected to show only little variation? I submit that ethnoarchaeological models are still useful in purely archaeological situations, despite their synchronicity. To evaluate this approach, I turn to the analysis of agricultural production, house lots, and household series in Yaxcaba, Yucatan.

YAXCABA AND THE MESOAMERICAN HOUSE LOT MODEL

Views of agricultural production and household organization in the tropical lowlands of Mesoamerica have undergone considerable modification. The principal agricultural strategy in the Maya Lowlands was traditionally described as extensive swidden cultivation in which a milpa plot is cleared, burned, and planted in maize, beans, squash, and other cultigens for two to three consecutive years. Declining productivity after the third year usually prompts the farmer to clear a new plot, and the previously cultivated land lies fallow for seven to ten years (Redfield and Villa Rojas 1934; Steggerda 1941). More recent work demonstrates that the system is more complicated. Modern and prehistoric Maya farmers cultivate a diversity of resources among a mosaic of locations including primary forest land, secondary forest, river levees, *rejolladas* (sinkholes that do not reach the water table), and other natural features that permit intensification (e.g. Fedick 1996; Schmidt 1980; Wilk 1991). They conform to the smallholder adaptation characteristic of many intensive agriculturalists worldwide (Netting 1993; Pyburn *et al.* 1998).

The spatial structure of agricultural production characteristic of the Mesoamerican tropics has been described as 'settlement agriculture' (Killion 1992b; Sanders and Killion 1992). According to this model, extensive cultivation is combined with intensive kitchen or house lot gardening as a part of an infield–outfield agricultural strategy. The intensity of land use is viewed as a continuum, divided between monocropped outfields (at a distance of greater than 45-minutes from the settlement), multicropped infields (located within a 45 minute walk from the residence), and the house lot garden. The settlement zone itself comprises the permanently and intensively cultivated sector within the system (Killion 1990: fig. 3).

The fundamental residence unit within settlements is the house lot or *solar*. *Solares* are large, bounded areas containing a dwelling area or structural core, a swept patio or clear area, and a garden area or toft zone (Deal 1985; Hayden and Cannon 1983, 1984; Killion 1987, 1990; Manzanilla and Barba 1990; Santley and Hirth 1993b). Generally these zones are concentrically arranged, with the dwelling area located near the centre (Killion 1990: fig. 6).

Some studies recognize further divisions within the house lot. In the Tuxtlas mountains of Veracruz, Killion (1987, 1990) describes an intermediate refuse zone located between the clear area and garden area. The degree to which refuse in the intermediate zone is dispersed or collected into discrete piles is related to the intensity with which the patio and lot are used for productive activities. Patio size also varies with the intensity of agricultural production on different plots. Large patios are prevalent for households that intensify agricultural production on infields near the settlement, whereas households that intensify their production on monocropped outfields have smaller patios within the house lot (Killion 1987, 1990).

Arnold (1987, 1991) shows that the presence of discrete refuse zones within the house compounds of ceramic craft specialists in the Tuxtlas is related to the simultaneous vs. sequential use of space and the intensity of production. Ancillary and animal structures may also form part of the structural core, as in the Tuxtlas, or be located further away from the dwelling towards the garden as in Yucatan (Killion 1990; Smyth 1990). Smyth (1988, 1990) indicates that among the Yucatec Maya of the Puuc region, house lots contain discrete maize washing areas at the edges of the patio near the garden. Storage structures, especially corn cribs, are located within the patio or within the dwelling. Among the highland Maya of Chiapas and Guatemala, Hayden and Cannon (1983, 1984) have identified provisional discard areas in the vicinity of the structural core where potentially useful materials are stored prior to reuse. Frequently, large pieces of broken pottery, bottles, and other items will be collected under furniture within the dwelling or along the outside walls of houses and ancillary structures. When the lot is abandoned, these items are often left behind (Deal 1985). Large refuse fragments also end up near fences and hedges, whereas hazardous waste, such as glass sherds, may be discarded in special areas or pits to minimize their hindrance of other activities.

Nevertheless, the three basic house lot components, dwelling–patio–garden, are common to all of the studies. Ethnoarchaeological research further demonstrates that variation in the relative sizes of these spatial components, particularly the ratio of the patio to garden area, is sensitive to the types and intensity of activities conducted both within and outside of the lot. Large patios, and more formalized refuse disposal in particular, result from the need for ample staging areas for agricultural or other production activities occurring near the community or within the house lot itself (Arnold 1987, 1991; Killion 1987, 1990). The relative proportions of house lot components are therefore useful indicators of variation in household productive strategies.

The creation and maintenance of the components within the lot hold implications for the distribution of refuse and can be recognized archaeologically through the analysis of inorganic debris and soil chemistry (Arnold 1987, 1990; Barba 1986; Manzanilla and Barba 1990; Smyth 1990; Tourtellot *et al.* 1989). The most common activity associated with house lot maintenance observed in all of the ethnoarchaeological studies is the sweeping of the patio, usually on a daily basis. This activity produces a pattern of low weight and small piece size refuse in the clear area and high weight, larger piece size refuse in the garden or toft zone. In some cases the garden zone contains high densities of refuse, distributed through the garden with organic debris which maintains soil fertility (Santley and Hirth 1993b: 6–7). In other cases, the garden is kept free of large pieces of detritus that would dull or break agricultural implements and hinder cultivation activities (Deal 1985; Hayden and Cannon 1983, 1984). The ethnoarchaeological studies suggest that the garden area can be differentiated from the patio on the basis of inorganic item weight and density in archaeological situations.

Agricultural production in Yaxcaba parish, 1750–1847

The situation in Yaxcaba parish during the late eighteenth and early nineteenth centuries presents no exceptions to the models of settlement agriculture or house lot spatial structure. The principal unit of residence within Yucatecan settlements is the house lot or *solar*. House lots are bounded by dry-laid limestone walls called *albarradas*, and they characteristically contain one or more apsidal or rectangular dwelling structures surrounded by a patio and a refuse-laden garden area. The garden zone resembles sheet midden and corresponds to intensively cultivated space used for horticultural endeavours, small livestock raising, and gardening. House lots arranged along streets according to the Spanish colonial grid plan are the basic unit of residence in early and late colonial period settlements (Alexander 1993, 1997; Hanson 1996) as well as in the present (Smyth 1990; SPP 1980).

The house lot also demonstrates considerable longevity in the region. House lots delimited by *albarradas* are recognizable at prehispanic sites in Yucatan, particularly at Cobá, Yaxuná, Dzibilchaltún, Chunchucmíl, Mayapan, and Cozumel (Alexander 1991; Bullard 1954; Folan *et al.* 1983; Friedel 1986; Friedel and Sabloff 1984; Manzanilla and Barba 1990; Vlcek *et al.* 1978). In other cases, analogous house lot components have been identified in the absence of lot walls. At Sayil, for example, dwellings and other ancillary structures are built atop large basal platforms, thought to have functioned as the patio, while the interstitial space between platforms is the likely location of garden zones (Killion *et al.* 1989; Tourtellot *et al.* 1989).

Central Yucatan and the Yaxcaba region are characterized by undulating, karst terrain, very shallow soils (15–30 cm deep), and a lack of surface water. Cenotes, collapse dolines that expose the water table, are the principal source of water, and *rejolladas* are common geologic features in the region and are frequently used for intensive horticulture (Gomez Pompa *et al.* 1990; Kepecs and Boucher 1996; Pool Novelo 1980; Schmidt 1980). Although Yucatecan agriculture cannot be strictly described as infield–outfield cultivation, Maya farmers in Yaxcaba currently plant milpas at varying distances from the settlement, between one and seven kilometres, and the diversity of cultigens in different milpa plots varies depending on soil characteristics (Arias Reyes 1980). Different cultigens within the solar are also spatially structured (Vara Morán 1980). In the karst environment, arable soils are frequently at a premium. Numerous colonial settlements in Yaxcaba parish were constructed over the remains of previous prehispanic settlement. Not only were the prehispanic settlements situated with access to water, but archaeological sites often contain the most productive soils and provide an accessible source of useful building materials.

The late eighteenth and early nineteenth centuries constituted a period of rapid change in Yaxcaba as the region became increasingly integrated with the expanding peninsular market economy driven by the policies of free trade (*comercio libre*) and the Bourbon political reforms (Farriss 1984; Patch 1993). From 1750 to the Caste War of 1847 the population of Yaxcaba parish nearly tripled (AME 1784, 1804, 1828, 1829). As a response to increased population density, the settlement expanded and dispersed from the two original colonial towns, Yaxcaba and Mopila, to establish numerous 'un-official' communities historically known as independent *ranchos* (Figure 6.1). The demographic recovery of the indigenous population also corresponded to the expansion of *haciendas*. *Haciendas* were Spanish–American owned estates engaged in cattle raising, and several were founded between 1784 and 1845. By 1800, the settlements formed a four-tiered hier-archy in the parish composed of the *cabecera* (municipal seat), Yaxcaba, auxil-iary towns (*pueblos*), independent *ran-chos*, and *haciendas*. Production centred around agriculture and cattle raising (BCCA 1778). Although wage labour and sharecropping occurred in Yaxcaba and on the *haciendas*, they were not prevalent, and craft specialization among parish households was minimal (Granado Baeza 1845).

Over this period, the number of *haciendas* increased by 24 per cent, yet only 10 per cent of the parish population

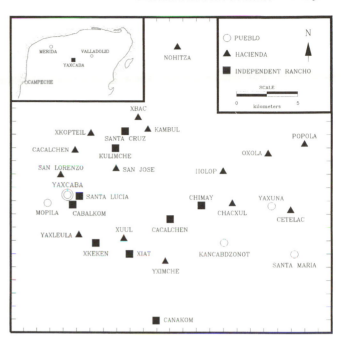

Figure 6.1 Yaxcaba Parish: location of the study area. Drawn by R. Alexander.

resided on the estates (Alexander 1993, 1997). Most of the population growth occurred in the *cabecera*, *pueblos*, and independent *ranchos*. The cattle *haciendas* became increasingly prevalent after Independence from Spain in 1821, when crown lands, previously available to anyone for use, became classified as vacant land subject to purchase (BCCA 1845; Farriss 1984; Reed 1964). The *hacienda* owners of Yaxcaba made claims for and purchased roughly 21 per cent of the land in the parish, and many of the claims bordered the communal lands of *pueblos* and independent *ranchos* (Alexander 1997; BCCA 1845). The expansion of the cattle *haciendas* at the expense of *pueblo* and independent *rancho* communities exacerbated land stress within the parish. It also inhibited the establishment of additional *rancho* settlements, such that further dispersal under the conditions of increasing population density was no longer a viable strategy for improving access to land (cf. Farriss 1978, 1984).

Attempts to integrate Yaxcaba with the peninsular market economy were short lived. Historical data indicate that the transition to a market-based economy was never completed but instead resulted in a protracted series of conflicts between *haciendas* and indigenous villages over land (Alexander 1993; Patch 1985, 1993). These frictions culminated in the Caste War of 1847. The Caste War is commonly interpreted as a revitalization movement in which rebel Maya attempted to throw off the yoke of foreign domination by means of armed resistance motivated through the proclamations of Juan de la Cruz and the cult of the talking cross (Bricker 1977, 1981; Cline 1950; Reed 1964; Rugeley 1996; Sullivan 1989). The revolt was largely successful, and at one point rebel Maya nearly gained control of the entire peninsula. The conflict was also protracted, and as a result a new religion with a separate priesthood and cult practices emerged from the movement (Bricker 1981: 87). Some Maya argue that the Caste War continues to this day (Sullivan 1989; Villa Rojas 1945). Yaxcaba was caught in the middle of the most violent conflicts, and between 1847 and 1855 the parish changed hands four times (Reed 1964). Although the

Caste War resulted in successful agrarian reform that eliminated most *haciendas* in the parish and re-established traditional patterns of land use (Bricker 1981), Yaxcaba parish also lost about 90 per cent of its population during the war, and all but seven of its original settlements were abandoned (Rejón 1862).

SITE STRUCTURE IN YAXCABA PARISH

In order to examine variation in settlement and site structure among communities and households within the parish, I implemented a multistage research design emphasizing survey, mapping, and surface collection. First, I used the list of communities pertaining to Yaxcaba parish in the *visitas pastorales* (pastoral visits) as a basis for delimiting the region for extensive survey (AME 1784, 1804, 1828, 1829). Each of the twenty-nine settlements listed in the historical records was located. Information collected for each settlement included a description of structures and features present at the site, its ecological setting, the location of water sources, an estimate of site size, the amount and stylistic characteristics of standing architecture, and any evidence of specialized functions within sites. Scale maps were made of the centres of all but three settlements using a compass and tape or a theodolite. All settlements in the extensive survey were classified into one of four archaeological categories (I–IV), on the basis of site size, the amount and function of masonry architecture, and site layout. The archaeological classes correspond respectively to the historical community types known as *cabeceras*, *pueblos*, *haciendas*, and independent *ranchos*.

On the basis of the information provided by the extensive survey, one *pueblo* (Mopila), one *hacienda* (Cetelac), and one independent *rancho* (Cacalchen) were selected for intensive survey. Abandonment of all three sites coincided with the Caste War, but the length of colonial occupation at the *pueblo*, Mopila (1581–1847), was longer than that of the *hacienda*, Cetelac (1773–1847), and the independent *rancho*, Cacalchen (1750–1847). Each of these sites also contained prehispanic components; platform mounds with superstructures were recorded during the intensive survey. Mopila showed evidence of Postclassic period (AD 1250–1545) occupation, while Cetelac and Cacalchen contained structures and artefactual material dating to the Early Classic period (AD 250–600). Cacalchen was also reoccupied by about fifteen families in the 1920s, but they returned to live in Yaxcaba in the late 1950s. Currently Mopila, Cacalchen, and Cetelac are used for extensive milpa cultivation, beekeeping, citrus cultivation, and occasionally for grazing and watering of individual cattle and horses by Maya living nearby.

Ninety to one hundred per cent of each site was mapped during the dry season using a Leitz EDM theodolite. Patterns of streets, house lots, individual dwellings, ancillary features, plazas and public architecture dating to the colonial occupations were clearly recognizable and recorded. Mopila and Cacalchen were 55 ha and 35 ha in size respectively. They consisted of house lots aligned along a grid pattern of streets arranged around a central plaza containing the principal water source for the community. The streets also widened at intervals creating small plaza areas, but these features were more common in Cacalchen than in Mopila. In Mopila, the main plaza contained a large church, the iglesia de San Mateo, and a *noria* (a well in which water is pumped to the surface with a windmill or with animal traction). Cacalchen lacked a church but contained three small shrines. Its principal water source was a large cenote. Both settlements had a walled cemetery located at the southern edge of the site.

Like most *haciendas* in the parish, Cetelac was about 35 ha in size and consisted of a large, two-storey, rectangular masonry house adjacent to a *noria*. Water troughs for livestock ran from the *noria* platform across the front of the house. Cetelac had four large livestock corrals surrounding the main house, and an additional apsidal masonry house was located near the front gate to one side of a central plaza. Surrounding the principal structures at the heart of the *hacienda* was an extensive system of *albarradas* that delimited additional corrals and the house lots of the resident workers. House lots to the west of the main house were aligned along streets, whereas lots to the east of the house beyond the largest corral were more irregular.

House lots in the three communities were large, often irregularly shaped areas. Most were overgrown with dense secondary vegetation, except for areas that had been burned in preparation for planting. When cleared of vegetation, we often found the remains of foundation braces for perishable houses as well as ancillary features such as pig sties, chicken coops, *arriates* (stones placed to protect tree roots), wells, *pilas* (water storage tanks), *eras* (irrigation berms), and *chich* (crushed rock) piles, all constructed of local limestone. Functions were attributed to the ancillary features on the basis of modern analogy. Contemporary Maya construct pig sties, chicken coops, *arriates*, and *pilas* out of limestone that are practically identical to the colonial examples recorded on survey. *Chich* piles, however, remain enigmatic. Functions attributed to *chich* piles in Yucatan include foundations for storage facilities (Killion *et al.* 1989; Smyth 1990) and stone mulch for protecting tree roots from soil erosion and moisture loss (Kepecs and Boucher 1996). The numbers and types of ancillary features are important clues for determining strategies of diversification and intensification of production within the house lot. Other than the structural core, however, house lot components such as the patio or garden could not be distinguished through surface survey.

Eleven house lots were selected by means of a stratified random sampling design for surface collection – four in Mopila, five in Cacalchen, and two in Cetelac. At Cetelac, areas surrounding the main house, *noria*, and ancillary structures, and plazas were also collected. Within each house lot, surface collection transects, consisting of 3 × 3 m squares continuously laid end to end, were placed to cross-cut structures, features, and different areas within the lot. The transects were cleared of all vegetation. The surface of each collection unit was scraped with a trowel, and the soil was screened through a one-eighth inch mesh. Artefacts of ceramic, chert, obsidian, shell, metal, bone, and glass were catalogued according to provenance and material type for subsequent analysis.

Surface collection transects were placed to cross-cut different sectors of the house lots, running through house structures and ancillary features. Assuming that the clear area surrounded the dwelling core and was maintained by daily sweeping, it was possible to delimit the extent of patio and garden areas by measuring the density of inorganic refuse in different areas of the lot. The house lot maintenance activities structured the location and density of colonial refuse and altered the pre-existing substrate of prehispanic refuse at the same time. The most common material recovered from the surface collections was ceramics, both prehispanic and colonial. The locations and extent of patio and garden areas were estimated by examining the fall-off patterns of average sherd weight and other artefacts across the transects. Although exposed bedrock was common within the house lots, most areas were covered with a thin layer of soil. Modification of the existing prehispanic substrate was also indicated. Not only was stone taken from nearby prehispanic mounds, but dirt containing prehispanic artefactual material was used for floor fill and possibly added to garden areas.

The structural core

At Mopila, Cacalchen, and Cetelac, the structural core was characterized by the presence of one or occasionally two semicircular, apsidal foundation braces (Figure 6.2). Within the area of the foundation braces, fill of crushed limestone and/or dirt remained, but floors had eroded. Metate fragments were often located along the edges of the foundation braces, and sometimes fragments of metal nails, latches, and hinges were found. Large values for ceramic frequency, weight, and average sherd weight were common in surface collection units located on or near the foundations

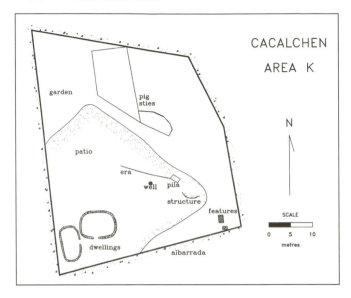

Figure 6.2 House lot K, Cacalchen, Yaxcaba parish. Drawn by R. Alexander.

of dwellings. Erosion of floors and floor fill in the colonial settlements is principally responsible for the large values of ceramics, and decomposition of the structures likely accounts for the distribution of metal artefacts. The broken metate fragments, however, might also indicate provisional discard areas (Deal 1985; Hayden and Cannon 1983). Ethnoarchaeological studies show that most refuse generated in the dwelling is also swept out the door, dumped next to the door, or thrown out the door into the patio or garden, and foot traffic near the dwelling tramples items into the underlying matrix (Arnold 1991: 129). Frequency and weight of inorganic refuse in the patio decreases with distance from the dwelling.

The scarcity of dwelling remains at these sites is unusual considering the length of their occupation. Many house lots contained no structural remains at all. Normally, house lots containing multiple structures and occupied by large populations are difficult to distinguish from the serial reuse of structures and the growth and decline of the domestic cycle over time (Moore and Gasco 1990). At Mopila, Cacalchen, and Cetelac, however, indications of the serial use of structures are absent. Although this pattern could indicate a small house lot population or the presence of nuclear families, the existence of completely perishable structures cannot be overlooked. On occasion, surface collection transects would cross portions of bedrock that had been filled or partially levelled, but where few foundation stones remained (Figure 6.2). Remaining foundation braces may represent cases where significant amounts of labour and materials were invested in house construction.

Contemporary Maya are also extremely thorough in collecting and reusing building materials from unoccupied structures, and the proximity of colonial and modern settlement in the Yaxcaba region may account for this pattern. If serial reuse of structures occurred, which is plausible especially at Mopila, reuse of materials from previously occupied dwellings was complete and included the removal of foundation stones. The structural core and ancillary features probably reflect the final configuration of structures within the house lot of the last occupants, as modified by post-abandonment processes (Deal 1985).

The patio and garden zones

Patios and garden areas within the house lots could be approximated by a fairly marked change in the size and density of ceramic remains, usually at the point where average sherd weight rose sharply, *c.* 3.5–4.0 g per sherd (Figure 6.2). A principal components analysis was conducted using ceramic frequency, ceramic weight, mean sherd weight, bone frequency, lithic frequency, metal frequency, and frequency of 'special' items such as glazed ceramics. The principal components most useful for distinguishing the patio from the garden and structural core usually displayed high loadings for mean sherd weight, metal, and frequency of special artefacts. When the value of the principal component was plotted for each unit across individual transects, it was possible to distinguish the structural core from the patio from the garden zone. Raw values for ceramic frequency and weight were less useful in this analysis. They proved somewhat more sensitive to topographic conditions, especially the degree of slope and amount of exposed bedrock. Rodent and other biological activity also affected the size of ceramic and lithic variables for some units given the thin soil conditions. Patios contained relatively small and light sherds as well as small bone fragments, whereas garden areas contained dense amounts of refuse resembling sheet midden. Lithics showed no distinct patterning between the two zones. The distribution of glass was also inconclusive, because most of the glass fragments proved modern. No intermediate refuse zones could be distinguished in this analysis.

The karst geological conditions suggest that the hindrance potential of large sherds in the cultivation process was probably less of a consideration in colonial settlements than retaining and augmenting soil within the lot (cf. Deal 1985; Hayden and Cannon 1983). Ancillary features, particularly pig sties and chicken coops, were located in garden areas and associated with very high densities of inorganic debris (Figure 6.2). *Pilas* and wells were often situated near patio edges (Figure 6.2). Among the Maya living in the Puuc region of Yucatan maize washing areas are indicated by their proximity to wells and *pilas*. Smyth (1988, 1990) suggests that because maize washing creates muddy areas and requires the undivided attention of the participant, these activities frequently take place at patio peripheries or in intermediate refuse disposal zones away from traffic.

Ethnoarchaeological studies indicate that smaller available work space correlates with the formalized arrangement of activity areas in scheduling and segregation of space (Arnold 1990; Hayden and Cannon 1983). The presence of numerous permanent constructions for penning livestock therefore might be expected in the smaller house lots, because the animals must be prevented from interfering with other activities occurring in the lot. This relationship, however, is not borne out for the Yaxcaba settlements. House lot size demonstrates no correlation with the numbers of ancillary features per lot, either within individual settlements or for all house lots among all three sites. The lack of correlation suggests that the greater numbers of ancillary features within some house lots, and particularly at Cacalchen, are not strictly a function of restricted residential space at the site. They likely indicate an actual difference in the household production strategy.

Unlike the structural core, the sizes of the patio and garden areas, as determined archaeologically, probably do not represent the final abandonment phase of the lot. Because the boundaries of the patio and garden expand or shrink over time according to the population of the house lot and in response to the different space needs of activities that take place in the lot, the relative sizes of these areas probably represent a mosaic of overlapping patios whose location and size has shifted over time. Given karst conditions, the patio area defined archaeologically probably represents the maximum combined extent of all patio areas over the life of the house lot, and the percentage of patio area within the house lot in this case seems to be correlated with the length of household series.

Site structure and differential access to land

Analysis of site structural patterns in house lots among Mopila, Cetelac, and Cacalchen revealed distinct differences in use of space. House lot size, the numbers of ancillary features within house lots, and patio size vary among the three sites (Kruskal Wallis tests, lot size $p < 0.002$; ancillary features $p < 0.03$; patio size $p < 0.05$).[1] The analysis suggests that different communities in the parish employed different strategies for coping with land stress and the changes wrought by *hacienda* expansion. Table 6.1 summarizes the site structural variation and historical information for each settlement.

Table 6.1 Comparison of population, land pressure, house lot size, ancillary features, and size of house lot components among three sites in Yaxcaba parish

Variable	Mopila	Cetelac	Cacalchen
Site size*	55	35	35
No. of house lots mapped	60	26	76
Mean house lot size	3,451	6,110	2,770
Mean no. of ancillary features per lot	0.217	0.346	0.645
No. of house lots surface collected	4	2	5
Mean garden size	1,934.8	5,069.5	1,664.8
Garden area (%)	50.9	73.7	61.8
Mean patio size[†]	1,967.8	1,807.5	730.0
Patio area (%)[†]	49.1	26.3	38.2
Mean no. metal artefacts per lot	33.5	2.0	8.0
Mean no. glazed ceramics per lot	20.0	3.75	1.75
Length of occupation[††]	266	74	97
Population growth§	155 to 342	8 to 51	184 to 634
Population density	6.22	1.28	18.11
Land pressure	Moderate	Very low	Acute

Notes: * Site size in hectares; all other measurements of area are in square metres.
   [†] Includes the area of the structural core.
   [††] In years.
   § Over the period 1784–1828.

House lots in Mopila were moderately large but contained relatively few ancillary features per lot (Table 6.1). *Chich* piles and *pilas* predominated over animal pens, which suggests a greater emphasis on arboriculture or storage than small livestock raising. Patios were large, but garden areas were also substantial. Throughout the colonial period, the inhabitants of Mopila were subject to tribute payments (AGN 1938; BCCA 1778; Gerhard 1979; UNM Scholes 1549, 1809). The church also regularly collected obventions, and Mopila's inhabitants paid the tithe on small livestock (BCCA 1778; Granado Baeza 1845). During the period of *hacienda* expansion, the interests of the church and state in the town's ability to meet its tax obligations probably afforded the community some protection over land-grabbing *hacienda* owners. Mopila had a long history of occupation, and the site was used as a permanent location for residential space for 266 years. The large proportion of patio area within Mopila house lots may reflect the stability of household series. During the period 1784 to 1828, population growth at Mopila was low compared to other sites in the parish. The *pueblo* and its communal lands were legitimately established.

The house lots of resident workers at Cetelac were extremely large, often created by modifying existing prehispanic *albarradas* (Table 6.1). They also contained relatively few ancillary structures per lot, but pig sties were the most numerous feature class. Patio areas were approximately the same size as those in Mopila, whereas garden areas were more extensive. Larger house lots were apparently constructed to provide for extended garden space.

Hacienda residents were sharecroppers who lacked access to land. The *hacienda* owner was responsible for his workers' tribute obligations and religious taxes. Cetelac had a very low rate of population growth, and land pressure among residents was very low. Resident workers, however, would have shared the land with the cattle of the estate, and consequently they would have needed to protect their crops from invasion by the cattle. Milpas could be securely planted at considerable distances from the *hacienda's* core or by fencing large parcels close to the house lot. At Cetelac, the large garden areas tentatively suggest that some milpa cultivation may have taken place in the house lot itself. The site was used as residential space from 1773 to 1847. In other periods it was most likely used for extensive swidden cultivation, apiculture, and livestock raising. The house lots probably reflect a short household series, approximately one or possibly two domestic cycles.

House lots at Cacalchen were very small but contained numerous ancillary structures per lot, especially animal pens (Table 6.1; Figure 6.2). Although the house lots were smaller than at Mopila and Cetelac, the total size of garden areas at Cacalchen was comparable. In a small lot, patio size (38.2 per cent of the lot) appears to have been sacrificed to maintain garden area. Cacalchen was used as residential space from about 1750 to 1847, and again from about 1925 to 1950. At other times the *rancho* reverted to extensive use for milpa cultivation and apiculture. Colonial period household series were therefore shorter than those at Mopila but longer than those at Cetelac.

Cacalchen lay just beyond the edges of civil and parochial jurisdiction. Tribute and obventions were rarely collected. *Rancho* inhabitants effectively engaged in a strategy that distanced them and their production from the extractive hands of the state and church. In the early nineteenth century, Cacalchen had a very high rate of population growth, and land pressure became acute. *Haciendas* claimed vacant land that directly bordered the communal lands of the community (BCCA 1846). House lots appear to have been subdivided to accommodate the fast growing population and prevent new inhabitants from residing on land near the settlement needed for infield milpa cultivation. The presence of larger numbers of ancillary features per house lot at Cacalchen suggests an intensification and diversification of house lot use less evident at Cetelac and Mopila. Intensively raising small livestock, as evidenced by the construction of permanent facilities for them, may have been an effective strategy (as it is today) that compensated for the scarcity of land, especially since the tithe on small livestock was not routinely assessed for *rancho* inhabitants.

The surface collections from house lots at Mopila, Cacalchen, and Cetelac yielded two classes of non-local items, metal and glazed ceramics, that could be chronologically assigned to the late 1700s and early 1800s. Variation in the quantities and distribution of these items permits a consideration of consumption within house lots and between sites, as well as the relationship of household consumption to political–economic structure. The amount of metal and glazed ceramic fragments recovered in the house lots actually refer to processes of discard, abandonment, and post-deposition for these artefacts (Deal 1985; Hayden and Cannon 1983; Schiffer 1987). Although these processes cannot be directly equated with consumption, they are roughly related, and, given the sampling conditions and procedures described above, the frequencies of these items will be used as an approximate measure of household consumption of non-local material culture.

Table 6.1 lists the mean frequency of metal artefacts and the mean frequency of glazed ceramics per house lot for each of the three settlements. Differences in the sampling fractions of surface collection areas between house lots and between sites are minimal. For Cetelac, these figures include artefacts collected in areas that correspond respectively to the main residence and extramural areas of the *hacienda*'s owner and the residence and extramural areas of the *hacienda*'s *mayoral* (caretaker). Both metal and glazed ceramics are present in significantly greater frequencies at house lots in Mopila than at the other two sites (Kruskal Wallis tests, metal $p < 0.012$; glazed ceramics $p < 0.020$).

The presence of metal and glazed ceramics among individual lots in Mopila also varies considerably. The maximum number of metal artefacts recovered from a single house lot is seventy-six, and the minimum number is eleven. For glazed ceramic fragments, the maximum is thirty-seven and the minimum is nine. House lots at Cacalchen generally demonstrate low frequencies of these non-local items, and variation among individual lots within the settlement is less than at Mopila. At Cetelac, the low frequencies of metal and glazed ceramics recovered from some units inside the main house of the *hacienda* probably can be attributed to the depositional context of the collection units which were located on top of roof-fall. The house lots of the *hacienda*'s resident workers demonstrate the lowest frequencies of metal and glazed ceramics of any house lots of the three sites.

This admittedly rough archaeological measure tentatively suggests that the consumption of non-local manufactures in the parish corresponds to the inhabitant's access to basic resources conditioned by each community's position in the political economic hierarchy. Historical information demonstrates that inhabitants of Mopila were more active in the regional economy than those of Cacalchen (Granado Baeza 1845), and consequently the archaeological evidence shows a greater presence of metal and glazed ceramics, along with variation in the amounts of those items between house lots, at Mopila. House lots and residential areas of *hacienda* dwellers, however, indicate a reduced frequency of non-local items, even though the *hacienda*'s connections to the colonial economy should have facilitated access to such products for the owner and his workers. Nevertheless, the permanent residents of Cetelac apparently did not consume these items in significantly greater quantities than *rancho* inhabitants. These patterns suggest that limitation of a household's access to land, and thereby its productive capacity, affected consumption of non-local utilitarian products.

COMPARISON OF RESULTS

A comparison of the site structural patterns in Yaxcaba's house lots with ethnoarchaeological house lot models and historical information about population, land stress, tax structure, and length of colonial occupation suggests a positive role for ethnoarchaeology in studies of prehistoric household organization. First, the components of the house lot model, the dwelling, patio, and garden zones, could be distinguished on the basis of the distribution of inorganic artefacts within house lots in Yaxcaba parish. Mopila, Cacalchen, and Cetelac also demonstrate variable lengths of occupation; yet even for Mopila, whose colonial occupation surpasses 250 years, house lot components were recognizable. Post-depositional noise in artefact distributions was present (see Deal 1985), but it did not completely obscure detection of patio and garden zones. Notably, length of occupation did not seem to affect detection of house lot components. In some cases house lot components in Mopila were clearer than in Cetelac. The use of aggregate data from successive co-residential groups, even in karst central Yucatan, demonstrates distinct patterning in the use of space within the lots.

Second, the comparison of site structural patterns among different settlements suggests that variation in house lot morphology is related to a community's or a co-residential group's access to basic resources. House lot residents in Mopila, Cacalchen, and Cetelac were agriculturalists who practised cultivation under different conditions of land stress and tax structure. Land constituted the critical basic resource necessary for production. Population density and access to land is reflected in several archaeological patterns that include: (1) the length of household series; (2) the size of the house lot; (3) the size of the garden area; (4) the numbers of ancillary features within house lots; and (5) consumption of non-locally produced metal and glazed ceramics. The size of the house lot is clearly related to population size and density. Large house lot size occurs under conditions of low rates of population growth, as at Cetelac, whereas small house lots occur in communities with high rates of population growth, such as Cacalchen. With the expansion of *haciendas* in Yaxcaba parish, communities were threatened with the loss of land used for milpa plots located at varying distances from the settlement. The size of the garden area is a measure of the intensity with which the settlement zone itself is used for agricultural production. For agriculturalists on the *hacienda*, who had all but lost independent access to land, the garden area within the house lot was critical. Similarly at Cacalchen, where land stress was acute, garden areas were used for intensive production not only of cultigens but also of pigs and chickens. At Mopila where access to land was secured by the town's long-term position as a community of taxpayers, garden areas were substantial but used less intensively for other activities than at Cacalchen and Cetelac.

Measures of the intensity of use and maintenance within individual house lots in Yaxcaba parish are somewhat more problematic. The size of the patio area, the dispersal or aggregation of refuse in the intermediate zone, and the formalization of the use of activity areas are the ethnoarchaeological indicators that suggest intensive use of the house lot as a staging area for near lot activities and production within the lot. In Yaxcaba parish, however, intermediate zones could not be distinguished in the distribution of non-organic artefacts. Also, the construction of permanent features for penning livestock – a more formalized use of space – did not correlate with house lot size. It is unclear how patio size relates to the use of the lot as a staging area. Generally, patio size seems to correspond to the site's length of occupation which suggests that the patio area is related to the length of the household series.

In colonial Yucatan, access to land was maintained by two forms of mobility known as dispersal and drift (Drennan 1988; Farriss 1978, 1984; Stone 1996). Dispersal refers to the establishment of satellite settlements around the congregated towns and the gradual movement of population to those settlements (Farriss 1978: 205). Drift is a process of intercommunity migration, usually in response to excessive labour drafts and civil and religious taxes (ibid.: 203). Restriction of access to land in Yaxcaba directly affected subsistence productivity and the household's ability to pay civil and religious taxes. Drift to established satellite settlements was a response that avoided both problems – it conferred greater access to land while avoiding tribute. Over the long term, establishing independent *rancho* settlements was an effective tactic that placed produce out of reach of civil and ecclesiastical authorities and avoided the excessive demands of the colonial regime.

These strategies are density dependent phenomena. Dispersal of settlement in Yaxcaba parish corresponded to episodes of population growth in situations where inhabitants needed to improve their access to land and maintain soil fertility (Drennan 1988; cf. Stone 1996). Under *hacienda* expansion, however, the historical evidence suggests that dispersal and the drift of population to independent *ranchos* ceased to be an effective means for coping with limited land. Continued dispersal did not occur and implied the need to adopt alternative strategies for contending with the increasingly limited availability of land. Intensification of production within the settlement zone was the response at Cacalchen and Cetelac.

From an examination of the sequences of occupation at Mopila, Cacalchen and Cetelac from the prehispanic period to the present, it appears that limited mobility and drift were fundamental ways of coping with short-term imbalances of population, land, and labour that affected agricultural production. Locations on the landscape may be classified according to their intensity of use. Yaxcaba's inhabitants intensively used the *cabecera* and the *pueblos* as permanent residential locations for house lots and kitchen gardening, whereas they used *haciendas* and independent *ranchos* sometimes for house lot residences and at other times for extensive swidden agriculture, apiculture, or stockraising. Yaxcaba and Mopila, for example, were occupied as permanent residential space from 1581 to the Caste War, whereas Cetelac and Cacalchen had more sporadic occupational histories. The length of household series, therefore, corresponds to the intensity of use of different places on the landscape and security of land tenure within community. The length of household series also expresses a relationship to a cycle of limited residential mobility, longer than the domestic cycle, among agriculturalists in this region.

CONCLUSION

The study of house lot site structure in Yaxcaba parish holds several implications for the use of ethnoarchaeological models in examining variation in prehistoric Mesoamerican household organization. First, it demonstrates that dwellings, patios, and gardens are recognizable for household series spanning more than 250 years, even in karst geomorphologic conditions. Second, it demonstrates that the organization of these components is sensitive to variation in the community's access to basic resources. Even though the inhabitants of Mopila, Cacalchen, and Cetelac were agriculturalists and expected to show relatively minor household variation, differences in land tenure were manifest in the sizes of gardens and patios, the numbers of ancillary features within lots, and the lengths of household series. Consumption of non-local items, metal and glazed ceramics, is also variable among the three communities. The community's position within the political economy likely conditioned the inhabitant's access to non-local materials and goods. Third, the study suggests that the length of household series is related to the intensity of use of specific portions of the landscape over time. The duration of occupation within house lots is not directly related to the length of a domestic cycle but to a longer period of residential mobility or drift between established towns and satellite communities.

Nevertheless, ethnoarchaeological models do present some problems in their application. Some aspects of site structure that relate to specific short-term conditions observed ethnographically are not readily distinguished in longer-term archaeological situations. The intensity of house lot maintenance, especially the use of the intermediate area, fluctuates according to the immediate needs of the household inhabitants. The degree to which the size of the patio relates to the need for using the house lot as a staging area for agricultural activities occurring off lot or whether patio size is related to the length of the lot's occupation is ambiguous.

These exceptions could be remedied if ethnoarchaeological investigations of households would reconsider the historical context of their ethnographic and archaeological observations. The temporal scale and periodicity of behavioural observations is crucial to understanding their impact on the archaeological record. By viewing ethnographic observations from a longer-term temporal stance, and considering the length of the household series as a variable that may not coincide with the development of the domestic cycle, ethnoarchaeological studies could begin to assess the relationship between rates of household change and the aggregate archaeological remains of household series. In advancing our knowledge of household morphology and adaptation, ethnoarchaeology and historical archaeology have the potential to reveal relationships among different temporal scales and cycles of change within household series that refined archaeological chronologies cannot.

ACKNOWLEDGEMENTS

My field research in Yaxcaba was made possible by the National Science Foundation (BNS-8813858), the Wenner Gren Foundation for Anthropological Research (Gr. 5089), and the Organization of American States. Their support is gratefully acknowledged.

NOTE

1 The Kruskal Wallis test is a non-parametric alternative to one-way analysis of variance based on the rank transformation of the variable under study. For cases where the assumptions required for one-way analysis of variance are not met, the Kruskal Wallis test evaluates the hypothesis that rank means are equal by calculating the H statistic which measures the degree to which the various sums of ranks for the variable differ from groups. The sampling distribution of H approximates the chi square (Blalock 1979: 367–9; Koopmans 1987: 397–404).

BIBLIOGRAPHY

Alexander, R. T. (1991) 'The Archaeology and Ethnohistory of Late Colonial Period Yaxcaba Parish, Yucatan, Mexico: Final Field Report 1988–1989 Season', Submitted to the Centro Regional de Yucatán, Instituto Nacional de Antropología e Historia, Mérida, Yucatán.

—— (1993) 'Colonial Period Archaeology of the Parroquia de Yaxcaba, Yucatan, Mexico: An Ethnohistorical and Site Structural Analysis', Unpublished Ph.D. dissertation, Department of Anthropology, University of New Mexico.

—— (1997) 'Late Colonial Period Settlement Patterns in Yaxcaba Parish, Yucatan, Mexico: Implications for the Distribution of Land and Population Before the Caste War', in J. Gasco, G. Smith and P. Fournier-Garcia (eds) *Approaches to the Historical Archaeology of Middle and South America*, Los Angeles: UCLA Institute of Archaeology, Monograph 38: 29–40.

Archivo General de la Nación (AGN) (1938) 'Incorporación a la real corona de las encomiendas de la Provincia de Yucatán. Distritos de las reales cajas de Mérida y Campeche', *Boletín del Archivo General de la Nación* 9, 4: 456–569 (Mexico).

Archivo de la Mitra Emeritense (AME) (1784) Visita a Yaxcabá, Visitas Pastorales 1783–1784 vol. 2, exp. 42, Cathedral Archive, Merida, Yucatan.

—— (1804) Visita a Yaxcabá, Visitas Pastorales 1803–1805 vol. 5, exp. 43, Cathedral Archive, Merida, Yucatan.

—— (1828) Yaxcabá, Selección Joaquín Arrigunaga Peon, caja 5, Ticul-Yotholin, Cathedral Archive, Merida, Yucatan.

—— (1829) Sotuta, Selección Joaquín Arrigunaga Peon, caja 4, Pencuyut-Teya, Cathedral Archive, Merida, Yucatan.

Arias Reyes, L. M. (1980) 'La Producción Milpera Actual en Yaxcabá, Yucatán' in *Seminario Sobre Producción Agrícola en Yucatán*, Mérida, Yucatán: Secretaria de Programación y Presupuesto (SPP): 259–304.

Arnold, P. J., III (1987) 'The Household Potters of Los Tuxtlas: An Ethnoarchaeological Study of Ceramic Production and Site Structure', Unpublished Ph.D. dissertation, Department of Anthropology, University of New Mexico.

—— (1990) 'The Organization of Refuse Disposal and Ceramic Production within Contemporary Mexican Houselots', *American Anthropologist* 92: 915–32.

—— (1991) *Domestic Ceramic Production and Spatial Organization: A Mexican Case Study in Ethnoarchaeology*, Cambridge: Cambridge University Press.

Arnold, P. J., III, and Santley, R. S. (1993) 'Household Ceramics Production at Middle Classic Period Matacapan', in R. S. Santley and K. G. Hirth (eds) *Prehispanic Domestic Units in Western Mesoamerica: Studies of the Household, Compound, and Residence*, Boca Raton: CRC Press: 227–48.

Ashmore, W. (1981) 'Some Issues of Method and Theory in Lowland Maya Settlement Archaeology', in W. Ashmore (ed.) *Lowland Maya Settlement Patterns*, Albuquerque: University of New Mexico Press 37–69.

Ashmore, W. and Wilk, R. R. (1988) 'Household and Community in the Mesoamerican Past', in R. R. Wilk and W. Ashmore (eds) *Household and Community in the Mesoamerican Past*, Albuquerque: University of New Mexico Press: 1–27.

Barba, L. (1986) 'La Química en el Estudio de Areas de Actividad', in L. Manzanilla (ed.) *Unidades Habitacionales Mesoamericanas y sus Areas de Actividad*, México D.F.: Instituto de Investigaciones Antropológicas, Universidad Nacional Autónoma de México: 21–39.

Biblioteca Cresencio Carrillo y Ancona (BCCA) (1778) Declaraciones de diezmos en el partido de Beneficios Altos y Bajos, son frutas de setenta y siete colectados en 1778 años, Mérida, Yucatán.

—— (1845) 1845a 1847 Registro de las denuncias de terrenos baldíos, Mérida, Yucatán.

Binford, L. R. (1978) *Nunamiut Ethnoarchaeology*, New York: Academic Press.

—— (1981) *Bones: Ancient Men and Modern Myths*, New York: Academic Press.

—— (1987) 'Researching Ambiguity: Frames of Reference and Site Structure', in S. Kent (ed.) *Method and Theory for Activity Area Research: An Ethnoarchaeological Approach*, New York: Columbia University Press: 449–512.

Blalock, H. M. Jr. (1979) *Social Statistics* (2nd revised edition), New York: McGraw-Hill Brook.

Blanton, R. E. (1994) *Houses and Households: A Comparative Study*, New York: Plenum Press.

Bricker, V. R. (1977) 'The Caste War of Yucatan: The History of a Myth and the Myth of History', in G. D. Jones (ed.) *Anthropology and History in Yucatan*, Austin: University of Texas Press: 251–58.

—— (1981) *The Indian Christ, The Indian King: The Historical Substrate of Maya Myth and Ritual*, Austin: University of Texas Press.

Bullard, W. R., Jr (1954) 'Boundary Walls and House Lots at Mayapan', Carnegie Institution of Washington, Department of Archaeology, Current Report no. 13, Washington, DC.

Chayanov, A. V. (1986) 'Peasant Farm Organization', in D. Thorner, B. Kerblay and R. E. F. Smith (eds) *A. V. Chayanov on the Theory of Peasant Economy*, Madison: University of Wisconsin Press: 29–269.

Clarke, D. L. (1972) 'A Provisional Model of an Iron Age Society and its Settlement System', in D. L. Clarke (ed.) *Models in Archaeology*, London: Methuen and Co. Ltd: 801–69.

—— (1977) 'Spatial Information in Archaeology', in D. L. Clarke (ed.) *Spatial Archaeology*, London: Academic Press: 1–32.

Cline, H. F. (1950) 'Related Studies in Early Nineteenth Century Yucatecan Social History', Microfilm Collection of Manuscripts on Middle American Cultural Anthropology no. 32, University of Chicago Library, Chicago, Illinois.

Cook, S. (1982) *Zapotec Stoneworkers: The Dynamics of Rural Simple Commodity Production in Modern Mexican Capitalism*, Washington, DC: University Press of America.

—— (1984) *Peasant Capitalist Industry: Piecework and Enterprise in Southern Mexican Brickyards*, Lanham: University Press of America.

Cook, S. and Binford, Leigh (1990) *Obliging Need: Rural Petty Industry in Mexican Capitalism*, Austin: University of Texas Press.

Cowgill, G. L. (1996) 'Discussion', *Ancient Mesoamerica* 7: 325–31.

Deal, M. (1983) 'Pottery Ethnoarchaeology Among the Tzeltal Maya', Unpublished Ph.D. dissertation, Department of Archaeology, Simon Fraser University, Burnaby, British Columbia.

—— (1985) 'Household Pottery Disposal in the Maya Highlands: An Ethnoarchaeological Interpretation', *Journal of Anthropological Archaeology* 4: 243–91.

—— (1988) 'Recognition of Ritual Pottery in Residential Units: An Ethnoarchaeological Model of the Maya Family Altar Tradition', in T. A. Lee, Jr and B. Hayden (eds) *Ethnoarchaeology Among the Highland Maya of Chiapas, Mexico*, Papers of the New World Archaeological Foundation no. 56, Provo: Brigham Young University: 61–89.

Dore, C. D. (1996) 'Built Environment Variability and Community Organization: Theory Building through Ethnoarchaeology in Xculoc, Campeche, Mexico', Ph.D. dissertation, Department of Anthropology, University of New Mexico, Albuquerque.

Drennan, R. (1988) 'Household Location and Compact versus Dispersed Settlement in Prehispanic Mesoamerica', in R. R. Wilk and W. Ashmore (eds) *Household and Community in the Mesoamerican Past*, Albuquerque: University of New Mexico Press: 273–93.

Evans, S. T. and Freter, A. C. (1996) 'Teotihuacan Valley, Mexico, Postclassic Chronology', *Ancient Mesoamerica* 7: 267–80.

Farriss, N. M. (1978) 'Nucleation versus Dispersal: The Dynamics of Population Movement in Colonial Yucatan', *Hispanic American Historical Review* 58: 187–216.

—— (1984) *Maya Society Under Colonial Rule: the Collective Enterprise of Survival*, Princeton, N.J.: Princeton University Press.

Fedick, S. (ed.) (1996) *The Managed Mosaic: Ancient Maya Agriculture and Resource Use*, Salt Lake City: University of Utah Press.

Folan, W. J., Kintz, E. R. and Fletcher, L. A. (1983) *Coba: A Classic Maya Metropolis*, New York: Academic Press.

Fortes, M. (1958) 'Introduction', in J. Goody (ed.) *The Developmental Cycle in Domestic Groups*, Cambridge: Cambridge University Press: 1–14.

Friedel, D. A. (1986) 'Yaxuna Archaeological Survey: A Report of the 1986 Field Season', Report submitted to the Committee for Research and Exploration, National Geographic Society, Washington, DC. Manuscript in possession of the author.

Friedel, D. A. and Sabloff, J. A. (1984) *Cozumel: Late Maya Settlement Patterns*, New York: Academic Press.

Gerhard, P. (1979) *The Southeast Frontier of New Spain*, Princeton, N.J.: Princeton University Press.

Gomez-Pompa, A., Flores, J. S. and Fernandez, M. A. (1990) 'The Sacred Cacao Groves of the Maya', *Latin American Antiquity* 1: 247–57.

Goody, J. (ed.) (1958) *The Developmental Cycle in Domestic Groups*, Cambridge Papers in Social Anthropology no. 1, Cambridge: Cambridge University Press.

Granado Baeza, B. (1845) Informe dado por el cura de Yaxcabá. Registro Yucateco, vol. 1, Colección Alfredo Barrera Vásquez, Centro Regional de Yucatán, INAH, Mérida, Yucatán.

Hammel, E. A. (1984) 'On the *** of Studying Household Form and Function', in R. McC. Netting, R. R. Wilk and E. J. Arnould (eds) *Households: Comparative and Historical Studies of the Domestic Group*, Berkeley: University of California Press: 29–43.

Hanson, C. A. (1996) 'The Hispanic Horizon in Yucatan: A Model of Franciscan Missionization', *Ancient Mesoamerica* 6: 15–28.

Hare, T. S. and Smith, M. E. (1996) 'A New Postclassic Chronology for Yautepec, Morelos', *Ancient Mesoamerica* 7: 281–97.

Haviland, W. A. (1966) 'Maya Settlement Patterns: A Critical Review', in M. A. Harrison and R. Wauchope (eds) *Archaeological Studies in Middle America*, Middle American Research Institute Publication no. 26, New Orleans: Tulane University: 21–47.

—— (1981) 'Dower Houses and Minor Centers at Tikal, Guatemala: An Investigation into the Identification of Valid Units in Settlement Hierarchies', in W. Ashmore (ed.) *Lowland Maya Settlement Patterns*, Albuquerque: University of New Mexico Press: 89–117.

—— (1988) 'Musical Hammocks at Tikal: Problems with Reconstructing Household Composition', in R. R. Wilk and W. Ashmore (eds) *Household and Community in the Mesoamerican Past*, Albuquerque: University of New Mexico Press: 121–34.

Hayden, B. (1988) 'The Coxoh Ethnoarchaeological Project', in T. A. Lee, Jr and B. Hayden (eds) *Ethnoarchaeology Among the Highland Maya of Chiapas, Mexico*, Papers of the New World Archaeological Foundation no. 56, Provo: Brigham Young University: 1–4.

Hayden, B. and Cannon, A. (1983) 'Where the Garbage Goes: Refuse Disposal in the Maya Highlands', *Journal of Anthropological Archaeology* 2: 117–63.

—— (1984) *The Structure of Material Systems: Ethnoarchaeology in the Maya Highlands*, Society for American Archaeology Paper no. 3, Washington, DC: Society for American Archaeology.

Hirth, K. G. (1993) 'The Household as an Analytical Unit: Problems in Method and Theory', in R. Santley and K. Hirth (eds) *Prehispanic Domestic Units in Western Mesoamerica: Studies of the Household, Compound, and Residence*, Boca Raton: CRC Press: 21–36.

Kepecs, S. and Boucher, S. (1996) 'The Cultivation of Rejolladas and Stonelands: New Evidence from Northeast Yucatan', in S. Fedick (ed.) *The Managed Mosaic: Ancient Maya Agriculture and Resource Use*, Salt Lake City: University of Utah Press: 69–91.

Killion, T. W. (1987) 'Agriculture and Residential Site Structure among Campesinos in Southern Veracruz Mexico: Building a Foundation for Archaeological Inference', Ph.D. Dissertation, Department of Anthropology, University of New Mexico.

—— (1990) 'Cultivation Intensity and Residential Site Structure: An Ethnoarchaeological Examination of Peasant Agriculture in the Sierra de los Tuxtlas, Veracruz, Mexico', *Latin American Antiquity* 1: 191–215.

—— (1992a) 'The Archaeology of Settlement Agriculture', in T. W. Killion (ed.) *Gardens in Prehistory: The Archaeology of Settlement Agriculture in Greater Mesoamerica*, Tuscaloosa: University of Alabama Press: 1–13.

—— (1992b) 'Residential Ethnoarchaeology and Ancient Site Structure: Contemporary Farming and Prehistoric Settlement Agriculture at Matacapan, Veracruz, Mexico', in T. W. Killion (ed.) *Gardens of Prehistory: The Archaeology of Settlement Agriculture in Greater Mesoamerica*, Tuscaloosa: University of Alabama Press:119–49.

Killion, T. W., Sabloff, J. A., Tourtellot, G. and Dunning, N. (1989) 'Intensive Surface Collection of Residential Clusters at Terminal Classic, Sayil, Yucatan, Mexico', *Journal of Field Archaeology* 16: 273–94.

Koopmans, L. H. (1987) *Introduction to Contemporary Statistical Methods* (2nd edition), Boston: PWS-Kent.

Lee, T. A., Jr and Bryant, D. D. (1988) 'The Colonial Coxoh Maya', in T. A. Lee, Jr and Hayden, B. (eds) *Ethnoarchaeology Among the Highland Maya of Chiapas, Mexico*, Papers of the New World Archaeological Foundation no. 56, Provo: Brigham Young University: 5–20.

Lee, T. A., Jr and Hayden, B. (eds) (1988) *Ethnoarchaeology Among the Highland Maya of Chiapas, Mexico*, Papers of the New World Archaeological Foundation no. 56, Provo: Brigham Young University.

Manzanilla, L. (ed.) (1986) *Unidades Habitacionales Mesoamericanas y sus Areas de Actividad*, México, DF: Instituto de Investigaciones Antropológicas, Universidad Nacional Autónoma de México.

Manzanilla, L. and Barba, L. (1990) 'The Study of Activities in Classic Households: Two Case Studies from Coba and Teotihuacan', *Ancient Mesoamerica* 1: 41–9.

Michels, J. W. (1979) *The Kaminaljuyu Chiefdom*, Monograph Series on Kaminaljuyu, University Park: The Pennsylvania State University Press.

Moore, J. D. and Gasco, J. L. (1990) 'Perishable Structures and Serial Dwellings from Coastal Chiapas: Implications for the Archaeology of Households', *Ancient Mesoamerica* 1: 205–12.

Netting, R. McC. (1993) *Smallholders, Householders: Farm Families and the Ecology of Intensive, Sustainable Agriculture*, Stanford: Stanford University Press.

Netting, R. McC., Wilk, R. R. and Arnould, E. J. (1984) 'Introduction', in R. McC. Netting, R. R. Wilk, and E. J. Arnould (eds) *Households: Comparative and Historical Studies of the Domestic Group*, Berkeley: University of California Press: xiii–xxxviii.

Nichols, D. L. and Charlton, T. H. (1996) 'The Postclassic Occupation at Otumba: A Chronological Assessment', *Ancient Mesoamerica* 7: 231–44.

O'Connell, J. F. (1995) 'Ethnoarchaeology Needs a General Theory of Behavior', *Journal of Archaeological Research* 3: 205–55.

Oswald, D. B. (1987) 'The Organization of Space in Residential Buildings: A Cross-Cultural Perspective', in S. Kent (ed.) *Method and Theory for Activity Area Research: An Ethnoarchaeological Approach*, New York: Columbia University Press: 295–344.

Patch, R. (ed.) (1985) 'Agrarian Change in Eighteenth-Century Yucatan', *Hispanic American Historical Review* 65, 1: 21–49.

—— (1993) *Maya and Spaniard in Yucatan*, Stanford: Stanford University Press.

Pool, C. A. and Santley, R. S. (1992) 'Middle Classic Pottery Economics in the Tuxtla Mountains, Southern Veracruz, Mexico', in G. J. Bey, III and C. A. Pool' *Ceramic Production and Distribution: An Integrated Approach*, Boulder: Westview Press: 205–34.

Pool Novelo, L. (1980) 'El Estudio de los Suelos Calcimórficos con Relación a la Producción Maicera', in *Seminario Sobre Producción Agrícola en Yucatán*, Mérida, Yucatán: Secretaria de Programación y Presupuesto (SPP): 393–424.

Pyburn, K. A., Dixon, B., Cook, P. and McNair, A. (1998) 'The Albion Island Settlement Pattern Project: Domination and Resistance in Early Classic Northern Belize', *Journal of Field Archaeology* 25, 1: 37–62.

Redfield, R. and Villa Rojos, A. (1934) *Chan Kom, A Maya Village*, Carnegie Institution of Washington Publication no. 448, Washington, DC.

Reed, N. (1964) *The Caste War of Yucatan*, Stanford: Stanford University Press.

Rejón, C. A. G. (1862) Memoria del Secretario General de Gobierno del Estado de Yucatán. Septiembre de 1862, Imprente José, Dolores Espinosa, Mérida. SPI.

Rugeley, T. (1996) *Yucatan's Maya Peasantry and the Origins of the Caste War*, Austin: University of Texas Press.

Sahlins, M. (1972) *Stone Age Economics*, New York: Aldine de Gruyter.

Sanders, W. T. and Killion, T. W. (1992) 'Factors Affecting Settlement Agriculture in the Ethnographic and Historic Record of Mesoamerica', in Th. W. Killion (ed.) *Gardens in Prehistory: The Archaeology of Settlement Agriculture in Greater Mesoamerica*, Tuscaloosa: University of Alabama Press: 14–31.

Santley, R. S. (1992) 'A Consideration of the Olmec Phenomenon in the Tuxtlas: Early Formative Settlement Pattern, Land Use, and Refuse Disposal at Matacapan, Vera Cruz, Mexico', in T. W. Killion (ed.) *Gardens of Prehistory: The Archaeology of Settlement Agriculture in Greater Mesoamerica*, Tuscaloosa: University of Alabama Press: 150–83.

—— (1994) 'The Economy of Ancient Matacapan', *Ancient Mesoamerica* 5: 243–66.

Santley, R. S. and Hirth, K. G. (eds) (1993a) *Prehispanic Domestic Units in Western Mesoamerica: Studies of the Household Compound and Residence*, Boca Raton: CRC Press.

—— (1993b) 'Household Studies in Western Mesoamerica', in R. S. Santley and K. G. Hirth (eds) *Prehispanic Domestic Units in Western Mesoamerica: Studies of the Household Compound and Residence*, Boca Raton: CRC Press: 3–17.

Santley, R. S. and Kneebone, R. R. (1993) 'Craft Specialization, Refuse Disposal, and the Creation of Spatial Archaeological Records in Prehispanic Mesoamerica', in R. S. Santley and K. G. Hirth (eds) *Prehispanic Domestic Units in Western Mesoamerica: Studies of the Household, Compound, and Residence*, Boca Raton: CRC Press: 37–63.

Stanley, R. S., Arnold, P. J., III and Pool, C. A. (1989) 'The Ceramics Production System at Matacapan, Vera Cruz, Mexico', *Journal of Field Archaeology* 16: 107–32.

Schiffer, M. B. (1987) *Formation Processes of the Archaeological Record*, Albuquerque: University of New Mexico Press.

Schmidt, P. (1980) 'La Producción agrícola prehistórica de los mayas', *Seminario sobre producción agrícola en Yucatán*, Mérida, Yucatán: Secretaria de Programación y Presupuesto (SPP): 39–82.

Secretaria de Programación y Presupuesto (SPP) (1980) *Seminario sobre producción agrícola en Yucatán*, Mérida, Yucatán: Secretaria de Programación y Presupuesto (SPP).

Smith, M. E. (1992a) 'Braudel's Temporal Rhythms and Chronology Theory in Archaeology', in A. B. Knapp (ed.) *Archaeology, Annales, and Ethnohistory*, Cambridge: Cambridge University Press: 223–34.

—— (1992b) *Archaeological Research at Aztec-period Rural Sites in Morelos, Mexico*, Pittsburgh: University of Pittsburgh Memoirs in Latin American Archaeology no. 4, University of Pittsburgh.

Smyth, M. (1988) 'Domestic Storage Behavior in the Puuc Region of Yucatan, Mexico: An Ethnoarchaeological Investigation', Unpublished Ph.D. dissertation, Department of Anthropology, University of New Mexico.

—— (1990) 'Maize Storage among the Puuc Maya: The Development of an Archaeological Method', *Ancient Mesoamerica* 1: 51–69.

Smyth, M. P. and Dore, C. D. (1992) 'Large-Site Archaeological Methods at Sayil, Yucatan, Mexico: Investigating Community Organization at a Prehispanic Maya Center', *Latin American Antiquity* 3: 3–21.

Steggerda, M. (1941) *The Maya Indians of Yucatan*, Carnegie Institution of Washington Publication no. 531, Washington, DC.

Stone, G. D. (1996) *Settlement Ecology: The Social and Spatial Organization of Kofyar Agriculture*, Tucson: University of Arizona Press.

Sullivan, P. (1989) *Unfinished Conversations: Mayas and Foreigners between Two Wars*, Berkeley: University of California Press.

Sutro, L. D. and Downing, T. E. (1988) 'A Step Toward a Grammar of Space: Domestic Space Use in Zapotec Villages', in R. R. Wilk and W. Ashmore (eds) *Household and Community in the Mesoamerican Past*, Albuquerque: University of New Mexico Press: 29–50.

Tourtellot, G. (1983) 'An Assessment of Classic Maya Household Composition', in E. Z. Vogt and R. M. Leventhal (eds) *Prehistoric Settlement Patterns: Essays in Honor of Gordon R. Willey*, Albuquerque: University of New Mexico Press: 35–54.

—— (1988) 'Developmental Cycles of Households and Houses at Seibal', in R. R. Wilk and W. Ashmore (eds) *Household and Community in the Mesoamerican Past*, Albuquerque: University of New Mexico Press: 97–120.

Tourtellot, G., Sabloff, J. A., McAnany, P. A., Killion, T. W., Dunning, N. P., Carmean, K., Palma, R. C., Dore, C. D., Beyer, B. F., Lopez Varela, S. L., Alvarez, C. P. and Wurtzburg, S. J., with an appendix by M. P. Smyth (1989) *Archaeological Investigations at Sayil, Yucatan, Mexico, Phase II: The 1987 Field Season*, Pittsburgh: Anthropological Papers, University of Pittsburgh.

University of New Mexico, Scholes Collection (UNM Scholes) (1549) Yucatecan Encomenderos. Notes on the document from the Archivo General de Indias, Guatemala 128. Archive 360, Box II–1, Maya, Item 12. Coronodo Room, Zimmerman Library, University of New Mexico, Albuquerque.

—— (1809) Relación de los pueblos de Yucatán, con el número de indios tributarios de cada uno, y la cantidad que pagan a la Real Hacienda según los subdelegados. Notes on the document from the Archivo General de la Nación, Mexico, Tierras 3556. Archive 360, Box II, Yucatan, Item 30. Coronado Room, Zimmerman Library, University of New Mexico, Albuquerque.

Vara Morán, A. (1980) 'La Dinámica de la Milpa en Yucatán: El Solar', *Seminario Sobre Producción Agrícola en Yucatán*, Mérida, Yucatán: Secretaria de Programación y Presupuesto (SPP): 305–42.

Villa Rojas, A. (1945) *The Maya of East Central Quintana Roo*, Carnegie Institution of Washington Publication no. 559, Washington, DC.

Vlcek, D. T., Garza de González, S. and Kurjack, E. B. (1978) 'Contemporary Farming and Ancient Maya Settlements: Some Disconcerting Evidence', in P. D. Harrison and B. L. Turner II (eds) *Prehispanic Maya Agriculture*, Albuquerque: University of New Mexico Press: 211–23.

Widmer, R. J. and Sheehy, J. J. (1990) 'Archaeological Implications of Architectural Changes in a Modern Potting Compound in Teotihuacan, Mexico', Paper presented at the 55th annual meeting of the Society for American Archaeology, Las Vegas.

Wilk, R. R. (1991) *Household Ecology, Economic Change and Domestic Life among the Kekchi Maya in Belize*, Tucson: University of Arizona Press.

Wilk, R. R. and Ashmore, W. (eds) (1988) *Household and Community in the Mesoamerican Past*, Albuquerque: University of New Mexico Press.

Wilk, R. R. and Netting, R. McC. (1984) 'Households: Changing Forms and Functions', in R. McC. Netting, R. R. Wilk and E. J. Arnould (eds) *Households: Comparative and Historical Studies of the Domestic Group*, Berkeley: University of California Press: 1–28.

Wilk, R. R. and Rathje, W. L. (1982a) 'Archaeology of the Household: Building a Prehistory of Domestic Life', *American Behavioral Scientist* 25, 6: 611–724.

Wilk, R. R. and Rathje, W. L. (1982b) 'Household Archaeology', in R. R. Wilk and W. L. Rathje (eds) 'Archaeology of the Household: Building a Prehistory of Domestic Life', *American Behavioral Scientist* 25, 6: 617–39.

Willey, G. R. and Leventhal, R. M. (1979) 'Prehistoric Settlement at Copan', in N. Hammond and G. R. Willey (eds) *Maya Archaeology and Ethnohistory*, Austin: University of Texas Press: 75–102.

Chapter Seven

The appetites of households in early Roman Britain

Karen Meadows

INTRODUCTION

The households in this chapter will be approached through an analysis of the culinary habits of their inhabitants. The settlements in question were situated along the Upper Thames Valley in southern England during a period of Roman conquest and rule. Structural remains of the houses are not villa-like;[1] no obvious floorplans have survived, in fact, a range of archaeological resources are required to confirm that these sites were places of habitation. As a consequence of their classification as 'native', settlements such as those found in the Valley are often used to exemplify 'native continuity' and/or low impact 'romanization'. I hope to provide a different view of the impact of conquest on these settlements by focusing on diet and consumption practices. An adjunct to this study has been the need to rethink a concept of households in which the 'house' is not the primary locus of study; I will also therefore suggest how settlements with little evidence of structures might provide a more integrated view of the household.

The Roman conquest of Britannia had an impact on the daily lives of the people who lived there. An obvious statement perhaps, but one which has yet to be incorporated into our accounts of the lives of the majority of the native population (Scott and Gaffney 1987: 85; Hingley 1997: 84). Discontentment with the polarization of 'romanization' versus 'native continuity' led me to consider whether the subtleties of diet and culinary practices can provide some insight into the early experiences of imperialism at the household level. As I have argued elsewhere, people of all backgrounds eat and drink in culturally specific ways and many of the items used to gauge the impact of Rome are those which are used when consuming food and alcohol (Meadows 1994, 1997). The majority of the settlements in the Upper Thames Valley during the early Roman period are considered 'native' rather than 'Roman' because of the way their settlements are structured and the nature of their consumption habits. The Valley is, therefore, an ideal region for the consideration of the impact of imperialism on native-type households. Although it was not anticipated at the time, the 'inconvenience' of the poor preservation of houses in the Valley during this period has been fundamental to my current approach to the study of households. Therefore, after a short introduction to the region, the first part of this chapter will concentrate on the exploration of households without the aid of houses. Following this, the consumption practices of various households will be analysed through the re-contextualization of the artefacts and remains surrounding eating and drinking.

THE UPPER THAMES VALLEY

The Upper Thames Valley cuts across southern-central England from the source of the Thames in the west, one hundred kilometres eastwards (see Figure 7.1). The region was within the first wave of the conquest after the Roman invasion of AD 43 (see Jones and Mattingly 1990: 66–7), although evidence of Roman and/or continental influence can be found in the late Iron Age (Miles 1986a: 50). There are also suggestions that the Valley may have crossed a number of late Iron Age tribal boundaries (Selwood 1984; although see Jones 1997; Lambrick 1992: 83). The Valley itself encompasses a flood plain which is flanked by a series of gravel terraces. Various small and large-scale excavations have shown that settlement density throughout the Valley was high during this period of political transition. This is also suggested by a series of contemporaneous crop marks (Robinson 1981; Miles 1982; Allen *et al.* 1984). Native-type settlements in the early Roman period are often identified by the presence of rectangular enclosures, fewer pits than in the late Iron Age, and in some cases, rectangular foundation slots as opposed to circular gullies. This is, however, a tenuous chronological distinction as the fine

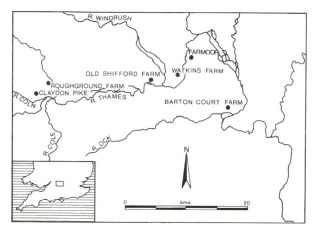

Figure 7.1 Map of the Upper Thames Valley and sites mentioned in chapter.
Drawn by C. Merony.

line that divides prehistory and history, although firm in the minds of some Romanists, is more difficult to isolate archaeologically (T. Allen pers. comm.). The Roman conquest is consequently not a fixed point in the archaeological recording of this region. This does not mean that we cannot consider the effects of imperialism by looking at settlements before and after the Roman invasion, but it does require that the focus be on the cumulative impact of the conquest, rather than trying to fit the archaeological record around specific historical events (Scott and Gaffney 1987: 86; Jones 1997).

The bias of research toward villas and urban areas is well known for Roman Britain (Hingley 1989: 4–5). For other types of settlements, it is as if by their classification as 'native' we somehow know what these types of settlements will divulge without excavation. Diversity in native type settlements or evidence of 'native discontinuity' (see Meadows 1997: 33) are subsumed by settlements that are better preserved and ultimately more Roman-like. Fortunately, many of the non-Roman-like settlements in the Upper Thames Valley were situated on gravel, and therefore have been excavated, in anticipation of gravel extraction, by the Oxford Archaeological Unit (the 'OAU'). Although there is now a bias towards excavated native settlements on the Valley's gravel terraces (Miles 1986a: 49; Lambrick 1992: 78), as native settlements throughout Roman Britain are being excavated (Drury 1982b: 1; Hingley 1989: 5) *and published*, it remains for us to incorporate them into our accounts of the impact of Roman imperialism. Indeed, until recently much of the academic interest in the archaeology of the Upper Thames Valley focused on the paucity of villas until late into the Roman period. Fulford comments that discussions about the Valley have been influenced by how we classify 'Roman' and 'native', and our emphasis on stone built 'villas' when the most plausible construction materials in the Upper Thames Valley – cob and timber – are not generally preserved (1992: 37; see also Miles 1989: 65; Allen *et al.* 1984). The implication is that we might be looking in the wrong place – structures rather than material culture – for evidence of 'romanization' (Fulford 1992: 29). Hingley has suggested instead that the Upper Thames Valley was occupied by more cooperative social groups whose ties to the community at large may have inhibited the development of Roman-type settlements after the conquest (1984a; 1988: 95, although see Haselgrove 1984; Lambrick 1992: 79–80). What distinguishes current approaches to the archaeology of the Upper hames Valley from other accounts of Roman Britain is that many of the basic assumptions that are made generally about rural settlements with regard to the presence and absence of romanized structures and material culture, are being challenged.

Households without houses

Any study of household archaeology in the Upper Thames Valley during the late Iron Age and early Roman periods is complicated by the poor preservation of structural features. What we find instead are pits, gullies, enclosure ditches and occasionally post-holes and house-slots. Beyond suggestions about shape and, if conditions permit, the types of materials used in their construction, the inner working of houses in the Upper Thames Valley is ambiguous (Allen *et al.* 1984). This contrasts with stone-built, villa-type structures found further afield where it is possible to reconstruct floorplans and, at times, infer specialized areas of the house. The types of innovative spatial and architectural analysis that typify the study of Romano-British villas (see E. Scott 1990; S. Scott 1994; Smith 1978) are not always appropriate for many of the native type settlements in Roman Britain (see also discussion in Boast and Evans 1986: 194). With the settlements in the Upper Thames Valley, we need to look beyond 'the house' in our investigation of the household. Essentially, this requires that any working definition of the term household has to fit the archaeology of the region. It would, for example, be difficult to restrict non-family or extended family members from the definition as it might not be possible to specify the living arrangements of particular residents. Equally, in the case of settlements which contain multiple buildings and/or households, it might not be possible to disentangle the many interactions within the settlement. This does not exclude the possibility of identifying areas of different or special status, of suggesting specific gender or family associations or of establishing particular practices associated with particular house sites in the Valley. They just do not feature in the definition. For the purposes of this chapter, when I refer to the 'household' I am referring to the 'group who *used* [my emphasis] and resided within a single house or group of closely related buildings' (Hingley 1990: 128).

The structures that we recreate out of gullies, post-holes and foundation slots are as susceptible to bias in interpretation as are the many other types of archaeological reconstruction (see articles in Drury 1982a). Low-lying sites in particular tend to have fluctuating water tables which affects the survival of structural features (Pryor 1983: 191). Pryor, for example, argues that our ideas about the organization of lowland settlements are prejudiced by examples of the less physically challenged upland settlements (ibid.: 190). Reynolds, in studying the archaeological movement of reconstructed Iron Age houses, has observed one instance when 'a post-built structure was altered to a ring gully structure by rats tunnelling under the wall and living in the space afforded by the wattle work' (1982: 176). He has many other such examples, as well as instances where a few seasons of ploughing have removed all traces of post-holes (ibid.: 190). Clearly, at sites where structures are poorly preserved, other aspects of habitation need to be considered (Pryor 1983: 197).

The establishment of households without floorplans is less ambiguous if the remains commonly associated with households, and the environmental data which reflect human settlement, are integrated. House sites at late Iron Age and early Roman Old Shifford Farm (one of the sites in this study) have been proposed through the concentration of burnt pottery and animal bones, clay impregnated with wattle, oven walls and charcoal at the terminals of particular enclosures within the settlement (Hey 1996: 105, 111). Environmental data were used to confirm habitation of a site at Farmoor which lacked structural evidence but exhibited a substantial increase in the number of beetles associated with timber in the Roman period. Species of dung beetle that congregate around vegetal refuse and animal dung were also seen as evidence for habitation at the site (Lambrick and Robinson 1979: 122, 117). No structures were recovered at early Roman Watkins Farm; however, the recovery of woodworm and bread beetles and high quantities of pottery was seen to 'suggest more than mucking out from a settlement elsewhere' (Allen 1990: 81). Artefacts and features that indicate a variety of activities done on a household scale, such as small-scale textile production, metalworking, food preparation and storage, and even the presence of human burials (Allen *et al.* 1993: 191), contribute to the establishment of domestic occupation (Hey 1996: 138). The hand-operated querns found at Roughground Farm and Old Shifford Farm, and the hearths and ovens recovered at Barton Court Farm, Old Shifford Farm and Roughground Farm (Allen *et al.* 1993: 191; Hey 1996; Miles 1986b) were all used to substantiate the case for habitation at the three settlements featured in this study.

The absence of floorplans also forces us to place more importance on the deposition of material culture in features throughout the settlement. How surrounding features 'behave' (Pryor 1983: 196) can reveal completely different aspects of life at a settlement than can a house examined in isolation. According to Rapoport, '[o]ne cannot merely consider a particular building because people do not live in, or act exclusively in, single buildings: they use various buildings, a variety of outdoor spaces, settlements, and whole regions' (1990: 12). This has been a criticism of the excavations of Romano-British villas where the primary locus of study has been the house rather than the whole estate (Gaffney and Tingle 1989: 3; Miles 1989: 60). A notable consequence of the poor preservation of houses is that more parts of the site have to be plotted and excavated to determine the nature of settlement. Analysis of the distribution of material culture around the site may help to substantiate the location of possible house sites (although see p. 114 below), but it also provides the means to contemplate the working of the household. The distribution of pots, bones and plants can, for example, be linked to ideas about cuisine and rites surrounding consumption and discard. In an integrated study of the household, all archaeological features, each artefact and biological residue, in fact every trace of habitation, takes on importance.

The remainder of this chapter will focus on the relationship between settlement structure and consumption. The contextual associations of the remnants of eating and drinking will be highlighted and discussed in a way that emphasizes the impact of the Roman conquest on the consumption practices of native-type households in the Upper Thames Valley. Such an approach incorporates the ideas and methods of a variety of specialists and is shaped by the various states of preservation, as well as excavation conditions. It is necessary therefore to acknowledge the many hands – both past and present – that have touched and continue to touch each settlement, including my own. In considering sites which have, for the most part, been excavated by the OAU, there is some consistency in the methods and issues which determine how each site is analysed, although the material from each settlement is still not technically comparable. However, it is ultimately through contrast that diversity and uniqueness is realized (Hingley 1984b: 86), and while I do not ignore the shortcomings of the various archaeological samples I nonetheless emphasize the points at which they diverge.

Structure: from rounded to rectangular
Despite their fragmentary appearance, pieced together by the remnants of habitation and the processes of decay, there were houses in the Upper Thames Valley. And, although it may not be possible or even appropriate to pinpoint exact moments of change, a number of native-type

settlements in the Valley were reorganized roughly around the time of the Roman conquest. As it is likely that people who lived in these settlements also constructed them, or at least had a hand in their organization, it might be assumed that their configuration was significant (Rippengal 1993: 93). The switch from rounded to rectangular houses is characteristic – though by no means universal (see Hingley 1997) – of the Roman period in southern England and is often viewed as a sign of Roman and/or continental influence. In the early Roman period the construction of rectangular buildings was more sporadic and as such interpretations of their presence often point to varying degrees of romanization. The term 'romanization', however, is misleading and its use as a barometer of change does not provide an adequate account of many of the structural changes that took place at settlements in the Upper Thames Valley during the early Roman period. The term also does not promote alternative explanations for the presence of Roman-style constructs. It has, for example, been suggested that the interior of rectangular structures might have been organised in a way that was more reminiscent of Iron Age circular structures, i.e. central public (cooking and eating) spaces and peripheral private (sleeping) spaces (Hingley 1990). Others, see the shift from rounded to rectangular as evidence of a profound change in mindset (Rippengal 1993), or as part of political strategy in response to the forces of imperialism (Lyons 1996). Conversely, the persistence of the round house is increasingly being considered as a statement of identity and resistance (Hingley 1997). The shape of a structure ought to be considered from within the social context of the whole settlement, and the reconfiguration of a settlement without an attendant change in house shape is as suggestive as a settlement whose composition during this period of political turmoil changes dramatically or appears on the outside to be little affected. As Wilk has remarked: 'The house . . . faces both inward and outward, to the household and to the rest of society' (1990: 40); this is equally true of the settlement.

Consumption

What and how we consume is socially, culturally, economically and politically motivated. The few studies which approach imperialism through the consumption habits of the conquered often focus on the otherwise neglected localized conditions of conquest and colonialism (see e.g. Hastorf 1990; Costin and Earle 1989; Brumfield 1987). As a number of these studies have shown, analysis of consumption at the household level can illustrate how imperialism might affect the daily rituals of habitation (Hastorf 1990; Costin and Earle 1989). Earlier in this chapter I mentioned that many of the Roman-like goods considered symbolic of the adoption of a romanized lifestyle – amphorae and their edible contents; food preparation wares such as mortaria; serving ware such as samian ware (*Terra sigillata*) – are associated with eating and drinking. In late Iron Age Britain the initial appearance of these types of goods is linked to the trading practices and political ambitions of the élite (Haselgrove 1989; Trow 1990; see also Dietler 1990). In the early Roman period their presence has been used to determine the extent that indigenous élites initially emulated and manipulated the customs of their Roman conquerors (Millett 1990). Roman-type ingredients and methods for procuring and preparing food have also been identified and used as indicators of a romanized lifestyle (Jones 1991). The prevalence of beef and pig rather than sheep at the more romanized settlements, for example, is thought to reflect the culinary habits of the Roman army, if not 'Romans' (King 1991). Particular types of dining custom have also been suggested for romanized and non-romanized peoples, i.e., the entertaining of guests within the villa using specialized vessels versus outside feasting and the eating – and especially drinking from large communal vessels – at the more native settlements (Blagg 1990: 206; Dannell 1979; Millett 1979; Meadows 1997; see also Okun 1989). A common explanation for changes in lifestyle is 'romanization' or conversely 'native continuity' if the settlement has not changed according to our expectations. Current critiques of the concept of romanization (Freeman 1993; Webster 1996; Hingley 1996; Barrett 1997; Mattingly 1997), however, argue for a more introspective analysis of the presence or absence of Roman-like material culture at all levels of the social hierarchy.

In the early Roman period, some of the Roman style wares 'trickled down' to the rest of the population, to the native settlements. It is unsatisfactory simply to place these settlements on a sliding scale of non-romanization, particularly if the significance of changes in or persistence of particular culinary customs has not been considered from within the overall context of the settlement itself. Miller has established that '[t]he point of a contextual analysis is that it relates apparently disparate sources of evidence to make each, in turn, the context for the others' (1985: 201). The procurement, preparation and consumption of food and drink encompasses most of the specializations of archaeology and reaches far beyond the dinner table. In Britain, in spite of the repeated requests over the years by bone, pot and plant specialists (Payne 1972: 80–1; Maltby 1981: 193; Hansen 1991; Darling 1989: 98; Hodder 1989: 271), archaeological remains are rarely integrated and rarely considered from within their excavated and social context. The focus is instead on the perceived value of particular ingredients and vessels disassociated from the circumstances of their use (Dietler 1990: 369; Sherratt 1987; Woolf 1993; Willis 1994; Mattingly 1997: 9). Hastorf has observed that 'some foods may change meanings by context, while other foods may have a constant meaning through all contexts' (1991: 135). Blanton has suggested that 'not only might it be possible to make fraudulent claims through consumption, but it might also be the case that goods could be subject to miscomprehension' (1994: 14). The consideration of the social contexts of material culture could potentially challenge many (if not most) of our current perceptions of Roman Britain.

SETTLEMENT STRUCTURE AND CONSUMPTION IN THE UPPER THAMES VALLEY

What follows is an account of work in progress; results and conclusions are therefore preliminary and inevitably subject to refinement. The structure of three native-type settlements in the Upper Thames Valley – Barton Court Farm, Old Shifford Farm and Roughground Farm – will be considered below. Following this, some of the distinctions in the types of artefacts and ingredients used in the consumption of food and drink will be introduced to facilitate a discussion of their contextual significance.

Barton Court Farm (Figure 7.2), was situated on the second gravel terrace and first settled in the late Iron Age. The settlement was reorganized in the early Roman period and subsequently abandoned and was not resettled until the late Roman period. The late Iron Age settlement had two occupation areas (separated by enclosures) both defined by the association of two closely connected structures, a circular gully and a series of irregular post-holes. The artefacts, animal and plant remains found in the gullies and in the associated pits, as well as the proximity of human burials, helped to further distinguish the settlement as a habitation site. In the early Roman period the settlement was reorganized on a completely different alignment, none of the earlier features were reused and a large, single, rectangular structure was established. As there is no obvious chronological break in the sequence of artefacts, and the early Roman period settlement was constructed on the same spot as the late Iron Age settlement, it has been suggested that occupation was probably continuous (Miles 1986b: 49; see also Ferrell 1995: 136). It is possible, therefore, that some of the material found in early Roman period contexts is residual. The types of artefacts and remains found in the house-slots and surrounding site enclosure are again consistent with habitation, although the nature of deposition for the two settlements was quite different.

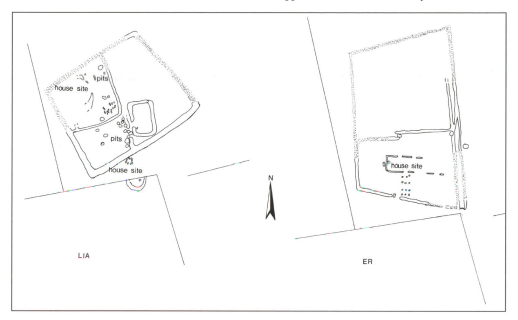

Figure 7.2 Barton Court Farm.
After Miles (1986b) with additions, drawn by B. Meadows.

Roughground Farm (Figure 7.3), also situated on the second gravel terrace, was settled and abandoned in the early Iron Age, was resettled in the early Roman period and occupied into the late Roman period. The early Roman settlement was characterized by a circular house enclosure with associated pits surrounded by a rectangular enclosure. Domestic material recovered in the terminals of the circular house enclosure differentiate the suggested house site from other features at the settlement. Away from the main occupation area is an elaborately marked cremation burial associated with a series of circular post-holes probably of early Iron Age. This early Roman settlement is quite different from that of neighbouring early Roman Claydon

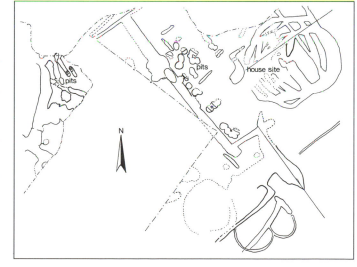

Figure 7.3 Roughground Farm.
After Allen *et al.* (1993), drawn by B. Meadows.

Pike which had a rectangular structure similar to that found at early Roman Barton Court Farm (Miles and Palmer 1983). Towards the end of the occupation of the early Roman settlement at Roughground Farm in the mid-second century a villa was constructed south of the earlier settlement.

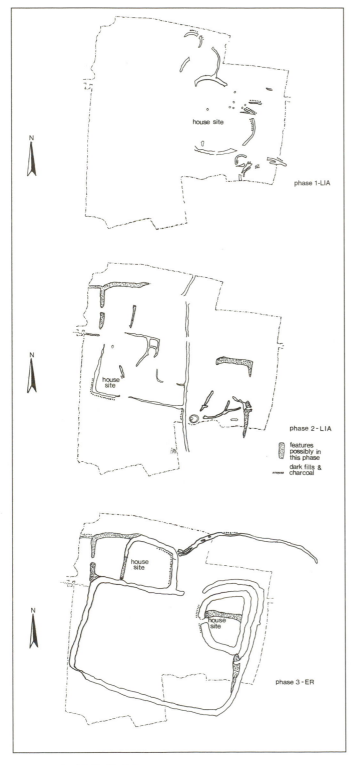

house site

phase 1-LIA

N

house
site

phase 2 - LIA

features
possibly in
this phase

dark fills &
charcoal

N

house
site

house
site

phase 3 - ER

N

Figure 7.4 Old Shifford Farm.
After Hey (1996), drawn by B. Meadows.

Old Shifford Farm (Figure 7.4), situated on the low-lying first gravel terrace, was first settled in the late Iron Age and was continuously occupied through to the early Roman period, when it was abandoned and subsequently resettled in the late Roman period. The cut-off points between the two late Iron Age phases and the early Roman occupation are more difficult to isolate, and the development of the settlement is described as 'probably more organic and continuous than a breakdown by phase indicates' (Hey 1996: 101).[2] Curvilinear enclosures and gullies were gradually superseded by more angular enclosures which were extended, and in some cases reused. By the early Roman period the settlement was enclosed by rectangular enclosure. Consequently, some of the material found in the various gullies and enclosures is mostly likely residual. Particular house sites have been suggested by the concentration of domestic debris, firstly in the terminals of the curvilinear gullies and later in the terminals of the sub-enclosures. The shape of the structures during the main phases of occupation is inconclusive. Wattle was recovered in each phase and judging from the contours of the gullies and sub-enclosures it is possible the structures were circular in the early phases and that one of the structures may have been rectangular in the early Roman phase, although this is speculative.

The containers

Barton Court Farm was my introduction to 'native' consumption practices in the Upper Thames Valley, although any archetypal position that this settlement may have held has since evaporated with the study of other 'native' settlements in the region. Preliminary observations of the pottery at the three sites in this study serves as a case in point (at each settlement it is the ceramic containers which have survived and on which this chapter will concentrate).[3]

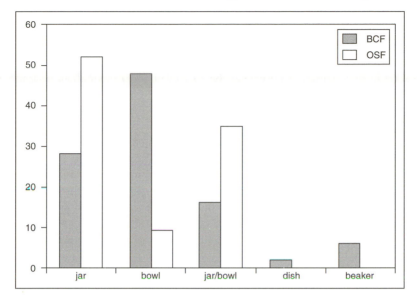

Figure 7.5 Percentages of identified late Iron Age pottery forms.

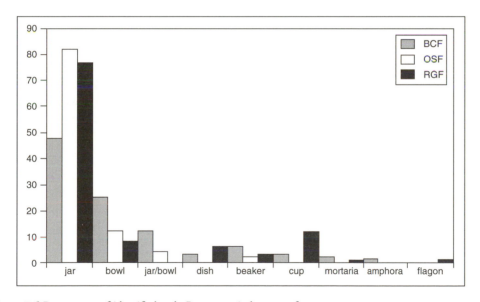

Figure 7.6 Percentages of identified early Roman period pottery forms.

The percentages of identified forms (Figure 7.5) at late Iron Age Barton Court Farm and Old Shifford Farm indicate a higher incidence of bowls at Barton Court Farm, which, together with the presence of dish forms and beakers, points to a more diversified repertoire of pottery forms at the settlement – forms that are commonly associated with the serving of food.

When we look at the early Roman period wares for all three settlements (Figure 7.6), both Barton Court Farm and Roughground Farm have a wider variety of wares, which include dishes, bowls, cups (some of which are samian ware), small amounts of mortaria and, at Barton Court, amphorae. Interestingly, many of the specialized wares associated with serving and especially drinking recovered at the earlier settlement at Barton Court Farm remain prominent at the early Roman period settlement. At Old Shifford Farm one beaker was identified, and while the types of jars and jar/bowls are similar to those recovered at the other two settlements the range in types of pots does not appear to include forms other than jars and, to a much lesser extent, bowls. No samian ware or mortaria were recovered at the settlement and a single sherd of amphora from a late Iron Age context is inconclusive. Indeed, compared to early Roman period sites in the area, Old Shifford had hardly any specialist wares (Booth in prep.). Specialized forms with specific uses, especially for serving food, are characteristic of the Roman period (Millett 1979). However, to conclude here that the pottery, and by association the dining practices, at Barton Court Farm and Roughground Farm was more romanized (in a native non-Roman kind of way!) than the pottery at Old Shifford is meaningless without the consideration of their context (Clarke 1996).

Some of the observed distinctions between vessel type also require further explanation. For instance, the association of jars with cooking and storage, and bowls with serving, is complicated by the problem in defining the point at which a bowl becomes a jar and vice versa (D. Miles pers. comm.). Burnt residues, for example, were found on jars at Roughground Farm whereas at Old Shifford they were found on bowls, jar/bowls and jars, an interesting distinction until you find that the majority of these forms would probably have been classified as jars at Roughground Farm (burnt residues were not recorded in the primary records at Barton Court Farm). The proportion of identified forms at Old Shifford was also comparatively low; however, the fabrics of both identified and non-identified forms at Old Shifford Farm are almost exclusively local. In the early Roman phase when vessels were increasingly wheel-thrown, the only example of non-local wares were handmade malvernian pots (Timby 1996: 126). Interestingly, when settlement at Old Shifford Farm was re-established in the third century, specialized forms such as beakers, tankards, dishes and Roman-style wares were only recovered in the latest phases of occupation. In contrast, the pottery recovered at early Roman Roughground and Barton Court farms consisted of both local and non-local wares. While the percentage of bowls at Barton Court Farm may be slightly exaggerated by the differing approaches to classifying forms, the settlement did have a significantly higher proportion of shallow bowls and beakers, whereas Roughground Farm had a higher proportion of cups and dishes. The possible significance of all of these contrasts will be considered below.

The ingredients

Bones

Most of the body parts of the four main domesticates were recovered at the three sites, which suggests that animals were being butchered at both the late Iron Age and early Roman settlements. Each settlement also appears to have had segregated pen-like areas, which suggests that animals may have been kept on site. The prevalence of cattle at the three early Roman settlements (Figure 7.7) may indicate a taste for meat commonly associated with the Romans, although high numbers of cattle at both late Iron Age Old Shifford and Barton Court farms complicate the making of such claims (Figure 7.8).

As well, in the Upper Thames Valley the prominence of particular species has generally been related to more long-standing traditions linked to the different elevations of the Valley (Wilson 1978; Robinson 1992; Lambrick 1992). The high percentage of horses at early Roman Old Shifford Farm, for example, is thought to be part of a trend in horse rearing seen at other low-lying settlements situated on the floodplain and first gravel terrace (Hey 1996: 170).

The butchered bones at Barton Court Farm and Old Shifford Farm (the record of butchery marks on the bones from Roughground Farm is at present inconclusive) indicate that animals

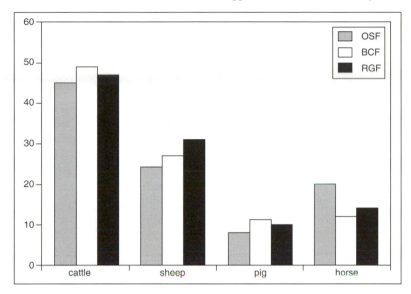

Figure 7.7 Percentages of identified early Roman animal species.

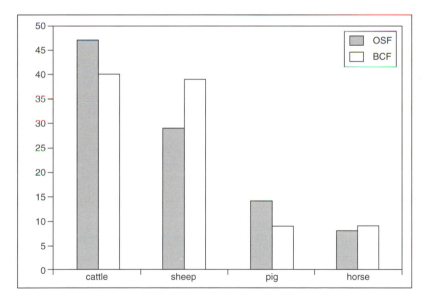

Figure 7.8 Percentages of identified late Iron Age animal species.

were separated into joints of meat using choppers and knives (Wilson 1986; Lange 1996). Fragments of knives have been recovered at Old Shifford Farm. There are also indications that bones were split for their marrow and that tongue, cheek meat and possibly the brain were also consumed. At Old Shifford only a small number of bones have cut marks and they were found primarily in the early Roman phase. These cut marks occurred mainly on the bones of cattle, and appear to represent the removal of skin and cheek meat and particularly the dismemberment of body parts. Although the points at which the bones were disarticulated are similar at both Old

Shifford and Barton Court farms, the methods used in separating the bones of the four main domesticates was more varied at Barton Court Farm where bones were chopped and cut in more or less equal measure. By the early Roman period there are suggestions that at Barton Court Farm more of the meat was filleted, while at Old Shifford Farm in each phase the evidence indicates pot cooking and roasting on the bone. Pig and horse were butchered in each phase at both Barton Court and Old Shifford, although the butchery of horses is more evident at both settlements in the early Roman period. Fewer of the major meat-bearing bones (vertebral column, humerus, femur, scapular, innominate bones – after Lange 1996) were butchered at Old Shifford, which suggests that horses were perhaps more consistently eaten at Barton Court Farm (although see p. 113 below). Initial observations of horse bones at Roughground Farm also indicate a comparatively large proportion of high meat yielding bones. The significance of wild species in the diet is inconclusive at this point, deer (all three sites), bird (Old Shifford and Barton Court) and fish bones (at Barton Court) have been recovered in small amounts and each probably contributed to the diet in a small, though not necessarily insignificant, way.

Plants

Plant remains were not recovered at Roughground Farm in the area of the site where the majority of early Roman settlement is evident. Findings in contexts associated with second-century villa layers indicating small numbers of spelt wheat are of interest, but are inconclusive in terms of what was being processed and/or consumed at the earlier settlement. Certainly the processing and consumption of grain was of particular significance to the settlement as seen in the deposit of querns in one area of the settlement (see p. 113 below). The two charred samples from a pit and a hearth at late Iron Age Barton Court Farm (no early Roman plant material was recovered) and the sixteen samples from the ditches and gullies at Old Shifford provide a small sampling of the types of plants that may have been consumed. At Barton Court Farm the two carbonized samples are dominated by cereals, with very small amounts of chaff and a variety of weed species. The most common cereal was spelt wheat, followed by six-row barley, bread wheat and small amounts of emmer wheat (Jones 1986). The presence of bread wheat in sizeable amounts is notable as its cultivation in the Valley is restricted; it is more labour intensive and has been associated with the more affluent segments of society (Jones 1989: 133; Allen *et al.* 1993: 176). At Old Shifford Farm, of the samples with more than twenty items, many could only be identified as arable. As with Barton Court Farm barley and wheat were the two most common cereals, with barley only slightly outnumbering wheat (only spelt wheat and six-row barley were identified to species); oats and small amounts of flax were present. The overall assemblage was also dominated by cereals, small amounts of chaff and a wide variety of weed species (Robinson 1996). The early Roman samples have higher numbers of cereals and chaff than in the earlier phases, but the numbers of items in each sample is generally small. The weed species for both settlements include edible weeds which allude to some of the possible variety of the diet (for criticism of how 'native' diet is generally portrayed see Reynolds 1995). Some of the species that may have been consumed include fat hen, common orache (Old Shifford and Barton Court) and black bindweed (Barton Court). Celtic bean was also found at Barton Court Farm, as was sorrel and knotgrass which are also used as dyes. Opium poppy was found in early Roman contexts at Old Shifford, which could have been used in the production of oil or possibly medicinally. Mint, parsley and wild turnip were also identified at the early Roman settlement. As to whether the two settlements were importers or producers of cereals, it is difficult to say; the plant specialists suggest that both are possibilities (Jones 1986; Robinson 1996; see also van der Veen 1991). What we can assume is that cereals and possibly other edible plant species were processed (querns have been recovered at both Old Shifford and Roughground Farms) and consumed on site.

CONTAINERS, INGREDIENTS, AND THEIR CONTEXTS

In between the recovery and identification of pottery, plants and animal bones, and the establishment of an economic basis for settlements, are the specific acts of eating, drinking and the rituals surrounding these everyday actions. The role that pottery plays in the actual distribution of food and drink is a relatively recent – and according to many pottery specialists long overdue (Howard 1981: 8; Sherratt 1987; Evans 1993: 95; Willis 1997; Rush 1997; Darling 1989) – factor in pottery analysis. Alternative explanations for characteristic animal and plant assemblages which take into account the possible importance of consumption and, for example, feasting, are also being offered (Gilbert and Singer 1982; Schuster Keswani 1994: 261; Rackham 1987: 47–8; Hansen 1991; Butler 1995; Hill 1995). The reconsideration of pot, bone and plant assemblages is particularly significant to small settlements, such as those in this study, which in spite of quite lengthy periods of occupation, often have modest assemblages and correspondingly small sample sizes. Instead of apologizing for the sizes of their samples, archaeologists are now considering the significance of their contextual configurations (Hill 1989, 1995). What follows is a selection of some of the more notable contextual associations recovered at the three sites in this study.

'Distinctive' deposits

At late Iron Age Barton Court Farm there are indications that the remains of particular meals – hearth stones, decorated bowls, beakers and articulated animal remains – were deposited in pits in and around one particular house site in the northern section of the settlement. At the reconfigured early Roman settlement, pits were less common and those that contained the possible remains of meals and/or libations were situated primarily at the periphery of the settlement away from the single house site, with the exception of a pit located inside the structure which contained serving ware. At early Roman Roughground Farm, west of the main living area, are a series of pits containing still functional rotary querns and pestles/hammerstones (one context for example has seven of these objects); a small selection of local jars and bowls; and significant numbers of animal bones. It is possible that these pits contain the remains of feasting with an agrarian theme. The contrast in types of artefacts that accompanied some of the deposits at early Roman Barton Court Farm (Roman pottery, brooches and coins) and Roughground Farm (local pottery and querns) is also notable. At low-lying Old Shifford Farm there was only a scattering of pits and they contained no animal bones and only one sherd of pottery. The absence of isolated groups of remains affects the identification of specific meals and/or events. However, it reinforces the importance of other features at the settlement when considering distinctive deposits. For example, do the limited amount of cut marks found primarily on cattle bones at early Roman Old Shifford indicate the special preparation of these animals before they were consumed? The correlation of separating bones through cutting through the ligaments, with the traditions of the Iron Age (Grant 1989: 141), is, in this context, particularly suggestive. Another possibility concerns the consumption of particular species in particular areas of the settlement. The eating of horse meat is less conclusive at both late Iron Age and early Roman Old Shifford Farm, except in the early Roman D-shaped house enclosure in which butchered meat-bearing bones and burnt bones have been found. It is possible that on occasion, at a time when they were gaining importance at the settlement, horses were also consumed. At Barton Court Farm, evidence for the butchery of horses was also minimal for the late Iron Age, but in the early Roman period butchered meat-bearing bones were found at the periphery of the settlement. The suggestion at both settlements is that at certain times and in certain places the eating of, and preparations for consumption of, particular species was differentiated.

At all three sites it is perhaps the accumulated material from the gullies and the ditches that provides images of some of the rituals of daily living. In both the late Iron Age and early Roman phases of Old Shifford Farm, pottery with cooking residues, meat-bearing animal bones, burnt bones, and clay oven fragments were concentrated around what are thought to be house enclosures, especially at the entrances. In the early Roman phase, increasing amounts of cereals were recovered from contexts associated with the two suggested house sites. Similar types of evidence for cooking, eating and drinking around the house sites was recovered at early Roman Roughground Farm and late Iron Age Barton Court Farm. Barton Court Farm has very little early Roman period food remains around the house itself, in contrast to Old Shifford Farm and Roughground Farm. The few artefacts and remains associated directly with the house are quite distinctive and include vessels linked to the serving of food (samian and non-samian shallow bowls and dishes); two door keys (signifying perhaps that doors were at times locked); and head and feet bones of various species deposited in the foundation slots of the structure. The absence of external hearths suggests that activities often associated with the house, such as cooking, were probably taking place inside; however, most of the residues from these activities, especially evidence of feasting, were situated at the boundaries of the settlement in the enclosure ditches. The deposition of the remnants of habitation and of eating and drinking is of course far from straightforward, and the vagaries of the archaeological record require that we do not take each context literally. It is for instance conjectured that domestic material in circular gullies and rectangular slots indicate house sites. If these features do not represent house sites, it is interesting that domestic material accumulated at the entrances of gullies and enclosures at each settlement except at early Roman Barton Court Farm, where there was the selective distribution of body parts in the foundation slots (see Parker Pearson 1996 on the importance of entrances in the Iron Age). It is these apparently distinctive concentrations of artefacts and remains that help to situate acts of eating and drinking within the context of tradition, mores and outside forces that govern the whole cycle of consumption, including procurement and discard (Barrett 1989; see Hill 1995; Grant 1991 for the rituals of 'ordinary' rubbish).

'Distinctive' settlements

Stepping back for a moment to consider the wider implications of some of these observations, I have approached early Roman period dietary and culinary practices from the position that the three sites housed people who were subject to direct and indirect forces of imperialism. Such a stance has a strong bearing on my interpretation of the three settlements and has led me to question the association of change with the concept of romanization. I have instead placed greater significance on the relationship between the restructuring of the settlements and the apparent changes in consumption practices.

Old Shifford Farm went from a non-enclosed settlement in the late Iron Age to an enclosed settlement with defined entrances by the early Roman period. Although the settlement was redefined, possibly reinforced, there are suggestions that some of the pre-existing customs and traditions that surround eating and drinking were also reinforced. The containers that held the ingredients, though increasingly wheel-made, were in each phase locally acquired and do not appear to diversify through time; the few pots from outside the local area were handmade and non-romanized. In each phase the remains of eating and drinking were concentrated around the house sites, although in the early Roman period there are indications that the two house sites may have been distinct from each other. Chaff was not recovered in the cereal samples in the more rectangular house site but was present in samples in the D-shaped house site. The only rotary quern was also recovered from this context. It was also in the D-shaped enclosure that the strongest evidence for the consumption of horse meat was recovered. This suggests that there might have been specialized areas for either preparing or possibly consuming food which may relate to the gender, age or rank of particular inhabitants (see Parker Pearson 1996). The narrow range in pottery might indicate the use of other types of containers (although see Evans 1989: 180), or possibly reflect the status of the inhabitants, although, in the context of the changes in settlement, the apparent indifference to, or total rejection of, Roman-like pottery (Timby 1996: 129) and the possible rejection of the consumption practices that are associated with them, is quite striking.

At Barton Court Farm, the settlement was also reconfigured in the early Roman period and entrances to the settlement appear similarly controlled. The arrangement of the living area of the settlement, however, changed dramatically. The two late Iron Age house sites, each with associated buildings, were in the early Roman period consolidated into a single, large rectangular structure. Roman-type pottery was utilized, and evidence of serving wares appears more clearly defined, including the use of small cups suggesting a different drinking practice. It is possible to view these changes in a number of ways. The adoption of a rectangular structure, the embracing of romanized dining practices, increases in the consumption of beef, and changes in the public rituals of consumption, could mark the rejection of the past and an acceptance of life under the Romans. An alternative explanation, one that is perhaps less mainstream, might view many of the changes as evidence that the inhabitants felt the need to protect the home. The apparent consolidation of 'the house' within a single building suggests that interaction between household members was also consolidated. The definition of public and private spaces, the possibility of locked doors, special(?) deposits of head and feet bones in the foundations slots of the house, the continued use of beakers and other specialized Iron Age wares, and the emphasis on settlement entrances and boundaries suggest that the relationship between the household and those outside of the household was being renegotiated. The adoption of specific Roman-like symbols may, therefore, have been integral to the protection of the settlement (see Lyons 1996; also comments by Mattingly 1997; Hingley 1997).

The limits of the Roman settlement at Roughground Farm are difficult to define and interpret, although the main living area was enclosed by a rectangular ditch. The site was not occupied in the late Iron Age, which makes the construction of a circular house particularly interesting when compared to examples of rectangular structures at neighbouring settlements (e.g. Claydon Pike which was occupied in both the late Iron Age and in the early Roman period). The positioning of an elaborate burial site next to an early Iron Age circular structure towards the end of the lifetime of the early Roman settlement is particularly suggestive. It is also interesting that of the three sites in this study it is only at Roughground Farm that occupation in the Roman period was continuous. Indeed, the site has a long history of villa construction which began with the demise of the early Roman settlement in the second century. Elements of both Barton Court Farm and Old Shifford Farm can be found at the early Roman period settlement. Residues of cooking, eating and drinking around the house site are similar to the patterning of artefacts and remains encountered at Old Shifford Farm. The range in pottery and the use of Roman-like containers, especially to prepare and serve food, are reminiscent of Barton Court Farm, and both settlements adopt customs associated with individualized drinking. It is a moot point as to whether the use of Roman-type pottery represents the active desire to emulate 'Roman' consumption practices, or is merely illustrative of what was available in the marketplace (Freeman 1993: 444; Cooper 1996). Clearly, we need to consider how the presence of Roman-style goods sits with other aspects of the settlement (Clarke 1996: 83). Why, for instance, was Roman-style pottery not recovered in the immediate vicinity of the house site or in the more distinctive deposits? Allen has suggested that the deposits of querns might have had a 'propitiatory significance' relating to the reorganization of the settlement and the establishment of a villa in the second century (Allen *et al.* 1993: 161).

As with the other two native sites, Roughground Farm is difficult to typecast; however, what is evident is that the establishment of a villa was a sufficiently important event to demand the commemoration of particular aspects of the past. Whether the movement from rounded to rectangular was done in celebration or with trepidation is at present difficult to ascertain.

CONCLUSION

The settlements in this study do not present a unified native voice. They were probably occupied at slightly different times and probably housed people of differing status with different agendas, different appetites and consequently different experiences of imperialism. Unfortunately, terms such as 'romanization' and 'native continuity' constrict the consideration of the variety of ways that people might have reacted to the conquest. The presence or absence of Roman-like structures and material culture must be contextualized. However, in order to recognize evidence of the experiences of imperialism, especially evidence for resistance, this evidence must first be acknowledged. Only then can it be 'seen' in the archaeological record. It was established earlier that this chapter is an account of work in progress. I am therefore in that most enviable of positions where observations are not yet expected to be conclusive. However, it should be apparent that I see a number of the changes in settlement pattern and consumption practices at the three sites in this study as evidence of a form of household resistance to the Romans. The recognition of resistance has not yet entered the mainstream of Romano-British archaeology (Webster 1996: 5); and while I do not expect everyone to see resistance in the above accounts I hope that I have presented a case for the reconsideration of how native settlements might have responded to encroachment by the Romans through conquest.

I began this chapter by suggesting how one of the obstacles to studying households in the Upper Thames Valley – the poor preservation of houses – can be partially resolved through focusing on more indirect evidence of human habitation. More than just a practical exercise in house detecting, this chapter has shown how the search for houses can provide a completely different perspective on the archaeological household by illustrating the need to both integrate the remains of habitation and consider the movement of people beyond the house.

ACKNOWLEDGEMENTS

I would like to thank Paul Booth, Jane Webster, Nick Cooper and Pim Allison for their invaluable comments on an earlier draft of this chapter. Conversations and correspondence with Tim Allen, David Jennings, Priscilla Lange, David Miles, Jane Timby and Bob Wilson have also contributed to this study, although any errors or omissions are my own. Thanks also to Colin Merony and Barbara Meadows for the drawing of Figures 7.1–5.

NOTES

1 I use the term 'villa-like' in much the same way that I use 'Roman-like' below, which is to acknowledge the malleability of Roman-style constructs in Roman Britain.
2 The two phases of late Iron Age pottery and bones were consequently consolidated to increase the size of each sample.
3 It is possible that wood and/or glass containers were used at each settlement. Contemporaneous, though non-stratified, fragments of glass bottles have been identified at Roughground Farm (Allen *et al.* 1993), and at Old Shifford Farm clay plates were recovered that may have been used to cover wooden containers (Hey 1996: 138).

BIBLIOGRAPHY

Allen, T. G. (1990) *An Iron Age and Romano-British Enclosed Settlement at Watkins Farm, Northmoor, Oxon*, Oxford: Thames Valley Landscapes: the Windrush Valley 1, Oxford: Oxford University Committee for Archaeology.

Allen, T. G., Miles, D. and Palmer, P. (1984) 'Iron Age buildings in the Upper Thames Region', in B. W. Cunliffe and D. Miles (eds) *Aspects of the Iron Age in Central Southern Britain*, Oxford: University of Oxford Committee Monograph 2: 89–101.

Allen, T. G., Darvill, T., Green, S. and Jones, M. (1993) *Excavations at Roughground Farm, Lechlade, Gloucestershre: A Prehistoric and Roman Landscape*, Oxford: The Oxford University Committee for Archaeology.

Barrett, J. C. (1989) 'Food, Gender and Metal: Questions of Social Reproduction', in M. L. Sorensen and R. Thomas (eds) *The Bronze–Iron Transition*, Oxford: British Archaeological Reports, International Series S483: 304–20.

—— (1997) 'Romanization: A Critical Comment', in D. J. Mattingly (ed.) *Dialogues in Roman Imperialism: Power, Discourse, and Discrepant Experience in the Roman Empire*, Portsmouth, R.I.: Journal of Roman Archaeology Supplementary Series no 23: 51–64.

Blagg, T. F. C. (1990) 'First-century Roman houses in Gaul and Britain', in T. F. C Blagg and M. Millett (eds) *The Early Roman Empire in the West*, Oxford: Oxbow Books: 194–209.

Blanton, R. E. (1994) *Houses and Households: A Comparative Study*, New York: Plenum Press.

Boast, R. and Evans, C. (1986) 'The Transformation of Space: Two Examples from British Prehistory', *Archaeological Review from Cambridge* 5, 2: 193–205.

Booth, P. (in prep.) 'Quantifying Status, Some Pottery Data from the Upper Thames Valley'.

Brumfield, E. M. (1987) 'Consumption and Politics at Aztec Huexotla', *American Anthropology* 89: 676–86.

Butler, S. (1995) 'Post-processual Palynology', *Scottish Archaeological Review* 9–10: 15–21.

Clarke, S. (1996) 'Acculturation and Continuity: Re-assessing the Significance of Romanization in the Hinterlands of Gloucester and Cirencester', in J. Webster and N. Cooper (eds) *Roman Imperialism: Post-Colonial Perspectives*, Leicester: Leicester Archaeology Monographs no. 3: 71–69.

Cooper, N. J. (1996) 'Searching for the Blank Generation: Consumer Choice in Roman and Post-Roman Britain', in J. Webster and N. Cooper (eds) *Roman Imperialism: Post-Colonial Perspectives*, Leicester: Leicester Archaeology Monographs no. 3: 85–98.

Costin, C. L. and Earle, T. (1989) 'Status Distinction and Legitimation of Power as Reflected in Changing Patterns of Consumption in Late Prehispanic Peru', *American Antiquity* 54: 691–714.

Dannell, G. G. (1979) 'Eating and Drinking in Pre-conquest Britain: The Evidence of Amphora and Samian Trading, and the Effect of the Invasion of Claudius', in B. C. Burnham and H. B. Burnham (eds) *Invasion and Response: The Case of Roman Britain*, Oxford: British Archaeological Reports, British Series 73: 177–84

Darling, M. J. (1989) 'Nice Fabric, Pity About the Form', *Journal of Roman Pottery Studies* 2: 98–101.

Dietler, M. (1990) 'Driven by Drink: The Role of Drinking in the Political Economy and the Case of Early Iron Age France', *Journal of Anthropological Archaeology* 9: 352–406.

Drury, P. J. (ed.) (1982a) *Structural Reconstruction. Approaches to the Interpretation of the Excavated Remains of Buildings*, Oxford: British Archaeological Reports, British Series 110.

—— (1982b) 'Introduction', in P. J. Drury (ed.) *Structural Reconstruction. Approaches to the Interpretation of the Excavated Remains of Buildings*, Oxford: British Archaeological Reports, British Series 110: 1–5.

Evans, C. (1989) 'Perishables and Worldly Goods – Artefact Decoration and Classification in Light of Wetland Research', *Oxford Journal of Archaeology* 8, 2: 179–201.

Evans, J. (1993) 'Pottery Function and Fine wares in the Roman North', *Journal of Roman Pottery Studies* 6: 95–118.

Ferrell, G. (1995) 'Space and Society: New Perspectives on the Iron Age of North-east England', in J. D. Hill and C. G. Cumberpatch (eds) *Different Iron Ages: Studies on the Iron Age in Temperate Europe*, Oxford, British Archaeological Reports International Series 602: 129–47.

Freeman, P. W. M. (1993) '"Romanisation" and Roman material culture', *Journal of Roman Archaeology* 6: 438–45.

Fulford, M. (1992) 'Iron Age to Roman: A Period of Radical Change on the Gravels', in M. Fulford and E. Nichols (eds) *Developing Landscapes of Lowland Britain. The Archaeology of the British Gravels: A Review*, London: The Society of Antiquaries of London, Occasional Papers 14: 23–38.

Gaffney, V. and Tingle, M. (1989) *The Maddle Farm Project. An Integrated Survey of Prehistoric and Roman Landscapes on the Berkshire Downs*, Oxford: British Archaeological Reports, British Series 200.

Gilbert, A. S. and Singer, B. H. (1982) 'Reassessing Zooarchaeological Quantification', *World Archaeology* 14, 1: 21–40.

Grant, A. (1989) 'Animals in Roman Britain', in M. Todd (ed.) *Research on Roman Britain – 1960–1989*, London: Society for the Promotion of Roman Studies (Britannia Monograph Series no. 11): 135–46

—— (1991) 'Economic or Symbolic? Animal and Ritual Behaviour', in P. Garwood, D. Jennings, R. Skeates and J. Toms (eds) *Sacred and Profane*, Oxford University Committee for Archaeology Monograph no. 32, Oxford: Oxbow Books: 109–14.

Hansen, J. M. (1991) 'Beyond Subsistence: Behavioural Reconstruction from Palaeoethnobotany', *Archaeological Review from Cambridge* 10, 1: 53–9.

Haselgrove, C. (1984) 'Comment on Hingley', *Scottish Archaeological Review* 3: 27–30.

—— (1989) 'The Later Iron Age in Southern Britain and Beyond', in M. Todd (ed.) *Research on Roman Britain – 1960–1989*, London: Society for the Promotion of Roman Studies (Britannia Monograph Series no. 11): 1–18.

Hastorf, C. A. (1990) 'The Effect of the Inka State on Sausa Agricultural Production and Crop Production', *American Antiquity* 55, 2: 262–90.

—— (1991) 'Gender, Space, and Food in Prehistory', in J. M. Gero and M. W. Conkey (eds) *Engendering Archaeology: Women and Prehistory*, Oxford: Basil Blackwell: 132–59.

Hey, G. (1996) 'Iron Age and Roman Settlement at Old Shifford Farm, Standlake', *Oxonensia* LXI: 93–175.

Hill, J. D. (1989) 'Re-thinking the Iron Age', *Scottish Archaeological Review* 6: 16–24.

—— (1995) *Ritual and Rubbish in the Iron Age of Wessex: A Study on the Formation of a Specific Archaeological Record*, Oxford: British Archaeological Report, British Series 242.

Hingley, R. (1984a) 'The Archaeology of Settlement and the Social Significance of Space', *Scottish Archaeological Review* 3: 22–7.

—— (1984b) 'Toward Social Analysis in Archaeology: Celtic Society in the Iron Age of the Upper Thames Valley (400–0 BC)', in B. W. Cunliffe and D. Miles (eds) *Aspects of the Iron Age in Central Southern Britain*, Oxford: University of Oxford Committee for Archaeology Monograph no. 2: 72–88.

—— (1988) 'The Influence of Rome on Indigenous Social Groups in the Upper Thames Valley', in R. F. J. Jones, J. H. F. Bloemers, S. L. Dyson and M. Biddle (eds) *First Millennium Papers: Western Europe in the First Millennium AD*, Oxford: British Archaeological Reports, International Series 401: 73–98.

—— (1989) *Rural Settlement in Roman Britain*, London: Seaby.

—— (1990) 'Domestic Organisation and Gender Relations, in Iron Age and Romano-British Households' in R. Samson (ed.) *The Social Archaeology of Houses*, Edinburgh: Edinburgh University Press: 125–47.

—— (1996) 'The "Legacy" of Rome: The Rise, Decline, and Fall of the Theory of Romanization', in J. Webster and N. Cooper (eds) *Roman Imperialism: Post-Colonial Perspectives*, Leicester: Leicester Archaeology Monographs no. 3: 35–48.

—— (1997) 'Resistance and Domination: Social Change in Roman Britain', in D. J. Mattingly (ed.) *Dialogues in Roman Imperialism: Power, Discourse, and Discrepant Experience in the Roman Empire*, Portsmouth, R.I.: Journal of Roman Archaeology Supplementary Series no. 23: 81–100.

Hodder, I. (1989) 'Writing Archaeology: Site Reports in Context', *Antiquity* 63: 268–74.

Howard, H. (1981) 'In the Wake of Distribution: Towards an Integrated Approach to Ceramic Studies in Prehistoric Britain', in H. Howard and E. L. Morris (eds) *Production and Distribution: A Ceramic Viewpoint*, Oxford: British Archaeological Reports, International Series 120: 1–30.

Jones, B. and Mattingly, D. (1990) *An Atlas of Roman Britain*, Oxford: Blackwell.

Jones, M (1986) 'The Carbonised Plant Remains', in D. Miles (ed.) *Archaeology at Barton Court Farm, Abingdon, Oxfordshire*, Oxford: Oxford Archaeological Unit Report 3, Council for British Archaeology Research Report no. 50, fiche 9: A1–B5.

—— (1989) 'Agriculture in Roman Britain: The Dynamics of Change', in M. Todd (ed.) *Research on Roman Britain – 1960–1989*, London: Society for the Promotion of Roman Studies (Britannia Monograph Series no. 11): 127–34.

—— (1991) 'Food Production and Consumption – Plants', in R. F. J. Jones (ed.) *Roman Britain: Recent Trends*, Sheffield: J. R. Collis Publications: 21–7.

Jones, S. (1997) *The Archaeology of Ethnicity: Constructing Identities in the Past and the Present*, London: Routledge.

King, A. C. (1991) 'Food Production and Consumption – Meat', in R. F. J. Jones (ed.) *Roman Britain: Recent Trends*, Sheffield: J. R. Collis Publications: 15–20.

Lambrick, G. (1992) 'The Development of Late Prehistoric and Roman Farming on the Thames Gravels', in M. Fulford and E. Nichols (eds) *The Archaeology of the British Gravels: A Review*, London: The Society of Antiquaries of London, Occasional Papers vol. 14: 78–105.

Lambrick, G. and Robinson, M. (1979) *Iron Age and Roman Riverside Settlements at Farmoor, Oxfordshire*, Oxford: Oxford Archaeological Unit Report 2 and Council for British Archaeology Research Report 32.

Lange, P. (1996) 'The Animal Bones', in G. Hey (ed.) 'Iron Age and Roman Settlement at Old Shifford Farm, Standlake', *Oxonensia* LXI: 93–175.

Lyons, D. (1996) 'The Politics of House Shape: Round vs. Rectangular Domestic Structures in Dela Compounds, Northern Cameroon', *Antiquity* 70: 351–67.

Maltby, M. (1981) 'Iron Age, Romano-British and Anglo-Saxon Animal Husbandry – A Review of the Faunal Evidence', in M. Jones and G. Dimbleby (eds) *The Environment of Man: The Iron Age to Anglo-Saxon period*, Oxford: British Archaeological Reports, British Series 87: 155–203.

Mattingly, D. J. (1997) 'Dialogues of Power and Experience in the Roman Empire', in D. J. Mattingly (ed.) *Dialogues in Roman Imperialism: Power, Discourse, and Discrepant Experiences in the Roman Empire*, Portsmouth, R.I.: Journal of Roman Archaeology Supplementary Series no. 23: 7–24.

Meadows, K. I. (1994) 'You Are What You Eat: Diet, Identity and Romanisation', in S. Cottam, D. Dungworth, S. Scott and J. Taylor (eds) *Proceedings of the Fourth Annual Theoretical Roman Archaeology Conference*, Oxford: Oxbow Books: 133–40.

—— (1997) 'Much Ado About Nothing: The Social Context of Eating and Drinking in Early Roman Britain', in C. Cumberpatch and P. Blinkhorn (eds) *Not So Much a Pot More a Way of Life: Recent Approaches to Artefact Studies*, Oxford: Oxbow Books: 21–35.

Miles, D. (1982) 'Confusion in the Countryside: Some Comments from the Upper Thames Region', in D. Miles (ed.) *The Romano-British Countryside: Studies in Rural Settlement and Economy*, Oxford: British Archaeological Reports, British Series 103(i): 53–79.

—— (1986a) 'The Iron Age', in G. Briggs, J. Cook and T. Rowley (eds) *The Archaeology of the Oxford Region*, Oxford: Oxford University Department for External Studies: 49–57.

—— (1986b) *Archaeology at Barton Court Farm, Abingdon, Oxfordshire*, Oxford: Oxford Archaeological Unit Report 3, Council for British Archaeology Research Report no. 50.

—— (1989) 'Villas and Variety: Aspects of Economy and Society in the Upper Thames Landscape', in K. Branigan and D. Miles (eds) *Villa Economies*, Sheffield: University of Sheffield Press: 60–71.

Miles, D. and Palmer, S. (1983) 'Claydon Pike', *Current Archaeology* 86: 88–92.

Miller, D. (1985) *Artefacts as Categories: A Study of Ceramic Variability in Central India*, Cambridge: Cambridge University Press.

Millett, M. (1979) 'An Approach to the Functional Interpretation of Pottery', in M. Millett (ed.) *Pottery and the Archaeologist*, London: Institute of Archaeology Occasional Publication no. 4: 35–48.

—— (1990) *The Romanization of Britain*, Cambridge: Cambridge University Press.

Okun, M. L. (1989) *The Early Roman Frontier in the Upper Rhine Area*, Oxford: British Archaeological Reports, International Series 547.

Payne, S. (1972) 'On the Interpretation of Bone Samples from Archaeological Sites', in E. S. Higgs (ed.) *Papers in Economic Prehistory*, Cambridge: Cambridge University Press: 65–81.

Parker Pearson, M. (1996) 'Food, Fertility and Front Doors in the First Millennium BC', in T. C. Champion and J. R. Collis (eds) *The Iron Age in Britain and Ireland: Recent Trends*, Sheffield, J. R. Collis Publications: 117–32.

Pryor, F. (1983) 'Gone, But Still Respected: Some Evidence for Iron Age House Platforms in Lowland England', *Oxford Journal of Archaeology* 2, 2: 189–98.

Rackham, J. (1987) 'Practicality and Realism in Archaeological Analysis and Interpretation', in C. F. Gaffney and V. L. Gaffney (eds) *Pragmatic Archaeology: Theory in Crisis?*, Oxford: British Archaeological Reports, British Series 167: 47–69.

Rapoport, A. (1990) 'Systems of Activities and Systems of Settings', in S. Kent (ed.) *Domestic Architecture and the Use of Space*, Cambridge: Cambridge University Press: 9–20.

Reynolds, P. J. (1982) 'Substructure to Superstructure', in P. J. Drury (ed.) *Structural Reconstruction. Approaches to the Interpretation of the Excavated Remains of Buildings*, Oxford: British Archaeological Reports, British Series 110: 173–98.

—— (1995) 'The Food of the Prehistoric Celts', in J. Wilkins, D. Harvey and M. Dobson (eds) *Food in Antiquity*, Exeter: Exeter University Press: 303–15.

Rippengal, R. (1993) 'Villas as a Key to Social Structure: Some Comments on Recent Approaches to the Romano-British Villa and Some Suggestions Towards an Alternative', in E. Scott (ed.) *Theoretical Roman Archaeology: First Conference Proceedings*, Aldershot: Avebury Press: 79–101.

Robinson, M. (1981) 'The Iron Age to early Saxon Environment of the Upper Thames Valley', in M. Jones and G. Dimbleby (eds) *The Environment of Man: the Iron Age to Anglo-Saxon Period*, Oxford: British Archaeological Reports, British Series 87: 251–86.

—— (1992) 'Environmental Archaeology of the River Gravels: Past Achievements and Future Directions', in M. Fulford and E. Nichols (eds) *The Archaeology of the British Gravels: A Review*, London: The Society of Antiquaries of London, Occasional Papers 14: 47–62.

—— (1996) 'Plant and Invertebrate Remains', in G. Hey (ed.) 'Iron Age and Roman Settlement at Old Shifford Farm, Standlake', *Oxonensia* LXI: 93–175.

Rush, P. (1997) 'Symbols, Pottery and Trade', in K. Meadows, C. Lemke and J. Heron (eds) *Proceedings of the Sixth Annual Theoretical Roman Archaeology Conference*, Oxford: Oxbow Books: 55–64.

Schuster Keswani, P. (1994) 'The Social Context of Animal Husbandry in Early Agricultural Societies: Ethnographic Insights and an Archaeological Example from Cyprus', *Journal of Anthropological Archaeology* 13: 255–77.

Scott, E. (1990) 'Romano-British Villas and the Social Construction of Space', in R. Samson (ed.) *The Social Archaeology of House*, Edinburgh: Edinburgh University Presss: 149–72.

Scott, E. and Gaffney V. L. (1987) 'Romano-British Villas: Practical Lessons for Tactical Fieldwork', in C. F. Gaffney and V. L. Gaffney (eds) *Pragmatic Archaeology: Theory in Crisis?*, Oxford: British Archaeological Reports, British Series 167: 83–8.

Scott, S. (1994) 'Patterns of Movement: Architectural Design and Visual Planning in the Romano-British Villa', in M. Locock (ed.) *Meaningful Architecture: Social Interpretation of Buildings*, Aldershot: Avebury Press: 86–98.

Selwood, L. (1984) 'Tribal Boundaries Viewed from the Perspective of Numismatic Evidence', in B. W. Cunliffe and D. Miles (eds) *Aspects of the Iron Age in Central Southern Britain*, Oxford: University of Oxford Committee Monograph 2:191–204.

Sherratt, A. G. (1987) 'Cups that Cheered', in W. H. Waldren and R. C. Kennard (eds) *Bell Beakers of the Western Mediterranean*, Oxford: British Archaeological Reports, International Series 331(i): 81–114.

Smith, J. T. (1978) 'Villas as a Key to Social Structure', in M. Todd (ed.) *Studies in the Romano-British Villa*, Leicester: Leicester University Press: 149–73.

Timby, J. R. (1996) 'The Pottery', in G. Hey (ed.) 'Iron Age and Roman Settlement at Old Shifford Farm, Standlake', *Oxonensia* LXI: 93–175.

Trow, S. D. (1990) 'By the Northern Shores of Ocean: Some Observations on Acculturation Process at the Edge of the Roman World', in T. Blagg and M. Millett (eds) *The Early Roman Empire in the West*, Oxford: Oxbow Books: 103–18.

Van der Veen, M. (1991) 'Consumption or Production? Agriculture in the Cambridgeshire Fens?', in J. Renfrew (ed.) *New Light on Early Farming. Recent Developments in Paleoethnobotany*, Edinburgh: Edinburgh University Press: 349–61.

Webster, J. (1996) 'Roman Imperialism and the "Post Imperial Age"', in J. Webster and N. Cooper (eds) *Roman Imperialism: Post-Colonial Perspectives*, Leicester: Leicester Archaeology Monographs no. 3: 1–17.

Wilk, R. R. (1990) 'The Built Environment and Consumer Decision', in S. Kent (ed.) *Domestic Architecture and the Use of Space*, Cambridge: Cambridge University Press: 34–42.

Willis, S. (1994) 'Roman Imports into Late Iron Age British Societies: Towards a Critique of Existing Models', in S. Cottam, D. Dungworth, S. Scott and J. Taylor (eds) *Proceedings of the Fourth Annual Theoretical Roman Archaeology Conference*, Oxford: Oxbow Books:141–50.

—— (1997) 'Samian: beyond dating', in K. I. Meadows, C. Lemke and Jo Heron (eds) *TRAC 96: Proceedings of the Sixth Annual Theoretical Roman Archaeology Conference Sheffield 1996*, Oxford: Oxbow Books: 38–54.

Wilson, B. (1978) 'The Animal Bones', in M. Parrington (ed.) *The Excavation of an Iron Age Settlement, Bronze Age Ring-Ditches and Roman Features at Ashville Trading Estate, Abingdon, Oxfordshire*, Oxford: Oxfordshire Archaeological Unit and the Council for British Archaeology: 110–39.

—— (1986) 'The Faunal Remains', in D. Miles (ed.) *Archaeology at Barton Court Farm, Abingdon, Oxfordshire*, Oxford: Oxford Archaeological Unit Report 3, Council British Archaeology Research Report no. 50, fiche 8: A1–G14.

Woolf, G. (1993) 'The Social Significance of Trade in Late Iron Age Europe', in S. Scarre and F. Healy (eds) *Trade and Exchange in Prehistoric Europe*, Oxford: Oxbow Books: 211–18.

Chapter Eight

Towards a feminist archaeology of households: Gender and household structure on the Australian goldfields

Susan Lawrence

INTRODUCTION

In arguing for the importance of household studies in archaeology, Wilk and Rathje (1982: 618) point out that the household is 'the most common social component of subsistence, the smallest and most abundant activity group', and by extension, one of the most fundamental units of archaeological analysis. Conkey and Spector (1984) make a similar argument for the fundamental role of gender as a principle which structures human activity and culture, and hence archaeology. Although both gender and households are basic to societies, it is only recently that there has been any explicit archaeological interest in studying the extent to which gender might effect patterns in the material remains of households. However, there is reason to expect that household archaeology could contribute to the archaeology of gender, and that an engendered archaeology could contribute to household studies by providing another point of access into the complex and dynamic nature of households.

An engendered archaeology begins with increasing the visibility of women (McBryde 1993: xi) and households have seemed a logical place to begin because the activities of women are particularly visible in the domestic domain. Tringham (1991: 101) notes that this is because the household is the minimal unit of social reproduction and as a result the presence of women there is guaranteed. She goes on to argue that 'The "household scale of analysis" is the vehicle with which we may possibly make the invisible women of prehistory and their production visible'. Similarly, Hardesty (1994: 136) argues that household analysis should provide important insights into the ways in which principles of gender organized modern western societies. This claim is based on the identification of women with the home in western ideologies since the early nineteenth century. However, there is some need for caution in making the link between households and women, particularly in historical contexts.

The association of women with domestic and men with public, which underlies many current discussions of gender, has its roots in the nineteenth century. Among the middle and upper classes paid work increasingly was done outside the home and by men, and the work that remained within the home was done by women and assumed social rather than economic significance (Cott 1977; Wall 1994; Welter 1966). These roles were idealized and given meaning in the doctrine of separate spheres in which men's work in the public arena and women's work in the private arena was mutually sustaining. These assumptions about gender roles pervade the documents historians and historical archaeologists use as sources, further contributing to the naturalization of the link between women and home. A critical examination of the roles of men and women in both the public and the private spheres challenges not only present paradigms but also overcomes some of the bias in contemporary accounts (McGaw 1989). While a consideration of gender in household studies will unquestionably increase the archaeological visibility of women, paradoxically it will only contribute to a further reification of the link between women and home unless there is an accompanying awareness of women's activities outside the domestic environment and of men's activities within it.

As Conkey (1993: 11) makes clear, feminist archaeology is explicitly not about finding women in the past: rather, it is about challenging and indeed transforming the entire archaeological endeavour by expanding and opening our methods of inquiry, by 'tak[ing] up critical perspectives on the scientistic reconstructions of the past'. That is, she advocates an engendered archaeology that is primarily concerned with modes of discourse. In so doing, Conkey is calling for a move beyond the simple identification of 'female' artefacts and the association of artefacts with particular genders. What is required is a greater awareness of the dynamic nature of gender as a process and its historical specificity (Conkey and Gero 1991: 9–10; Purser 1991: 13; Wylie 1991: 34).

Methodological approaches to the archaeological study of gender are still developing and most continue to be concerned with increasing the visibility of women. It has been repeatedly stated that there is no easy way of 'finding' women in the archaeological record, as there is no easy way of 'finding' men (Conkey 1993: 3; Seifert 1991: 2). However, a fundamental tenet of any feminist archaeology is that gender, like status and other symbolic and social constructs, is neither inaccessible through the archaeological record nor absent from existing discussions about the past (Conkey and Gero 1991: 4; Conkey and Spector 1984; Wylie 1991: 31–3; ibid. 1992: 16). That being the case, methodologies must be devised that facilitate identifying associations between gender and material remains, just as inferences are already made based on associations between artefacts and social status, ethnicity, and power. To make any meaningful and defensible inferences involves establishing the social context of the material remains and under what conditions any associations might pertain. Making such inferences based on the data is a way to begin to examine women's lives in the past satisfactorily and to demonstrate the kind of historical specificity called for.

The inclusion of substantive, data-based analyses is critical if feminist archaeology is to make a lasting contribution because challenging existing discursive structures without 'adding women' is as insufficient a gendered archaeology as is that of doing the archaeology of women without a feminist critical stance. The 1980s and 1990s have been dominated by critical challenges to processual and systemic archaeology, yet as both Engelstad (1991) and Spencer-Wood (1991) have shown, while post-processual and critical archaeology, like feminist archaeology, seek to open space for alternative voices and new means of discourse, neither explicitly includes either gender or women and both are manifestly non-feminist.

Feminist studies of households have taken several forms. There are numerous analyses of the gendered use of space (Chase 1991; Donley-Reid 1987, 1990; Gibb and King 1991; Hodder 1983; Lyons 1989; Small 1991; Tringham 1991), but artefact studies are less common. The latter have approached the problem of methodology from two perspectives. Signature studies have sought to identify archaeological signatures for households occupied by single- and mixed-sex groups. While some of these studies (e.g. Lydon 1993; Starbuck 1994) have been limited to discussions of specific artefacts associated with the presence of women, others have described patterns observed in the entire assemblage at household sites. Seifert (1991, 1994) has used functional categories to compare assemblages from all-female brothels to those of neighbouring working-class family homes in nineteenth-century Washington, DC. Blee (1991) has used similar techniques in a study of households in the American West. She compared assemblages from family households, all-male households and brothels and found that while food preparation, consumption and storage items dominated the family assemblages, the all-male assemblages were dominated by personal and male-specific items, and alcohol items and female-specific items dominated the brothel sites. The kind of pattern delineation attempted in these studies is more useful than observing the presence or absence of individual artefacts linked with a particular sex because the patterns indicate that there are clear and meaningful ways in which gender structures household activity and that these structures are visible archaeologically.

However, such studies are hampered by what Tringham (1991: 97) calls 'a misunderstanding as to what an engendered [archaeology] should comprise'. That misunderstanding consists of a reliance on logical positivism which restricts enquiry to that which can be demonstrated by recourse to a body of 'factual' data. Because signature studies do not move beyond the observable differences in archaeological assemblages, they do not explore the social processes surrounding the assemblages. This is not to say that interpretation is not constrained by the archaeological data, which it must be (Wylie 1992), but rather that interpretation arises out of the details of the data, and is then used to inform broader perspectives. As Kryder-Reid (1994: 97) writes, 'the analysis of gender is not the discovery of a group identity or an artefact assemblage but rather is the discovery of the formation of that identity and the process by which those artefacts are made meaningful'. Broader approaches to the study of gender in household assemblages incorporate such a perspective.

Interpretive studies use the identification of patterns, either in assemblages or groups of artefacts, to examine and make visible gender in social structures. Archaeological data is the starting point for such studies but meaningful analyses are possible even when archaeological data is restricted. In a study of Native Alaskan women's involvement in the fur trade in Russian America for example, Jackson (1994) identifies cloth and clothing paraphernalia as key artefacts for understanding the role of women. However, she is not content merely to use those artefacts to establish the presence of women. Rather, she examines the ways in which women traded cloth, were the recipients of traded cloth, and manufactured garments from the cloth. A numerically insignificant number of archaeologically preserved items provides access to a wide range of key issues related to colonial encounters, and Jackson (ibid.: 49) is able to conclude that 'however few items there are in archaeological assemblages, this complex should not be shortchanged in future examinations of historical sites in Russian America'. Similarly, Kryder-Reid (1994) is able to produce an elegant discussion of the construction of gender roles in an all-male religious community despite being unable to conclusively associate artefacts with groups of residents. Instead, tasks and spaces are identified and linked to gendered roles associated with lay brothers and priests. In this way she is able to demonstrate that in the absence of women, lay brothers took on not only traditionally feminine domestic work but also a female ideology of submissiveness and purity within the community.

Analyses like these expand the potential for the gendered study of households by situating artefacts and assemblages within a broader social context. In this chapter a similar approach is taken in order to discern the role of gender in households on the Australian goldfields in the nineteenth century, and in particular on the Moorabool diggings, a site 60 km west of Melbourne, Victoria (Figure 8.1) and typical of the small, temporary camps that arose on diggings. Archaeologically visible households in the settlement are described and evidence for the presence of women leads to a discussion of the ways in which gender structured household composition,

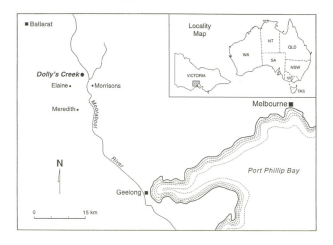

Figure 8.1 The location of Dolly's Creek and Morrisons, collectively known as the Moorabool diggings. Drawn by S. Lawrence, re-drawn on CAD by Ming Wei.

subsistence patterns, and material culture within the settlement. It is argued that this is important not only for identifying women and increasing their visibility but also for facilitating an analysis of gender as a historical process.

THE MOORABOOL DIGGINGS AND THE GOLD RUSH

The gold rush of the nineteenth century was global in extent and unprecedented in scale. The rush began with the discovery of gold in California in 1848 which precipitated a series of discoveries in countries around the Pacific rim. It spanned several generations from the first Californian discoveries to the final rush to the Klondike in 1896 and stimulated mass migrations of people, drawing gold seekers from western Europe and eastern North America and directing them to lands on the edges of expanding colonial territories, including the western United States, western Canada, New Zealand, Australia, and South Africa. These migrations resulted in rapid population growth in the colonial lands, and while much of it was temporary, people remained in sufficient numbers to significantly alter the shape of settlement. California attracted only 400 migrants from the eastern United States in 1848, but in 1849 after the discovery of gold it attracted 90,000 (Holliday 1981: 26). Similarly, in 1851 after fifteen years of European migration to Victoria the population had only grown to 77,000 inhabitants. By 1861, after a decade of gold rushes, the population had risen to 541,000 (Serle 1963: 382).

Gold was discovered in the colony of Victoria in 1851, shortly after discoveries to the north in New South Wales. Both discoveries were made by men who had been on the Californian diggings (Blainey 1963). For the first few months the Victorian rush was confined to a small number of rich diggings around Ballarat, Bendigo and Castlemaine but it was the discovery of gold in a multitude of other locations that really consolidated the colony's role in the gold rush because they perpetuated the excitement and adventure and continued to attract new participants. The immediate effect of the discoveries was to throw the colony into disarray by drawing the existing population to the goldfields and by attracting thousands of immigrants. Over 90,000 people a year arrived in Victoria by sea in 1852 and 1853, and it took several years for any semblance of normalcy to be re-established (Serle 1963: 383–5). Longer-term effects were particularly evident in the economy, and in the size and distribution of the population. The economy became more diversified and a number of industries, including agriculture, metalworking, timber getting, and manufacturing began to challenge the traditional dominance of wool and gold (Bate 1978: 17; Powell 1970: 112; Serle 1963: 230–1). The white population of the colony, which had been small, ethnically British, and thinly distributed, also underwent a number of changes. In the 1850s, the main decade of the rush, it increased in size and saw the addition of significant numbers of people of Chinese, continental European, and American background. In addition, the gold rush drew the population into the interior of the colony and away from the coastal cities and towns. Gold created two major inland cities, many large towns, and countless smaller towns and villages.

Payable gold at Dolly's Creek was announced in April of 1857 and people began moving to the field (*Geelong Advertiser* [GA]; *Reports of the Mining Surveyors* [MSR]). Shortly thereafter gold was

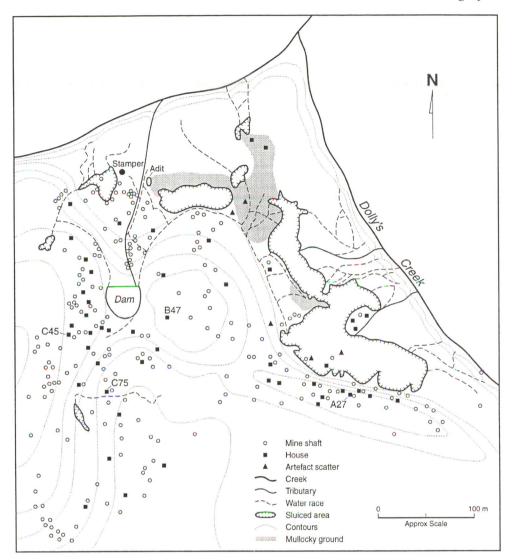

Figure 8.2 The study area of Dolly's Creek.
Drawn by S. Lawrence, re-drawn on CAD by Ming Wei.

also discovered on nearby Tea Tree Creek and at Morrisons along the Moorabool river, and the three together became known as the Moorabool diggings. Between 100 and 200 people went to the diggings at the time of discovery and the population gradually increased to a peak of nearly 700 people in 1861. However, the rush quickly passed leaving only a handful of people on the field throughout the 1860s and 1870s. By the 1880s activity had shifted to deep lead mines along the banks of the Moorabool river at Morrisons and to quartz reefs in the vicinity of Elaine, a few kilometres to the west. Although Morrisons and Elaine continued into the twentieth century, the settlement at Dolly's Creek was virtually abandoned and the area gazetted as a permanent reserve for the growth and preservation of timber in 1888.

Industrially the Moorabool diggings was a small-scale alluvial field with gold-bearing gravels thinly deposited through the region, lying from 0.5 m to 6 m below the surface. In the documentary records the diggings are frequently referred to as a good 'poor man's field'. This was a common term used to describe fields where the returns were low but steady. Diffuse but reasonable quantities of gold made fields like the Moorabool workable for a steady wage but did not produce large fortunes. The deposit was not rich enough to create a massive rush or to sustain a substantial permanent settlement, but it was enough to hold a small number of people for a few years. As a result the settlement was characterized by ephemeral structures and a transient population. People came and went both seasonally and over a period of years as other rushes and other industries provided temporarily more lucrative sources of income. Rates were collected and electoral roles maintained but the settlement was never surveyed or incorporated and the most frequent form of government contact was through the person of the Mining Surveyor.

Archaeological remains of the diggings include the sluices, races and mine shafts of the alluvial workings, as well as at least sixty fireplaces where huts once stood (Figure 8.2). Fieldwork on the site between 1990 and 1992 resulted in the intensive survey and mapping of industrial and domestic remains at the settlement and the excavation of four habitation sites, including dwellings and associated rubbish pits. Altogether nearly 14,000 artefacts were recovered from the 86 m² excavated in total (Lawrence 1995). Written evidence of the community is more fragmentary. Some official government records such as the quarterly *Reports of the Mining Surveyor* provide detailed information about aspects of the community but other records, such as mining leases and manuscript censuses, have been lost or destroyed. The tabulated census for the colony survives and is useful in some years, but in others the Moorabool is grouped with other, larger communities and so becomes invisible. Occasional columns in the *Geelong Advertiser* provide fleeting glimpses of community activity, as do inquests and court cases. Literary sources on the gold rush are abundant and rich, as the period was extensively recorded by contemporaries who wrote letters, diaries, and memoirs, and made sketches and paintings as well. Although none relate specifically to the Moorabool, these more peripheral sources provide contextual information necessary for interpretation.

HOUSEHOLD ARCHITECTURE AND GOODS

Individual households occupied camp sites incorporating one or more small structures made of a combination of calico, timber and stone. During the archaeological survey of the settlement in 1990 sixty-four such camp sites were identified, and four, designated A27, B47, C75 and C45, were selected for excavation. Structures and midden deposits were sampled at each. Variation in architectural forms and amongst the artefact assemblages suggests that two household sites were used solely or primarily for domestic residential purposes and that at the other two sites residential elements and commercial activity were combined. Of the latter sites, one was a residence/pub and one was a residence/pub/store. The distribution of personal artefacts indicates that two of the households included women and at these sites the domestic elements of the assemblages were significantly different to those from the single-sex households.

Rough, temporary structures are characteristic of gold rush architecture. Buildings that were simple in design but highly variable in form and material resulted from the practices of transient miners who employed expedient methods to build, transport, and rebuild homes. Artists and writers have provided many descriptions of homes on the goldfields which indicate what those on the Moorabool may have been like. On the diggings buildings were generally portable and hastily constructed of calico, blankets, timber, bark, and whatever other materials were at hand. The Clacy party at Bendigo in 1852 lived at first in canvas tents purchased in Melbourne and later built a shelter using branches from a nearby tree as tent poles while blankets carried in the swags formed the tent (Clacy 1963: 85). Antoine Fauchery (1965: 60) described his tent of canvas and branch poles as a 'white forage cap'. Pictorial evidence of similar tents is featured in the work of other goldfields artists including S. T. Gill and Edward Snell (Gill 1982; Griffiths 1988). Some impression of the range of buildings on the Moorabool is conveyed in the census of 1861. The census-taker categorized houses by type of building material and by number of rooms and also recorded how many people were living in each type of house. In all, 215 houses housed 619 residents of the diggings (a further sixty-two residents were unaccounted for here). Of these homes, fifty-four were of wood or stone but the majority, 161, were of bark or calico.

Tents were defined in the census as any building with a calico roof, so it is possible that some 'tents' would have had bark or timber walls and glass windows; there was archaeological evidence of this at three of the houses excavated. Most people recorded in the census lived in tents and only 200 people lived in wood or stone buildings. The number of people per house was higher in the wooden buildings, however, with on average 3.7 people living in each building compared to 2.6 people living in each tent. Those figures give a deceptive impression of relative crowding because most of the wooden buildings were larger than the calico and bark homes. Of the 161 tents and bark huts, only forty had more than one room while, of the fifty-four wood or stone buildings, forty-eight had more than one room. It is apparent that

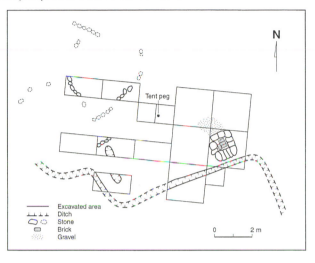

Figure 8.3 Site plan of House C75, Dolly's Creek. Drawn by S. Lawrence, re-drawn on CAD by Ming Wei.

fabric was a significant indicator of capital investment in the settlement. Those people willing to build in the more permanent materials also determined to make the extra effort and bear the extra expense of enlarging their dwellings.

Archaeological evidence provides more detail about the nature of the dwellings. The architectural remains at the two residential-only sites that were excavated are typical of the simple one room tents. The location of the buildings is indicated by the presence of several features, including collapsed quartzite fireplaces, one or more levelled pads cut into the hillsides, and drainage ditches dug around the exterior of the pads. At one site, C75, there is evidence of a single structure, including a fireplace situated at one end of a pad and several drainage ditches (Figure 8.3). At B47 there is evidence of two structures, one of which had a fireplace while the other, a few metres downhill to the west, was erected on a levelled pad with drainage ditches on two sides (Figure 8.4). The pads at C75 and B47 were the same size, 5 × 3.5 m, and the fireplace structure at B47 was of similar dimensions. Nails used in the timber tent frames and tacks used to fasten calico in place were found at both sites, but the presence also of window glass indicates that, while calico may have been used in the walls and roof, there was nevertheless sufficient framing to support at least one window at each structure.

There are two reasons for assuming that the two structures at B47 are part of a single related complex. At all of the sixty-four house sites recorded in the survey there was 50–100 m between nearest neighbours, a distance consistent with the 20 perche (500 m^2) allotments granted under the terms of the Miner's Right, or licence to mine. The proximity of the two structures at B47, which were only 6 m apart, suggests that they were built on the same allotment. In addition only one structure had a fireplace, which also suggests that they were built and used together.

When several miners were working together and sharing accommodation, cooking was often done in a single shared tent with a fireplace, and sleeping tents for individuals did not require fireplaces. Complexes comprised of several tent pads, only one of which had a fireplace, have been documented on California goldfields sites (Tordoff and Seldner 1987: 58–61). Additional tents for sleeping or storage was one way of increasing the available living space, and the presence of two structures rather than one at B47 suggests that greater separation of activities was possible there than at the typical one room dwellings. The census-taker on the Moorabool may have counted the extra tents as extra rooms, as twenty-five tents were listed with more than one room. However, multi-roomed tents could also be purchased by those with extra resources who wished to improve their living conditions. One example, from the Bendigo diggings, was owned by a family group of three adults and one infant who had a tent with 'two nice square apartments with a lobby between and a distinct door to each' (Lane and Serle 1990: 26). One room served as general purpose kitchen/ parlour/dining room, while the other was the bedroom of the married couple and their child. Each room had its own fireplace and the parlour had a window as well.

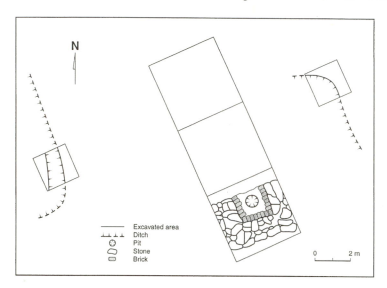

Figure 8.4 Site plan of House B47, Dolly's Creek.
Drawn by S. Lawrence, re-drawn on CAD by Ming Wei.

The tents on the Moorbool were built on hill slopes and at both sites ditches were found that had been dug to channel rainwater away from the interior of the buildings, a practice also referred to in written accounts (Griffiths 1988: 304; Korzelinski 1979: 57). The ditches show how the residents experimented to find the best way of diverting rainwater around the tents. At C75, the first attempt was a shallow scooped ditch dug along the uphill side of the tent. This soon proved inadequate however and a second, longer, ditch was built which lay further from the tent and which carried the water to a point far from the tent itself. This second ditch was deeper than the first and had straight sides and a flat, level base, and was lined with rubble and sheets of iron and tin.

The fireplaces were the dominant architectural feature in both dwellings, occupying one end of the tent, either adjacent to or opposite the door. The fireplaces were built of roughly shaped quartzite blocks held together by mud mortar. They stood about 1 m high and, based on the quantity of rubble found on the sites, probably had wooden or corrugated iron chimneys. Tents on the cold and rainy Ballarat field sketched by Eugene Von Guerard also had fireplaces of cobbles and mud and these were often topped with a barrel to provide additional height for the chimney (Tippin 1982: 21, 51 and pl. XII). It was not necessary to construct a built-in fireplace and from documentary and pictorial sources it can be inferred that many tents had no fireplace (Clacy 1963: 63; Griffiths 1988: 291, 305, 315). Where only a short stay was expected it was more expedient simply to put up a canvas tent and cook outdoors over an open fire. However, fireplaces were commonly built when either long-term or winter occupation was planned. Fireplaces were sometimes made of stones or sods, sometimes of wood, and sometimes of green bullock hides stretched around branches, though the latter varieties often caught fire (Griffiths 1988: 60; Sussex 1989: 24).

At B47, an experienced stone mason built a particularly strong and substantial fireplace. Inside the firebox a single row of bricks laid along the base of the walls provided a convenient ledge on which to rest a grate or a kettle. The fireplace excavated at C75 was not as expertly nor as substantially built as at B47 but it was carefully maintained. The quartzite blocks were held together with a mud mortar made from the local soils and the surface was given a finish of kaolin. Kaolin, or pipeclay, was one of the materials found in the mine shafts on the Moorabool and it must have been brought from the mines to the house. When the pipeclay was combined with water a whitewash was created that was then applied to the fireplace. This practice was common on the diggings. Elsie Bayard, who grew up at Dolly's Creek in the early years of the twentieth century, recalls her mother's daily chore of whitewashing the fireplace with pipeclay brought from her father's mine in a hessian sack (E. Bayard pers. comm.). Other women on other goldfields also cleaned and brightened their homes in this way. One woman on Tasmania's Lisle goldfield recalled that

> The whitest of pipeclay was used as a wash for the fireplaces and housekeepers would search for the best and carefully remove any yellow pieces from their whiting buckets so that the final result would be most immaculately snowy.
>
> (Edwards 1952, quoted in Coroneos 1993: 166)

As the fireplaces physically dominated the tents, whitening them would have significantly lightened the interiors.

These two dwellings on the Moorabool diggings had similar artefact assemblages, in addition to the architectural similarities. Because the settlement was an ephemeral one, the houses were occupied for only short periods of time and there was little opportunity for large quantities of refuse to accumulate. The archaeological deposits are therefore thin and sparse and so artefacts from house floor and midden deposits at each site have been combined for the purposes of analysis. Ceramic cross-mends between the two types of deposit at each site and mean dates for the deposits derived from all datable artefacts were used to establish that they were contemporaneous. The assemblages are characterized by a predominance of architectural items, a large and diverse range of ceramics and faunal remains, a small number of personal items, and comparatively few alcohol bottles.

Architectural items such as nails, tacks, and fragments of window glass made up 77 per cent of the assemblage from B47 and were also the largest category at C75 where 37 per cent of the assemblage was architectural (Table 8.1). Tablewares and faunal remains were also large categories in both assemblages. Ceramic items represented included at least seventeen vessels at B47 and a minimum of forty-three vessels at C75, more vessels than at either of the other two sites. Tablewares, consisting of plates, teacups, saucers and teapots were the most common forms and a small number of food storage and preparation vessels such as jugs and bowls were also represented. There were no toiletry items in either assemblage. All of the tablewares were common, inexpensive earthenwares but the decorative patterns were diverse and colourful. The majority of the forty-three different designs were transfer printed in blue, mauve, sepia, green, or mulberry. Faunal remains, 7 per cent of the assemblage at C75 and 9 per cent of the assemblage at B74, were also diverse and included chicken, cow, goat, pig, and sheep bone. Personal items were present in both assemblages in very small quantities. Buttons, jewellery and footware comprised less than 1 per cent of either assemblage. Alcohol bottles were also represented, but made up less than 10 per cent of the assemblages, in marked contrast to the commercial/residential assemblages at the other two

Table 8.1 Moorabool diggings: distribution of artefacts from excavated house sites

Identification	C75 No.	%	B47 No.	%	A27 No.	%	C45 No.	%
Nails	629	33.5	915	77.5	70	5.53	1,077	14.6
Door hardware	1	0.05	1	0.08	0	0	22	0.3
Window glass	61	3.25	1	0.08	11	0.87	144	1.95
Tableware	193	10.3	51	4.32	20	1.58	154	2.08
Cookware	1	0.05	0	0	0	0	17	0.23
Metal containers	4	0.21	0	0	16	1.26	415	5.61
Glass containers	306	16.3	24	2.03	226	17.9	229	3.1
Ceramic containers	43	2.29	2	0.17	0	0	25	0.34
Soda water bottles	6	0.32	1	0.08	0	0	23	0.31
Condiment bottles	0	0	0	0	0	0	16	0.22
Medicine bottles	9	0.48	1	0.08	0	0	63	0.85
Faunal remains	119	6.35	105	8.9	26	2.05	38	0.51
Lamp parts	0	0	0	0	2	0.16	150	2.03
Furnishings	1	0.05	0	0	0	0	2	0.03
Clothing	6	0.32	3	0.25	0	0	20	0.27
Footware	1	0.05	1	0.08	0	0	17	0.23
Tobacco items	19	1.01	13	1.1	1	0.08	9	0.12
Alcohol items	135	7.2	57	4.83	888	70.1	3,767	51
Ammunition	0	0	1	0.08	0	0	0	0
Horse items	5	0.27	0	0	0	0	6	0.08
Stationery	18	0.96	2	0.17	0	0	3	0.04
Sewing items	2	0.11	1	0.08	0	0	1	0.01
Tools	316	16.9	1	0.08	6	0.47	1,121	15.2
Coins	0	0	0	0	0	0	2	0.03
Total	1,875	100	1,180	100	1,266	100	7,321	100

sites. Only five alcohol bottles and one medicine bottle were represented at B47, while four alcohol bottles and one medicine bottle were represented at C75.

There is nothing about either of these two sites, with their simple canvas buildings, their solid fireplaces, and their diverse artefact assemblages, to suggest that they were anything other than residences. However, at the other two sites both architectural and artefactual evidence indicates that the sites had more specialized functions in addition to domestic activities. At A27 surviving architectural remains indicate that it was a tent structure with a fireplace, similar to those at the domestic sites. The principal difference from those sites is in the artefact assemblage which is dominated by alcohol bottles. A minimum of twenty alcohol bottles and one medicine bottle are represented in the assemblage, 70 per cent of which is alcohol bottle glass. Because of the quantity of bottles the site has been identified as a pub. However, poor preservation of the archaeological remains at this site has made more detailed analysis of either structure or artefacts impossible.

Preservation was much better at the fourth site, C45. This has also been identified as a pub, and possibly one which operated as a shop as well, which was not uncommon on the goldfields. Both the assemblage and the architecture at C45 are markedly different to the residential pattern. The site included at least two buildings, both built partially of stone (Figure 8.5). Only a corner of one building survives but the footings of the other remain in reasonable condition. The latter was a one room structure 3.5 m long and 2 m wide, with at least two glass windows and a wooden door with iron hinges, a lock, and a brass doorknob. Gaps in the stonework and fragments of window glass *in situ* as they had fallen indicated that the door and one window were located along one long wall of the building. A stone and brick fireplace formed the short wall to the right of the door. The lower part of the walls consisted of roughly cut blocks of quartz, quartzite, and conglomerate bound with mud mortar, and would have stood to a height of between 0.5 m and 1 m. Above the stonework the upper part of the walls and the roof were probably made of bark or calico supported by a wooden frame, as is suggested by the presence of nails, tacks and several large iron spikes. Further evidence of the building technique was provided by one fragment of wall covering found. The fragment consisted of multiple layers of differing material. On the exterior was a sheet of tin followed by a layer of stiff embossed cardboard, several layers of newspaper, a layer of hessian, and, finally, on the interior surface, patterned wallpaper (Figure 8.6). The building may have begun as canvas with tin added on the exterior as waterproofing and card, newspaper, and then wallpaper successively added as interior decoration.

The sturdy construction of the buildings at C45 requires some explanation. It would have taken greater time, effort and money to construct such solid structures of stone and wood than to erect the normal canvas dwelling, and whoever did so must have had good reason. Operating a business would be just such a reason, as the strong walls and door would have afforded security which was of particular concern to storekeepers and publicans. Tent stores on the goldfields were frequently robbed by thieves who used knives to cut through the canvas walls at the back of the store and then pulled goods through the holes (Korzelinski 1979: 137). The prevention of robberies would have been a priority for storekeepers and would have justified the use of more substantial construction than was used by ordinary householders. At C45 both the stone around the lower portion of the walls and the strong locks and doors may be seen as security measures taken to protect a shop and its contents.

Further evidence of commercial activities at this site is found in the artefact assemblage. As at A27, a major proportion of the assemblage is alcohol bottle glass, in this case 48 per cent of the assemblage, with at least eighty-five bottles represented. It is this preponderance of alcohol which suggests that the site was a pub. However, the variety and quantity of other goods at C45, including the presence of multiples of many items, has led to its identification as a store as well. Evidence of stock includes five shovels, three wedges, four food tins, four salad oil bottles and six medicine bottles. None of the other assemblages included duplication of items on this scale. Bulk packaging of foodstuffs is also evident in the presence of iron hoops from wooden casks and a brass tap used for dispensing liquids from casks. Other aspects of the assemblage are similar to those at C75 and B47, suggesting that the site had a residential role as well as a commercial one, but it was common for storekeepers to live in their shops (Sussex 1989: 17, 25). Fragmented crockery and faunal remains suggest household rubbish rather than shop goods, and a number of personal items including buttons, jewellery and footwear also suggest a residence.

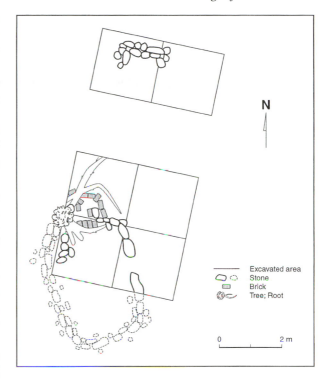

Figure 8.5 Site plan of House C45, Dolly's Creek. Drawn by S. Lawrence, re-drawn on CAD by Ming Wei.

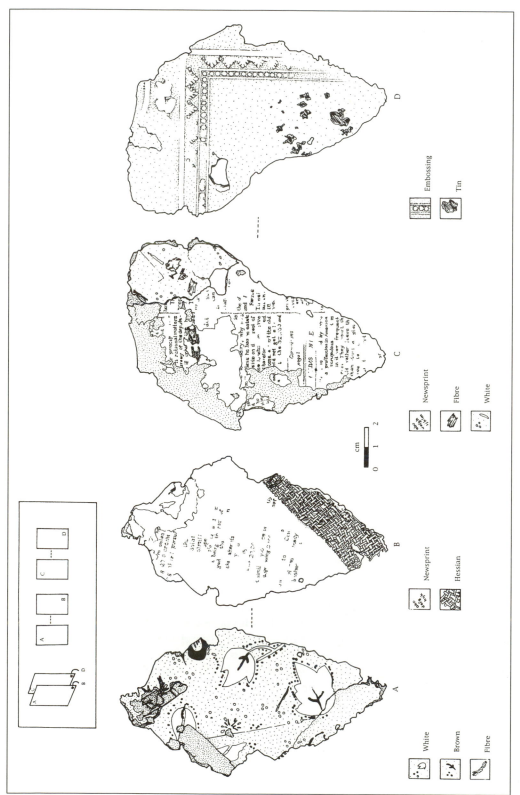

Figure 8.6 Fragment of wall covering from House C45, Dolly's Creek. The fragment is a composite of wallpaper, hessian, newsprint and embossed cardboard. A sheet of tin was attached to the cardboard. Drawing by Michelle Denny.

HOUSEHOLDS WITH WOMEN

The analysis of structures and assemblages from households on the Moorabool diggings has led to the identification of household function, but more interesting are differences in the material life of households that can be correlated with differences in the gender composition of the households. Because dress and adornment are attributes directly related to gender identities, personal artefacts are the clearest archaeological indicators of the presence of men, women, or children. While three of the four household assemblages included personal items, only two included gender-specific items belonging to women. One of the two sites with women's belongings was the residential site C75, where the heel of a woman's shoe and a pressed tin brooch were found, while at the residence/pub/store, C45, a black glass ball button, a pressed tin clasp, and a woman's gold wedding band were found.

The assemblages from the two sites where women's possessions were found were qualitatively different to those at A27 and B47, which further suggests that women were part of the households there rather than simply visitors. In addition to the presence of personal objects belonging to women, both assemblages included a wide range of artefacts associated with home furnishings and tablewares. While the tablewares from the single-sex households consisted only of fragmentary transfer printed underglazed ceramic plates and cups, at C75 they also included a stemmed glass serving dish, two pressed glass bowls, a tumbler, a teapot, and a knife and fork. At C45 tablewares included ceramic plates and cups, glass tumblers, a stemmed glass, a fork and two spoons. Furnishings at C45 included several parts of a kerosene lamp, two different styles of drawer pull and a fragment of wallpaper, while at C75 an ornate cast brass mantel clock case (Figure 8.7) was found and the fireplace was given an interior coating of pipeclay. Neither of the other assemblages contained any furnishing items. The significance of the composition of the assemblages associated with women will be addressed below (pp. 136–8).

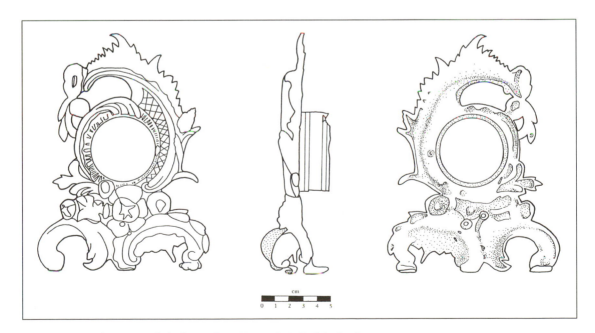

Figure 8.7 Cast brass mantel clock case from House C75, Dolly's Creek. Drawn by Michelle Denny.

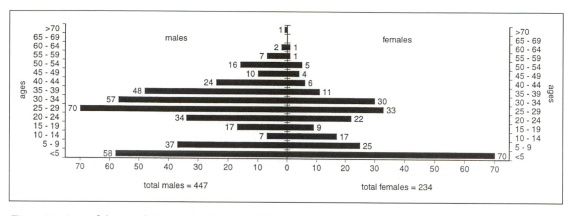

Figure 8.8 Ages of the population on the Moorabool diggings in 1861, based on figures in the Census of Victoria.

The differences between the assemblages at the sites where women's personal goods were found and those where they were not suggest differences in household composition. Two of the households apparently included both women and men and the only members of the other two households were male. While it is possible that women were present at A27 and B47 and their possessions were not recovered during the excavations, it would be expected that if this were the case the remainder of the assemblages would be similar to those at C75 and C45. Instead, there are marked differences in both quality and quantity of goods across a range of categories. For this reason it is argued that, in this case, the absence of women's possessions from two assemblages does indicate that women were not part of those households.

The identification of female-specific items in two of the four assemblages prompted a closer examination of other evidence about the community's residents. Further evidence of the number of women present on the diggings is provided by the Victorian colonial census of 1861, and both artefacts and documents challenge the traditional historical characterization of the gold rush as a predominantly male event (Bate 1978: 21, 41; Blainey 1963; Goodman 1994). In April of 1861 the census-taker recorded that 681 people lived in the settlement, half either women or children below the age of 15 (Figure 8.8). Most of the adults were young, 65 per cent of the men being less than 40 and 86 per cent of the women. Of the 122 adult women 100 stated that they were or had been married. Widows comprised only 2 per cent of the married women in the whole of Grant County, of which Dolly's Creek was a part, and it can be assumed that the number of widows at Dolly's itself was similarly small. As women were less likely than men to be on the diggings without their spouses, it seems probable that the number of married women was close to the number of married men living with their wives on the goldfield. Thus most of the women and a good many of the men were living as part of a couple and most of the couples probably had children, as there were just over two children for every married woman in the settlement and most of the women were of child-bearing age. Although there is no evidence from comparable 'poor man's diggings', evidence from larger towns suggests that this pattern is not unusual for the Victorian fields as a whole (Fahey 1983; Grimshaw and Fahey 1982; Grimshaw and Willet 1980; Philipp 1987).

The number of women and children present had a significant effect on household structure. The census-taker in 1861 also recorded dwellings, of which there were 232 on the Moorabool. With a total population of 681, this suggests an average of 2.9 people per dwelling, and as co-residence is the principal means by which households are identified archaeologically it is assumed that the number of dwellings reflects an equal number of households. Average household size may not adequately reflect household composition however. When the number of couples and children living in nuclear families are considered household size changes to approximately 4.1 people in each nuclear family group and two people in each of the remaining households which were composed primarily of adult males. However, the family households may have been even larger, incorporating unmarried siblings, adult children, and domestic help and, in consequence, the number of single person households smaller. While these figures are speculative, they do provide some indication of the kinds of households that might have been found in the settlement. Other documents provide evidence of the role within the community of kin relationships that linked individual households.

Many historians and anthropologists have shown that in frontier situations connections forged between individuals as the result of marriage are instrumental in both cementing and initiating economic and political relationships (Derry 1992; Purser 1991; Russell 1994). In areas of recent settlement instant extended families of multiple brothers-, sisters-, and cousins-in-law provided social and business contacts and support in times of distress. In such circumstances neither men nor women necessarily experienced gold fields as places of hostile or indifferent strangers. Both sexes frequently travelled in family groups and continued to experience the companionship and support that had been familiar to them before migrating. Derry (1992) has been able to link kin networks with settlement patterns and material culture in frontier Alabama, but the paucity of documentary records precludes that kind of analysis here. However, it is still possible to recapture something of the dense network of kin ties that underlay the otherwise disconnected community structure of the Moorabool, and women's lives in particular were shaped by a network of kin structures that they created and maintained.

Ties of marriage connected the new mining settlement with the pre-existing pastoral community. George Beech Silvester arrived in the mining town of Morrisons in 1859, opened a store, and was made the community's first postmaster (GA 14 June 1859). Nine years later his status in the area was sufficient to enable him to marry Hughina Morrison, daughter of the squatter Hugh Morrison after whom the settlement was named (GA 14 February 1868). Marriage into such an important landowning family no doubt further increased Silvester's prestige in the community. Women from farming families also married men in the mining settlements, incorporating transient gold seekers into the obligation and exchange networks of the agricultural community. The McCormack family provides one example of the rapid creation of a large extended family. Mary McCormack's husband Thomas Haines had come to Morrisons as a miner, although he later took up a selection and became a dairy farmer (Morrison's Cemetery Records). Mary's father and her three brothers were also miners, one of whom, William, married Sarah Lavery whose father John was a farmer at Morrison's (Morrison's Cemetery Records). The marriages of these two women made the Lavery, McCormack and Haines households into a clan, providing workmates and companionship for both men and women.

SUBSISTENCE PATTERNS

Women and also children in the households had implications for the subsistence strategies employed. On the goldfields, subsistence was centred on mining, and 87 per cent of the men recorded in the 1861 census identified themselves primarily as miners. For many, however, mining was only one part of a broader subsistence strategy. Periods on the diggings were frequently interspersed with timber cutting, labouring, or a range of other odd jobs. Men moved between jobs as they moved between diggings, mining on one field, keeping store on the next, or turning to a previous trade. Farming provided another supplement to mining income, particularly after the initial rush period when land was gradually opened for selection. McGowan (1992: 46) reports that on subsistence goldfields in New South Wales the rhythms of the agricultural cycle began to influence the course of mining, and excavated washdirt was left piled on claims during the harvest period as miners worked their selections. Other miners were able to take up selections close to the diggings and could schedule activities at both places during each day as, for example, did one miner in Victoria who spent eight hours a day mining and three hours a day erecting farm buildings and fences (Evans 1975: 45).

The pooled efforts of the entire family were required to make this combination of mining and farming successful. Sons assisted fathers on the mines but the day-to-day running of the farm was commonly the responsibility of mothers and daughters. This pattern is demonstrated by the Lewis family in Victoria and the Lawson family in New South Wales. Both families lived on selections near goldfields and in both cases the men were absent for extended periods prospecting and mining. The women and young children worked on the farms, ploughing and planting, raising cattle for sale, and maintaining dairy herds and vegetable gardens. It was the food and cash from these enterprises rather than income from mining that sustained the families (ibid.: 8–9; Matthews 1987: 113–14).

Archaeological evidence provides further clues about the symbiotic relationship between subsistence mining and subsistence farming. The goldfields diet is popularly characterized as comprising little but mutton chops and damper. However, faunal remains from the excavations included eggshell and the bones of rabbits, chickens, pigs, cows, and goats, as well as sheep. Keeping domestic animals and growing vegetables on the diggings was possible because one of the terms of the Miner's Right was a 20 perche (500 m²) allotment on which to build a hut. Women, and also children, provided the labour that made small-scale production on such plots feasible. Selling surplus eggs and butter was one way in which women supplemented the family income. The cooperation required to successfully maintain such an operation is just one example of the importance of the family or household group as the unit of production for subsistence miners, few of whom were able to survive on the efforts of one individual alone.

The role of women in productive agricultural labour hints at the range of economic tasks in which women were engaged. Contemporary letters and diaries provide further evidence of these tasks. In addition to the ubiquitous tasks of bearing and raising children, cleaning house, shopping, cooking, sewing, and doing the laundry, contemporary commentators recorded that women ran shops and sold sly grog, or illicit alcohol, bought gold, and worked family claims. Economic labour was only one component of women's work however, and an equally important component being that of social labour, both at the community level and in the home. Feminist historians (Lake 1986; McGaw 1989) have pointed to the role of women in initiating and maintaining community institutions such as churches and schools, and Hardesty (1994) in the United States and McGowan in New South Wales (1992) have cited the presence of such structures archaeologically as indications of the exertions of women in mining settlements. On the Moorabool diggings three churches, three schools, and a continuous round of concerts, picnics, and dances reported in the local newspaper are evidence of the work of women in that community. Another important social task which fell to goldfield women as much as it did to their sisters in cities was the maintenance of the family's social identity through entertaining and display, both of which involved informed purchasing of consumer goods and the creation of an appropriate domestic environment. Evidence of this social labour is seen in the material culture of the household assemblages associated with women.

HOUSEHOLD GOODS

While the presence of women's belongings cannot be used to identify residential-only sites, there is strong evidence for the association of women with particular forms of activity, and in particular with the maintenance of the household's cultural identity. One version of cultural identity that was particularly prominent during the nineteenth century was that of domesticity which valorized the sanctity and unity of the family and celebrated morality and respectability (Lake 1986; Russell 1994; Summers 1975; Welter 1966). Women in particular were identified as guardians of these values and of the home, which was the physical site at which esteem for these values was most fully expressed. In addition to exercising responsibility for matters such as family health, education, and morals, women were responsible for the physical environment of the home itself. Wall (1994: 134–5) has argued that from the early 1800s young American women were being socialized as consumers skilled in acquiring the goods necessary for furnishing a home in a way that would create an appropriate domestic setting. A similar process was taking place in Australia where Russell (1994) has demonstrated that in mid-century Melbourne a considerable portion of the socialization and education of young, middle-class girls was devoted to the acquisition of skills in interpreting the complex messages of morality, respectability, and status embodied in the material culture of dress and home furnishings.

Goods are an important component of what Bourdieu (1984: 4) has termed our cultural competence, an ability to operate comfortably and appropriately within a given social milieu, and which is only acquired as a result of long familiarity with and exposure to that milieu. Blanton (1994: 9–11) has described the canonical and indexical functions of houses within this system of cultural competence and his argument can be extended to other forms of consumer goods, and particularly to household furnishings. Houses communicate canonically by serving as a material frame which continuously reinforces social divisions and categorical oppositions. That is, for those living in the house it both embodies the social identity of the household and acts as a reminder of it. Indexical functions of the house communicate this household identity to outsiders. Furnishings similarly structure and reinforce social relationships within the household and, through the process of entertaining and visiting, are used to negotiate the household's position *vis-à-vis* others. Houses have the ability to be read in isolation because due to their cost and visibility they are less liable to produce incorrect readings (Blanton 1994: 13). However, other goods are most reliable, and most meaningful, when considered collectively (Douglas and Isherwood 1978: 5–12; McCracken 1990: 121).

Furnishings and consumer goods in the assemblages from the two households associated with women suggest the household identities that they embodied. The assemblages from all four households are meagre and the goods represented limited in number and poor in quality. However, particularly at the two family sites they revealed a diversity of form and function extending well beyond the basic goods necessary for subsistence in a short-term diggings camp. Ceramic tablewares, pressed glass stemmed bowls, gilded clock cases, floral wallpaper (Figure 8.6), and even whitewashed fireplaces transformed temporary tents on the diggings into respectable Victorian parlours suitable for entertaining guests and reinforcing the moral standards of the household. To a stranger on the goldfields the symbolic message of the goods may have been overlooked or misread, but to other residents they would have been clearly understood.

In diaries and letters written by women on the goldfields descriptions of similar arrangements indicate recognition and approval. Diarist Ellen Clacy described two tent homes on the Bendigo diggings in 1852 (Clacy 1963: 55, 56). At the first tent she saw that 'the tins are as bright as silver, there are sheets as well as blankets on the beds, and perhaps a clean counterpane, with the addition of a dry sack or piece of carpet on the ground'. In contrast, at another tent nearby, 'a block of wood forms a table, and this is the only furniture; many dispense with that. The bedding, which is laid on the ground, serves to sit upon. Tin plates and pannikins . . . compose the tea service.' The passages provide an emic understanding of the attitudes and ideologies that gave the rooms meaning. Both homes were sparsely furnished with beds, tin dishes and a table, but one was clearly more acceptable to Clacy than was the other. Other women made similar efforts to improve their surroundings. In 1855 Emily Skinner camped with her husband and baby in a tent on the Woolshed diggings, and although the tent was not as comfortable as their slab hut had been on the previous diggings, nevertheless 'We lined the tent with green baize, and it was really pretty and comfortable' (Duyker 1995: 64). In the winter, with

> the snug tent warmly lined and with a blazing fire in the wide fireplace, it was cosy enough. Our men were first rate bush carpenters, and had made several articles of furniture: cupboard, safe, tables and some really comfortable chairs. They looked quite nice when cushioned and covered with neat chintz, and we spread bags and matting over the earthen floor.
>
> (Duyker 1995: 75)

Written descriptions and physical evidence indicate that women on the goldfields were actively using material culture to assert the respectable status of their households.

CONCLUSION

This chapter contributes to an emerging feminist archaeology of households in two ways. First, it presents empirical evidence of ways in which household assemblages associated with both men and women differ from those associated only with men. Because most analyses of household assemblages have not considered gender as a structuring principle, this kind of data is not yet widely available. Differences between the four households in this study can be partially interpreted as the result of functional differences: alcohol bottles and multiple items at two sites suggest that they were used as pubs and or stores as well as residences, while the absence of these items at the other two sites suggests residential-only use. However, these functions do not explain all of the differences apparent, which become understandable only when gender is considered as a possible variable. The distribution of women's personal belongings is correlated with the distribution of certain items related to household furnishing which are associated with a cultural identity valuing domesticity. While this identity is specific to the mid-nineteenth century and cannot be extended in time or to other cultures, its identification in the material record, and its association with women, suggests that similarly gendered patterns might be identifiable in other contexts.

The second contribution is the use of the empirical data as a point of departure for the consideration of other issues concerning gender as a structuring principle in the diggings. The use of gender as a category of analysis increases the visibility of women, but more significantly demonstrates the complexities of goldfields households. Household composition, kin networks, and subsistence strategies take on new dimensions when women are made more visible. Approximately 50 per cent of the households on the Moorabool included women, which made possible the formation of extended families who drew households together for social and economic purposes. Alternative subsistence strategies that diversified the diet and economically underpinned small-scale mining were also made possible by women who tended gardens and manufactured dairy products. Material culture was part of the negotiation of gender roles and domestic environments were made meaningful within a system of cultural values of which gender was an integral part. This broader interpretation challenges the traditional depiction of goldfields as male-dominated societies and demonstrates the power of including gender in the archaeological study of households.

BIBLIOGRAPHY

Bate, W. (1978) *Lucky City: The First Generation at Ballarat*, Carlton: Melbourne University Press.

Blainey, G. (1963) *The Rush that Never Ended*, Carlton: Melbourne University Press.

Blanton, R. (1994) *Houses and Households: A Comparative Study*, New York: Plenum Press.

Blee, C. H. (1991) 'Sorting Functionally-Mixed Artifact Assemblages with Multiple Regression: A Comparative Study in Historical Archaeology', Unpublished Ph.D. thesis, University of Colorado.

Bourdieu, P. (1984) *Distinction: A Social Critique of the Judgement of Taste*, trans. R. Nice, Cambridge, Mass.: Harvard University Press.

Census of Victoria, 1861, State Library of Victoria.

Chase, S. (1991) 'Polygyny, Architecture and Meaning', in D. Walde and N. Willows (eds) *The Archaeology of Gender: Proceedings of the 22nd Annual Chacmool Conference*, Calgary: The University of Calgary: 150–8.

Clacy, Mrs C. (1963) *A Lady's Visit to the Gold Diggings of Australia in 1852–53*, Melbourne: Lansdowne Press (first published London, 1853).

Conkey, M. (1993) 'Making the Connections: Feminist Theory and Archaeologies of Gender', in H. du Cros and L. Smith (eds) *Women in Archaeology: A Feminist Critique*, Occasional Papers in Prehistory no. 23, Department of Prehistory, Research School of Pacific Studies, Canberra: The Australian National University: 3–15.

Conkey, M. and Gero, J. (1991) 'Tensions, Pluralities and Engendering Archaeology: An Introduction to Women and Prehistory', in J. Gero and M. Conkey (eds) *Engendering Archaeology: Women and Prehistory*, Cambridge: Basil Blackwell: 3–30.

Conkey, M. and Spector, J. (1984) 'Archaeology and the Study of Gender', in M. Schiffer (ed.) *Advances in Archaeological Method and Theory 7*, New York: Academic Press: 1–38.

Coroneos, C. (1993) 'A Poor Man's Diggings: An Archaeological Survey of the Lisle Denison Goldfields', Unpublished report prepared for the Forestry Commission, Hobart, and the Queen Victoria Museum and Art Gallery, Launceston.

Cott, N. (1977) *The Bonds of Womanhood: 'Woman's Sphere' in New England 1780–1835*, New Haven: Yale University Press.

Derry, L. (1992) 'Fathers and Daughters: Land Ownership, Kinship Structure, and Social Space in Old Cahawba', in A. Yentsch and M. Beaudry (eds) *The Art and Mystery of Historical Archaeology: Essays in Honor of James Deetz*, Ann Arbor: CRC Press: 215–28.

Donley-Reid, L. (1987) 'Life in the Swahili Town House Reveals the Symbolic Meaning of Spaces and Artefact Assemblages', *The African Archaeological Review* 5: 181–92.

—— (1990) 'The Power of Swahili Porcelain, Beads and Pottery', in S. Nelson and A. Kehoe (eds) *Powers of Observation: Alternative Views in Archaeology*, Washington, DC: American Anthropological Association: 47–59.

Douglas, M. and Isherwood, B. (1978) *The World of Goods: Towards an Anthropology of Consumption*, Ringwood: Penguin.

Duyker, E. (ed.) (1995) *A Woman on the Goldfields: Recollections of Emily Skinner, 1857–1878*, Carlton: Melbourne University Press.

Engelstad, E. (1991) 'Images of Power and Contradiction: Feminist Theory and Post-Processual Archaeology', *Antiquity* 65: 502–14.

Evans, W. (1975) *Diary of a Welsh Swagman 1869–1894*, Melbourne: Macmillan.

Fauchery, A. (1965) *Letters from a Miner in Australia*, Melbourne: Georgia House.

Fahey, C. (1983) 'Bendigo 1881–1901: A Demographic Portrait of a Victorian Provincial Town', *Australia 1988*, Bulletin 11: 88–107.

Geelong Advertiser (GA)

Gibb, J. and King, J. (1991) 'Gender, Activity Areas, and Homelots in the 17th Century Chesapeake Region', *Historical Archaeology* 25, 4: 109–31.

Gill, S. T. (1982) *The Victorian Goldfields 1852–3: An Original Album*, M. Cannon (ed.), South Yarra: Currey O'Neil for the Library Council of Victoria.

Goodman, D. (1994) *Gold Seeking: Victoria and California in the 1850s*, Sydney: Allen and Unwin.

Griffiths, T. (ed.) (1988) *The Life and Adventures of Edward Snell*, North Ryde: Angus and Robertson.

Grimshaw, P. and Fahey, C. (1982) 'Family and Community in Nineteenth Century Castlemaine', *Australia 1988*, Bulletin 9: 88–125.

Grimshaw, P. and Willet, G. (1980) 'Family Structure in Colonial Australia: An Exploration in Family History', *Australia 1988*, Bulletin 4: 5–27.

Hardesty, D. (1994) 'Class, Gender Strategies, and Material Culture in the Mining West' in E. Scott (ed.) *Those of Little Note: Gender, Race and Class in Historical Archaeology*, Tucson and London: University of Arizona Press: 129–48.

Hodder, I. (1983) 'Burials, Houses, Women and Men in the European Neolithic', in D. Miller and C. Tilley (eds) *Ideology, Power, and Prehistory*, Cambridge: Cambridge University Press: 51–63.

Holliday, J. (1981) *The World Rushed In: The California Gold Rush Experience*, New York: Simon and Schuster.

Jackson, L. (1994) 'Cloth, Clothing and Related Paraphernalia: A Key to Gender Visibility in the Archaeological Record of Russian America', in E. Scott (ed.) *Those of Little Note: Gender, Race and Class in Historical Archaeology*, Tucson and London: University of Arizona Press: 27–54.

Korzelinski, S. (1979) *Memoirs of Gold Digging in Australia*, trans. and ed. S. Robe, St Lucia: University of Queensland Press.

Kryder-Reid, E. (1994) '"With Manly Courage": Reading the Construction of Gender in a Nineteenth-Century Religious Community' in E. Scott (ed.) *Those of Little Note: Gender, Race and Class in Historical Archaeology*, Tucson and London: University of Arizona Press: 97–114.

Lake, M. (1986) 'The Politics of Respectability: Identifying the Masculinist Context', *Historical Studies* 22, 86: 116–31.

Lane, T. and Serle, J. (1990) *Australians at Home*, Melbourne: Oxford University Press.

Lawrence, S. (1995) 'No Abiding City: The Archaeology and History of an Ephemeral Mining Settlement', Unpublished Ph.D. thesis, La Trobe University.

Lydon, J. (1993) 'Task Differentiation in Historical Archaeology: Sewing as Material Culture', in H. du Cros and L. Smith (eds) *Women in Archaeology: A Feminist Critique*, Occasional Papers in Prehistory no. 23, Department of Prehistory, Research School of Pacific Studies, Canberra: The Australian National University: 129–37.

Lyons, D. (1989) 'Men's Houses: Women's Spaces: The Spatial Ordering of Households in Doulo, North Cameroon', in S. MacEachern, D. Archer and R. Garvin (eds) *Households and Communities*, Proceedings of the 21st Annual Chacmool Conference, The University of Calgary: 108–15.

McBryde, I. (1993) '"In Her Right Place . . . "? Women in Archaeology, Past and Present', in H. du Cros and L. Smith (eds) *Women in Archaeology: A Feminist Critique*, Occasional Papers in Prehistory no. 23, Department of Prehistory, Research School of Pacific Studies, Canberra: The Australian National University: xi–xv.

McCracken, G. (1990) *Culture and Consumption*, Bloomington: Indiana University Press (first published 1988).

McGaw, J. (1989) 'No Passive Victims, No Separate Spheres: A Feminist Perspective on Technology's History', in S. Cutcliffe and R. Post (eds) *In Context: History and the History of Technology, Essays in Honour of Melvin Kranzberg*, Research in Technology Studies vol. 1, Bethlehem: Lehigh University Press, Bethlehem, and London and Toronto: Associated University Presses: 172–91.

McGowan, B. (1992) 'Aspects of Gold Mining and Mining Communities in the Shoalhaven Area of New South Wales: An Archaeological and Historical Study', *Australasian Historical Archaeology* 10: 43–55.

Matthews, B. (1987) *Louisa*, Fitzroy: McPhee Gribble/Penguin Books.

Morrison's Cemetery Records, Ballan Historical Society, Ballan, Victoria.

Philipp, J. (1987) *A Poor Man's Diggings: Mining and Community at Bethanga, Victoria, 1875–1912*, Melbourne: Hyland House.

Powell, J. (1970) *The Public Lands of Australia Felix: Settlement and Land Appraisal in Victoria 1834–91 with Special Reference to the Western Plains*, Melbourne: Oxford University Press.

Purser, M. (1991) '"Several Paradise Ladies are Visiting in Town": Gender Strategies in the Early Industrial West', *Historical Archaeology* 25, 4: 6–16.

Reports of the Mining Surveyors (MSR) (1857–1888) Department of Industry, Technology, and Natural Resources, Victoria.

Russell, P. (1994) *A Wish of Distinction: Colonial Gentility and Femininity*, Carlton: Melbourne University Press.

Seifert, D. (1991) 'Introduction', *Historical Archaeology* 25, 4: 1–5.

—— (1994) 'Mrs. Starr's Profession', in E. Scott (ed.) *Those of Little Note: Gender, Race and Class in Historical Archaeology*, Tucson and London: University of Arizona Press: 149–74.

Serle, G. (1963) *The Gold Age: A History of the Colony of Victoria, 1851–1861*, Carlton: Melbourne University Press.

Small, D. (1991) 'Initial Study of the Structure of Women's Seclusion in the Archaeological Past', in D.

Walde and N. Willows (eds) *The Archaeology of Gender: Proceedings of the 22nd Annual Chacmool Conference*, Calgary: The University of Calgary: 336–42.

Spencer-Wood, S. (1991) 'Towards a Feminist Historical Archaeology of the Construction of Gender', in D. Walde and N. Willows (eds) *The Archaeology of Gender: Proceedings of the 22nd Annual Chacmool Conference*, Calgary: The University of Calgary: 234–44.

Starbuck, D. (1994) 'The Identification of Gender at Northern Military Sites of the Late Eighteenth Century', in E. Scott (ed.) *Those of Little Note: Gender, Race and Class in Historical Archaeology*, Tucson and London: University of Arizona Press: 115–28.

Summers, A. (1975) *Damned Whores and God's Police: The Colonisation of Women in Australia*, Ringwood: Penguin Books.

Sussex, L. (1989) *The Fortunes of Mary Fortune*, Ringwood: Penguin Books.

Tippin, M. (ed.) (1982) *An Artist on the Goldfields: The Diary of Eugene Von Guerard*, South Yarra: Curry O'Neil.

Tordoff, J. and Seldner, D. (1987) 'Cottonwood Creek Project Shasta and Tehama Counties, California: Dutch Gulch Lake Excavation at Thirteen Historic Sites in the Cottonwood Mining District', Unpublished report for the US Army Corps of Engineers, Sacramento.

Tringham, R. (1991) 'Households with Faces: The Challenge of Gender in Prehistoric Architectural Remains', in J. Gero and M. Conkey (eds) *Engendering Archaeology: Women and Prehistory*, Cambridge: Basil Blackwell: 93–131.

Wall, D. (1994) *The Archaeology of Gender: Separating the Spheres in Urban America*, New York: Plenum Press.

Welter, B. (1966) 'The Cult of True Womanhood: 1820–1860', *American Quarterly* 18: 151–74.

Wilk, R. and Rathje, W. (1982) 'Household Archaeology', in R. Wilk and W. Rathje (eds) 'Archaeology of the Household: Building a Prehistory of Domestic Life', *American Behavioral Scientist* 25, 6: 617–640 .

Wylie, A. (1991) 'Gender Theory and the Archaeological Record: Why Is There No Archaeology of Gender?', in J. Gero and M. Conkey (eds) *Engendering Archaeology: Women and Prehistory*, Cambridge: Basil Blackwell: 31–54.

—— (1992) 'The Interplay of Evidential Constraints and Political Interests: Recent Archaeological Research on Gender', *American Antiquity* 57, 1: 15–35.

Chapter Nine

Spatial and behavioural negotiation in Classical Athenian city houses

Marilyn Y. Goldberg

The places and situations in which men and women negotiated with each other and with the norms of accepted behaviour provide an interesting focus in an investigation of any society. Classical Athens is no exception. Up until recently, however, our focus has been less on actual practice than on the norms and ideals of behaviour expressed in our sources; and in our examination of these norms and ideas, we have concentrated on the distinctions that separated men and women and the societal constraints under which they lived. Evidence that has survived to give us information about Athenians living in city houses can be analysed more fruitfully with regard to the situations in which actual practice conformed or deviated from ideals. To my mind, an understanding of the recursive nature of people and their social environment is very helpful in explaining the complexities of life in Athenian houses. Where norms and behaviour apparently contradicted each other, we can look for negotiation. The courtyard of an Athenian house was clearly one such place and there undoubtedly were others, both inside houses and out. The first section of this chapter is an introduction to the history of the study of gendered space in Athenian households. The second section examines the physical reconstructions of gendered spaces. The third section discusses the ways the spaces in the household may actually have functioned.

HISTORY OF THE STUDY OF GENDERED SPACE IN ATHENIAN HOUSEHOLDS

Until recently, the way we have interpreted the archaeological remains of Athenian houses has been not only simplistic, but biased as well. First of all, the archaeological material has taken second place to the evidence derived from literature and other written documents, documents that are, in fact, few in number. This reliance on written sources was made easier by the limitations of the archaeological data, a small number of houses that are badly preserved and not yet well published. The physical evidence was seen as a confirmation of what we had learned via the written. The reliance on men's written documents that emphasize ideals over practice has led classicists and archaeologists to assume that all houses had separate women's quarters and a male *andron*, even though less wealthy houses may not have had a single room always used as an *andron* or fixed women's quarters. It has long been accepted that the *andron*, which is clearly marked out by certain architectural characteristics in houses and on Athenian vases by its occupants and furniture, was the place where men attended *symposia*. Remains confirm texts. Or so it seems. But what about the houses we have found that do not have the particular architectural features that have been understood to signal an *andron*? Does the absence of these hallmarks mean that some families had no rooms that were used only by men? Did the Athenian families living in houses that did have what we have called *androns* consider them male space, as the etymology of the word seems to indicate? If they did so, were the rooms in practice not used by women or at least citizen women? For we know that any characterization of the space as male would have been in some ways a fiction, even in the fifth century, since *hetairai* and flute girls attended at least some *symposia.*

What did Athenians consider female space? Was the whole house considered female space, as the frequently used dichotomies male/public:female/private would seem to indicate? If so, where does the *andron* fit into this pattern? Are the women's rooms, which are also mentioned in texts, the analogue of the *andron* and, if so, where are they? The *gunaikonitis* or, literally, place for women, is the word translated as women's quarters. The word appears in relatively few ancient texts written during the fifth and fourth centuries – not surprisingly, since the majority of ancient texts from this period cover the business of men and not women. In one court case the Greek orator Lysias (1.9.3) mentions that in the defendant's house the *gunaikonitis* was originally upstairs, until it was moved downstairs. This passage suggests that women's rooms did not occupy a fixed space. In another case of Lysias (3.6.4) the accused is said to have broken into a house and entered the *gunaikonitis* in a drunken search for a boy slave. If this passage is taken at face value, the Athenians in the jury were expected to have found it not unusual that a boy slave might be in the women's rooms. Aristophanes in his comedy *The Thesmophoriazousai* (414), a play about women celebrating a women's only religious festival, mentions the *gunaikonitis*. He puts a speech into the mouth of an unnamed woman, blaming the tragedian Euripides for slandering women and causing men to place bars and bolts on the *gunaikonitis* to keep women from committing adultery. The implication is that bars and bolts were an innovation and unusual. Xenophon of Athens, who wrote a treatise on the management of a country estate, *Oeconomicus*, also uses the word (9.5.2, 9.6.5), but since he discusses a country estate and not a city house, the specific use of the word is not relevant in this discussion, which is limited to urban domestic structures.

How are we to interpret the statement that certain women were embarrassed to be seen at home even by their male relatives (Lysias 3.6–7)? It certainly does not mean that women lived in seclusion inside their houses (Cohen 1989, 1991). These questions, because they arise out of a consideration of gender and space, permit and even compel us to re-examine Athenian households and to make use of more recent trends in interpretation (Brown 1993: 259–61; Conkey and Williams 1991; di Leonardo 1991; Schmitt Pantel 1994: 470–1; Talalay 1994: 174–5).

The most fruitful approaches, to my mind, share the characteristic of emphasizing the recursive nature of culture and human behaviour (Cohen 1991: chs 2–4, 6; Conkey 1990; Dougherty 1995; Kent 1990; Knapp 1992; Moreland 1992; Nevett 1995). Some recognize that both the written information about women's and men's spaces and the archaeological record itself are the result of the interaction of cultural patterns and actions by individuals (Hodder 1991, 1992; Shanks and Tilley 1987; Sourvinou-Inwood 1991). Others recognize that this interaction needs to be considered in terms of space and in terms of time as well (Foley 1981; Foxhall 1994; Nevett 1995; Rapoport 1990). Most also acknowledge that the history we scholars write when we interpret household data is the result of an interaction, but this time of our own culture and our own personal values with those of the past (Brown 1993; Sourvinou-Inwood 1991; Talalay 1994). Because I focus on interaction, I see Athenian households as places of integration, places where individuals who were separated by gender distinctions, as well as by sex and family and class, negotiated norms and space. The courtyard, certainly the defining feature of Athenian houses, was one of the chief sites of this integration (Jameson 1990b: 179), but it was not the only one. In this chapter I am limiting myself to examples of houses actually in the city of Athens, rather than country houses as well. I thereby can avoid having to take into account distinctions that undoubtedly existed between city life and life in the country.

In the 1960s and 1970s archaeologists who used the methods of New Archaeology and classicists who were influenced by French structuralism focused our attention on the ways in which environmental and cultural patterns constrain the behaviour of individuals. The New Archaeologists concentrated on the interaction of ecological and cultural systems and the patterns that they produced in the archaeological record (Brown 1993: 248–9, Gilchrist 1991; Kent 1990; Moreland 1992: 115). The traditional explanation for the Athenian courtyard house, that it was a product of environmental considerations, fits this method of interpretation, although antedating it considerably. This explanation, that climate determines the style of the house, has been accepted almost without question by modern scholars, in large part because it was proposed by the very influential Roman architect Vitruvius (6.1), who wrote a treatise on architecture at the end of the first century BCE or the early part of the next century. Yet as we now know from the excavated remains of Greek houses, his description of the Greek house (6.2) is hardly accurate, especially for houses built three or four hundred years before the architect's own time. The Athenian courtyard house did provide light and ventilation, combined with warmth in the winter and shade in the hot summer, in a city where dense housing made privacy important. If the houses had any windows on the street at all, the openings were probably small and high on the wall. However, using a similar explanatory method, house plans could be said to have been shaped by the Athenian economic system as well. To a large extent Athenian society consisted of households of farmers for whom there was an unequal distribution of good land. As a result, the courtyards of city houses, as well as those of country ones, served as enclosed yards to ensure the protection of the household property.

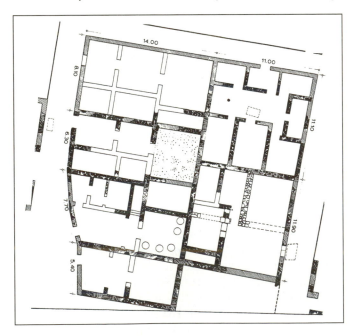

Figure 9.1 Plan of block of houses on the north slope of the Areopagus, Athens. Cesspools indicated by rectangles formed by dashed lines. North at top of plan.
After Travlos (1971: 396 fig. 509). Reproduced with permission of Greenwood Publishing Group, Inc., Westport, Conn. Copyright by Verlag Ernst Waasmuth.

Structuralists have given priority to patterns of paradigmatic thought that are observable in written documents and in material remains. In these paradigms gender is of prime importance and has been related to physical space most frequently in the dichotomous analogies, male/public/outside:female/private/inside. In the most influential expression of this structuralist approach, Vernant argued that the opposition of Hestia and Hermes was part of a set of societal norms that contrasted male and female space. He writes that Hestia was marked by the central hearth in the courtyard and Hermes by the herm outside the front door, both features that are mentioned in literary sources (Vernant 1983). These are features for which we have only some archaeological confirmation. A few houses have evidence for fixed hearths, although never in the courtyards. And although a few herms have survived, none were found by house doors. In the analogy above the whole house is defined as female. Scholars of gender recognize that these analogies also reflected relationships of power, that the patriarchal structure of Athenian society was clearly reproduced in the hierarchical ordering of these analogies (DuBois 1991; Keuls 1985; Sourvinou-Inwood 1995; Tyrrell 1984). The female side was normally devalued in order to justify women's exclusion from political power conducted in the Agora.

We owe our thanks to Walker for having written the first examination of the archaeological evidence for Athenian houses in the light of a gendered division of space (Figure 9.2). She too saw the cultural pattern of divided male and female space as an organizing principle of a house. In addition, she also took into account the literary evidence that seems to speak of the seclusion of women within 'women's quarters'. In the light of this additional evidence, she provided plans of the houses to show that the interior of the house consisted of separate male and female space (Walker 1983; see also Fantham *et al.* 1994). For her, courtyards were sometimes part of female space and sometimes part of male space. Hoepfner and Schwander used the same organizing principle and literary evidence to reconstruct the women's quarters on the second floor of a block of houses in the Piraeus (Hoepfner and Schwander 1994: 22–50, fig. 33). Because they do not speak in terms of gendered space, it is not clear how they would have defined the courtyard. They do presume the existence of women's quarters and place them on the second floor. Would the courtyard, as a result, have belonged to men or been considered male?

To my mind these interpretations of the house or part of the house as female space share certain characteristics that make their results flawed. First of all, their focus is predominantly or even solely on the importance of the pattern of opposition of male and female and its reflection in the household (cf. Goldberg 1998a, 1998b; Lamphere 1993). Second, they give primacy to written evidence and do not see that the archaeological evidence is equally as important and worthy of its own separate study, as Nevett has argued (1994). Third, they assume rules for gender behaviour and then cite only those that document the pattern of gendered opposition, thereby inviting circular logic. Fourth, in relying so heavily on literary evidence, some do not take into account the fact that written evidence itself was socially constructed and frequently reflects the ideals and norms of a particular class, as well as gender (Goldberg 1998b; Nevett 1995). It is difficult to say whether the standards of the élite were shared by *hoi polloi* as well, although the power of the standards of a dominant group should not be

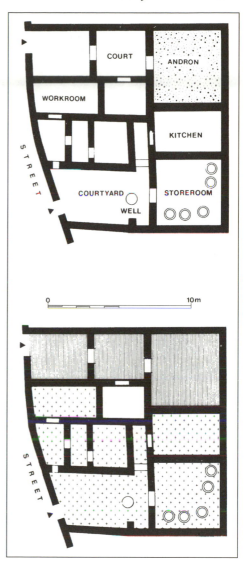

Figure 9.2 Walker's plans of two houses from same block on the north slope of the Areopagus, Athens (two central houses on the left in Figure 9.1). Top: indicating the use of rooms. Below: women's quarters marked by +; rooms used by men shaded. North at the top of both plans.

After Walker (1983: 87 figs 6.2a–b). Copyright 1983 by Croom Helm. Reproduced with the permission of Routledge.

ignored. Fifth, although these approaches do take into account the fact that societal norms found in this written evidence were attempts to validate power by 'naturalizing' it, they are less concerned with the way that cultural and physical boundaries were negotiated than they are with the boundaries themselves (Sanders 1990). We know that women certainly worked in the courtyard, the most public place of the house, and also that they went out in public on different occasions (see pp. 157–8). How did they manipulate societal norms to do so?

Sixth, as has been frequently emphasized, women are not an undifferentiated group (e.g. Versnel 1987). Surely some standards of behaviour must have differed depending on the age and status of the woman and men involved. And finally, the assumptions about public and private and women's seclusion, at times, have been coloured by the cultural heritage of the modern scholar. Western European Orientalism and the nineteenth-century understanding of what the separation of public and private means have blurred the cultural specificity of the particular ways men and women interacted at home in Athens in the Classical period (Ahmed 1982; Blok 1987; Conkey and Williams 1991; Goldberg 1998b; Hodder 1991). In her chapter in this volume, Spencer-Wood discusses how Victorian élite gender ideology was projected on the reconstruction of Classical houses into gender segregated areas. In some cases, as Sourvinou-Inwood has recently pointed out, ethnographic comparisons of women of ancient Athens with women in 'modern Mediterranean cultures' have also been used without precision (Sourvinou-Inwood 1995).

Some of these problems arise from a devaluation of individual agency in the face of striking cultural patterning, whether the individual is the ancient Greek man or woman or the investigator of today. Others arise from the uncritical assumption that social patterns can be described by analogies that are expressed in terms of dichotomous oppositions and that these oppositions are all equivalent to each other (e.g. Hodder 1987, cf. Foxhall 1989; Gilchrist 1991; Goldberg 1998a, 1998b; Lloyd 1966; Saxonhouse 1992). It may quite well be that patterned oppositional thinking did exist in Athens by the fifth century, although I am not at all sure how pervasive it would have been. Certainly such a pattern confirmed the more powerful position of a citizen man. But it is also true that if we repeatedly use analogies based on opposition, we lose sight of intermediary categories, categories that deserve to be thought of as more than just interstitial. To give two obvious examples, in the analogies of gender and space cited above, where is religion, the 'social glue' of Athens? Women participated in and served as priestesses for the most public celebrations in Athens: religious festivals. Or where do guest friends, *xenoi*, fit into the pattern? For *xenoi* were, in part, family friends and had access to their friends' houses; yet they were not members of that household. Moreover it is also true that individual agency is as important a focus as cultural norms, a point emphasized by post-colonialist and feminist scholars (Burke 1991; Conkey and Williams 1991). If individual agency is not a focus we can all too easily overlook the fact that people are not only constrained by social customs but also can create and subvert them (Abu-Lughod 1990). Without such a focus, we get a picture of women or other members of non-dominant groups as passive, as always acted upon and never as cultural agents (Ahmed 1982; Hodder 1991; Talalay 1994).

RECONSTRUCTIONS OF HOUSEHOLD GENDERED SPACES

Both Nevett and Jameson have focused our attention on the importance of considering Greek houses by looking at the archaeological evidence in its own right (Jameson 1990a, 1990b; Nevett 1994, 1995). Nevett has shown that environmental concerns alone cannot explain the organization of the house. Jameson has pointed out how little the archaeological remains confirm the gendering of space. Even hearths and herms are more noticeable by their absence from Athenian houses, despite Hoepfner and Schwander's placement of a hearth in the main living room of every

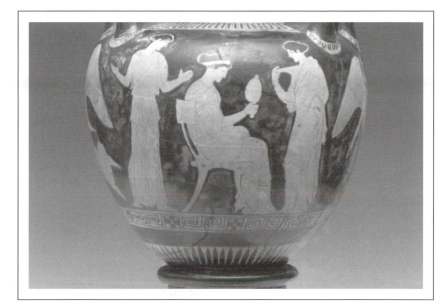

Figure 9.3 Body of Athenian vase, with a woman seated on a chair and looking in a mirror, and two attendants. A *lebes gamikos* (*c.* 440 BCE). David M. Robinson Collection, University Museums, University of Mississippi. Photo: Museum.

Figure 9.4 Drawing of Athenian vase, a *stamnos* now lost, with a woman on the left looking back towards two women folding cloth. Cloth and mirror hanging on the wall. Another cloth on a stool and a storage chest to the right. By the Copenhagen Painter (*c.* 450 BCE). After Gerhard (1840: pl. 301).

house in their reconstruction of a block in fifth century Piraeus (Hoepfner and Schwander 1994: 39–41 figs 31, 33; Jameson 1990b: 193–4; Kent 1990: 105–6). Both Nevett and Jameson have argued that women certainly worked in the courtyard. Nevett has shown that men, even non-family men, certainly had to walk through that space to the *andron*, if there was one. Small has drawn our attention to the cultural specificity of the separation of male and female space, the variations in the patterns of women's separation from men in different societies (Small 1991). He has demonstrated the importance of considering the actual archaeological markers of space and what they tell us about conceptualizations of space. These interpretations all add to our understanding of the way people acted in Athenian houses.

When we compare the ancient Athenian normative standard of public space as male and private space as female with women's lived experiences, we see a paradox. This paradox points out clearly who owned that standard. Women's place was not always at home for slave women or women too poor to have had slaves, who had to fetch water if they didn't have a well at home, or women who were wet-nurses or midwives or vendors (Demosthenes, *Euboulides* 31, 34; Aristophanes, *Acharnanians* 478, *Wasps* 497, 1380–92, *Frogs* 1346, *Lysistrata* 445, 447–8, *Thesmophoriazousai*

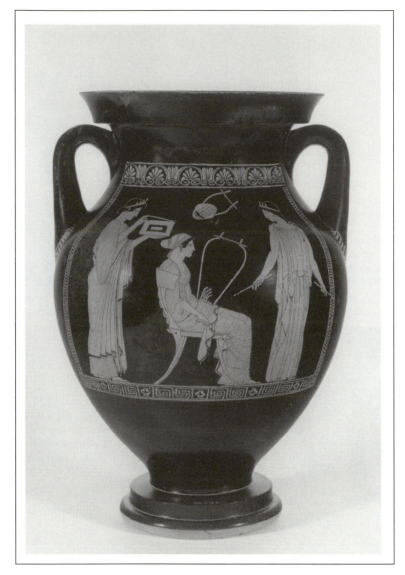

Figure 9.5 Athenian amphora with a woman seated on a chair and playing a barbiton, a woman to the left looking into a box and a woman to the right holding double flutes. By the Niobid Painter (*c.* 460–450 BCE).
With permission of the Walters Art Gallery, Baltimore (inv. no. 48.2712).
Photo: Museum.

346ff., 447ff.). Discourses of gender and class and status certainly intersected to shape the standard (Goldberg 1998b; Humphreys 1993: xiv). Nonetheless the dominant aristocratic men, who controlled the means of defining the image of the home as women's place, had real power in limiting the majority of women to work at home, whether in their own homes or in those of their masters or clients. In this competitive society, men's honour depended on this standard (Small 1991: 340–1). In addition this identification of a normative conceptualization of space is synchronic, not diachronic. By its very nature this normative standard obscures historical change.

What women did was not unchanging through time. For example, how many women, who would never have had to work outside their homes before the Peloponnesian War, were forced to do so during and after the war (Cohen 1991: 150–1)? Demosthenes (*Euboulides* 45) mentions that some women were forced into field labour when economic conditions in Athens had worsened.

Likewise we can also compare the ideal of separate men's and women's spaces within the house with lived reality in order to investigate similar issues. On the basis of the written evidence, it does sound as if there was a room that was limited to use by citizen men, the *andron*, and there was a room or set of rooms, the *gunaikonitis*, to which women were restricted. Archaeological evidence seems to confirm this ideal image. On vases we see men reclining on couches at *symposia*. Since literary texts identify the room where these drinking parties were held as the *andron*, scholars have assumed that vases showing men and their companions at parties are scenes that take place in such a room. We look at some houses and we can identify this room as an *andron* by certain architectural features, a raised platform that held the dining couches and an off-centre door to accommodate them, or finer treatment of the flooring (e.g. Figure 9.1, second house from the top on the left). Women on vases are often shown seated or standing in space, usually assumed to be the women's quarters, surrounded with typical women's possessions like chairs and wool baskets and mirrors and boxes (Figures 9.3–5). Scholars have labelled this space 'the women's quarters'.

Where were the women's quarters?

When Walker turned her attention to the physical remains of Greek houses in a search for the *gunaikonitis*, she divided up some Athenian houses into men's and women's areas in order to show the actual location of this female space. The best known of her examples is part of a block of houses, at the north foot of the Areopagus and south of the South Stoa in the Athenian Agora (Figure 9.2). Walker considered the entrance area into the northern section of the house male space, as she did the courtyard and the room behind it, since this last room was identified by the excavators as a possible *andron* (Thompson 1959: 101). The rooms around the southern courtyard she considered the women's quarters (Nevett 1995: 13; Walker 1983). Others have put the women's quarters on the second floor, as have Hoepfner and Schwander, already mentioned above, who have published such detailed reconstructions of a block of houses in the Piraeus, the harbour town of Athens, of the fifth century BCE (Hoepfner and Schwander 1994). So too did Lauter-Bufe and Lauter (1971) who published a house on the Pnyx of the type they have called *Flügelhofhaus*.

In houses that have been excavated, almost no rooms are marked out in the archaeological record as having had a concentration of what we call women's objects, like mirrors or jewellery boxes. In many cases the finds have not been published; at best there are passing references to selected objects. Given the value of these objects, surely they would have been noted by excavators. On the other hand this very value makes their absence not surprising, for the inhabitants of the houses probably removed their valuable possessions prior to the abandonment of the house. In only two Athenian houses have numbers of loomweights been found together to indicate a fixed place where that most characteristic of women's activities – weaving – took place (Jameson 1990b: 186). And this fact is not the result of poor preservation, since loomweights survive very well, although they are just the kind of artefact whose worth was not considered important by excavators. It seems likely, however, that looms were portable, just as pieces of furniture and other household objects were. They could be moved out to the courtyard into the warm winter sunlight or back into the cool of the sun dried brick rooms in the hot summer. Even beds could be moved, at least to judge by stories that tell of bedrooms that were moved or created. In Lysias 1, we hear of a wife who moved downstairs to sleep with her new baby for convenience.

In Plato's *Protagoras* a storeroom was converted into a bedroom for visitors. Much of the evidence seems to suggest, in fact, that many rooms did not have a purpose that was fixed and that furniture could be moved around to suit the occasion (Jameson 1990a, 1990b).

Loomweights were found in one of the houses under consideration in this chapter, in the block south of the Agora used by Walker (Figures 9.1–2). Unfortunately the excavation reports for these houses are extremely sketchy and often quite confused (Thompson 1959). Rarely are the find-spots of the artefacts listed, nor can the written texts describing the building phases be correlated with the published ground plans. In some cases, many of the artefacts are not reported at all. In fact the lack of accuracy and attention to detail in the publications of these and other houses excavated is striking, especially in comparison with the reports of the excavations of the public buildings in the neighboring Agora. These problems point to a general devaluation of ancient Athenian domestic architecture and the more mundane artefacts of household use, thus replicating the power bias of the ancient Athenian élites.

Nine loomweights were found in one room, a small chamber 'bordering the street at the very middle of the west side of the block' (Figure 9.1; Thompson 1959: 100). But it is unclear to which room the excavator refers. Walker seems to have assumed that the excavator meant the larger room in the middle of the block, which she labelled 'workroom' (Figure 9.2). Yet this room is not small. The excavator may have meant the small room just below Walker's workroom. Unfortunately the relationship of either of these rooms to each other or to their surroundings is very unclear. The excavators described this block as originally, in the fifth century, having consisted of four houses and two open yards at the south end of the block (Figure 9.1). Yet the publication did not make at all clear the earlier, fifth-century demarcation of the two houses on the west side of the block, where the loomweight room is located. Walker postulated a doorway connecting her workroom with the rooms to the south and thus forming one of the original four houses mentioned by the excavators (Figure 9.2). These rooms were part of her women's quarters. The resulting house had two doors opening onto the street and two courtyards. In the official publication of the block, however, the architect Travlos drew a solid wall between the workroom and the room to the south, thereby showing two houses instead of one (Figure 9.1). Possibly we can take Walker's plan as the state of the block in the fifth century and that of Travlos as that at the end of the fourth century, although Travlos dated the houses in his plan to the fifth century. Yet that fifth-century house would be unique, to my knowledge, because it has two doors opening on the same street and two courtyards connected to them. And in any case there is no reason that the loomweight room did not serve many purposes or that weaving did not take place elsewhere at times, for example, in the courtyard in the wintertime to catch the light and warmth. Studies of depositional histories of houses have alerted us that a find-spot does not necessarily indicate place of use (LaMotta and Schiffer, Chapter 2, this volume). Probably women wove in the room in which the loomweights were found at times. Only in this sense can we call it a loomroom or part of the women's quarters.

Nor can we always put women's quarters on the second floor. We have no evidence that all Greek houses had them (Jameson 1990b: 179–81; Morgan 1985: 117; Nevett 1994: 103). It is important for us to remember that Jones, who has given us such useful, three-dimensional drawings of Attic houses with two storeys, himself said that these were sketches, not precise reconstructions (Jones 1975).

In reality, women were not kept in seclusion in women's quarters (Cohen 1989, 1991). Nor do our texts, despite the mention of the *gunaikonitis*, provide evidence of a fixed space for such rooms (see p. 143 above; Jameson 1990b; Nevett 1994, 1995). The evidence of vase paintings also points to a lack of fixed space. We are lucky that these depictions show furnishings, since these artefacts are so important in identifying the use of rooms (Rapoport 1990). In all likelihood many of the objects depicted on these vases actually were the possessions of a wife, her dowry or the gifts given by her family to her new household (Lissarrague 1995; Oakley and Sinos 1993: 7; Schaps 1979: 9–16.) Nonetheless the vases need to be considered carefully.

On vases we see women who are surrounded by part of the moveable furnishings that tell the story of what some women did when they were together. An Athenian vase painter working *c.* 440 BCE chose two typically 'female' objects – a mirror and a chair – to set the scene on the body of a bridal vase (Figure 9.3). Although we are probably correct in assuming this particular scene shows a bride preparing for her wedding because of the type of vase on which it is shown, chairs and mirrors occur in other depictions of women (Figures 9.4–5). Other typical women's furnishings are related to the archetypal women's work of making clothing and bedding from wool. Frequently the process of woolmaking is indicated by a specially shaped wool basket or a spindle. In other cases the finished product, the cloth itself, and the chest in which it was stored indicate this activity that was central to women's lives, as can be seen on a now lost water jar painted in the first quarter of the fifth century (Figure 9.4). So prominent are chests and wool-working to the lives of Athenian women that one of the themes of the first museum exhibit on women in Classical Greece took as one of its main themes 'Containers and Textiles as Metaphors for Women' (Reeder 1995). It is interesting to note that this scene of women folding cloth is shown on a vase shape associated with women, just as was the vase in Figure 9.3. One of the jobs of women in Classical Athens was fetching water, although it is not to be presumed that upper-class women had to do this chore themselves; they had slave women who drew the water for the household. An Athenian painter working *c.* 460–450 showed women in quite different activities (ones which are rarely shown on vases and for which we have little written evidence), but again decorated the scenes with 'women's' chairs and boxes (Figure 9.5). On this vase, the seated woman in the centre holds a musical instrument, the woman to the left holds a box and her companion to the right carries a double flute. This musicmaking was not characterized as 'women's work' by Classical Athenian men, but it seems to have been part of the lives of some upper-class women. Although as far as we know Athens produced no women poets until the third century BCE, there is no reason to suppose that at least some élite Athenian women could not perform the poetry compositions of others.

But these vases cannot be understood as photographs (cf. Conkey 1990: 12–13). Rather it is as if the vase painter had been a set designer who had the aim of presenting in a clear and economical manner a stage set. This set was to be read; that is, to be understood to mean 'women acting together'. To achieve this goal, the painter added as visual cues the objects that were known to belong to women. This is not the same as saying that the scenes show the inside of the woman's quarters of the house. Rather they are what Sourvinou-Inwood calls a conceptual area (Sourvinou-Inwood 1991: 110). We are seeing the work of vase painters who were raised in a society and working for a clientele that thought of space as gendered. The presence of boxes and mirrors signalled that women were not, for example, in the Bouleuterion or the Tholos taking part in governmental affairs; they were not in what was considered male space. The painters, however, made their own choices about how to express this concept visually from their own knowledge of free women's actual possessions. The individual agency of the painter should not be forgotten, as both Osborne and Sourvinou-Inwood have argued in such different ways (Osborne 1991; Sourvinou-Inwood 1991). We also can see how the vase painter was 'setting the stage' for a play about wealthier Athenians. These were the Athenians who had colonnaded entryways or courtyards in their houses and had fine chairs and jewellery boxes and well-dressed servants (Demosthenes xxvii, *Against Aphobos*; House of Kallias: Plato, *Protagoras* 314–15D; Wycherley 1978: 187 n.33). This 'normative' house is only one of a number of different kinds of houses in the archaeological evidence. Many people did not have this standard of living.

Where was the *andron?*

Certainly not all Athenian houses had *androns,* if by that we mean rooms with the distinctive architectural features mentioned earlier. A good many did not, as far as we can tell from our small sample. Of a group of three houses of the late fourth century on the north-east slope of the Areopagos (Figure 9.6; Jones 1975: 85 fig. 7A; Nevett 1995: 14) the centre house did have an *andron,* whereas the smaller house to the right of it did not. The room to the lower right of the colonnaded courtyard in the centre house had a raised platform for the placement of couches, which have been drawn by the excavator. The excavators were not certain whether a room in the left house was an *andron;* it had a hearth (indicated by a rectangle) and an off-centre door. There may have been no *androns* in houses C and D in the Industrial District (Jones 1975: 73 fig. 3; Nevett 1995: 14–15). Some houses may have had *androns* at one time and not in others. It has been conjectured, on the basis of the special treatment of the floor, that there was an *andron* in the rather large house with loomweights used by Walker, i.e. in the proposed fifth-century phase of the block (Figure 9.2). Yet by 300 BCE the house had been divided into two and this room had become the only large room in a much smaller house (Figure 9.1). It does not seem likely that in so restricted a house there would have been enough rooms for one to have been restricted to a single function.

To complicate matters even further, the fact that some houses did not have the architectural features that we equate with an *andron* does not necessarily mean that men did not have the exclusive use of one room in such houses, at least some of the time. Admittedly, it would have been more cumbersome to carry dining couches from room to room than it was to carry chairs and boxes and baskets. Yet such couches may have been used only by the wealthy. In any case, we have already seen that beds could be moved around the house. Certainly other furnishings, ones that were signs of female space to the painters of and audiences for Attic vases, were portable. Rather than telling us about the fixed nature of women's quarters, Lysias 1, which told of the new mother moving downstairs with her baby, may instead be taken as support for an *andron* that was

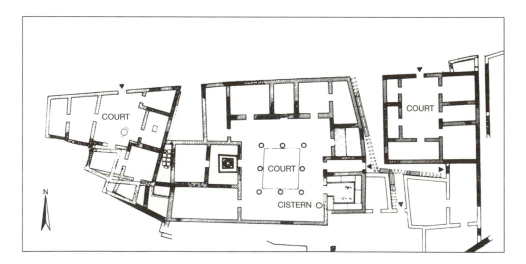

Figure 9.6 Plan of three houses on the north-east slope of the Areopagus, Athens. Central house with two rooms with decorated floors. Left house with circular well in courtyard and a hearth, indicated by small rectangle.
After Camp (1986: 148 fig. 127). Copyright 1986 by Thames and Hudson. Reproduced with permission of the author and Thames and Hudson.

a shifting rather than fixed space. For when the mother moved downstairs, the *andron* was moved upstairs (Jameson 1990b: 187–8; Morgan 1985: 118; Walker 1983: 83).

Furthermore, women had to work outside of 'the women's quarters', even if such spaces did exist in some houses. Women had to make frequent use of the courtyard on the ground floors, whether or not there were second floors. It was the woman's job to process the wool and grains and vegetables and fruits produced on her family's land into sustenance and clothing and bedding for her family. Much of the messy parts of this would have been done in the courtyard (Jameson 1990a, 1990b). Some women had the use of wells in their courtyards, for example in House C (Jones 1975: 73 fig. 3) and in the leftmost of the three houses on the north-east slope of the Areopagos (Figure 9.6). A vase from the period shows a woman getting water from a well very like the one in these courtyards (Lyon 1989: fig. 41). At some times women must have been working right inside the front door of some houses, for instance the rightmost house of Figure 9.6 or houses on the Pnyx that are of the *Flügelhofhaus* type (Jones 1975: 89 fig. 8; Lauter-Bufe and Lauter 1971: fig. 3) or the houses of Simon and Mikion and Menon in the south-west corner of the Agora (Jones 1975: 69 fig. 2, 128 figs 22.1–2).

THE ACTUAL FUNCTIONING OF HOUSEHOLD SPACE

The controllers of the image that confirmed a separation of men and women were most probably aristocratic men and quite possibly aristocratic women, as well as other men who had accepted the values of this class and had the wealth to do so. For this standard had the possibility of being met in the houses of only the wealthier segment of society, just as the elaborate *symposia* we know from vase paintings and from philosophical discourses belonged to the same, limited milieu (Humphreys 1993: xiv; Jameson 1990b: 190; Nevett 1995). Furthermore, not all those families who were wealthy enough to have had rooms specifically for dining couches maintained such a strictly gendered separation of space; that is, if the reconstruction of an *andron* in the *Flügelhofhaus* cited above is correct. There we see a well-built house with a front door that opens directly onto the courtyard and also a room with provisions for the couches that we associate with an *andron*.

On the other hand, the normative standard of men's and women's places did arise out of quite real and unequal power relationships. Furthermore, as Humphries has emphasized, we must not forget that the Athenian man had a great deal of physical power over his wife and children (Humphreys 1993: xxv–xxvi). It is possible, as Sourvinou-Inwood maintains, that even in household religious matters, women were subordinate to men (Sourvinou-Inwood 1995). And most women did spend much of their time at home. To add to this complicated picture, it certainly is striking that at the same time there also was a societal norm, seemingly antithetical to the one that gave to women the world of the house. This other standard affirmed the importance of Athenian women in communal religious rites enacted in public space. This norm has no place in the dichotomous analogies that chararacterize outside space and public life as male and inside space and domestic life as female (Goldberg 1998b).

It is also important to consider not only the contradictions produced by a comparison of norm and practice, but also the places where women and men negotiated with these contradictions. Different kinds of evidence can be brought forward to show ways in which ancient Greek women could have manipulated their traditional roles to react against standards that put so much emphasis on their domestic role inside their houses (cf. Abu-Lughod 1990). The recent investigations of the subjects of women at the public well/fountain and women and mourning have given us very interesting results because they use this approach (Cohen 1989, 1991; Foley 1993). Some Athenian women also accommodated themselves to the ideal by working outside their homes, but at the homes of others, as wet-nurses and midwives. And the women vendors, for example, whom we know from the plays of Aristophanes, may not have cared a fig for the ideal, and instead were quite happy to have work where they sold fruit and not their bodies.

Was the house really women's space?

Athenian houses were physical spaces where women did interact with each other, with men and with societal norms. Nevett's emphasis on the courtyard and the street door as the two essential features of Athenian houses has advanced this discussion immensely. The door to the street was the major architectural feature that marked a separation of space in the archaeological record and in actuality (Sanders 1990: 65; Small 1991). Front doors may have been the only substantial ones in Athenian city houses. These doors had not only functional, but also economic worth. Two surviving written sources tell us of the importance of doors and other woodwork to the Athenians who fled their homes in the countryside ahead of their enemy in the Peloponnesian War. These families knew the value of wood, for they took the wood of their houses with them if they were able (Thucydides ii.14.1; *Hellenica Oxyrhinchia* 17(12): 4–5).

Some vase painters seized on the prominence of the door and made this architectural feature their marker of separation of inside from out. One door that these artists painted was the front door of the house as it was seen from the outside, from an indeterminate space in the painted field of the vase, which in 'real life' would have been the street. It is also possible that, at times, the door and the outside wall of the house served as a kind of bulletin board for a family to announce to outsiders family events like a wedding (Oakley and Sinos 1993: 21, 34 fig. 79). Significantly, this door did not separate women from men. It separated household members from non-household members, as both Small and Nevett have argued, but on the basis of evidence from different cultures. The analogy should read outside/stranger : inside/household member. That this analogy has only recently been articulated for Athenian domestic architecture signals the danger in expressing relationships in dichotomous analogies that are all considered equivalent to each other. Yet even this, more recently expressed analogy obscures distinctions. For rules of behaviour may have varied depending on the sex and the class of both the stranger and the family member.

Vase painters seem to have painted another door, the partly open door into the marriage chamber, which was signalled by an elegantly covered bed (Oakley and Sinos 1993: 35–7). The space that can be labelled 'outside' of the door in this type of representation is not so clear. Sometimes it is filled with women and is clearly in a courtyard or else in a more indeterminate space, which should also be inside a house (Lyon 1989: fig. 124, 140; Oakley and Sinos 1993: fig. 129). At other times the bridegroom, accompanied by the women attendants of the bride, lead the bride toward this room. Sometimes they clearly are outside of the house and at others inside (Oakley and Sinos 1993: figs 105–7). The door to the bridal chamber had great symbolic value and like the front door it stood for the house, *pars pro toto* (Sourvinou-Inwood 1991: 71). The door to the marriage chamber, however, does not seem to have been physically substantial, unless it always occurred on now lost second floors. In fact, the lack of evidence for interior doors in Athenian city houses suggests that none of them were substantial.

Some houses, like Houses C and D in the Industrial District (Jones 1975: 73 fig. 3) or the centre of the block of three houses on the Areopagus (Figure 9.6), had an entrance hall or an off-centre door that maximized the privacy of the house (Nevett 1995). Strangers would not have been able to see into the courtyard from the street, even if the front door were open; nor could a person who was making a purchase at a store, for example the one next to the front door of House C (Jones 1975: 73 fig. 3). Other houses did not have off-centre doors or entrance corridors. Sometimes these houses are less luxurious than their neighbours, like the two outer houses in the block of three on the Areopagus (Figure 9.6) or the House of Simon on the edge of the

Agora (Jones 1975: fig. 22.1). Other houses, like the *Flügelhofhaus* on the Pnyx, although not particularly large, do have other architectural pretensions such as an *andron*, as we have seen (Lauter-Bufe and Lauter 1971: 111–12 fig. 3). Yet here too the front door opened right on the courtyard. These arrangements may mean that the separation of the domestic activities of the household from strangers was less strictly enforced in some households; or it may mean that this separation was not a custom of some households at all (Nevett 1995). Possibly these families did not belong to the aristocratic class. In some instances these families may have been poorer ones who had few choices in their small houses. In other instances they may have been metics, i.e. aliens resident in Athens, or wealthy non-aristocratic Athenian citizens with their own customs. Interestingly, living in one *Flügelhofhaus* at some point in time was a family for whom the separation of non-family members from women working inside the house seems not to have been a concern, seemingly in contradiction to the élite norm. Yet the family had a room for drinking parties which, apparently at least, was in the aristocratic style.

Strange men, however, did enter even houses with doorways protecting the interior of the house from the street viewer (Lysias 1; Jameson 1990b: 183). Only in the case of Walker's hypothetical reconstruction of the fifth-century phases of her houses (Figure 9.2) or in the case of the central house on the Areopagus (Figure 9.6) could men have entered into what she designates as the men's areas without moving through the women's courtyard. As indicated earlier, however, Walker's reconstruction is highly problematical. In some cases aristocratic men had to enter a courtyard where women might be working if the men were on their way to *symposia* in houses with couch-rooms. Nevett has shown how the architectural arrangement of these houses made this occurrence almost inevitable. And this despite the fact that the norm said that women do not come into contact with men who are not family members. A man who came to discuss business with the husband of a house would have had to go through the courtyard of his house to do so, wherever the *andron* was. Men of much lower status also entered the courtyard, such as the man who came to clean out the cesspool for compost in a house in the block south of the South Stoa (Figure 9.1; Jones 1975: 83 fig. 6A; Owens 1983). In this instance we have not only the literary references to this civic garbage pickup, but the actual remains of cesspools in the houses (Owens 1983).

In households where the men had the wealth and leisure to have *symposia*, *xenoi*, who were not relatives nor exactly strangers either, came to drinking parties and also had to go through the courtyard to get to the couch-room. These *xenoi* do not fit into our oppositional categories at all (Nevett 1994: 108–9). It is possible that some of these men may have been able to come and go in their friends' houses and mingle with members of the household (Cohen 1991). In houses that were also stores or workshops, courtyards served men and even women purchasers, as well as the inhabitants of the house. The House of Simon belonged to a cobbler and his customers would have come into the courtyard or even inside the building to buy new shoes (Jones 1975: 68–71; Thompson 1980; Thompson and Wycherley 1972: 173–85), as a girl and her father are doing on an Attic vase (Thompson 1980). We are probably to imagine the scene on another vase, on which a woman is buying perfume, as taking place in a perfume store (Lyon 1989: fig. 11). The girl in the cobbler scene was presumably of citizen rank to judge by the depiction of her father. The woman purchasing oil may have been a slave, if we assume that wealthy women of citizen rank did not go out to shop without an escort and we also assume that the vase painter intended to show all the participants in a real practice.

Did behavioural conventions influence the use of space?

The organization of the house itself presents us with a paradox. In fact, the courtyard was the site where men and women, family members and strangers interacted with each other, where they had to play out their cultural customs on real ground. When strange men did enter the courtyard, women may have for that time removed themselves from the courtyard and gone into one of the rooms, an example of the principle of scheduling of space (Nevett 1994: 109). Behaviour is a far more important indicator of the use of space than fixed architectural elements (Rapoport 1990). Women may have followed other behavioural conventions such as lowering their eyes, turning away or lifting their drapery to hide their eyes. When non-family men came inside they, too, may have 'ignored' these working women in some behavioural way. Women may have adopted different practices, depending on their own status or that of the stranger, whether man or woman, slave, metic or free. And how would a wife have behaved when a courtesan, a *hetaira*, came into her husband's house for a drinking party? Would women have been more likely to avoid the presence of free men or slave, non-Athenian or Athenian? Although one situation we know from Lysias (3, 6–7) suggests the contrary, there is little likelihood that the women of the house would have had to remove themselves or hide their faces when male family members came into the house. As a good lawyer, Lysias was exaggerating the purity of the women of the household in order to make the arrival of the accused seem even more dastardly. We know it was the custom for men and women family members to celebrate together during parts of wedding feasts and mourn together during parts of funerals (Oakley and Sinos 1993: 22 = *PCG* V 184–5; Foley 1981). It is also a possibility worthy of at least consideration that households in the same neighbourhoods may have formed fictive families and, consequently, that neighbour men would have been treated as family members (Small 1991: 339), as may have close associates of the husband.

Did time influence the use of space?

Much of the day, it would seem that the courtyard and the whole house did belong to the women, both slave and free, and young children of both sexes. Even the *andron*, if there was one, had to be cleaned and tidied after the previous day's *symposium*. The men were in the fields or in the *agora*. Yet at the beginning of the working day of the farming season, in more prosperous households, men would have filled that space as they gathered their equipment and perhaps animals before going out to the field; and so would they again on their return at the end of the day. In less prosperous families, it may have been only the husband who went out to work his land. There is no reason to believe that men and women of the house were not sharing that space as they decided and allotted their chores in the morning or compared notes at dusk. Certainly they shared household rituals, like libations, which were repeated on a daily basis, and made sacrifices in the courtyard and elsewhere. In the short winters, perhaps some men stayed at home during the day, doing things like repairing their tools and meeting with friends and associates or coming and going from business or politics or exercise in the city. If a house was also a workshop and store without separate entrances into the house itself and into the commercial area, the space of the courtyard would have had to have been negotiated throughout the day when both women and men needed light and water for their tasks and customers were making purchases. In other houses, occasional or regular drinking parties would have caused shifting negotiations of the courtyard space.

We may have evidence that men and women of citizen rank dined at the same feast, at times in the house of the father of a bride before the bride was taken to her husband's house. This custom seems to contradict the evidence recorded in our courtcase about what seems to me a suspiciously modest household, one in which the women shielded themselves from the presence of even their male relatives (Lysias 3, 6–7). Where would the apparently customary marriage feast, so notable for its absence in Attic vase paintings, have taken place? If both men and women of citizen rank ate reclining on couches, a practice for which I find no reference, it could have been in the *andron*. If women ate while seated in chairs and only the men reclined, there would not have been enough room in an *andron* for couches and chairs and tables for the food. Dentzer cites examples of Attic vases that show a woman seated on a throne and a man on a couch and comments on the rarity of this combination (Dentzer 1982: 123–5). The visual representations that show men and women dining together in this manner do not necessarily refer to real practice, however. One scene from a vase with this distinction in practice for men and women shows divine couples (Nevett 1994: 109 fig. 5.3). Yet Schmitt Pantel and Schnapp have identified the seated women on another vase as a courtesan (Schmitt Pantel and Schnapp 1982: 61 no. 14). Attic reliefs (Dentzer 1982: pls 75–82) may heroize the couple by showing them in this manner and thereby likening them to the iconography of Near Eastern kings and queens. On the other hand, aristocratic couples may indeed have dined in this manner on some occasions. Possibly some houses had two formal rooms to accommodate two different kinds of celebrations. One house, the middle of this block of three from the Areopagos, has two rooms with decorated floors, the couch-room to the lower right of the courtyard and a second room to the left (Figure 9.6). One may have been a family banquet room, the other the *andron*. But this was a particularly elegant house. In other circumstances the courtyard may have accommodated the feasters, whether on couches or chairs. And the very rich may have held this feast in a sanctuary (Oakley and Sinos 1993: 22–3). Schmitt Pantel has provided a discussion of public banqueting contexts (Schmitt Pantel 1992).

CONCLUSIONS

In looking at how men and women, strangers and families, used the central space of the house, I have been examining the physical spaces where norm and practice interacted, but it is not possible for me to do so without also taking into account the importance of both behaviour and time (Rapoport 1990; Knapp 1992). For the house is not only a physical space, but a space whose use varies with time (Bourdieu 1966). The portable nature of most of the furnishings of an Athenian house meant that the rooms and courtyard were probably used in different ways at different times. The locations of women's rooms, marriage chambers and even *andrones* seem not to have been fixed permanently by architectural structure in many cases. Patterns of use would have varied according to different kinds of time – for example, the cyclical time of repeating work days or of the agricultural season or of a person's life cycle or the even longer cycle of a sequence of generations living in the same house (Foxhall 1989; Nevett 1995: 20). We hear from Aeschines (1.124) how a house served different functions through this longer period of time. Consider for a moment the cyclical time of the annual religious calendar. On days when great festivals were celebrated, possibly only slaves were at home. During the Thesmophoria, on the other hand, only men and female slaves could have been at home, since free women spent three days outside together at this celebration. The life cycles of the members of the household would have affected the way people used it. New members – a bride, a slave, an infant – were accepted into the household and the courtyard was where their membership was first recognized. Family members died and their bodies passed through the courtyard in the procession to the cemetery. And then there were more episodic events like the business call or the *symposium* or the compost pickup, or far longer extents of time like the intergenerational changes likely in households where an Athenian husband was usually much older than his wife.

A consideration of behaviour brings us to the question of the ownership of the rules governing the use of space in the Athenian house. We know that the husband owned the house and even some of its inhabitants. Legally almost all the power rested in the hands of the husband. But traditional customs, not always clear in legal evidence, may also have provided a wife a sort of counterbalance to her husband's control. Lin Foxhall has suggested ways that some married women of citizen rank may have been influential in the management of their households (Foxhall

1989). They owed this power to the leverage they had because their dowries helped in the survival of their households. Women may also have received respect and authority because of their effectiveness in creating a well-run household. Certainly the skill of Athenian women in making textiles was held in high esteem and to the Greeks weaving was a metaphor for human resourcefulness (Barber 1994: 242). These women were using their traditional roles in a way that seems to run counter to their legal status. Certainly in some other cultures, women have been able to appropriate the ideology that assigned them the household as their sphere to then argue that they should control the rules about how people, including men, were to behave in their space (Spencer-Wood, Chapter 10, this volume). It is interesting to entertain the possibility that, on some occasions when family women and men were together, Athenian wives may have influenced the rules of behaviour.

Women did spend a lot of their time at home. And the image of women's place at home was a strong one, all the more so since Classical Athens had a relatively small and homogeneous population. Yet the population of Athens was not so homogeneous that distinctions based on class and status did not have an effect on the playing out of this image in daily life. Women also went outside for many reasons, as we know. There was another image of women's place; women's place was also at public worship. Women were in an unequal power relationship in which societal norms explained why they did not have control of their own city-state or even, to some extent, their own bodies. On the other hand, there is no reason to deny that they were capable of manipulating the social restrictions that the aristocratic and male-dominated culture placed upon them. An examination of the spaces in which women and men acted or could have acted shows us how they lived their own lives in the elaborate dance that we all do when we express our own personalities that have been moulded by our own cultural circumstances. It shows us that the household, rather than being a place of isolation for women, was an important site of social integration for many different members of the Athenian community. We also see how tenuous is the evidence that has been used to support exclusively female and male spaces in Classical Athenian households.

ACKNOWLEDGEMENTS

I would like to thank my student Melanie Pereira for her help with this chapter.

BIBLIOGRAPHY

Abu-Lughod, L. (1990) 'The Romance of Resistance: Tracing Transformations of Power Through Bedouin Women', *American Ethnologist* 17: 41–55.

Aeschines, *The Speeches of Aeschines* (trans. Charles Darwin Adams 1919), Cambridge, Mass.: Loeb edition.

Ahmed, L. (1982) 'Western Ethnocentrism and Perceptions of the Harem', *Feminist Studies* 8, 3: 521–34.

Aristophanes (trans. Benjamin Bickley Rogers 1924), vols 1, 2, Cambridge, Mass.: Loeb edition.

Barber, E. (1994) *Women's Work: The First 20,000 Years*, New York: Norton.

Blok, J. (1987) 'Sexual Asymmetry: A Historiographical Essay', in J. Blok and P. Mason (eds) *Sexual Asymmetry*, Amsterdam: Gieben: 1–58.

Brown, S. (1993) 'Feminist Research in Archaeology: What Does It Mean and Why Is It Taking So Long?', in N. Rabinowitz and A. Richlin (eds) *Feminist Theory and the Classics*, London: Routledge: 238–71.

Bourdieu, P. (1966) 'The Sentiment of Honor in Kabyle Society', in J. Peristiany (ed.) *Honor and Shame: The Values of Mediterranean Society*, Chicago: University of Chicago Press: 191–241.

Burke, E. (1991) *Struggle and Survival in the Modern Middle East*, New Haven: Yale University Press.

Camp, J. (1986) *The Athenian Agora*, London:Thames and Hudson.

Cohen, D. (1989) 'Seclusion, Separation and the Status of Women in Classical Athens', *Greece and Rome* 36: 3–15.

—— (1991) *Law, Sexuality and Society: The Enforcement of Morals in Classical Athens*, Cambridge: Cambridge University Press.

Conkey, M. (1990) 'Experimenting with Style in Archaeology: Some Historical and Theoretical Issues', in M. Conkey and C. Hastorf (eds) *The Uses of Style in Archaeology*, Cambridge: Cambridge University Press: 5–17.

—— (1991) 'Does It Make a Difference: Feminist Thinking and Archaeologies of Gender', in D. Walde and D. Willows (eds) *The Archaeology of Gender: Proceedings of the 22nd Annual Chacmool Conference*, Calgary: University of Calgary: 24–33.

Conkey, M. and Williams, S. (1991) 'Original Narratives: The Political Economy of Gender in Archaeology', in M. di Leonardo (ed.) *Gender at the Crossroads of Knowledge: Feminist Anthropology in the Postmodern Era*, Berkeley, Los Angeles: University of California Press: 102–39.

Demosthenes, *Private Orations* (2 vols) (trans. A. T Murray 1936, 1939), Cambridge, Mass.: Loeb edition.

Dentzer, J.-M. (1982) *Le motif du banquet couché dans le proche-orient et le monde grec du VIIe au IVe siècle av. J.C.*, Rome: École française de Rome.

di Leonardo, M. (1991) 'Introduction: Gender, Culture and Political Economy', in M. di Leonardo (ed.) *Gender at the Crossroads of Knowledge: Feminist Anthropology in the Postmodern Era*, Berkeley, Los Angeles: University of California Press: i–xii.

Dougherty, C. (1995) 'War Memorials: The Politics of Public Mourning', in *Abstracts of the 127th Annual Meeting of the American Philological Association*, Worcester, Mass.: American Philological Association: 32.

DuBois, P. (1991) *Centaurs and Amazons: Women and the Prehistory of the Great Chain of Being*, Ann Arbor: University of Michigan Press.

Fantham, E., Foley, P., Kampen, N., Pomeroy, S. and Shapiro, H. A. (1994) *Women in the Classical World*, Oxford: Oxford University Press.

Foley, H. (1981) 'The Conception of Women in Athenian Drama', in H. Foley (ed.) *Reflections of Women in Antiquity*, New York: Gordon and Breach: 127–68.

—— (1993) 'The Politics of Tragic Lamentation', in A. Sommerstein *et al.* (eds) *Tragedy, Comedy and the Polis*, Bari: Levante: 101–44.

Foxhall, L. (1989) 'Household, Gender and Property in Classical Athens', *Classical Quarterly* 39: 22–44.

—— (1994) 'Pandora Unbound. A Feminist Critique of Foucault's *History of Sexuality*', in A. Cornwall and N. Lindisfarne (eds) *Dislocating Masculinity. Comparative Ethnographies*, London: Routledge: 133–46.

Gerhard, E. (1840) *Auserlesene griechische Vasenbilder* 4, Berlin.

Gilchrist, R. (1991) 'Women's Archaeology? Political Feminism, Gender Theory and Historical Revision', *Antiquity* 65: 495–501.

Goldberg, M. (1998a) 'The Amazon Myth and Gender Studies', in K. Hartswick and M. Sturgeon (eds) *Stephanos: Papers in Honor of Brunilde Sismondo Ridgway*, Philadelphia: University of Pennsylvania Press: 89–100.

—— (1998b) 'Deceptive Dichotomy: Two Case Studies', in M. Casey (ed.) *Redefining Archaeology: Feminist Perspectives. 3rd Australian Women in Archaeology Conference*, Canberra: Australian National University Press: 107–12.

Hodder, I. (1987) *The Archaeology of Contextual Meanings*, Cambridge: Cambridge University Press.

—— (1991) *Reading the Past* (2nd edition), Cambridge: Cambridge University Press.

—— (1992) *Theory and Practice in Archaeology*, London: Routledge.

Hoepfner, W. and Schwander, E.-L. (1994) *Haus und Stadt im klassischen Griechenland*, Munich: Deutscher Kunstverlag.

Humphreys, S. (1993) *The Family, Women and Death* (2nd edition) Ann Arbor: University of Michigan Press.

Jameson, M. (1990a) 'Domestic Space in the Greek City-state', in S. Kent (ed.) *Domestic Architecture and the Use of Space*, Cambridge: Cambridge University Press: 92–113.

—— (1990b) 'Private Space and the Greek City', in O. Murray and S. Price (eds) *The Greek City from Homer to Alexander*, Oxford: Oxford University Press: 171–95.

Jones, J. (1975) 'Town and Country Houses of Attica in Classical Times', in H. Mussche, P. Spitaels and F. Goemaere-De Poerck (eds) *Thorikos and the Laurion in Archaic and Classical Times. Miscellanea Graeca* 1, Ghent: Belgian Archaeological Mission in Greece: 63–140.

Kent, S. (1990) 'Activity Areas and Architecture: An Interdisciplinary View of the Relationship Between Use of Space and Domestic Built Environments', in S. Kent (ed.) *Domestic Architecture and the Use of Space*, Cambridge: Cambridge University Press: 1–8.

Knapp, A. B. (1992) 'Archaeology and *Annales*: Time, Space and Change', in A. B. Knapp (ed.) *Archaeology, Annales and Ethnohistory*, Cambridge: Cambridge University Press: 1–21.

Keuls, E. (1985) *The Reign of the Phallus: Sexual Politics in Ancient Athens*, New York: Harper and Row.

Lamphere, L. (1993) 'The Domestic Sphere of Women and the Public World of Men: The Strengths and Limitations of an Anthropological Dichotomy', in C. Brettell and C. Sargent (eds) *Gender in Cross Cultural Perspective*, Englewood Cliffs, N.J.: Prentice-Hall: 82–92.

Lauter-Bufe, H. and Lauter, H. (1971) 'Wohnhäuser und Stadtviertel des klassischen Athen', *Deutsches Archäologische Institut. Athenische Abteilungen* 86: 109–24.

Lissarrague, F. (1995) 'Women, Boxes, Containers: Some Signs and Metaphors', in E. Reeder *et al.*, *Pandora: Women in Classical Greece*, Princeton: Princeton University Press: 91–101.

Lloyd, G. E. R. (1966) *Polarity and Analogy, Two Types of Argumentation in Early Greek Thought*, Cambridge: Cambridge University Press.

Lyon, D. (trans.) (1989) *City of Images: Iconography and Society in Ancient Greece*, Princeton: Princeton University Press.

Lysias (W. R. M. Lamb trans. 1960) Cambridge, Mass.: Loeb edition.

Moreland, J. (1992) 'Restoring the Dialectic: Settlement Patterns and Documents in Medieval Central Italy, in A. B. Knapp (ed.) *Archaeology, Annales and Ethnohistory*, Cambridge: Cambridge University Press: 112–29.

Morgan, G. (1985) 'Euphiletos's Lysias I', *Transactions of the American Philological Association* 112: 115–23.

Nevett, L. (1994) 'Separation or Seclusion: Towards an Archaeolgocial Approach to Investigating Women in the Greek Household in the Fifth to Third Centuries B.C.', in M. Parker Pearson and C. Richards (eds) *Architecture and Order: Approaches to Social Space*, London: Routledge: 98–112.

—— (1995) 'Gender Relations in the Classical Greek Household: The Archaeological Evidence', *Annual of the British Archaeological School in Athens* 90: 1–29.

Oakley, J. and Sinos, R. (1993) *The Wedding in Ancient Athens*, Madison: University of Wisconsin Press.

Osborne, R. (1991) 'Whose Image and Superscription Is This?', *Arion* 3rd ser. 1, 2: 255–75.

Owens, E. (1983) 'The *Koprologoi* at Athens in the Fifth and Fourth Centuries B.C.', *Classical Quarterly* n.s. 33: 44–50.

Plato, *Dialogues* (B. Jowett trans. 1, n.d.), New York: Bigelow Press.

Rapoport, A. (1990) 'Systems of Activities and Systems of Settings', in S. Kent (ed.) *Domestic Architecture and the Use of Space*, Cambridge: Cambridge University Press: 9–20.

Reeder, E. (ed.) (1995) *Pandora: Women in Classical Greece*, Princeton: Princeton University Press.

Sanders, D. (1990) 'Behavioral Conventions and Archaeology: Methods for the Analysis of Ancient Architecture', in S. Kent (ed.) *Domestic Architecture and the Use of Space*, Cambridge: Cambridge University Press: 43–72.

Saxonhouse, A. (1992) 'Introduction – Public and Private: The Paradigm's Power', in B. Garlick, S. Dixon and P. Allen (eds) *Stereotypes of Women in Power: Historical Perspectives*, New York: Greenwood Press: 1–12.

Schaps, D. (1979) *The Economic Rights of Women*, Edinburgh: Edinburgh University Press.

Schmitt Pantel, P. (1992) *La Cité au Banquet*, Rome: École française de Rome.

—— (1994) 'Women and Ancient History', in P. Schmitt Pantel (ed.) *A History of Women: From Ancient Goddesses to Christian Saints*, Cambridge, Mass.: Belknap Press: 464–72.

Schmitt Pantel, P. and Schnapp, A. (1982) 'Image et societé in Gréce ancienne', *Revue archéologique*: 57–74.

Shanks, M. and Tilley, C. (1987) *Re-Constructing Archaeology: Theory and Practice*, London: Routledge.

Small, D. (1991) 'Initial Study of the Structure of Women's Seclusion in the Archaeological Past', in D. Walde and D. Willows (eds) *The Archaeology of Gender: Proceedings of the 22nd Annual Chacmool Conference*, Calgary: University of Calgary: 336–42.

Sourvinou-Inwood, C. (1991) '*Reading*' Greek Culture: Texts and Images, Rituals and Myths*, Oxford: Oxford University Press.

—— (1995) 'Male and Female, Public and Private, Ancient and Modern', in E. Reeder (ed.) *Pandora: Women in Classical Greece*, Princeton: Princeton University Press: 111–22.

Talalay, L. (1994) 'A Feminist Boomerang: The Great Goddess and Greek Prehistory', *Gender and History* 6: 165–83.

Thompson, D. (1980) 'The House of Simon the Shoemaker', *Archaeology* 13: 234–40.

Thompson, H. (1959) 'Activities in the Athenian Agora: 1958', *Hesperia* 28: 98–103.

Thompson, H. and Wycherley, R. (1972) *The Athenian Agora* 14, *The Agora of Athens*, Princeton: Princeton University Press.

Thucydides, *The Complete Writings of Thucydides* (R. Crawley trans. 1934) New York: Modern Library.

Travlos, J. (1971) *Pictorial Dictionary of Ancient Athens*, Tübingen: Verlag Ernst Waasmuth.

Tyrrell, W. B. (1984) *Amazons, A Study in Athenian Mythmaking*, Baltimore: Johns Hopkins University Press.

Vernant, J. P. (1983) 'Hestia–Hermes: the Religious Expression of Space and Movement in Ancient Greece', in J. P. Vernant, *Myth and Thought*, London: Routledge and Kegan Paul: 127–75.

Versnel, H. S. (1987) 'Wife and Helpmate: Women of Ancient Athens in Anthropological Perspective', in J. Blok and P. Mason (eds) *Sexual Asymmetry*, Amsterdam: Gieben: 59–86.

Vitruvius, *The Ten Books on Architecture* (Morris Hicky Morgan trans. 1914) Cambridge, Mass.: Dover Press.

Walde, D. and Willows, D. (eds) (1991) *The Archaeology of Gender: Proceedings of the 22nd Annual Chacmool Conference*, Calgary: University of Calgary.

Walker, S. (1983) 'Women and Housing in Classical Greece', in A. Cameron and A. Kuhrt (eds) *Images of Women in Antiquity*, London: Routledge and Kegan Paul: 81–91.

Wycherley, R. E. (1978) *The Stones of Athens*, Princeton: Princeton University Press.

Xenophon, *Oeconomicus, A Social and Historical Commentary* (Sarah B. Pomeroy trans. 1994) Oxford: Clarendon Press.

Young, R. (1951) 'An Industrial District of Ancient Athens', *Hesperia* 20: 135–288.

Chapter Ten

The world their household: Changing meanings of the domestic sphere in the nineteenth century

Suzanne M. Spencer-Wood

This chapter shows how our understanding of household activities in other cultures has been shaped by archaeological projections of an élite Victorian gender ideology as the universal gender system from early prehistory through Classical cultures to the nineteenth century. Archaeologists have created distorted constructions of past cultures by selecting and interpreting evidence to validate an assumed gender dichotomy. Feminist theory and research has questioned assumed stereotypes, revealing previously overlooked evidence of multiple diverse gender ideologies and practices from prehistory to the present. This chapter demonstrates that the élite Victorian gender ideology was not even universal in the nineteenth century.

The first section of this chapter discusses how feminist theoretical critiques have revealed androcentric biases produced by projecting Victorian-derived modern gender stereotypes as universal. Partial understandings of the past have been created by dichotomizing cultural activities into dominant-public-male versus subordinate-domestic-female roles. Feminist theorizing has revealed that belief in the reality of dualistic gender ideology is supported at deeper levels by language and an epistemological belief in the universality of structuralist binary thinking (Spencer-Wood 1993). The next section discusses how nineteenth-century classicists legitimated their élite Victorian gender ideology by claiming it originated in Classical Greece. Feminist research is presented showing that a gender dichotomy was not universally espoused or practised in Classical Greece. The last section discusses some alternative nineteenth-century gender ideologies and practices in Europe and the United States that created a diversity of new types of archaeological sites, including kitchenless houses and public kitchens. The diversity of Victorian women's public cooperative housekeeping enterprises raises questions about whether it is always possible to define the household as distinctly separate from the community.

FEMINIST CRITIQUES OF MALE-BIASED FRAMEWORKS

Starting in the 1970s third-wave feminist analyses have revealed how a self-reinforcing structure of Victorian-derived androcentrism deeply permeates all aspects of western culture, including anthropology, archaeology, scientific epistemology, language, and values. Multiple levels of male bias support and reinforce each other in a comprehensive androcentric system of thought that is represented as objective in ungendered text and discourse. As a result most of us have at some point unconsciously used widely accepted but androcentric paradigms, methodology, models, assumptions or taxonomies. Androcentrism can be most simply defined as an ideology of sexist prejudice resulting from a male-centred point of view. Androcentrism constructs gender in a universal structural dichotomy between opposed gender stereotypes. In androcentric ideology men are identified as public, cultural, rational, active, powerful, superior and naturally dominant over women, who are devalued as subordinate, domestic, natural, emotional, powerless, passive and inferior. Women and households have been devalued to the point that they have often been excluded entirely from large-scale constructions of the past in apparently objective ungendered text. Androcentric archaeology and anthropology are fundamentally political in supporting the oppression of women in the present by creating partial distorted constructions of cultures that represent male dominance and female subordination as universal, natural, and inevitable (Spencer-Wood 1992a). This section discusses feminist critiques of androcentric biases at a number of levels, from supposedly ungendered text and discourse, through constructions of cultures in gender dichotomies, to the underlying epistemology of structuralism.

The disappearance of women and households in androcentric ungendered discourse

The political standpoint of an individual or group is revealed by the questions that are not asked as much as the questions that are asked. Traditionally most archaeological research has not explicitly considered gender, although it is a foundational cultural construct that structures all social life. Supposedly objective ungendered text, discourse, constructions of cultures and evolution reveal unquestioned sexist assumptions about gender. Prior to feminist archaeology gender was not researched as a cultural construct because it was unproblematically reduced to biologically determined models of sex in which weak domestic women were dependent on strong public men (Harding 1987a: 299). According to this ideology, because men are dominant their viewpoints and behaviour are of primary importance, while domestic women are subordinate and unimportant. Therefore, supposedly ungendered constructions of other cultures usually represent men's behaviours and viewpoints as those of the whole society, often masked as cultural norms (Conkey and Spector 1984: 4). The primacy and dominance of men over women is reinforced at the deepest cultural level by the linguistic convention of always putting men before women. Further, women disappear and are excluded from the past by the linguistic convention of using male nouns and pronouns to represent androcentric text and discourse as ungendered and universal (Spencer-Wood 1991a). Women and children often disappear from the past in ungendered text that purports to represent them but is actually exclusively about men.

The tradition of subsuming women and children within male-biased language extends as well to male-defined categories. For instance, in historical archaeology households usually have been identified only by the male head (Spencer-Wood 1991a). This continues the historic western cultural practice in which each man legally controlled and represented 'his' household of women and children in the public community of men (Rowbotham 1973: 4, 43, 48–50, 55–6). Women and children have disappeared, not only in male-defined households but also in classes defined according to men's occupations by economists, historians and archaeologists (Spencer-Wood 1991a: 236). At the larger scale cultures are often defined according to male-controlled social, political and economic structures. Households and women disappear as they are subsumed in classes. For instance, Henretta's (1971) androcentric research on the social structure of colonial Boston only discussed men, their sons, and their occupations, as if households, women and girls didn't exist. Henretta ignored female-domestic households and families as unimportant to men's public history. Yet colonial women in households produced significant quantities of goods for public sale, including textiles, butter, eggs and chickens. Further, many houses included rooms where public sales occurred, whether stores, craft shops, or print shops such as Ben Franklin's in Philadelphia. Often women worked in household stores, in craft shops, and in the industrial system of 'putting out' to households the production of goods such as shoes and straw hats. Widows usually became proprietors of household businesses after their husbands died (Wertheimer 1977: 12–20, 51). Androcentric bias in ungendered text and discourse is often apparent from the fact that only men are mentioned, excluding women's contributions to history.

Henretta exemplifies the fundamental assumption among androcentric historians and anthropologists: what men did was always more important and powerful than what women did. Some early feminist anthropologists analysed how androcentric anthropologists produced male-biased ethnographies by accepting the viewpoints of male informants as the monolithic truth for a culture (Rohrlich-Leavitt *et al.* 1975). Men have been viewed by many anthropologists and historians as the only important social agents, the makers of male-defined large-scale political history. This definition of what is important in the past limits research questions to men's public actions and excludes women and households from the past because they are assumed to be only domestic and therefore irrelevant to history by definition. Thus women and households have disappeared in androcentric constructions of the past as sequences of men's public events, including wars, conquests, and kings.

In processual archaeology those questions considered most important and accorded the highest status have been male-defined and limited to the identification of ungendered large-scale public external variables considered to determine small-scale internal socio-cultural variables such as ethnicity, class, and gender (Wylie 1991a, critiquing Binford 1983: 221). Many large-scale external causal variables are androcentrically assumed to be controlled by men, such as exploration, wars, trade, and governmental or religious cultural contacts. The systems theory model of culture has focused research on large-scale processes in functional perspective, making small-group actions, roles and choices invisible as sources of cultural change (Conkey and Spector 1984: 22–3). Large-scale public constructions of the past subsume and therefore exclude from consideration the essential contributions of households to economies, social and political systems. Prior to feminist critique and research household archaeology was considered a less important small-scale topic due to its association with women. Households were not often explicitly related to larger scale descriptions of cultural systems. The widely used systems model of culture supported the focus on ungendered constructions of the past at the large public scale by not including subsystems for gender or households (Wylie 1991b). Gender has often been included in the social subsystem. However, this limitation is problematic because gender and households are fundamental to the construction and operation of all cultural structures, including economic and political subsystems. Yet it is common to exclude mention of households in large-scale ungendered descriptions of subsistence systems, classes, or political systems. The large-scale focus is on men's public activities, whether hunting, agriculture, production of goods for trade or political leadership. The household is subsumed under these ungendered but male-represented categories and is seldom mentioned at the large scale.

Projecting the ideology of dichotomies as the universal reality

Large-scale cultural processes, cross-cultural generalizations, theories, methods and questions are considered most important in the search for scientific laws of culture change. At a deeper epistemological level the positivistic paradigm of science used in the 'new' archaeology is based on a historically situated gender ideology. In the eighteenth century Descartes drew from the gender ideology opposing rational man versus emotional woman to create the ideology that objectivity is opposed to subjectivity (Bordo 1986). Yet the subjective elements in the objective scientific method include the selection of research question, data, and methods of analysis that together determine research results (Longino and Doell 1983). Claims that the scientific method is absolutely objective have been bolstered by the use of omniscient language that removes the subjective observer, making it difficult to reveal assumptions masked in passive voice statements that 'The data show this to be true' (Spencer-Wood 1993: 130). However, the interpretation of meanings of data are shaped by theory and method. Androcentric frameworks, assumptions and methods that classify data as either domestic or public can create the finding of a sexual division of labour as the result of circular reasoning (shown by Kennedy and Watson 1991).

Starting in the 1970s some feminist anthropologists and archaeologists began to critique androcentric biases involved in the explicit construction of gender as a universal structural dichotomy, in which public active men dominated women who were devalued as domestic, passive, and subordinate (e.g. Reiter 1975). This practice of reproducing androcentric models and assumptions by explicitly constructing gender in sexist dichotomies has been called the 'add women and stir' approach (Bunch 1987: 140). In prehistoric archaeology's classic construction of early hominid evolution, men supposedly evolved larger brains as a result of their important hunting roles, while women remained unevolved because they were only gatherers and child rearers at the home base (Washburn and Lancaster 1968). The modern devaluation of women's domestic roles resulted in the devaluation of prehistoric women's complex knowledge and roles that were essential for the survival and evolution of hominids. In a 1971 groundbreaking feminist article Linton critiqued the lack of evidence supporting the Man the Hunter construction of early hominid social life that portrayed women as limited to domestic roles at the home base, dependent on men to bring home the bacon and firewood. This critique applies equally well to the more recent construction of Man the Scavenger, which only slightly modified the Man the Hunter myth. Subsequent research on modern hunter-gatherers that form the closest analogy for early hominids has shown that women's gathering comprises the vast majority of the diet (Lee 1968). Further, feminists have also critiqued androcentric evolutionists who have emphasized the male-associated mechanism of individual competition and survival of the fittest (Gross and Averill 1983; Tanner 1981: 3, 6, 23). The importance of the female-associated principle of cooperation in women's activities, including gathering and child-rearing has been overlooked (Tanner and Zihlman 1976). Androcentric archaeologists have only considered men's cooperaive hunting or scavenging and meat sharing to be important in human evolution (e.g. Washburn and Lancaster 1968; Jolly and Plog 1986: 277–9).

The construction of cultures, evolution, and science in simplistic dichotomies is supported at an epistemological level by structuralism, which considers dualistic either/or thinking to be the universally natural pattern of thought. The widespread acceptance of structuralism has resulted in monolithic constructions of cultures as sets of dichotomies (e.g. Deetz 1988), even in post-processualism, although it was strongly influenced at the theoretical level by feminist critiques of dichotomies and concerns for individual social agency (Hodder 1987: 6–9; 1992: 84–5). Structuralist thinking classifies the diversity of human cultural behaviour into either one or the other of only two categories that are constructed as polar opposites. Unfortunately, some early attempts to engender other cultures used a structuralist methodology that resulted in monolithic categorizations of women as domestic and subordinate to dominant public men. In Rosaldo and Lamphere's 1974 edited volume they and other authors such as Ortner uncritically used an over-generalizing cross-cultural methodology to find universal dominance by public men and subordination and devaluation of domestic women (Ortner 1974; Rosaldo 1974: 23, 29, 35, 41; Rosaldo and Lamphere 1974: 4, 8, 13–14). This exemplifies how some early feminists reinforced gender stereotypes by uncritically accepting male-biased frameworks, methods, ethnographies and data. The ranking inherent in the creation of dualistic oppositions in binary structuralist thinking results in the high status accorded large-scale male–public constructions of the past and the low status accorded small-scale female–domestic pasts.

Dichotomized constructions of household roles and spaces

Gender dichotomies, structuralist thinking and methods can produce distorted constructions of households in a number of ways. First, the dichotomizing of gender into male–public and female–domestic spheres results in the *a priori* categorization of all household tasks as domestic, although many public tasks and events can occur in households, such as production of goods for public sale, public waged labour (as in taking in laundry and the putting-out system), production of public labour, and public entertainments from political receptions to parties, dinners and teas (Spencer-Wood 1996: 399; 1991a: 237). Second, dualistic gender ideology is often simplistically projected as actual practice so that household tasks and roles are unproblematically assigned to women. Even when it is acknowledged that both genders had household roles, they are commonly constructed as structurally opposed in a static normative sexual division of labour. Documented dualistic gender ideology is uncritically accepted as historic reality and is projected onto archaeological data (e.g. Jameson 1987). Within the structuralist framework of gender dichotomy household spaces, features and artefacts are assigned fixed mutually exclusive identities as either male or female (critiqued by both Allison and Goldberg, this volume). The subjectivity of structuralist constructions of gender and households is usually masked in apparently objective text using the passive voice of omniscient authority to claim that artefacts, features and spaces associated with men were, by definition, public, while those associated with women were domestic. In sum, concepts of gender and the household are not problematized except by feminists (e.g. Nelson 1997; Reiter 1975: 12–16; Stine 1991).

In historical archaeology Yentsch (1991) similarly projected this idealistic gender dichotomy onto American colonial households, monolithically categorizing the front parlour, dining room, white ceramics and other tableware as male, public and cultural versus women's domestic kitchen space where nature was processed in earthen-coloured pottery. This could have been a useful critique of the categorization of households as solely domestic, but instead the mutual exclusivity of the male–public versus female–domestic dichotomy was just imposed on household material culture. The problem with this framework is that women as well as men displayed their status to 'public' outsiders in the parlour and hosted 'public' dinners in the dining room. Household spaces were used for public activities at least as much by women as by men. Women often hosted 'public' teas where they displayed their social status to women and sometimes men from other households. Women's and men's public activities in the home often overlapped in the same spaces. In addition, by the nineteenth-century upper- and middle-class homes often included separate men's parlours and women's parlours where each gender could publicly display their social status and wealth to people outside the household. Yet in the distorted double standard of dualistic gender ideology men's parlours are labelled public while women's parlours are labelled domestic. Finally, men were also not always excluded from household kitchens and pantries, since high status was expressed by having male black servants to serve public meals (e.g. the [male] butler's pantry).

Inclusive feminist frameworks

Many feminists have thrown off the bonds of structuralist thinking that dichotomizes cultures into mutually exclusive *either* male–public *or* female–domestic activities, roles, artefacts, and spaces. The actual complexity and diversity in real gender systems can seldom be accurately represented by simplistic dichotomies. Instead, I have suggested a more open-minded inclusive *both/and* contextually situated epistemology that more objectively analyses all the evidence to determine whether it supports a whole range of gender behaviours. I've proposed modelling diversity in any dimension as a continuum that includes all the shades of grey between the two ends of the range of variation, whether two supposed opposites or the beginning and end of a historical developmental continuum (Spencer-Wood 1992b). For instance, the social dimension of degree of gender segregation in household behaviours, spaces or artefacts can each be modelled as a continuum from complete spatial separation of women's and men's activities, artefacts or spaces at one end, to complete flexibility in gender roles and multiple uses of artefacts and spaces at the other end. Between these two poles the continuum includes the whole range of variation possible in combining gender-segregated and shared household spaces and artefacts. Tasks and artefacts that were not gender segregated can overlap in household spaces that also include gender-segregated tasks and artefacts. Feminists in this volume critique the *a priori* fixed classification of household spaces and artefacts as either male–public or female–domestic. Instead households are problematized, and evidence is sought to determine whether there are gender-fixed and/or multiple flexible uses of household artefacts and spaces.

Feminists have critiqued gender stereotypes basically in two ways: evidence has been found that women as well as men were important powerful cultural agents both (1) in the domestic sphere and (2) in the public sphere, even in male-dominated cultures. Most feminists, while not denying evidence of male domination and oppression of women in many situations, have also sought and found evidence of women's many sources of social and cultural power. Feminists have argued that women's public positions cannot be dismissed as exceptions, but instead invalidate the identification of women as only domestic. However, fewer feminists have challenged the solely male–public definition of importance by showing that women's domestic roles were important by themselves and not just for what they contributed to public history (Spencer-Wood 1993).

Differentiating gender ideologies from practices

The universality of gender stereotypes can be further critiqued by differentiating gender ideology from reality. Gender ideals constructed in stereotypes and dichotomies do not represent the full diversity, complexity and flexibility in actually practised gender roles and behaviours (Spencer-Wood 1991b, 1994). The linguistic root of the confusion of ideals with practice is the definition of a role as 'the characteristic and expected social behavior of an individual' which represents ideals and normative practice as monolithic synonyms, ignoring variation in individual behaviour that is the basis for processes of culture change. Since the culturally constructed categories of women and men both included important domestic as well as public actors, the idealistic gender dichotomy did not exist as a monolithic reality (Spencer-Wood 1993: 128).

The gender dichotomy between public men versus domestic women can also be critiqued as only one gender ideology, albeit a dominant one, among many gender ideologies. Many people today have other gender ideologies that support women in working outside the home and support male contributions to housework. Not only are there many alternative ideologies today, there were also a number of alternative ideologies in the past. Feminists have shown that the meaning of the female–domestic versus male–public dichotomy changed through time and was only one among a variety of gender ideologies.

THE LEGITIMATION OF ÉLITE VICTORIAN IDEOLOGY BY CLASSICAL ARCHAEOLOGY

This section discusses feminist critiques of the use of Classical scholarship to materially legitimate modern and Victorian gender stereotypes as universal. In 1980 Rosaldo critiqued the universalization of modern gender stereotypes by revealing their roots in the élite Victorian gender ideology of separate spheres for dominant public men versus subordinate domestic women.

Subsequently feminist historians have shown that this dominant gender ideology was only one of many nineteenth-century gender ideologies (see pp. 170–3). The Victorian separate spheres gender ideology was dominant because it was espoused by most people in the upper and middle classes (Spencer-Wood 1991b: 223). Most nineteenth-century scholars were élite men who believed in the superiority of western culture and projected their Victorian separate spheres gender ideology to dichotomize classical cultures into mutually exclusive male–public versus female–domestic spheres, spaces and artefacts (critiqued by Nixon 1994: 8–13).

This ideology was supported by the structuralist school in anthropology founded in the 1880s by Lévi-Strauss, and by earlier Enlightenment philosophers from Descartes to Locke and Rousseau (Nye 1988: 6). Nineteenth-century male scholars materially legitimated their élite Victorian gender ideology by tracing its descent from the misogynist Classical Greek gender ideology exemplified in Aristotle's writings, which had been recorded and passed down to Victorians through a long line of male scholars in exclusively male academic institutions. Further, Victorian classicists uncritically accepted male-dominated Classical gender ideology as historic reality and proceeded with structuralist interpretations of Classical artefacts and spaces at sites, including house sites, as either male–public or female–domestic (critiqued for Greece by Goldberg and for Romans by Allison, this volume).

Universalizing one Classical gender ideology

A number of feminist critiques apply to the Victorian constructions of Classical cultures that have been maintained in the male-dominated field of the classics. First, double androcentric biases were created by Victorian men's sexism plus the biases in using only Classical male writers' viewpoints to construct the supposedly universal norms or behaviours of Classical cultures. Cantarella (1987) identified a tradition of Classical Greek misogynist philosophers who argued that women's virtues were domestic and physical rather than intellectual while men's virtues included rational thought and the ability to govern, justifying the legal exclusion of women from education and formal politics. Classical Greek ideologies arguing that men's public roles were more important than women's domestic roles are certainly questionable given the fact that the entire society was dependent on women's domestic production of cloth as well as food. Accomplished weavers were highly valued by most Greeks. Fine cloth was a gift for the Gods, and the fine patterns in clothing were depicted in vase paintings and in sculpture, including a Parthenon frieze (Blundell 1995: 141).

The diversity of Classical Greek gender ideologies

Second, more recent feminist research has revealed that the Classical Greek misogynist gender ideology, while possibly dominant among men, was not the gender ideology espoused by all men and women. Feminists have found some evidence of Greek women's alternative gender ideologies in exclusively female rituals to the Goddess Demeter and the God Dionysus (Blundell 1995: 163–9; Winkler 1990: 189). Cantarella contrasted Classical Greek misogynist male philosophers, including Aristotle, with the more egalitarian diverse views of the Socratic school, the Cynic school, the Pythagoreans and Plato. Socrates' gender ideology held that women could be the intellectual equals of men, in support of female scholars such as Aspasia. Further, the Cynics and Pythagoreans took the revolutionary position that women and men had the same virtues, so that women had the capacity publicly to govern society (Cantarella 1987: 52–61). Plato, in *The Republic* completed *c.* 380 BC, proposed that the state be governed cooperatively by an élite group of women and men who would live communally and avoid worldly corruption by owning no possessions and being kept in poverty and asceticism by those they governed. Because Plato believed that only reproductive sexual differences were innate, élite women and men would be afforded the same education and opportunities for achievement. Individual households, property, families and marriage would be abolished in favour of eugenic breeding and cooperative nurseries and childcare (Blundell 1995: 181–3). However, this governing commune was to be supported by slaves from the lower class. The egalitarian social organization Plato proposed for this utopian élite commune was the opposite of the dominant Classical Greek gender ideology and many practices that sought to limit women's roles and their education to private households.

Diversity in gender practices in ancient Greece

Third, Classical Greek women exemplify how actual practice was not limited to ideals specified in the dominant gender ideology. For instance, evidence indicates that the ideal of female seclusion in households was not really practised. Greek women's important religious roles both in the household and in public were acknowledged and recorded by men. Women were indispensable in household rituals because they maintained family stability. This important domestic role was extended into women's sacred practices that created community cohesion. Women were predominantly responsible for funerary rituals and were publicly prominent participants in religious cults. Further, women usually served as priestesses to Goddesses, and also served as oracular agents for two male gods – Zeus at Dodona and the most important Classical oracular shrine to Apollo at Delphi. Priestess was the only public office open to women within the dominant Classical ideology. Classical Athens had priestesses for more than forty major cults. Further, the priestess of Athena Polias, Athens' patron deity, officiated at the most important of the state festivals and at times had the power to influence political decisions. Only women were allowed to participate in a festival in honour of Demeter, the goddess of corn and cultivation, which was central to the state religion (Blundell 1995: 134–5, 160–5). In sum, Classical Greek women were not secluded in households, but had a variety of public religious powers both in the supposedly male–public sphere as well as in the female–domestic sphere of the household.

Further, some Classical Greek women held other public positions. Several renowned Greek poets were women, despite the lack of education for women. A number of Greek women philosophers were educated beyond their domestic duties and some practised their egalitarian beliefs in relationships with male egalitarian philosophers or with women. Finally, a few women had political power, including queens, a magistrate, and even some female warriors and leaders of armies in the Hellenistic period (Cantarella 1987: 57, 63–76, 91–3).

Summary

This section has shown how nineteenth-century classicists inaccurately projected their élite Victorian gender ideology as actual practice throughout Classical Greece. In addition, scholars legitimated their élite Victorian gender ideology that devalued women as domestic, irrational and subordinate, by tracing it to Aristotle. Further, the similar dominant Classical Greek gender ideology was considered universal, overlooking the diversity of alternative gender ideologies by both men and women. Men have needed to legitimate their dominance because some women and men have contested male dominance from Classical Greece (Cantarella 1987: 56), through medieval times and the seventeenth century through the twentieth century (Lerner 1993).

This section has shown that a richer understanding of Classical Greek cultural complexities is generated by feminist critiques and research on the diversity in gender ideologies and actual practices. In this volume, both Allison and Goldberg reject the projection of élite Victorian gender ideology to universally segregate Classical households into mutually exclusive *either* male–public *or* female–domestic spaces and artefacts. Instead they each found that most household spaces included both female and male activities, supporting a feminist both/and inclusive approach.

ALTERNATIVE VICTORIAN GENDER IDEOLOGIES AND PRACTICES

The rest of this chapter argues that the élite Victorian ideology of nineteenth-century classicists cannot be considered a universal gender structure because it wasn't even universally espoused or practised by nineteenth-century Americans or Europeans. Ideals of women's exclusive domesticity were practised neither by working women nor by middle- and upper-class women who delegated child rearing to servants. Further, large numbers of people rejected the dominant Victorian gender ideology that devalued women as inferior and subordinate and made them economically dependent on men while exploiting their domestic labour. For instance, many working women and middle-class reformers rejected the élite Victorian ideal of idle domestic womanhood as sinful and instead extolled the virtues and godliness of labour.

Overview of domestic reform

This section discusses a wide variety of social movements that I call 'domestic reform' because they sought through diverse gender ideologies and practices to transform western culture by raising the status of women and domestic labour to be equal to the status of men and public labour. Traditional histories that focus on the male public sphere largely overlook women's domestic reform movements as private organizations insignificant to history. Domestic reform was researched by feminist historians starting in the late 1970s, and in 1981 Hayden categorized a number of women's reform movements as 'material feminists'. I have coined the term 'domestic reformers' for these movements because many reformers opposed female suffrage at least initially and their reforms were directed at re-forming the household or domestic sphere (Hayden 1981; Spencer-Wood 1987, 1991b). Because women's domestic sphere was defined in relation to men's public sphere, redefining the domestic sphere also meant redefining the public sphere, resulting in the transformation of western culture and gender ideology from the nineteenth century into the twentieth century.

Domestic reformers were mostly middle-class women and some men who changed dominant Victorian ideology by redefining women's domestic sphere in relation to men's public sphere. The reformers resisted male dominance by arguing that women should control an expanded household that included both the domestic sphere and parts of the public sphere. In a number of different ways the reformers conflated the meanings of domestic and public by making the domestic sphere public and the public sphere domestic. The boundary between the supposedly separate gender spheres blurred as they were combined fundamentally in two ways (Spencer-Wood 1991b, 1994).

First, domestic reformers made parts of the domestic sphere public by transforming many of women's household tasks into public female professions which were acceptable for women within the dominant gender ideology because they were arguably 'domestic' professions. Domestic reformers argued that just as women were innately best suited to take care of the private family and household, women were also best suited to be the caretakers or mothers of the community-as-household (Robertson 1982: 166; Spencer-Wood 1991b). By extending women's private household roles into the public community, domestic reformers created a powerful positive solution to the fundamental nineteenth-century social problem of 'whether the existence of the marital family is compatible with that of the universal family which the term "Community" signifies' (Smith 1979: 238). Cooperative housekeeping expanded the meaning of 'family' and 'household' from private homes to the public community. Second, domestic reformers applied men's public sphere rational thinking, scientific methods and technology to both private and public households in order to transform housework into a profession equivalent to men's public professions. The professionalization of housework was symbolized and implemented with special scientific equipment and classes and schools in domestic science, scientific cooking, housekeeping and home economics. In sum, the reformers sought to raise women's status by transforming domestic work into women's professions both in the private household and in the public sphere (Spencer-Wood 1991b).

Reformers socialized many household tasks to create women's public housekeeping co-operatives, in which individual women cooperated for the rational efficient production of household tasks and products. Cooperatives resisted male-dominated individual households in which the same tasks were repeated by each woman in isolation. The idea of public housekeeping cooperatives spread from Europe to the United States in the late eighteenth century and in the nineteenth, often as a result of American women's experiences and observations when studying or visiting in Europe. Cooperatives included day nurseries, kindergartens, playgrounds, cooking, dining, and laundry cooperatives, working women's cooperative homes, public kitchens, and social settlements. The reformers symbolized and implemented the professionalization of domestic tasks by founding industrial schools for girls and adult schools and classes that created higher levels of female teaching professions, such as college professors in home economics and early childhood education (e.g. kindergartens, Montessori, etc.). By socializing aspects of housework in the public sphere the reformers created many women's public professions that are still major female-dominated professions today such as kindergarten and nursery school teaching, home economics, nursing, nutrition, social work and public health. Domestic reformers also successfully argued that some male-dominated professions should become female-dominated because women's supposedly innate domestic abilities made them better suited than men to be grade-school teachers, sales clerks, typists, secretaries, bank tellers and telephone operators (Anderson and Zinsser 1988: 177, 193–6, 246, 389, 393–4; Hayden 1981; Robertson 1982: 395–6, 398, 423–4, 444–6, 452–3).

Documentary and material evidence shows that domestic reform movements taken together transformed western culture by redefining the dominant gender ideology to make it acceptable for women to work in what was considered men's public sphere. Further, domestic reform movements were instrumental in creating a majority for female suffrage in Britain and in the United States. The effectiveness and importance of a wide variety of domestic reform organizations and programmes is amply demonstrated by their rapid growth in numbers and membership, their spread across the western world, and the long-term utility of many of these social service organizations up to the present day (Spencer-Wood 1991b).

Domestic reform ideologies

Domestic reform was supported by a great diversity of ideologies, but was united by some shared beliefs. The belief that every aspect of social life had 'domestic meaning' (Leach 1980: 209) redefined the household and domestic reform activities as virtually unlimited. Most domestic reformers believed in the Cult of True Womanhood (Welter 1966) or Domesticity that defined women as domestic, but combined it with Enlightenment egalitarian beliefs and the democratic ideology of the American and French republics (ideologically drawing on men's Classical education stressing the socio-politics of the Greek and Roman worlds), to create an ideology of equality between women's domestic sphere and men's public sphere. Domestic reformers combined Enlightenment beliefs in the perfectibility of society with the development of science to advocate perfecting housework tasks by rationalizing them with efficient scientific methods and equipment. Applying rational, scientific principles to housework was also supported by the popular 'religion of science' that viewed scientific laws of nature and principles of order as manifestations of the symmetry and harmony of God's creation (Leach 1980: 136; Turner 1985: 181–3).

In cooperative housekeeping movements, women applied their domestic values and superior morality to reform what they saw as the corruption and sin resulting from capitalism and usury in men's public sphere (Cott 1977: 66–8; Robertson 1982: 13–19, 31–2; Welter 1974: 145–6). Their goal, as president of the Women's Christian Temperance Union Frances Willard put it, was to 'make the whole world homelike' (Hayden 1981: 153). Evangelical Christian reformers sought to reform and perfect society for the second coming of Christ in the Millennium (Porterfield 1980: 99–120, 155–88). Evangelical Christians rejected Puritanical beliefs in original sin and predestination to transform American culture with beliefs in original purity and the possibility of redemption and salvation through good deeds and benevolence, including many domestic reform institutions. The socialization of household tasks into public housekeeping cooperatives in communes and in urban areas was supported by utopian religious ideology about community families and households, Enlightenment perfectionist and egalitarian beliefs, Communitarian Socialist beliefs in the scientific efficiency of collective labour, and Plato's philosophy of an élite egalitarian cooperative, proposed in *The Republic* (Hayden 1981; Holloway 1966: 24).

American historians, in most cases feminists, have identified a number of cults that ideologically supported domestic reform in both America and Europe. The status of women and their household roles was raised by the Cult of True Womanhood, or Domesticity, the Cult of Home Religion, and the Cult of Republican Motherhood. Women's public professions were legitimated and supported by Republicanism, the Cult of Single Blessedness and the Cult of Real Womanhood. The Cult of Domesticity argued that women's domesticity made them superior to men both in domestic ability and morally. Reformers resisted male dominance in the household by arguing that women's supposedly innately superior domestic abilities made them better suited to control their domestic sphere. Women's superior morality was established because their domestic sphere was separated from the supposedly sinful capitalism and usury in men's public sphere (Robertson 1982: 13–19; Welter 1966). This logically led to the Cult of Home Religion which advocated household worship in the more moral domestic sphere (Handlin 1979: 4–19). The reformers created the Cult of Republican Motherhood to argue for women's equal rights to education as the mothers of the next generation of male democratic leaders, extending American and French egalitarian democratic ideals from men to women (Beecher 1841; Robertson 1982: 15–17). These cults raised the status of women and their domestic roles in the household.

Women's public professions were legitimated and supported by Republicanism, the Cult of Single Blessedness and the Cult of Real Womanhood. From Republicanism some women argued that they were public independent republics deserving suffrage, in resistance to the *femme coverte* tradition of married men representing their wives (Hymowitz and Weissman 1978: 22–5). Both republican ideology and religious ideology about the high status of nuns as the brides of Christ were the background to the development of the Cult of Single Blessedness in 1780, which advocated that women not marry but instead become economically independent through public professions, to redress the economic dependence on men that made women subordinate. And in fact the proportion of unmarried women in America increased from approximately 7 per cent in the 1830s to approximately 11 per cent in 1870 (Chambers-Schiller 1984: 3–5, 21–3). As late as the 1910s a newspaper article asked whether most employed women ascribed to the 'Cult of Single Blessedness' and pointed out that most women journalists were married (*Chronicle Telegraph* 1891) In the second half of the nineteenth century the Cult of Real Womanhood advocated that women should be educated, marry carefully, maintain health and physical fitness, and be trained for a profession in case they should need to support their families (Cogan 1989).

These ideologies supported educational, economic, and physical sources of power for women and the development of women's public professions by domestic reformers. My research has revealed how women reformers created and drew on such alternative ideologies of equality to change the meaning of the domestic/public dichotomy in élite Victorian gender ideology. Using an inclusive feminist approach I seek not simply to validate materially any single historic gender ideology, but ask instead what the evidence indicates about the extent to which the variety of alternative gender ideologies affected material culture used in actual historic behaviours.

Historical archaeology of domestic reform

A historical archaeology of domestic reform is particularly useful because reform ideologies were symbolized and implemented with material culture. Further, both documentary data and archaeological data need to be analysed conjunctively in order to develop an understanding of how ideologies were realized in actual practices of domestic reform. The documents of domestic reform are largely prescriptive, detailing ideal religious or scientific material culture to be used to symbolize and implement different ideologies of domestic reform. Ideologies and prescriptions of ideal material culture are important contributions to ideological and intellectual histories, but must not be mistaken for actual practices. Archaeological research on the material culture and built environments actually used for domestic reform can provide insights into the relationships between ideals and practices. Material culture and architecture used to implement domestic reform may be found above or below ground, or in the few documents and depictions concerning the actual operation of domestic reform institutions, enterprises, and programmes. More domestic reform material culture may be excavated in site yards in poor or rural neighbourhoods that lacked municipal trash collection, and in site yards used by children who were more likely to lose artefacts than were adults.

In many cases it may be difficult or impossible to distinguish architecture or material culture used in domestic reform from ordinary domestic architecture or equipment. However, by using documents to identify and locate domestic reform sites archaeological excavation can be used to determine the extent to which ordinary material culture or ideal domestic reform artefacts and architecture were used at these sites. Both innovative and ordinary material culture were consciously given new meanings to symbolize and implement domestic reform. This corresponds well with a material feminist approach that views material culture not simply as a product or reflection of cultural behaviour or ideology but as an active social agent shaping behaviour. Domestic reform also demonstrates how cultural materials, buildings, and spaces have no fixed meaning or gender identity, but rather change meanings in different subcultural contexts. These meanings may only be ascertained through the synergistic contextual interpretation of documents and material culture which is the essence of historical archaeology.

The rest of this chapter will reveal that domestic reform was not monolithic, but included a wide variety of social movements and reformers who espoused many different gender ideologies and operated a great diversity of institutions, organizations, and programmes. Examples of the diversity of domestic reform ideologies, practices, architecture and distinctive material culture will be discussed in sequence for public housekeeping cooperatives in communal societies, followed by urban public housekeeping cooperatives with or without kitchenless houses or apartments, and finally domestic reform of the household.

Public communal households

The earliest domestic reform movements were European communal societies of the seventeenth century that combined heretical religious ideologies with socialism and communalism. Many communes were heretical sects that emigrated to America to avoid persecution by state churches. Socialist communes were often founded first in Europe and then replicated in America. The most renowned heretical sect with cooperative housekeeping that fled to America were the Shakers, who founded nineteen Societies from Maine to Kentucky (1774–1826) under the leadership of

Ann Lee, who in 1759 had become a leader of the Shakers in England (which was founded by a married couple, Holloway 1966: 55–9). Other heretical sects that fled Europe to found communes with cooperative housekeeping in the United States included three Harmony Society towns (founded by George Rapp 1805–24), and seven Amana Inspirationist communes (founded by women and men, starting 1855) that still thrive today. An American heretic, John H. Noyes, founded the three towns of the Oneida Perfectionists (1847–78). The most renowned socialist communal experiments included a few Fourierist Phalanxes and Owenite communities in Europe and in the United States: fifteen Owenite communes (1820s–1830), Brook Farm (1841–6), and thirty Fourierist Associations (1840–60), which combined science and religion (Hayden 1981: 33–9). Communes often influenced each other, as exemplified by the inspiration the Oneida Perfectionists gained from Brook Farm, Shaker communalism, and Socialism, while rejecting Fourierism. People in communal societies felt that they could not reform the whole society and therefore withdrew to form a perfect cooperative society in miniature – a heaven on earth (Hayden 1981: 96; Holloway 1966: 34–5, 184–5).

Commune ideologies

The egalitarian ideologies of communes were drawn from a great historical depth and diversity of sources. The diverse egalitarian ideologies of religious communes developed from different interpretations of the Bible, especially Christ's Sermon on the Mount, the Apostolic communal church, Gnosticism brought back from the Crusades, Deism, and books such as St Thomas More's *Utopia*, which derived almost entirely from the élite commune proposed in Plato's *Republic*. Socialist communes combined the 'religion of science', Enlightenment egalitarian ideology, and Communitarian Socialism that also drew on the ideology in Plato's *Republic*. Thus most communes believed in gender, racial and ethnic equality as well as communal property, but differed from Plato by abolishing slavery in any form. The great diversity in egalitarian communal ideologies can be illustrated by a few examples. The Shakers believed that God was bisexual and created female and male 'in our image'. Biblical authority for the absence of marriage in Heaven was interpreted by the Shakers and most other heretical sects to justify celibacy, while the Oneidans interpreted the same text to justify promiscuity. Fourier's 'religion of science' belief that God created a harmonious universe was combined with a fanciful scheme of cosmological evolution, including seas turning into lemonade, polyandry with concubinage, and 'attractive industry' on a cooperative basis (Holloway 1966: 18, 24, 64, 134–42, 104, 182–3). While both Owen and Fourier believed that character was shaped by environment rather than heredity, Fourier went beyond Owenite arguments for gender equality through collective housekeeping by claiming that 'The degree of emancipation of women is the natural measure of general emancipation' and 'the extension of the privileges of women is the fundamental cause of all social progress' (Hayden 1981: 33–5).

Commune gender practices

The egalitarian ideologies of communal societies were practised by women who transformed domestic production into public cooperative housekeeping that was equal in status to men's cooperative agricultural and craft production. Some communes permitted or practised some form of marriage, but most religious communes practised celibacy and asceticism that with egalitarian cooperative living had a long tradition in Christian monasteries, nunneries, abbeys and heretical sects (Holloway 1966). Men and women often worked in gender-segregated groups. Despite egalitarian ideologies, women were usually paid less than men (Hayden 1981: 39). Women cooperatively performed most household tasks and produced goods such as clothing, milk, butter, cheese, vegetables, fruit and eggs, while men worked cooperatively in fields, craftshops and mills to produce goods such as meat, grain, flour, lumber, buildings, and furniture. In a few communes, such as the Social Palace in Guise, France, and at Oneida, both genders worked in communal factories that provided strong economic bases for these communes (Hayden 1981: 37; Holloway 1966: 188–9).

Most communes were founded and led by men, although a few were founded and led by women or leaders of both genders. My feminist both/and approach can be used to model the diversity in gendered leadership practices as a continuum from exclusively male leadership at one extreme to female leadership at the other extreme, with the shared leadership of the Shakers in between. The diversity of communal governments can be modelled on a continuum from completely autocratic at one end to entirely democratic at the other end, with many communes falling somewhere in between. These two leadership practices intersect at different points along these continuums to model the autocratic male leadership of George Rapp, the mixed gender autocratic leadership of the Shakers, the partial democracy (for men and unmarried women) of the Amana Inspirationists, and the consensus government of the Oneidans (Holloway 1966: 59, 67–8, 95, 172, 192).

Archaeology of communal households

Archaeologists can gain information about the degree of cooperation, centralization and segmentation of tasks in communes from the size and configuration of buildings. Applying my inclusive both/and feminist paradigm, degree of cooperative architecture can be modelled on a continuum from private households at one end to public community cooperative households at the other end, with combinations in between. The social dimension of degree of centralization can also be modelled on a continuum measuring the number of cooperative tasks performed in single large buildings versus the number of cooperative tasks in separate buildings. The kinds of cooperative tasks in different buildings may be indicated by types of artefacts lost or discarded near buildings. Most communes segregated cooperative tasks into different buildings to some extent. Many communes, especially religious sects, were organized as one community household in a large structure. In the United States, Shaker 'families', the Oneida Perfectionists, and Fourierists lived in large buildings with cooperative facilities including at least a kitchen, dining room and meeting room, plus separate buildings for other cooperatives. In the early 1860s the Oneida Perfectionists constructed a single building that housed mixed gender living quarters as well as the cooperative kitchen, dining hall, workshops and a nursery. The cooperative laundry and older childcare were in separate buildings, as well as the carpentry shop, barns, and factories. A Fourierist Phalanstery building for cooperative living often included a laundry and bakery, while the Shakers used separate buildings.

Excavations at American Shaker villages have uncovered the foundations of buildings used for cooperative housekeeping by a Shaker 'family' that had gender-segregated living quarters. Excavation uncovered the huge stone base of a large fireplace/stove for cooperative cooking, large pots and serving dishes for cooperative eating, as well as artefacts in other structures indicating cooperative weaving and education (Vaillancourt 1983). The Amana Inspirationists built separate small kitchenless houses of four apartments each that would leave clusters of small foundations around a larger cooperative house for every fifty residents with a large kitchen and chimney base, dining room, and laundry that might be identifiable if large soapstone sinks remained. Nearby were communal kindergartens, schools and workshops. The Rappites built family row houses with private kitchens that would leave a long subdivided foundation with a small chimney base in each unit, plus a large cooperative building foundation with a large chimney base for coopera-tively cooking of feasts. The Fourierist Social Palace built in 1859 at Guise, France, housed 350 ironworkers and their families in large buildings containing separate family apartments with private kitchens, plus separate buildings for a public community cooperative bakery, café, schools, theatre, restaurant and butcher shop. The largest central apartment house included a cooperative nursery and kindergarten specially designed for children (Hayden 1981: 37–45, 96).

Archaeologists might also find remains indicating the extent of use of material culture specifically invented for cooperative housekeeping in communes. Innovative equipment and toys could be found from kindergartens or infant schools, often in separate buildings at a number of communes, including Owenite communities (Scotland 1800–24 and United States 1820s–30), the Social Palace in France, Fourierist Phalansteries, Brook Farm, Oneida, and Amana (Hayden 1981: 38, 48, 97). Shaker inventions for increasing the efficiency of cooperative housekeeping that might leave distinctive archaeological remains included a washing machine, the common clothespin, an apple peeler and corer, a pea sheller, a cheese press, a round oven, and a conical stove for heating irons. At the Social Palace in France reformers created laundry tubs that expelled water by spinning, bathtubs with adjustable bottoms for children or adults, and innovations in heating, lighting and ventilation. Oneida used the latest heating, lighting and sanitation devices and invented an improved washing machine, a mop wringer, an institutional potato peeler, and a 'lazy susan' to facilitate food service (Hayden 1976: 23, 197–8, 200; 1981: 48, 120). Archaeology might also contribute information about the degree to which communes sold their labour-saving innovations as well as innovative toys to outsiders.

Public cooperative households

The idea of cooperative housekeeping spread from communitarian socialist ideology and communes to cooperative hotels and apartments. Fourier's early call for shared facilities in Parisian apartment buildings was followed by designs for cooperative apartments by American reformer Melusina Fay Pierce in 1869 and subsequent designs by a number of mostly male architects that were constructed in cities from Boston and New York to London, Paris and Moscow. Starting in the 1870s middle- and upper-class cooperative apartment hotels offered collective dining, and cooking, laundry, housework, and childcare by servants, transforming the stigmatized occupation of domestic service into higher status hourly waged occupations with regular hours. Some hotels also offered private dining rooms and kitchens in the apartments. Apartment hotels offered economies through cooperative domestic services and women were freed from organizing servants so they could organize social movements such as domestic reform. Some commercial cooperative hotels were also constructed for single working women who were willing to pay for cooperative parlours, dining rooms, cooking, and laundry. Socialist and communist workers' organizations hired architects to design a number of cooperative apartment houses, starting in the United States in the 1910s and in Paris and Moscow by the 1920s. Workers cooperatively built and owned these apartment houses and paid for cooperative domestic services such as dining clubs, tea rooms, cafeterias or restaurants, bakeries, day nurseries, kindergartens, playgrounds, and laundries. Some included libraries, auditoriums, schools, and health centres, as well as tailors, butchers, and grocery stores (Buchli 1996: 10; Hayden 1981: 69–86, 254–9).

Non-commercial cooperative homes for the increasing numbers of single working women in the 1890s were either organized by working women or by domestic reformers. Working women sometimes arranged to live together, cooperatively sharing housework and rent and supporting each other in times of unemployment and strikes, as at the Jane Club in Chicago. Women reformers and religious orders created non-profit cooperative homes for working women in order to prevent the financial and sexual exploitation of women by unscrupulous commercial boarding-house keepers. Cooperative homes for working women were the most widespread type of cooperative housekeeping institution, including both religious and non-sectarian homes. The most widespread and numerous type of cooperative home for working women which also offered educational classes and employment services were the YWCA homes. Modelled after the YMCA, the first YWCA was created in London in 1855, thence spreading to America and Australia. The YWCA offered not only cooperative dining rooms, kitchens, parlours and laundries, but also lecture halls, class rooms, reading rooms, gymnasiums, cafés and club rooms (King 1885: 205; Wilson 1979: 99).

College-educated women and men reformers cooperatively lived in social settlement houses in poor neighbourhoods in order to offer poor families a wide variety of programmes. Settlement houses run by male reformers in London inspired Jane Addams to found the first American settlement house in 1889 in Chicago, which started a large movement in the United States. Women reformers sought to alleviate working women's double burden of work and housework by offering childcare and education in cooperative day nurseries and kindergartens. To prepare the unskilled, mostly immigrant, poor to become employed citizens, settlements and industrial schools operated by women and/or men offered classes in subjects ranging from mathematics and English, to printing, typing, dressmaking, cooking, housekeeping and domestic science. Classes were included both for children and for adults, sometimes segregated by gender. Programmes to keep latchkey children from the immoral temptations of the streets after school included playgrounds, gardens and clubs in subjects such as history, biology, music, dancing and reading (Addams [1910]1981; Woods and Kennedy 1911).

Possible archaeological remains of cooperative hotels, apartments and cooperative households of working women or men include some of the largest urban structures, often with facilities for cooperative cooking and laundry in the basement, which might leave large footings and remains of large-scale equipment. Some artefacts might be lost in the yards of working-class cooperative apartments in poor neighbourhoods with inadequate rubbish collection. Artifacts most likely to be lost at industrial schools and settlement site yards are small items used in sewing, such as needles, pins and thimbles, and children's items, such as safety pins and toys from kindergartens.

Public cooperative housekeeping enterprises

Domestic reformers also founded cooperative housekeeping enterprises outside of cooperative households. In most cases public cooperative housekeeping enterprises did not completely replace private housekeeping in homes. Rather, household tasks were separately socialized in cooperative institutions, including neighbourhood cooperative kitchens, dining cooperatives, cooked food delivery services, public kitchens, day nurseries, and kindergartens.

Childcare cooperatives

The idea of day nurseries that provided physical care for infants spread from French crèches run by nuns to nurseries in communes and day nurseries as separate institutions. Later in the nineteenth-century day nurseries often included kindergarten classes for older children (Snyder 1972: 9–12 19–21, 41, 58; Steinfels 1973: 34–9, 42–55; Beer 1942: 33–41, 48–51, 144–51). Following Robert Owen's innovations in developmental childhood education for working mothers at his Institute for the Formation of Character (1800–24) in Scotland, the kindergarten was invented in 1837 in Germany by Friedrich Froebel (Hayden 1981: 33, 97–9). He developed the kindergarten ideology of discovery learning through which children harmoniously developed their God-given mental and physical capacities by playing with specially designed educational toys, called Froebelian gifts (Figure 10.1). Starting in 1838 German immigrants founded German-language kindergartens in the United States. The American kindergarten movement was led by Elizabeth Peabody, who founded the first English-speaking kindergarten in Boston in 1860. Around the turn of the century Italian Maria Montessori created Montessori schools that stressed more structured individualized learning of skills and scientific principles. Although some

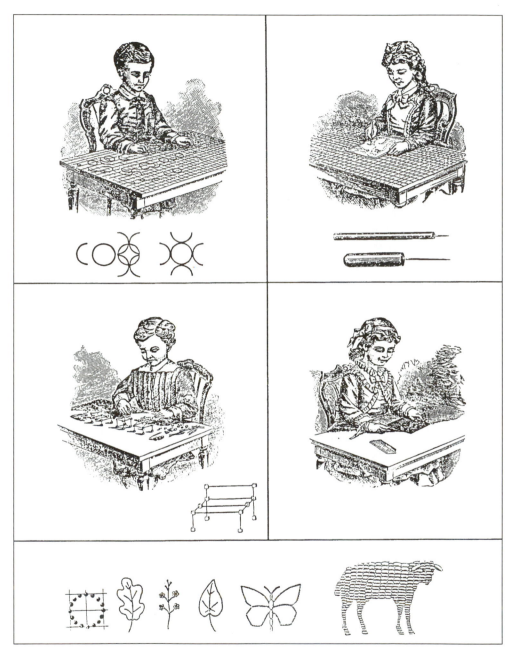

Figure 10.1 Advertisements for Froebel kindergarten gifts with durable parts that archaeologists could find in excavation.
Peabody and Mann (1877): (Publisher's Ads 1884) 14, 16–18, 21, 26, 36–37.

American women educators translated and advocated Montessori's methods in the 1910s, and a 1913 American lecture tour by Montessori was sponsored by notables including Thomas Edison, Alexander Graham Bell and Margaret Wilson (the President's daughter), Froebel's more playful and socially oriented kindergartens continued to predominate (Howes *et al.* 1939: 290). Montessori developed her own special equipment for teaching shape distinctions, mathematics and principles of physics.

Archaeologists might find some of the special Froebelian or Montessori equipment in the yards of kindergartens or schools because small children are more likely to lose artefacts than are adults. Kindergarten equipment included small blocks, metal circles, model parts, pricking and weaving needles, as well as shells and seeds that could easily be lost in site yards (Figure 10.1). The amount of use and curation of these special artefacts will affect how many are found in contrast to ordinary toys, indicating to what extent ordinary and special equipment were used.

Public cooperative kitchens

Public cooperative kitchens were charitable institutions established to feed the poor, nutritiously and scientifically at low or no cost. The first public kitchens were in European almshouses such as the Munich House of Industry founded in 1790 by Count Rumford in order to make experiments in feeding the poor 'scientifically' with his innovative efficient stove design. Public kitchens were also founded as separate cooperative institutions in Vienna, Leipzig and Berlin, where a soup kitchen for the poor was founded in 1866 by Lina Morgenstern. A similar philanthropic kitchen, or *cucini populari*, was founded in Modena, Italy. In the United States Ellen Swallow Richards and Mary Hinman Abel drew on these earlier public cooperative kitchens to found the New England Kitchen in 1890 in Boston, followed by the Rumford Kitchen exhibited at the World's Columbian Exposition in 1893. The resulting publicity led to the spread of public cooperative kitchens to many other cities in the United States. Public kitchens used scientific weights and measures and Aladdin Ovens that slowly cooked food with the heat of gas lamps funnelled into metal-lined insulated boxes with shelves on which dishes of food were stacked (Figure 10.2). Few archaeological remains are expected at the sites of public kitchens because of municipal rubbish collection and the concern of domestic reformers for sanitation. Remains in community dumps would usually be difficult to distinguish from laboratory equipment in some cases and domestic equipment in others. Remains might be found of special equipment for transporting cooked food from public kitchens to working-class homes, including metal dishes and insulated metal containers (Hayden 1981: 155–9).

In neighbourhood cooperative kitchens, including dining clubs and cooked food delivery services, meals were cooperatively prepared for a number of families who either ate together in dining cooperatives or received delivery of their meals at their individual houses. Communes such as the Rappites that had individual family houses with kitchens as well as a cooperative community kitchen and dining room were precedents for neighbourhood cooperative kitchens and dining rooms,

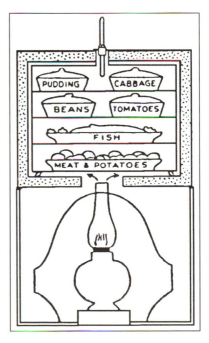

Figure 10.2 The Aladdin oven. Kinne and Cooley (1917: 43).

usually set up in an ordinary house. Usually a middle-class member of a dining cooperative would oversee servants who cooperatively produced meals for the other middle-class households who were members of the dining cooperative. Cooperative kitchens and cooked food delivery services both transformed an aspect of low-status domestic service into a higher waged occupation with regular, though still long, hours. The precedents for cooked food delivery services included cook shops that sold hot food in Europe and the United States and the urban English custom of taking family roasts or cakes to be baked in bakers' ovens. Cooked food delivery services first developed in Europe and then spread to the United States, where in 1868 Harriet Beecher Stowe published an article about her cooked-food-delivery experience from living in Europe. Community cooperative kitchens were given added impetus by World War I kitchens in Europe, especially the 1,000 National Kitchens in English cities, and mobile kitchens established in trams in Halifax, England and in devastated areas of France.

Cooked food delivery services and public kitchens both used large pots to cook food and packed food for transport in covered metal dishes nested inside special insulated buckets. Municipal garbage collection and the concern of domestic reformers for sanitation make it unlikely that archaeologists would excavate much evidence of this special equipment in site yards of middle-class cooperatives, although parts of this special transportation equipment might be found in urban dumps. Ordinary domestic archaeological remains can be expected from the less frequent working-class community cooperative kitchens, because a family's children usually delivered the cooked food packed in canning jars inside oatmeal cartons insulated with newspaper. Inadequate rubbish collection in poor urban areas might result in unusual amounts of canning jars and large food preparation and cooking containers and utensils in the yards of working-class cooperative kitchens (Hayden 1981: 60–2, 207–26).

Community cooperatives and kitchenless households

As the urban middle class moved from city apartments, sometimes with cooperative housekeeping services, into more private individual suburban houses, domestic reformers built on the idea of dining clubs to create suburban neighbourhood cooperatives, sometimes in conjunction with kitchenless houses. American reformers such as Marie Howland, Edward Bellamy and Charlotte Perkins Gilman inspired both American and European architects to design and build a number of experimental neighbourhoods of kitchenless houses with central cooperatives. English architect Ebenezer Howard became renowned for his Garden City town plan, for which he and his associates designed the Cooperative Quadrangle – a square of attached kitchenless row houses with a central dining room, kitchen and laundry in one corner. Between 1909 and 1924 Howard's architectural firm designed four Cooperative Quadrangles that were built in London suburbs. Some were reminiscent of university quadrangles, and Tudor revival architectural style was frequently used to evoke the coherence of pre-industrial villages. Domestic services were supplied by paid employees, who in some cases were supervised by lady tenants who took turns as unpaid managers. Howard, as well as Fourier, influenced French cooperative housing designs. In the United States, kitchenless houses with central cooperatives were built in a few summer communities for affluent New Yorkers. For instance, in 1922 Ruth M. Adams designed Yelping Hill Connecticut's seven kitchenless houses, some Tudor style, and remodelled an old barn as a community centre with a cooperative kitchen, dining room, living room, childcare, and guest quarters. Inspired by Howard's Garden City, two architects in California, the Heineman brothers, in 1910 designed the bungalow court – moderately priced single and double bungalows bordering a centre garden with a central building housing a sewing room and laundry over a covered play area (Hayden 1981: 230–9, 260–3). Archaeologists could easily distinguish the configuration of Cooperative Quadrangles and bungalow courts.

Archaeological survey of domestic reform sites in Boston

My survey of over 120 Boston domestic reform sites founded from 1860 to 1925 shows how the rapid growth of women's cooperative housekeeping enterprises physically contested male dominance on the public landscape and moved the built environment toward gender equality. Further, women's public professions and institutions grew to dominate parts of many public urban landscapes, in contrast to the ideal of an exclusively male public-sphere landscape (Spencer-Wood 1994). Public and private were physically conflated as reformers built prominent public institutions in residential neighbourhoods, while housing other public cooperative housekeeping enterprises in typical domestic structures.

The survey further revealed geographical relationships between the reformers and participants in reform. Some reformers lived in settlement houses in poor immigrant neighbourhoods where they offered cooperative childcare and numerous educational programmes. Other reformers lived in private homes or cooperative hotels in posh neighbourhoods and volunteered or worked in schools for cooking and housekeeping, or in cooperatives in nearby poor neighbourhoods. With a feminist approach I sought and found evidence that participants in reform were not passive, but negotiated with reformers for programmes and material culture that would meet their needs (Spencer-Wood 1987, 1994). For instance, working-class families protested the bland north eastern United States 'Yankee' menu offered them at public kitchens, saying 'You can't make a Yankee out of me by making me eat that', and 'I'd ruther eat what I'd ruther' (Addams [1910]1981: 102). The reformers responded by offering more ethnic dishes that were not slow-cooked in the scientific Aladdin oven until they lost flavour. Archaeological evidence may indicate the extent to which this oven and its scientific cooking methods were actually used in enterprises such as public kitchens and cooking cooperatives (Figure 10.2; Spencer-Wood 1991b).

Domestic reform of the private household

My research on American domestic reform of the household, conducted within this larger context, shows how reformers conflated women's domestic roles with men's public roles. Rational principles, scientific methods and equipment used by men in their public businesses were adapted by women reformers and applied to organize and mechanize housework for increased efficiency. In contrast to histories that have portrayed women only as consumers of men's household inventions (e.g. Lifshey 1973; Wright 1964), feminist research has revealed that some women earned income as early as the 1860s by inventing, patenting and sometimes undertaking factory production of their scientific designs for household equipment such as a stove, a washing machine, irons and sewing devices (Macdonald 1992: 38–47, 60–3, 196, 385–6, 393).

Women's domestic reform ideology was instrumental in applying rational scientific methods and equipment to housework. In domestic advice manuals reformers presented pictures and drawings of innovative equipment arranged to increase the efficiency and healthiness of housework in both middle-class and working-class homes. The evidence that women's domestic manuals both verbally and materially transformed gender ideology and relationships corrects male-centred histories that did not consider women's domestic advice literature important.

The American woman's home, by Beecher and Stowe

The earliest domestic reform ideology appeared in the most popular mid-nineteenth-century domestic manuals by Catherine Beecher and her famous sister, Harriet Beecher Stowe. Drawing on the ideology of Republican Motherhood, which pointed out the importance of the profession of motherhood in raising tomorrow's male political leaders, their aim was to 'elevate both the honor and remuneration' of women's household tasks to professions 'as much desired and respected as are the most honored professions of men'. This goal was materially symbolized and

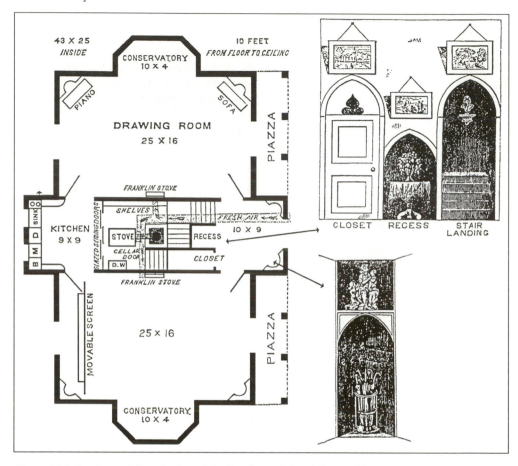

Figure 10.3 Beecher and Stowe's plan of the first floor of their 'Christian' house. Beecher and Stowe ([1869] 1985: 26–7).

implemented by raising the kitchen from its frequent location in the basement to a central position on the more public ground floor. Kitchen doors for shutting in cooking smells could be opened at other times, expressing the interconnectedness of the domestic sphere (Figure 10.3). The rational arrangement of furniture and equipment supposedly expressed the order and harmony in 'divine nature'. Innovative shelf boxes stored materials beneath working surfaces while hooks and shelves above held cooking utensils and dining tableware (Figure 10.4).

Beecher and Stowe used the popular Cult of Home Religion to raise women's domestic role to the exclusively male status of a minister, and elevated food preparation and service as analogous to communion. They justified their and other women's house designs by quoting the Bible: 'The wise woman buildeth her house.' Reformers drew on evangelical Protestantism to contend that women were naturally more pious and moral due to their closeness to God and nature in a domestic sphere separated from a men's capitalistic public sphere which was corrupted by the sin of usury. Women's supposedly innately superior domestic morality was symbolized with a cruciform house, gothic furnishings, gothic doorways, gothic corner niches with religious statues, and romantic religious and bucolic pictures. A Gothic arched central recess in the entrance hall held the small round table that with a Bible was the normative symbol for family communion in the church of the home. The Beecher sisters designed a public entry space filled with symbols of the pre-eminence of woman's role as minister of the home church. They also designed a bow-windowed conservatory in each of the two ground-floor rooms, where they recommended that women and children grow houseplants, bringing God's nature into the home (Figure 10.3). The simple house design did not include a large men's parlour separate from the usually smaller women's parlour which in wealthy Victorian houses physically expressed the relative status of the separate female domestic and male public spheres. Instead Beecher and Stowe contended that woman should control the entire domestic sphere and cooperatively organize her children's labour as the 'sovereign of her empire' (Beecher and Stowe [1869]1985: 17–36, 222, 442–5; Handlin 1979: 4–19).

The archaeology of household domestic reform

Archaeologists excavating house sites often find flowerpots without

Figure 10.4 A view of part of Beecher and Stowe's rational kitchen design, shown on the left in plan in Figure 10. 3.
Beecher and Stowe ([1869] 1985: 34).

realizing that they could symbolize the Cult of Home Religion. Gothic and floral designs popular on mid-nineteenth-century household tableware also symbolized women's supposedly naturally superior piety. Of course household ceramic choices could also be driven by cost, availability, aesthetics, or some combination of factors (Spencer-Wood 1996: 419–20).

Archaeologists may be able to contribute to the important question of to what extent documented ideal domestic reform equipment and designs for the home were actually used, and by whom. This may be indicated in historic documents, photos, or above ground material culture. The preserved historic house of Harriet Beecher Stowe in Hartford, Connecticut, includes some kitchen furniture similar to what she and her sister recommended. Archaeologists may find material evidence of the undocumented extent to which other people implemented distinctive foundation features and artefacts in the basement design, including the ice closet, the washtub drains, water pipes, laundry stove and the drying rack.

Further developments in efficient arrangements of furniture and equipment in Christine Frederick's early twentieth-century domestic manual include photographs of designs she and some friends implemented in their houses. Frederick's basement laundry materially organized the process from a laundry shute to sorting table to large metal tubs, a washing machine, and a metal drying rack heated by a stove, followed by an ironing board, mangle and table for folding clean

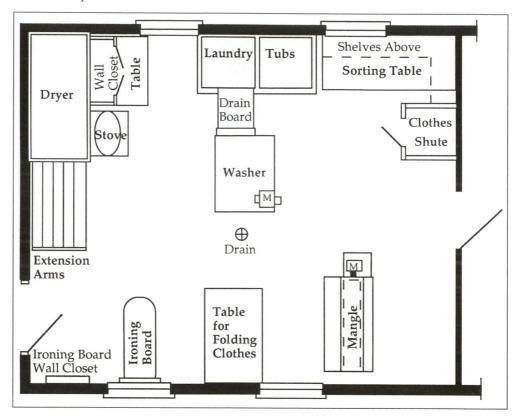

Figure 10.5 Frederick's laundry was designed for an efficient sequence of tasks.
Beecher and Stowe ([1869] 1985): after Frederick (1923: 224).

clothes (Figure 10.5). Archaeologists could find many parts of large metal laundry equipment in rural or town dumps. Frederick's kitchen was arranged on one side for food preparation, from a refrigerator raised by a dumbwaiter from the basement to kitchen, to a cabinet which Frederick invented and which integrated cupboards with a work surface, to a metal oil stove, and a serving table over a fireless cooker chest in which food was slowly cooked by heated soapstones beneath insulated buckets. The other side of the kitchen included a table for stacking dishes next to a sink with drainboards, and shelves and closets for storing clean dishes. Frederick and her friends, the Noyes at Oneida, also hung utensils on the walls, and had dishwashers and vacuum cleaners (Frederick 1923: 32, 64, 98, 110, 114).

The question of to what extent domestic reformers' designs were adopted in other households is seldom documented. Cohen's research found that the simple wood furniture suggested by reformers was not adopted by most of the working class, which sought plush furniture and carpets as high status furnishings (Cohen 1980). Frederick showed photos of her kitchen designs implemented both in a large kitchen and in a small apartment (Frederick 1923: 40, 178). Ellen Swallow Richards in her manual on the cost of housing illustrated a remodelled apartment kitchen that included some of her suggestions to facilitate sanitation, such as a sheet lignolith floor laid up the wall a few inches, glass shelves, and a glass table. However, aside from hanging pots under the glass table and a cooking range with overhead shelves and boiler, this kitchen did not implement reformers' designs for efficiently arranging domestic equipment (Richards 1905: 70–2).

Archaeologists might find evidence of the degree of adoption of innovative domestic equipment advocated by reformers by excavating community dumps or house sites in rural or poor neighbourhoods that lacked municipal garbage collection. However, the degree to which ordinary domestic utensils and equipment were used to implement reform could not be identified without documenting reform sites, as I have in my surveys of Boston and Cambridge (Spencer-Wood 1987, 1991b, 1994, 1996).

CONCLUSION

This chapter has critiqued the universal construction of past cultures in the shape of Victorian-derived gender stereotypes. An assumed gender dichotomy between dominant–public–men versus subordinate–domestic–women has been legitimated by projecting its origin back to early hominid social organization, despite the lack of any supporting evidence. Further, the belief in a gender dichotomy between rational men versus emotional women led to the construction of other structuralist oppositions, such as objectivity versus subjectivity. Archaeological theory and method are permeated with the binary thinking embedded in structuralism and the scientific method.

Feminists have shown that modern gender dichotomies are largely derived from the dominant élite Victorian gender ideology of separate spheres. Nineteenth-century scholars legitimated their élite gender ideology by tracing its origins to the dominant misogynist Classical Greek philosophy. However, feminist research has revealed that Classical women and men espoused a diversity of gender ideologies. Further, women had important public as well as domestic gender roles and practices.

Feminists have debunked the claimed universality of Victorian gender dichotomies with research revealing the change and diversity both in gender ideologies and in actual gendered behaviours in many cultures. Feminist research shows how men's dominant binary gender ideology has been contested by alternative gender ideologies which have sought more egalitarian gender roles and relationships throughout history. Further, feminist research has demonstrated that women had important roles in both domestic and public spheres from ancient times until the present day.

This chapter has shown how nineteenth-century western culture, gender ideology and practice were materially transformed by alternative domestic reform ideologies and practices. The diversity of domestic reform gender ideologies had roots in Classical Greek philosophies, as well as fundamentalist Christian beliefs. Victorian women's domestic reform ideologies redefined and conflated the meanings of domestic and public to successfully contest the exclusion of women from the public sphere, creating a large number of female public professions that were acceptable within the dominant ideology because they could be labelled 'domestic'. Further, women and men reformers combined the supposedly separate female/domestic and male/public spheres to argue that women's housework should be a paid profession equivalent to men's professions.

Public cooperative housekeeping enterprises that socialized private household tasks challenged any unitary definition of the household as exclusively familial and private. Cooperative house-keeping institutions materially blurred the distinction between community and family household. Communes created economically cohesive community-scale households. Kitchenless houses and apartments also materially changed the traditional definition of a household.

In this chapter feminist questions revealing the diversity of Victorian and Classical Greek ideologies and behaviour have challenged monolithic definitions of *the* gender roles, *the* gender ideology, or *the* typical household in a culture. Further, feminist critiques of binary thinking have revealed how sexist gender ideology has been selectively reproduced and represented as *the* universal ideology and practice from ancient Greece to the twentieth century. Androcentric constructions of the unitary gender ideology and norms of a culture, region, or time period, can be corrected with feminist theory, methods and research on the diversity in cultural ideologies, practices and material culture.

ACKNOWLEDGEMENTS

I would like to thank Dr Allison for commenting on this chapter and editing it for publication. I would also like to thank librarians who assisted me in finding sources of information at the Schlesinger Library on the History of Women in America at Radcliffe College, at the Massachusetts Institute of Technology Archives, at the Simmons College Archives, and at Wellesley College.

BIBLIOGRAPHY

Addams, J. ([1910]1981) *Twenty Years at Hull-House*, New York: New American Library.
Anderson, B. S. and Zinsser, J. P. (1988) *A History of Their Own: Women in Europe from Prehistory to the Present* II, New York: Harper and Row.
Beecher, C. E. (1841) *A Treatise on Domestic Economy*, New York: Marsh, Capen, Lyon and Webb.
Beecher, C. E. and Stowe, H. B. ([1869]1985) *The American Woman's Home, or Principles of Domestic Science*, New York: J. B. Ford and Co.
Beer, E. S. (1942) *The Day Nursery*, War Edn, New York: E. P. Dutton.
Binford, L. R. (1983) *Working at Archaeology*, New York: Academic Press.
Blundell, S. (1995) *Women in Ancient Greece*, London: British Museum Press.
Bordo, S. (1986) 'The Cartesian Masculinization of Thought', *Signs* 11, 3: 439–56.
Buchli, V. A. (1996) *The Battle Against Microbes and Counter-Revolutionaries: The Soviet Domestic Front (1920–1931)*, unpublished Harriman Institute Certificate Essay, Columbia University.
Bunch, C. (1987) *Passionate Politics: Essays 1968–1986 – Feminist Theory in Action*, New York: St. Martin's Press.
Cantarella, E. (1987) *Pandora's Daughters: The Role and Status of Women in Greek and Roman Antiquity*, Baltimore: Johns Hopkins University Press.
Chambers-Schiller, L. V. (1984) *Liberty a Better Husband. Single Women in America: The Generations of 1780–1840*, New Haven: Yale University Press.
Chronicle Telegraph (1891) *Literary Learns Mr. Bok Proves that Love and Literature are Not at War: Matrons and Spinsters*, January 18, Pittsburgh. In Andrews Scrap Album of Laura C. Holloway Langford, in the Shaker Collection, Joseph Downs Collection of Manuscripts and Printed Ephemera, The Winterthur Library, Henry Francis Du Pont Winterthur Museum, Winterthur, Delaware.
Cogan, F. B. (1989) *All-American Girl: The Ideal of Real Womanhood in Mid-Nineteenth-Century America*, Athens: University of Georgia Press.
Cohen, L. (1980) 'Embellishing a Life of Labor: An Interpretation of the Material Culture of American Working-Class Homes, 1885–1915', *Journal of American Culture* 3, 4: 752–5.
Conkey, M. W. and Spector, J. D. (1984) 'Archaeology and the Study of Gender', *Advances in Archaeological Method and Theory* 7: 1–38.
Cott, N. F. (1977) *The Bonds of Womanhood: 'Woman's Sphere' in New England, 1780–1835*, New Haven: Yale University Press.
Deetz, J. F. (1988) 'Material Culture and Worldview in Colonial Anglo-America', in Mark P. Leone and Parker B. Potter, Jr (eds) *The Recovery of Meaning: Historical Archaeology in the Eastern United States*, Washington, DC: Smithsonian Institution Press.
Dubrow, G. L. (1991) 'Preserving Her Heritage: American Landmarks of Women's History' II, Unpublished Ph.D. dissertation, University of California, Los Angeles.
Frederick, C. (1923) *Household Engineering: Scientific Management in the Home* (5th edition), Chicago: American School of Home Economics.
Gittell, M. and Shtob, T. (1980) 'Changing Women's Roles in Political Volunteerism and Reform of the City', *Signs* 5, 3 (suppl.): S67–80.
Gross, M. and Averill, M. B. (1983) 'Evolution and Patriarchal Myths of Scarcity and Competition', in

S. Harding and M. Hintikka (eds) *Discovering Reality. Feminist Perspectives on Epistemology, Metaphysics, Methodology, and Philosophy of Science*, Dordrecht: Reidel.

Handlin, D. P. (1979) *The American Home: Architecture and Society, 1815–1915*, Boston: Little Brown and Co.

Harding, S. (1987a) 'The Instability of the Analytical Categories of Feminist Theory', in S. Harding and J. F. O'Barr (eds) *Sex and Scientific Inquiry*, Chicago: University of Chicago Press.

Hayden, D. (1976) *Seven American Utopias: The Architecture of Communitarian Socialism, 1790–1975*. Cambridge: Massachusetts Institute of Technology Press.

—— (1981) *The Grand Domestic Revolution: A History of Feminist Designs for American Homes, Neighborhoods, and Cities*, Cambridge: Massachusetts Institute of Technology Press.

Henretta, J. A. (1971) 'Economic Development and Social Structure in Colonial Boston', in R. W. Fogel and S. W. Engerman (eds) *The Reinterpretation of American Economic History*, New York: Harper and Row.

Hodder, I. (1987) 'The Contextual Analysis of Symbolic Meanings', in I. Hodder (ed.) *In The Archaeology of Contextual Meanings*, Cambridge: Cambridge University Press.

—— (1992) *Theory and Practice in Archaeology*, London: Routledge.

Holloway, M. (1966) *Heavens on Earth: Utopian Communities in America 1680–1880* (2nd edition), New York: Dover.

Howes, D., Braun, M. L. and Garvey, R. (eds) (1939) *American Women: The Standard Biographical Dictionary of Notable Women* III 1939–40, Los Angeles: American Publications.

Hymowitz, C. and Weissman, M. (1978) *A History of Women in America*, New York: Bantam.

Jameson, R. (1987) 'Purity and Power at the Victorian Dinner Party', in I. Hodder (ed.) *The Archaeology of Contextual Meanings*, Cambridge: Cambridge University Press.

Jolly, C. J. and Plog, F. (1986) *Physical Anthropology and Archeology* (4th edition), New York: Alfred A. Knopf.

Kennedy, M. C. and. Watson, P. J. (1991) 'The Development of Horticulture in the Eastern Woodlands of North America: Women's Role', in J. M. Gero and M. W. Conkey (eds) *Engendering Archaeology: Women in Prehistory*, Oxford: Basil Blackwell.

King, M. (1885) *King's Handbook of Boston, 1885*, Cambridge, Mass.: Moses King.

Kinne, H. and Cooley, A. M. (1917) *Foods and Household Management: A Textbook of the Household Arts*, New York: Macmillan.

Leach, W. (1980) *True Love and Perfect Union: The Feminist Reform of Sex and Society*, New York: Basic Books.

Lee, R. B. (1968) 'What Hunters Do for a Living, or, How to Make Out on Scarce Resources', in R. B. Lee and I. DeVore (eds) *Man the Hunter*, Chicago: Aldine.

Lerner, G. (1993) *The Creation of Feminist Consciousness: From the Middle Ages to Eighteen-seventy*, New York: Oxford University Press.

Lifshey, E. (1973) *The Housewares Story: A History of the American Housewares Industry*, Chicago: National Housewares Manufacturers.

Linton, S. (1971) 'Woman the Gatherer: Male Bias in Anthropology', in S. Jacobs (ed.) *Women in Perspective: A Guide for Cross-Cultural Studies*, Urbana: University of Illinois Press.

Longino, H. and Doell, R. (1983) 'Body, Bias and Behavior: A Comparative Analysis of Reasoning in Two Areas of Biological Science', *Signs* 9, 2: 206–27.

Macdonald, A. L. (1992) *Feminine Ingenuity: Women and Invention in America*, New York: Ballantine Books.

Nelson, S. M. (1997) *Gender in Archaeology: Analyzing Power and Prestige*, Walnut Creek: Altamira Press.

Nixon, L. (1994) 'Gender Bias in Archaeology', in L. J. Archer, S. Fischler and M. Wyke (eds) *Women in Ancient Societies: An Illusion of the Night*, London: Macmillan.

Nye, A. (1988) *Feminist Theory and the Philosophies of Man*, New York: Routledge.

Ortner, S. B. (1974) 'Is Female to Male as Nature Is to Culture?', in M. Z. Rosaldo and L. Lamphere (eds) *Woman, Culture, and Society*, Stanford: Stanford University Press.

Peabody, E. P. and Mann, M. (1877) *Guide to the Kindergarten and Intermediate Class; and Moral Culture of Infancy*, New York: E. Steiger.

Porterfield, A. (1980) *Feminine Spirituality in America*, Philadelphia: Temple University Press.

Reiter, R. R. (1975) 'Introduction', in R. R. Reiter (ed.) *Toward an Anthropology of Women*, London: Monthly Review Press.

Richards, E. H. (1905) *The Cost of Shelter*, New York: John Wiley and Sons.

Robertson, P. (1982) *An Experience of Women: Pattern and Change in Nineteenth-Century Europe*, Philadelphia: Temple University Press.

Rohrlich-Leavitt R., Sykes, B. and Weatherford, E. (1975) 'Aboriginal Woman: Male and Female Anthropological Perspectives', in R. R. Reiter (ed.) *Toward an Anthropology of Women*, London: Monthly Review Press.

Rosaldo, M. Z. (1974) 'Woman, Culture and Society: A Theoretical Overview', in M. Z. Rosaldo and L. Lamphere (eds) *Woman, Culture, and Society*, Stanford: Stanford University Press.

—— (1980) 'The Use and Abuse of Anthropology: Reflections on Feminism and Cross-cultural Understanding', *Signs* 5, 3: 389–417.

Rosaldo, M. Z. and Lamphere, L. (1974) 'Introduction', in M. Z. Rosaldo and L. Lamphere (eds) *Woman, Culture, and Society*, Stanford: Stanford University Press.

Rowbotham, S. (1973) *Hidden From History: Rediscovering Women in History from the 17th Century to the Present*, London: Pluto Press.

Smith, D. S. (1979) 'Family Limitation, Sexual Control, and Domestic Feminism in Victorian America', in N. F. Cott and E. H. Pleck (eds) *A Heritage of Her Own*, New York: Simon and Schuster.

Snyder, A. (1972) *Dauntless Women in Childhood Education 1856–1931*, Washington, DC: Association for Childhood Education International.

Spencer-Wood, S. (1987) 'A Survey of Domestic Reform Movement Sites in Boston and Cambridge, ca. 1865–1905', *Historical Archaeology* 21, 2: 7–36.

—— (1991a) 'Towards a Feminist Historical Archaeology of the Construction of Gender', in D. Walde and N. D. Willows (eds) *The Archaeology of Gender: Proceedings of the 22nd [1989] Chacmool Conference*, Calgary: University of Calgary Archaeological Association.

—— (1991b) 'Towards an Historical Archaeology of Domestic Reform', in R. M. McGuire and R. Paynter (eds) *The Archaeology of Inequality*, Oxford: Basil Blackwell.

—— (1992a) 'A Feminist Agenda for Non-sexist Archaeology', in L. A. Wandsnider (ed.) *Quandaries and Quests: Visions of Archaeology's Future*, Carbondale: South Illinois University Press.

—— (1992b) 'Introduction to Critiques of Historical Archaeology', Paper presented at the 1992 Annual Society for Historical Archaeology Conference, Kingston, January 6.

—— (1993) 'Toward the Further Development of Feminist Historical Archaeology', *World Archaeological Bulletin* 7: 118–36.

—— (1994) 'Diversity in 19th Century Domestic Reform: Relationships Among Classes and Ethnic Groups', in E. M. Scott (ed.) *Those 'Of Little Note': Gender, Race and Class in Historical Archaeology*, Tucson: University of Arizona Press.

—— (1996) 'Feminist Historical Archaeology and the Transformation of American Culture by Domestic Reform Movements, 1840–1925', in L. A. De Cunzo and B. L. Herman (eds) *Historical Archaeology and the Study of American Culture*, Knoxville: Winterthur Museum and University of Tennessee.

Steinfels, M. O. (1973) *Who's Minding the Children?*, New York: Simon and Schuster.

Stine, L. F. (1991) 'Early 20th Century Gender Roles: Perceptions from the Farm', *The Archaeology of Gender: Proceedings of the 22nd [1989] Annual Chacmool Conference*, Calgary: University of Calgary Archaeological Association: 496–501.

Tanner, N. M. (1981) *On Becoming Human*, Cambridge: Cambridge University Press.

Tanner, N. and Zihlman, A. (1976) 'Women in Evolution. Part I: Innovation and Selection in Human Origins', *Signs* 1, 3 (part 1): 585–608.

Turner, J. (1985) *Without God, Without Creed. The Origins of Unbelief in America*, Baltimore: Johns Hopkins University Press.

Vaillancourt, D. R. (1983) 'Archaeological Excavations at the North Family Dwelling House Site, Hancock Shaker Village, Town of Hancock, Berkshire County, Massachusetts', Unpublished manuscript, Project, Rensselaer Polytechnic Institute, Troy, New York.

Washburn S. L. and Lancaster, C. S. (1968) 'The Evolution of Hunting', in R. B. Lee and I. DeVore (eds) *Man the Hunter*, Chicago: Aldine.

Welter, B. (1966) 'The Cult of True Womanhood: 1820–1860', *American Quarterly* 18, 2 (part 1): 151–74.

—— (1974) 'The Feminization of American Religion: 1800–1860', in M. Hartman and L. W. Banner (eds) *Clio's Consciousness Raised: New Perspectives on the History of Women*, New York: Harper Colophon Books.

Wertheimer, B. M. (1977) *We Were There: The Story of Working Women in America*, New York: Pantheon Books.

Wilson, M. G. (1979) *The American Woman in Transition: The Urban Influence, 1870–1920*, Westport, Conn.: Greenwood Press.

Winkler, J. J. (1990) *The Constraints of Desire. The Anthropology of Sex and Gender in Ancient Greece*, London: Routledge.

Woods, R. A. and Kennedy, A. J. (eds) (1911) *Handbook of Settlements*, New York: Charities Publications Committee.

Wright, L. (1964) *Home Fires Burning: The History of Domestic Heating and Cooking*, London: Routledge and Kegan Paul.

Wylie, A. (1991a) 'Gender Theory and the Archaeological Record: Why Is There No Archaeology of Gender?', in J. M. Gero and M. W. Conkey (eds), *Engendering Archaeology: Women and Prehistory*, Oxford: Basil Blackwell.

—— (1991b) 'Feminist Critiques and Archaeological Challenges', in D. Wade and N. D. Willows (eds) *The Archaeology of Gender: Proceedings of the 22nd Annual Chacmool Conference*, Calgary: University of Calgary Archaeological Association.

Yentsch, A. E. (1991) 'The Symbolic Divisions of Pottery: Sex-Related Attributes of English and Anglo-American Household Pots', in R. H. McGuire and R. Paynter (eds) *The Archaeology of Inequality*, Oxford: Basil Blackwell.

Chapter Eleven

Discussion: Comments from a classicist

Eleanor Leach

> Society can only have lawful relations to space if society already possesses its own intrinsic spatial dimension; and likewise space can only be lawfully related to society if it can carry these spatial dimensions in its very form . . . Society must be described in terms of its intrinsic spatiality; space must be described in its intrinsic sociality.
>
> (Hillier and Hanson 1984: 26)

Goethe was initially 'surprised' by the small scale and compactness of Pompeii with its 'narrow streets and small windowless houses whose only light came from their entrances and open arcades'(Goethe 1982: 189). Only after he had obtained entry, in the following week, to the Museum at Portici where portable finds were being stored, did his vision of the site expand by the view of 'objects that were part and parcel of their owners' daily lives' (ibid.: 203). Then, in his imagination the houses appeared simultaneously 'more cramped and more spacious'; more cramped because he now saw them filled with objects, and more spacious because of the beauty of the objects themselves. It was not simply paintings that he saw – of these he had already experienced a sampling within the houses themselves – but the collection commonly called *instrumentum domesticum* which the excavators had preserved selectively and with some care. To these the poet, well schooled by his reading of Winckelmann, responded with eloquent aesthetic appreciation: 'these were decorated with such art and grace that they enriched and enlarged the mind in a way that even the physical space of the largest room cannot do'. The objects that thus caught his imagination were decorated jars and lamps:

> There was one beautiful jar, for example with an exquisitely wrought rim which, on closer inspection, turned out to be two hinged semicircular handles, by which the vessel could be lifted and carried with ease. The lamps are decorated with as many masks and scrolls of foliage as they have wicks, so that each flame illuminates a different work of art. There were high, slender bronze pedestals, evidently intended as lamp stands. The lamps, which were suspended from the ceiling were hung with all sorts of cunningly wrought figures which surprise and delight the eye as they swing and dangle.
>
> (Goethe 1982: 203)

Leaving aesthetics aside, the confidence that a selection of objects could provide a reliable index to modes of life scarcely originated with Goethe, but had long since been incorporated into antiquarian research. On this premise in the earlier eighteenth century, the Abbe Bernard de Montfaucon based his pioneering work on ancient culture, the three volume *Antiquity Explained and Represented in Sculptures*, a work initially undertaken for the purpose of glossing difficult allusions in literary texts by reference to material objects, which had expanded virtually *sua sponte* into a massive compilation of Greek and Roman customs and activities. The reliability of this reconstructive premise and the development of methodologies needed to correct and redirect it is the central theme of the essays that Penelope Allison has brought together here. Collectively these are paradigmatic of the pervasive disposition of current archaeological thinking to modify the simple evaluation of material evidence by theoretical examination of interpretive assumptions and processes. Proceeding on the common conviction that 'households are essential building blocks in the reconstruction of past societies', the writers explore the various interpretive processes needed to translate archaeological records into social texts. To this end the essays have a common focus on the practical problem of understanding find-spots and reading the process of assemblage formation. Singly their various inquiries extend into larger questions of the spatial dynamic of households, the mechanics of production and consumption, gender visibility, communal structure. While dealing with a variety of situations ranging from two examples of volcanic inter-ruption to the gradual discontinuation of Greek Halieis and from a site where dung beetles are the only indicator of former habitation to a reformist movement in ongoing Boston society, the authors approach each other in their scepticism towards cultural generalizations based upon methodological or ideological preconceptions and their commitment to discover appropriate structures within which to examine specific materials.

To a certain extent one may see the assemblage of these essays as radiating from a Pompeian centre in response to the questions that Allison's own work in reconstructing domestic assemblages from excavation archives has opened, but this orientation is fully appropriate to the influential position of Pompeii in the development of European archaeology as the first site to offer the possibility of contextualizing ancient life. Dr Allison has asked me to comment on these essays from a classicist's point of view, which inevitably leads to foregrounding certain issues at the expense of others. For a classicist one predominant issue towards which household archaeology leads is the demarcation of public and private spaces within houses, a topic which, having attracted much recent attention, remains controversial for its tendency to bring out both structural and symbolic patterns with a generalizing authority that may leave inadequate room for the modification of concrete evidence. The essays here offer many examples of such modifications and I want to examine these with particular emphasis on matters of limits and boundaries, looking from traditional boundary fixing to more experimental boundary crossings in several of the societies here considered. Needless to say considerable literary evidence comes into play, thus generating within the interpretive realm another boundary question concerning the extent to which this should enter into archaeological analysis of ancient society.

Paradoxically, as Pompeianists themselves know, the accessible site, even in combination with its *instrumentum domesticum* has never supplied as much useful information about the processes of life as one might expect. At the heart of the problematic lies the 'Pompeii principle, the notion that an abruptly interrupted social process displays an ideal and legible record of normative activity'. Realistically, however, when viewed in the light of papers concerned with assemblage formation and forms of household abandonment (LaMotta and Schiffer, Ault and Nevett, McKee) Pompeii would emerge as the last site to which the Pompeii principle can profitably be applied. The purest example of rapid abandonment is, of course the Cerén site in El Salvador where, in the face of a catastrophic eruption, the villagers left behind practically all household and personal goods, including some objects of value, and many of these in places where they had been used. The difference is apparent between this fugitive population and the Pompeians, some of whom inadvertently sacrificed their lives to saving their valued objects. Also, unlike these Pompeians, whose site was declared an official disaster relief area by the imperial government, the Cerén villagers did not return to their buried homes for salvage. But even in this rapidly abandoned site with its exceptionally legible stratigraphy, the archaeological record is partially shaped by discard. In addition to a final resting place for useless objects in a communal midden, the site provides examples of ingenious recycling strategies that alter the function of everyday objects, such as handles from broken pottery re-employed to fasten doors. Contrasting this archaeological record with that of the more deliberately abandoned Greek sites that Ault and Nevett discuss we find a place for Pompeii in between since it contains some undisturbed assemblages, some seasonal storage that is hard to distinguish from displacement caused by repair operations, and much archaeological intervention of a kind that presnt day excavators deplore. In their survey of the problems of documentation and publication presented by sites with abundant artefacts, Ault and Nevett show that certain difficulties that Pompeian excavators once confronted are also recognized by contemporary archaeologists. Any Pompeian scholar will find much to learn from LaMotta and Schiffer's typology of the various situations within which objects may be abandoned or discarded. Consideration of these ordinary methods of discard in Pompeian studies might seem like a salubrious antidote to the attention that has traditionally gravitated towards the more luxurious finds.

Charged with the twofold onus of representing (however inappropriately) Roman life in general and dramatizing the site and its history for popular audiences, Pompeian interpretation has tended to reinforce assumptions rather than question them, often conventionalizing and transmitting insecurely constructed inferences as real facts. This is especially true where spatial usage is concerned. A glance at Montfaucon's pre-Pompeian effort (1720–2) to understand architectural terminology or visualize spatial organization on the basis of unaided textual evidence shows its virtual impossibility. 'Tis not a little difficult', he wrote, 'to know precisely what the atrium was and wherein it differed from the impluvium or court where the rain-water discharged itself' (II.62). Although this conundrum will provoke the laughter of a present day classicist or even a ninth grader whose Latin studies include a 'Roman cultural component', the subsequent availability of Pompeian house plans to resolve the antiquarian's puzzlement has resulted in the transmission of a set of formulaic architectural definitions from one exposition to another. Vitruvius is the source most commonly invoked for the naming and definition of spaces; his prescriptions for the sizing of the *atrium, tablinum* and *alae* are adapted to this purpose with the ensuing result that he is made the authority to back up much that he does not actually say (e.g. Clarke 1992).

Allison's own work (1992) enters into this nexus as an attempt to move the determination of spatial usage in Pompeii away from its conventional grounding in literary sources towards material culture. The preliminary step has involved a recontextualization of objects in their original find-spots through the study of archaeological records. Although the records, she has found, were perhaps better than expected, assumptions concerning identification and location upon which they were founded have proved more complex.

She has opened up a large number of problems arising from the traditional methodologies used. One set of problems stems from the use of literary information in identification, not only of Vitruvius as the canonical source for the naming of spaces but also of ancient lexicography as a source for the identification of objects. As Allison demonstrates in her sampling of Daremberg/Saglio's Pompeian lexicographical treasure hunt, the hierarchical pre-eminence of *atrium* space is often invoked as a *basis* of object identification, and thus used to reinforce stereotyped ideas of Roman life. In speaking of the *arca* and the *cartibulum*, her motto is to distrust dictionaries, and with this I must readily agree although on somewhat different grounds. Some of the ancient sources from which lexicographers derive their definitions are in themselves speculative in so far as their authors may be trying to explain or recover meanings that have already gone out of common use. The oblong, single-legged *cartibulum* of Varro's *De Lingua Latina* is a good example, since the passage in which this identification appears happens to be the sole occurrence of the word in all written Latin texts. This is taking the *difficilior lectio* with a vengeance. Small wonder that tables of this description are no more frequent in Pompeian houses than is the term in Latin texts. Romans commonly call their tables *mensae*.

Another set of problems stems from analogy. Goethe entered this realm when he noted that the small houses of present day Naples resembled those from Pompeii. Over the years, however, the communication between local workmen and archaeologists has resulted in the widespread use of contemporary practice as a basis for Pompeian identification. Jashemski (1987: 74) often resorted to analogy to corroborate the validity of planting methods deduced from her garden excavations. There is a difference however between arboriculture within conditions of soil and climate that have remained more or less the same over the centuries, and culinary practices subject to cultural change – not to mention the *abbeveratoio* that excavators labelled as an ancient bird feeder. Although Lesbia's sparrow and Melior's parrot do indeed bear witness to at least an occasional Roman weakness for pet birds, it does seem unlikely that these pampered fowls will have drunk from the very same type of vessel as might be sold in the petshops of modern Pompeii.

Allison comments on the tendency of archaeology to privilege architecture over assemblages, a point on which the number of her contributors are agreed, but they are equally in agreement concerning the complexity of the relationship between dwellings as the containers of habitation and the internal dynamics of households. The point is repeatedly made that archaeologists do not excavate households, but merely the potential for reconstructing them. While architecture may enclose domestic spaces, it does not necessarily confine household activities, which may in different ways spill over into areas of the community: the political community as we know from the Classical world or a community of production as seen in Mesoamerican and early British sites. A common problem confronting household archaeologists is the need for mediating instruments to cut through the silences that distance physical remains from patterns of life. Especially to the archaeologist who digs houses of non-literary societies, ethnography seems to occupy a position equivalent to that of history and literary texts for the classicist. Furthermore, as several discussions make clear, the use of ethnoarchaeological models may be no less controversial than reading archaeology from written history. Allison mentions the potentially prescriptive nature of such applications and their tendencies towards generalizations. Alexander defends the usefulness of ethnoarcheology in its bearing on site structure. Her study of architecture, land and implements in eighteenth-century Mesoamerican households resembles Pompeian archaeology by its interest in identifying spaces, and on this basis the relationship of households to their communities. Similar attempts have recently been made for Pompeii (Laurence 1995; Wallace-Hadrill 1991; Robinson 1996), whose diversity of architectural configurations makes it particularly problematic. Spatial itineraries of Pompeii (Eschebach 1970; La Torre 1988) are open to criticism for their arbitrary manner of dealing with difficult uncanonical spaces. Databases give volume as a primary index of wealth and social status, but this mechanical criterion requires qualification by such specific circumstances as the concentration of status symbols within compact house plans. Certainly a diagrammatic plotting of spatial dimensions can indicate the overall distribution of wealth and poverty throughout the city, but such figures are less useful in assigning determinations of social character to the nine 'Regiones' used to map the urban topography, since these divisions bear no inherent relationship to Pompeian social organization, but merely comprise a system created by archaeologists for convenient reference. Although major thoroughfares, as Wallace-Hadrill (1991) commonsensically pointed out, may attract a high degree of commercial activity, they provide equally an advantageous situation for the politically ambitious. Within the individual *insulae*, or socially evolved units, making up our 'regions', actual kinds of structure and activity are mixed. Robinson (1996) is right in looking to neighbourhoods as a structuring basis for Pompeian demography, as Ling (1997) specifically demonstrates by his detailed study of the Insula of the Menander.

The division of domestic space into men's and women's uses (a larger matter than simply quarters) is at the very heart of our understanding of social structures, whether in economic or other terms. It can be either practical or symbolic or both. Also, as Parker Pearson and Richards (1994) demonstrate by a broad range of coverage ranging from neolithic houses in Britain to the American south, it can appear quite independently of certain aspects of social sophistication. It can be affected by the relationship between the house and its economic production, and also by the relationship of family structure and fertility to the symbolic conceptualization of the cosmos. As a general principle these authors formulate that the more 'private' the life of the dwelling, the more likely is interior space to involve separation. Neither the demarcation of public and private nor considerations of gender are inevitably requisite to considerations of household archaeology. McKee does not attempt to identify the sex of workers in the communal or individual buildings of the Cerén site, and Alexander's study of Spanish colonial households places no emphasis on gender. From the femininist point of view, even the most sophisticated societies may count as non-literary; a point implicitly recognized by the employment of the term 'visibility' with reference to the traces of women's activities in household archaeology. The application is obvious, however, to questions of Greek domestic spaces where interpreters are working with the principle of social separation of the sexes and its resultant consequences for definition of public and private as well as interior/exterior; the entry granted to strangers and the conduct of subsistence activities. Consequently preconceptions concerning the interrelationships of the sexes in Antiquity have deeply influenced concepts of domestic space before investigation actually begins.

For the rigidity with which the concept of a segregated interior and the confinement of women has been applied to ideas of Greek domesticity much blame can be placed upon the uncritical acceptance of Vitruvius' brief picture of the Greek house (6.7), created with contrast in mind, as being less adapted to the official reception of visitors than the Roman. In his schematization a colonnaded peristyle reached by a long passageway has at its back a suite of rooms adapted to textile production and surrounded by symmetrically placed sleeping chambers and other spaces for dining. Collectively these form the gynaceum. In an effort to authenticate this floor plan, the Morgan translation of Vitruvius (1914: 187) illustrates with a model from Delos, but this model is misleading on two counts: first because of the high degree of romanization affecting Delian society, and second because this floor plan bears little resemblance to the Classical Greek houses that we have come to know in such cities as Athens and Olynthus which Goldberg discusses here, and which have also been considered by Nevett (1994) and by Jameson (1990). Needless to say the builders and owners of these Athenian town houses had never read Vitruvius, nor did the Roman architect appear conversant with the type. Instead of the paved peristyle Vitruvius features, these genuinely Greek houses are oriented around central courtyards which served multiple purposes. It is also hard to tell whether the evidence of literary passages is helpful or confusing, especially with reference to the very well-known case treated by Lysias which involves moving the quarters of a woman recently in childbirth from the upper to the lower floors of the house.

Goldberg's chapter represents the new wave of Greek spatial investigation that has questioned that once canonical feature of the 'women's quarters' in the Greek house on the empirical grounds that many recently excavated houses show no place for it, in contrast to their inclusion of a very recognizable *andron*. As her incorporation of the word 'behavioural' into her title indicates, the issue of men's and women's uses may exist in independence of men's and women's specific quarters. What we are looking for may not be spatial patterns but more elusive conduct patterns, as, for instance, how the women of the house might have behaved in the presence of entering males. Likewise her emphasis on the integration of the household is conceptually important to the Greek articulated notion of the *oikos* as a social and civic unit. As Jameson (1990) has noted, and also Pomeroy in her new commentary on Xenophon (1994: 58–67, 292–9), such considerations tend to lessen the gender dichotomy derived from some literary sources. Goldberg focuses upon the courtyard as the area of critical household activities where economic necessity may enter into the determination of priorities as well as the relative power balance of men and women. From this emphasis emerges the possibility of a strong link between spatial usage and economic patterns, partially related to the extent to which the household in question employed servants or depended upon the industry of its women for the services fundamental to everyday life. Clearly it would seem that the less prosperous Greek women must have engaged on a daily basis in household labours situated within the courtyard, and also have made trips outside the house. Thus the concept that emerges from Goldberg's discussion that I particularly want to emphasize here is the concept of negotiated space as the practical embodiment of social power relationships.

Negotiated space seems very much the principle in the Roman world. As late as the work of Amedeo Maiuri and the topographical compilation of Tatiana Warsher, the notion that Pompeian houses ought to contain separate women's quarters held force, to the extent that any cluster of interconnected rooms got the label of *gynaceum*. A recent combination of social and literary studies has exploded this as being out of keeping with the general nature of Roman domestic life. A multitude of written sources present Roman matrons dining with their husbands, while Asconius' reference to the loom of a Roman matron in the *atrium* as an ethical status symbol (*in Milonianum* 38) can suggest that characteristic female activities such as weaving could contribute signifying value to the construction of a noble family image. In this light one may consider Allison's remarks on the discovery of loomweights in the Pompeian space. Laurence (1994: 129–32) has proposed a daily sequence of spatial genderings within the household activities of the Roman élite based upon the male custom of spending parts of the day in the Forum or the baths.

While some of the households here presented are genderless, the question of public and private is endemic to feminist household archaeology with its attendant implications for the social position of women. Deliberately coordinating her comments with those of Goldberg, Suzanne Spencer-Wood faults the legacy of male dominated Classical scholarship whose interaction with nineteenth-century bourgeois premises has polarized characterizations of male and female natures and spheres of activity which the widespread contemporary incorporation of binary structuralism into anthropological methodology has even more deeply entrenched. Her discussion of spatial function and gender roles in Victorian Boston challenges the stereotypical opposition between 'public, cultural and dominant males' and 'domestic, natural, and subordinate' women even as this pattern came to be challenged within the structure of upper-class society itself. From the perspective of a New England childhood, raised on the novels of Louisa May Alcott and gravitating to journalist and reformer Margaret Fuller as a teenage role model, I have no trouble in bringing literary evidence to bear on the question of diverse gender ideologies within that world, while the concept of women as the creators of culture and of women's work being both distinct and equivalent to men's work is scarcely foreign.

Nonetheless the point strikes me that the culturally creative role of the female is itself an élitist concept and this is what makes the work of the social reformer particularly interesting as she moves to redefine the entire nature of public/private activity and boundaries. Here we see the beginnings of a cultural transformation still actively working itself out within our own society. Of course the larger context for this redefinition of women's roles is one created by such contemporaneous social and economic movements as the transformation of scientific discovery into practical technology and the regularization of professions across boundaries of class and gender as a hierarchy responsive to social mobility.

At the same time these activities, while broadening the sphere of women's influence beyond the domestic shell, inevitably canonize some of women's hitherto private roles as appropriate public activities, and even salaried activities, in conformity with codes of decorum and with the élitist readiness to yield the guardianship of culture to women. While this idea clearly pertains to upper-class women's possession of an *otium* that encourages socially enhancing activities as pastimes, it is also transferable across classes and physical contexts. There is a potentiallly interesting inter-association between Spencer-Wood's established Boston families and the environmentally displaced households of Susan Lawrence's Australian goldfields operating within wholly different economic parameters. Here the need for family subsistence erases all barriers to women's extra-domestic activity, as they and their children share in agricultural duties with their men. Even in these physically makeshift habitations, however, traces of gentility in material culture distinguish women's presences from the exclusively masculine, and bear witness to feminine aesthetic drive as a means of creating continuity with civilized environments left behind. Journals and diaries, women's familiar instruments of observation and expression, provide important testimony not only to the valuation placed upon material amenities but also to feminine social activity in promoting a sense of community in an isolated environment.

Returning to the topic of public and private spaces raised as a preliminary, these perspectives opened by these essays give much evidence against the use of fixed patterns as they look from traditional boundary fixing to more experimental boundary crossings in several of the societies here considered. Like the practices of discard and reuse in household economy, social boundary crossing may be the creation of physical and material circumstances. In this area also the specifics of individual situations must be allowed full play in the reformulation or reformation of cultural generalizations. As an interrelationship between the 'internal space' of society and the physical spaces it structures, boundary crossing challenges the demarcation of public and private identities in the same manner that it challenges the interassociation of interior and exterior spaces. No less, however, is it applicable to the readiness of scholarship to admit modifications and to perceive possibilities of useful interchange.

These few comments scarcely exhaust the possibilities of comparative dialogue opened by this collection of essays. While the authors themselves have initiated the dialogue in responding to one another's methodological problems and solutions, their beginnings only invite active continuation by every user in drawing conclusions and finding comparisons relevant to his/her own particular field of inquiry.

BIBLIOGRAPHY

Allison, P. M. (1993) 'How Do We Identify the Use of Space in Roman Houses?', in E. M. Moormann (ed.) *Functional and Spatial Analysis of Ancient Wall Painting*, Proceedings of the Fifth International Congress on Ancient Wall Painting, Amsterdam, 8–12 September 1992, Publications of the Dutch Institute in Rome, *Stichtung BABesch* 3: 1–8.
—— (1992) 'The Distribution of Pompeian House Contents and its Significance' I and II, Ann Arbor: University Microfilms no. 9400463 (1994).
Clarke, J. R. (1992) *The Houses of Roman Italy 100 BC–AD 200: Ritual, Space and Decoration*, Berkeley: University of California Press.
Eschebach, H. (1970) *Die Städtebauliche Entwicklung des antiken Pompeji*, Mitteilungen des Deutschen Archäologischen Instituts, Römische Abteilungen Supplement 17, Heidelberg: F. H. Kerle.
Goethe, Johann Wolfgang von (1982) *Italian Journey: 1786–1788*, trans. W. H. Auden and E. Meyer, San Francisco: North Point Press (reprint).

Hillier, B. and Hanson, J. (1984) *The Social Logic of Space*, Cambridge: Cambridge University Press.

Jameson, M. (1990) 'Domestic Space in the Greek City-state', in Susan Kent (ed.) *Domestic Architecture and the Use of Space: An Inter-disciplinary Cross-cultural Study*, Cambridge: Cambridge University Press: 92–113.

Jashemski, W. (1987) 'Recently Excavated Gardens and Cultivated Land in the Villas at Boscoreale and Oplontis', in E. B. Macdougall (ed.) *Ancient Roman Villa Gardens*, Dumbarton Oaks Colloquium on the History of Landscape Architecture X, Washington, DC: Dumbarton Oaks Research Library and Collection: 31–76.

La Torre, G. F. (1988) 'Gli impianti commerciali ed artigianali nel tessuto urbano di Pompei', in A. De Simone, *Pompeii: l'informatica al servizio di una città antica* 1–2, Rome: L'Erma di Bretschneider: 75–102.

Laurence, R. (1994) *Roman Pompeii: Space and Society*, London and New York: Routledge

—— (1995) 'The Organization of Space in Pompeii', in T. J. Cornell and K. Lomas (eds) *Urban Society in Roman Italy*, London: University College: 63–78.

Ling, R. (1997) *The Insula of the Menander at Pompeii I: The Structures*, Oxford: Clarendon Press.

Montfaucon, Bernard de (1721–2) *Antiquity Explained and Represented in Sculptures*, trans. D. Humphreys, 3 vols, New York and London: Garland Publisher (reprinted 1976).

Morgan, M. H. (trans.) (1914) *Vitruvius: The Ten Books on Architecture*, Cambridge, Mass. (reprint New York 1960).

Nevett, L. (1994) 'Separation or Seclusion? Towards an Archaeological Approach to Investigating Women in the Greek Household in the Fifth to Third Centuries B.C.' in M. Parker Pearson and C. Richards, *Architecture and Order: Approaches to Social Space*, London: Routledge: 98–112.

Parker Pearson, M. and Richards, C. (1994) *Architecture and Order: Approaches to Social Space*, London: Routledge.

Pomeroy, S. (1994) *Xenophon, Oeconomicus, A Social and Historical Commentary*, Oxford: Clarendon Press.

Robinson, D. (1996) 'The Social Texture of Pompeii', in S. Bon and R. Jones (eds) *Sequence and Space in Pompeii*, Oxford: Oxbow Books: 135–44.

Wallace-Hadrill, A. (1988) 'The Social Structure of the Roman House', *Papers of the British School at Rome* 56: 43–97.

Wallace-Hadrill, A. (1991) 'Elites and Trade in the Roman Town', in J. Rich and A. Wallace-Hadrill (eds) *City and Country in the Ancient World*, London: Routledge: 241–72.

—— (1995) 'Public Honor and Private Shame: The Urban Texture of Pompeii', in T. J. Cornell and K. Lomas (eds) *Urban Society in Roman Italy*, London: University College: 39–62.

Warsher, T. (1949) *Codex Topigraphicus Pompeianus* VI x, Unpublished manuscript in Rome.

—— (1951) *Codex Topigraphicus Pompeianus* VI viii, vols 1–4, Unpublished manuscript in Rome.

Index

Page numbers in bold denote illustrations

Linton, S. 165
literary: evidence 145, 191; sources 7, 126, 144, 192, 195 *see also* documentary, text
Loma Caldera volcano 32
Longacre, William A. 36
loomweights: Athenian households 149, 150, 152; Pompeian households 195; Roman households in Britain 70–1
Lysias 143, 149, 152, 156, 194

McCormack family 135
McGowan, B. 135–6
machines, domestic 8, 170–1, 181
Maiuri, Amedeo 195
maize washing 89
male: association with public 11, 121–2; dominance of 13, 138, 162–3, 165–72, 181, 195; as head of household 4, 9–10, 163
Man the Hunter 165
Man the Scavenger 165
marriage: Moorabool diggings 135
marriage chamber, Athenian 154
Marxist systems 8
material culture: reading of 7–8 *see also* Roman material culture
Maya 21, 85, 87, 88
Maya Lowlands 13, 82
meat 110–12
Melbourne 137
Mesoamerica 78–94, 193; agricultural production 82–3; application of ethnoarchaeological models 13, 78, 79–80, 92, 94; dwelling-patio-garden components 83; reasons for lack of changes in household strategies of prehistoric 82; *see also* Yaxcaba
Mexicans 5
Mexico 7, 12, 78 *see also* Yaxcaba
mid-level theory 2 *see also* systems theory
midwives 147, 154
Miller, C. D. 32
Miller, D. 4, 7–8, 9, 106
mining: combination of farming and 136; goldfields 135–6
mobility: drift and dispersal 93; residential 12, 93, 94, social 196
Mogollon pueblo 24
Montessori, Maria 177, 179
Montfaucon, Bernard de 191, 192
Montgomery, B.K. 24
Moorabool diggings (Australia) 7, 123, 124–38; ages of the population 134; archaeological remains and artefacts 126; architecture and buildings 126–8, 130–1; artefact assemblages 129–30, 131, 133, 137; composition and size of households 134–5; discovery of gold 124–5; evidence of commercial activities 130–1; and fireplaces 127, 128–9, 133; gold deposits

125–6; household size 134–5; households with women 133–5; increase in population 125; kin relationships 135; living in tents 126, 127, 128, 137–8; location 124; marriage 135; work of women 136–7, 138
Moore, J. and Scott, E. 10
Mopila 86, 87, 88, 90, 91, 92, 93, 94
morality: women as guardians of 11, 137
More, St Thomas 174
Morgenstern, Lina 179
Morrison, Hughina 135
Morrisons 125, 135
mortaria 105, 109, **109**, 110
mortuary ritual 24
Moscow 176
Motherhood, Republican 172, 181
moulds 66–7
Mt. Vesuvius 58
Munich House of Industry 179
Murray, P. 21

Navajo 10, 23
New Archaeology 43, 144
New South Wales 135–6
noira (well) 86
North America 23
North American scholarship 15
'nostalgia effect' 21–2
Noyes, John H. 174
nurseries 177

objectivity: and subjectivity 164–5, 185
oikos 195
Old Shifford Farm 103–4, 106, 108, 114–15; butchered bones 110–11, 111–12; cereals 112; containers 109, 110; deposits 113, 114; map **108**
Old World archaeology 6
Olynthus 46
Oneida Perfectionists 174, 175, 176
Orientalism 146
Osborne, R. 151
ovens 179, 181
Owen, Robert 177
Owenite communities 174, 176
Oxford Archaeological Unit 102

Pader, Ellen 5
painting 13 *see also* vase-painting, Athenian
Paris 176
Parker Pearson, M. and Richards, C. 194
patios 83, 84, 87, 88–9, 90, 91, 92
Peabody, Elizabeth 177
Peloponnese 7
Peloponnesian War 149, 154
Pernice, Erich 66
philosophy: Classical Greek 185 *see also* Plato